OPERATIONAL AND THEORETICAL ASPECTS OF INTRAMURAL-RECREATIONAL SPORTS

edited by

THOMAS P. SATTLER
University of Illinois—Chicago Circle

PETER J. GRAHAM
Northeastern University

DON C. BAILEY
North Texas State University

Leisure Press
P.O. Box 3
West Point, N.Y. 10996

A publication of Leisure Press.
P.O. Box 3, West Point, N.Y. 10996
Copyright © 1978 by the National Intramural-Recreational Sports Association
All rights reserved. Printed in the U.S.A.

ISBN 0-918438-44-6

CONTENTS

CHAPTER IV: PUBLIC RELATIONS AND PUBLICITY

CHAPTER V: RESEARCH

CHAPTER VI: INTRAMURAL-RECREATIONAL SPORTS PERSONNEL: LEADERSHIP AND ADMINISTRATION

PREFACE

Western society is in the midst of casting aside the "Protestant Work Ethic" and replacing it with a much more leisure-oriented philosophy of life. Concurrent with this philosophic transformation, members of academic communities are calling upon intramural—recreational sports programs to expand and diversify their program offerings in an effort to afford all members of the community multiple opportunities to satisfy their leisure needs and to acquire a positive recreational "high."

To successfully meet this challenge, intramural—recreational sports personnel must be perpetually cognizant of the ever changing leisure needs of their clientele. Moreover, they must be able to identify and be willing to institute appropriate program changes necessary to accomodate the expanding variety of clientele leisure needs. During this era of sexual, racial, and cultural integration, technicological revolution, and significant demographic change, intramural—recreational sports personnel who fail to maintain an awareness and comprehension of contemporary issues will ultimately become victims to that which Toffler describes as "future shock."

The people who provide leadership for intramural—recreational sports programs at institutions, installations and communities around the country gather once each year in a national meeting to share their common successes and problems. The framework for this conclave is designated the National Intramural—Recreational Sports Association Annual Conference. The leadership personnel come from all segments of the industry including sports participants, student leaders, students preparing for the profession and professionals. Many years of experience are represented and the experience of individuals ranges from that of first contact with intramural—recreational sports to directors of programs with several decades of developed expertise. The organization itself has been in operation for twenty eight years.

A formal program of activities is conducted at each annual conference, and a part of this program consists of the formalized presentation of ideas, procedures, research and philosophies pertaining to the profession. The quality of presentations varies and the topics are diverse. The editors have studied all presentations and made a careful selection of papers for inclusion in this publication. The papers included represent the individual author and do not necessarily represent the collective position of the National Intramural-Recreational Sports Association membership. The authors of the various papers are to be commended for their efforts in sharing the knowledge they have gained through both study and experience. The opportunity for many to benefit from their instruction will be their reward. The officers and collective membership of the National Intramural-Recreational Sports Association are to be complimented for providing the forum through which the ideas, procedures, research, and philosophies of these individuals can be expressed.

It is the intent of this volume to assist intramural—recreational sports personnel with the development and maintenance of diversified programs—programs designed to reflect and provide for the recreational needs of the clientele being served. We believe that this book contains some of the most current information available.

The editors are indebted to the contributing authors for their experiences and expertise. The editors wish to dedicate this book to all of those devoted individuals associated with intramural—recreational sports programs.

Thomas P. Sattler
Chicago, Illinois
Peter J. Graham
Boston, Massachusetts
Don C. Bailey
Denton, Texas

CHAPTER I

Philosophical and Historical Considerations

THE CHANGING COLLEGE STUDENT: NEW DIRECTIONS FOR INTRAMURAL-RECREATIONAL SPORTS PROGRAMS

Peter J. Graham, ED.D., Northeastern University

How does one describe the college student of the future? This is a topic of vital concern to all educational leaders responsible for establishing the future directions of higher education. The topic is also of equal importance to administrators of collegiate intramural-recreational sports and activity programs for it is the responsibility of this group of educators to define the types of leisure-time recreational programs to be made available for the student of the future.

If the programming challenges of the future are to be successfully met, advance planning is going to be an absolute necessity. However, prior to commencing any meaningful planning an analysis of projective and descriptive demographic population data must be made relative to the future student clientele toward whom collegiate intramural-recreational sports and activity programs will be directed.

There are three major factors which will have a significant affect upon the future directions taken by collegiate intramural-recreational sports and activity programs. They are (1) population trends, (2) educational interests, and (3) changing student leisure-time interests.

Population Trends

In June of 1969, *U.S. News and World Report* published an article which focused on changing student enrollments in the United States. Contained in the article were the following predictions (June 9, pp. 9-10):

(1) Elementary school enrollments would peak in the 1969 school year and would then start to decline.

(2) High school enrollments would continue to grow slowly reaching a peak about 1977 and would then begin to decline.

(3) College and university enrollments would continue to grow for years to come.

(4) Total spending for education in the United States would continue to rise at a rapid rate.

Figure 1 illustrates the predicted enrollment patterns for elementary school students. A review of Figure 1 reveals that for grade school enrollments (K-8), a drop of 4,648,000 students was estimated to occur between the years of 1968-1980.

Figure 2 shows that during this same time-frame, high school enrollments (9-12) were expected to sustain a decline of 1,448,000 students. But, as Figure 3 depicts, within this same period of time, the number of students enrolled at colleges and universities was projected to increase by 4,380,000.

Figure 1
UPS AND DOWNS IN ENROLLMENTS......
GRADE SCHOOLS: Headed Down
(through grade 8)

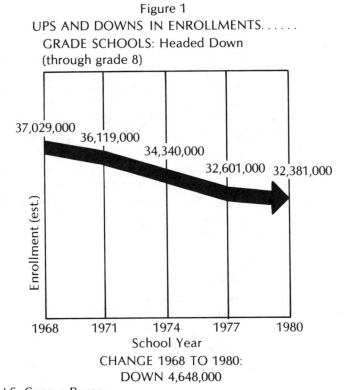

CHANGE 1968 TO 1980:
DOWN 4,648,000

Source: U.S. Census Bureau

10

Figure 2
HIGH SCHOOLS: Up, Then Down
(grades 9-12)

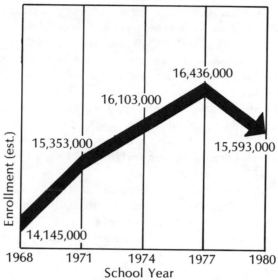

CHANGE 1968 TO 1980: UP 1,448,000
Source: U.S. Census Bureau

Figure 3
COLLEGES: Steady Rise

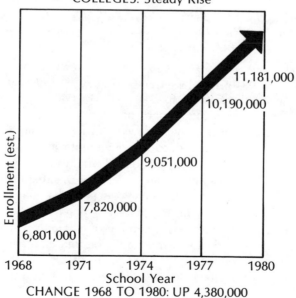

CHANGE 1968 TO 1980: UP 4,380,000
Source: U.S. Census Bureau

From the data above, it should be readily apparent that the 1968 predictions have been fairly accurate. In the first five years of the predictive period, student enrollments tended to agree with those forecasted. However, during the past five years, enrollment prognastications have been somewhat under estimated. Elementary and secondary school student populations have dwindled faster than anticipated and the number of collegiate students has risen at a rate greater than that expected. Also, the forecast that the funds expended on education would continue to increase has shown a relative degree of accuracy over the past five years. But, the escalating costs of education have risen so fast that significant problems have been encountered, especially in higher education. From spring, 1970, to fall, 1976, one hundred-thirteen private institutions of higher education have either closed or shifted to public control (*The Chronicle of Higher Education*, November 21, 1977).

Where do we stand today? As forecasted in 1968, the number of pre-school aged children has dropped dramatically in the United States in the past decade. An NBC televised news report (February 10, 1977) noted that the pre-school segment of the nation's population had dropped by 10% during the past six years. In 1978, the average family in the United States had only 1.8 children.

The 1977, February 28th issue of *Time* magazine reported that:

> *Since 1957 the fertility rate has dropped from a peak of 3.76 children per woman to a record low of 1.75 last year (1967). Though the birth rate may rise in the next 30 years, it is highly improbable that Americans in the foreseeable future will again engage in the great procreational spree of the post war years. The baby boom has become a bust.* (p. 71).

And, in the February 28, 1977 issue of *Newsweek* it was reported that, "There have been so few births that the number of children 13 and under has dropped by 7.6 million since 1970." (p. 51).

The rapid depletion in the number of "traditional" school aged people (5-22 years old) could be effectively slowed down (or possibly even reversed) if another baby boom were to occur. At one point some demographers, but very few, held the belief that a mini-boom would be noted in the United States birth rate. The reasoning behind this belief was that once the children born during the post war baby boom grew old enough to have babies of their own, the birth rate would again soar, thus creating an "echo" of the earlier boon. Yet, even though the present number of women of child bearing age have far exceeded that of the past decade, the total number of births have not increased as evidenced by the 1978 figure of 1.8 children per family.

Philip Hauser of the University of Chicago's Population Research Center states:

If another baby boom is going to happen at all, it will have to hap-
pen soon. The eldest women (those born during the 1947-57 baby
boom) are now reaching 30. Its pretty well known that if a woman
is going to have children, she'd better have them by her mid-30's.
(Newsweek, February 28, 1977, p. 55)

Thus, as Hauser and others see it, if the baby boom "echo" has not occurred by 1982, it probably never will.

Concomitant with the declining birth rate, the proportion of "older" peo- ple in the United States has been steadily increasing. No longer can America be characterized as a representative of the "youth" or "pepsi" culture. To verify this fact, simply reflect upon the advertisements currently employed by the Pepsi Cola Company. Notice that they have changed considerably from those presented but a few years ago. Where once teen-agers and those in their early 20's were prominently, almost exclusively, featured, the current casts are composed of a whole spectrum of ages—with the greatest em- phasis being upon the more mature segments of society. Business executives constantly study the changes in demographic data and have become quite sensitive to any shifts evidenced in the population profile.

Consequently, when the current changes in the nation's demographic pro- file were evidenced, business concerns reacted immediately by introducing appropriate changes in their product promotional efforts. Business has done what we in the field of intramural-recreational sports and activity program- ming must do: they have made whatever changes are necessary to make their product attractive to present and future clientele.

Education Interests

A number of changes have taken place in recent years with respect to stu- dent's educational interests. These changes range from the type of educa- tional institution preferred to the subject area of major concentration.

In the past few years, students have demonstrated a growing preference toward two-year institutions of higher education. Although the number of college and university students continues to expand, the greatest gains in enrollments have been experienced by community colleges and two-year professional institutions. In the December 19, 1977 issue of *The Chronicle of Higher Education* it was reported that:

The largest one-year [in student enrollments] were in two-year in-
stitutions (up 5.2 per cent). . . . This fall, public two-year colleges
reported 5.8 per cent more new freshmen, while private two-year
institutions reported an increase of 9.1 per cent. (p. 6)

And, of course, when the percentage of the student market electing two-year institutions expands, a corresponding decrease in four-year institution enrollments must be anticipated.

Another recent change concerns the number of women enrolled at institutions of higher education. Historically, males have composed the largest segment of the collegiate student body. However, this is no longer true. According to the *The Chronicle of Higher Education* (January 9, 1978) female students were responsible for 93 percent of the enrollment growth experienced by colleges and universities in 1977. Women accounted for 49 percent of the total higher education student body: women constitute 46 percent of the full-time and 52 percent of the part-time student population. In 1977, women outnumbered men among 18- and 19-year-olds attending colleges and universities throughout the nation. The United States Census Bureau reports that ten years ago women represented 40 percent of the collegiate student body; 35 percent twenty years ago; and, 29 percent thirty years ago.

The number of "non-traditional" college students represents a third area in which significant changes have been evidenced in recent years. According to *The Chronicle of Higher Education* (August 8, 1977, p. 2), "College attendance by persons at least 35 years old remained fairly stable—at about 1.2 million—following a 50 per cent increase from 1973-75." The rapid growth in the "non-traditional" student enrollment may possibly be attributed to one of several factors:

(1) More people are returning to school to acquire the sophisticated skills so necessary to "keep pace" with our highly technological society.

(2) Because of technological advancements many persons, out of necessity, are preparing themselves for mid-life career changes.

(3) A greater number of women are pursuing educational degrees either while raising or after having raised a family.

Part-time students represent a fourth area in which a substantial change has been noted. In the December 19, 1977 issue of *The Chronicle of Higher Education* it was noted that the 1977 student enrollments reflect a 6 percent increase, "among part-time students." (p. 6) A study conducted by the State of Illinois produced data indicating that one of every three adults in the state had taken at least one continuing education course of some kind within the past two years. As reported in the February 21, 1978 issue of *The Chronicle of Higher Education*, "Nearly two-thirds of those taking courses for credit were working toward a degree, license, or certificate." (p. 6)

Finally, a fifth area in which change has been observed is related to the subject areas chosen for major academic pursuit. This change has been especially evident within the past ten years. Between 1969-70 and 1975-76 the percentage of undergraduate students majoring in the humanities and social sciences dropped by a significant level. According to data collected by the Carnegie Council in Policy Studies on Higher Education, as reported

14

in the December 19, 1977 issue of *The Chronicle of Higher Education*, social science majors decreased from 18 percent in 1969-70 to 8 percent in 1975-76. During the same time-frame, humanity majors fell from 9 percent to 5 percent. The report further stated:

> *The data indicate that undergraduate programs in professional areas — including business administration, education, agriculture, architecture, journalism, and some occupational fields — were the chief beneficiaries of the shift in undergraduate preferences. The production of students majoring in those fields rose from 38 to 58 per cent.* (p. 7)

Figure 4 presents the data generated by each of the Carnegie studies.

Figure 4

MAJOR	1969-70	1975-76
PROFESSIONS	38%	58%
SOCIAL SCIENCES	18%	8%
HUMANITIES	9%	5%
BIOLOGICAL SCIENCES	5%	7%
PHYSICAL SCIENCES	7%	8%
ARTS	6%	6%
OTHER	17%	8%

The Chronicle of Higher Education, December 19, 1977, p. 7.

Changes in Student Leisure-Time Interests

In recent years, collegiate students have exhibited a change in their leisure-time activity preferences. Interest appears to have shifted, even if just minimally, from the traditional activity areas of competitive sport such as football, basketball, and wrestling (activities which for so long have characterized intramural-recreational sport programs) toward the newer emerging activities such as skateboarding, frisbee, water polo, orienteering, and the so called high-risk activities.

Although a significant amount of overlapping is found in those leisure-time activities preferred by the various age groups of students, each group does display certain differences in activity preferences. And certainly this is to be expected due to the fact that each group has certain need areas which a responsive and sensitive intramural-recreational sports and activity program ought to be directing its efforts toward satisfying.

For the most part, the traditional age college student continues to demonstrate a strong interest for participation in highly competitive, direct competition activities such as football, ice hockey, soccer, wrestling, and so forth. Yet, within this group there has been evidence of a tendency to seek out participation opportunities in "contemporary" team, dual, and individual activities. And many of these activities are pursued in terms of indirect competition. With the diversity of sport activities available today, there can be no question that the leisure-time activity horizons of the collegiate student of the 1970's is much greater and broader than that of students 10 or 20 years ago.

Leisure-time activity interests of women, especially collegiate women, have experienced substantial change in recent years. Graham (1975) noted that in the past:

> Women and girls have been characterized by the Victorian image—physically weak, dependent upon the male, and abhorred by the thought of engaging in physical competition amongst themselves. (p. 259)

However, no longer are women willing to accept passive recreation roles. They have cast off the female sociological stereotype, at least with respect to their interests in participating in sport and physical activities. Today, women are demanding opportunities to participate in the same types of sports and activities as those afforded males.

This shift in social philosophy has enabled female students to pursue a whole host of activities which until recent years had been primarily dominated by males. Concurrently, women have demonstrated a substantial interest toward participating in high-risk activities such as football, ice hockey, wrestling, hang gliding, technical rock climbing, martial arts, and so on.

The full-time student population, however, is not totally composed of traditional college age students. In ever increasing numbers older, more mature individuals are returning to the college campuses throughout the nation. In their pursuit of academic study, these individuals are often seeking to advance their technological knowledge or to "re-tool" themselves in preparation for a mid-life career change. We can anticipate the number of students in this catagory to continue to swell as time goes on. Toffler (1970) in his book, *Future Shock*, notes that it will not be uncommon in the future for people to change their professional careers two, three, even four times in a lifetime.

Leisure-time activity preferences for members of the returning, older college student group tend to be somewhat different than those of the traditional age group. These students are much more into the "life-time" sports. They tend to shun the highly competitive, physically demanding activities. Team activities are less in demand while dual and individual activities are extremely popular. Many members of this student category have a high degree of concern for participation in physical fitness programs.

The part-time student can not be classified into one single category. Students comprising the part-time student body represent all segments of the population—young, middle-age, and older citizens. One thing they do have in common, however, is that for the large majorty of part-time students, their time on campus is usually limited. Therefore, although an individual student might be interested in participating in intramural-recreational sports and activities, his/her needs may not be fully met because of time conflicts between activity schedules and his/her class schedule.

Ramifications

What does the changing characteristics of the college student population mean to future intramural-recreational sports and activity programs? In essence it appears to indicate that in the very near future, if not already, directors of college programs are going to be faced with the task of attempting to provide leisure-time activity programs designed to meet the needs of a diverse clientele. No longer will the traditional program format suffice.

To adequately meet the recreational needs of collegiate students in the future, intramural-recreational sports and activity directors are going to have to develop and maintain multi-phased programs. Incorporated into each institution's program must be sports and activities designed to meet the needs of a specific segment of the student clientele. Using basketball as an example, the program of the future is going to require that a highly competitive, direct competition tournament be sponsored for the traditional age student, a "low key" recreational tournament be provided for the older student, and a drop-in, unstructured program be established to provide for the part-time student.

Furthermore, activities are going to have to be offered for both males, females, and on a co-rec basis. The types of activities are going to have to change as student interests dictate. Directors are going to have to be much more attentive to the wishes of all students, not just the traditional student.

Finally, no longer will intramural-recreational sports and activity programs be able to maintain the traditional late afternoon, early evening mode of operation. If the needs of all students are to be adequately met, then programs are going to have to be scheduled throughout the day and evening. This is going to require a reallocation of facility use priority. Achievement of this goal is going to necessitate close cooperation among physical education, athletic, and intramural-recreational sports and activity administrators.

In essence, the changes taking place in the demographic characteristics of the collegiate student population should result in intramural-recreational programs playing a greater and more important role in the collegiate society. Program directors are going to face a continual challenge to develop programs that adequately provide for the leisure-time needs of each student group.

REFERENCES

Graham, Peter J. "Title IX: Human Rights in School Sports," *Twenty-Sixth Annual Conference Proceedings*, National Intramural-Recreational Sports Association, 1975.

— — —. *Newsweek*, February 28, 1977.

— — —. *The Chronicle of Higher Education*, August 8, 1977.

— — —. *The Chronicle of Higher Education*, November 1, 1977.

— — —. *The Chronicle of Higher Education*, December 19, 1977.

— — —. *The Chronicle of Higher Education*, January 9, 1978.

— — —. *The Chronicle of Higher Education*, February 21, 1978.

— — —. *Time,* February 28, 1977.

Toffler, Alvin. *Future Shock.* New York: Random House, 1970.

— — —. *U.S. News and World Report,* June 9, 1969.

THE PARADOXES OF PLAY

Francis M. Rokosz, Wichita State University
Wichita, Kansas 67208

In previous writings[26] [27] [28] [29], this author has protested the structuring of intramural sports programs on the basis of the varsity athletics model. Amplified here are some of the bases for complaint and proposals for change, as well as several new thoughts for consideration.

This paper is constructed around eight paradoxes (or incongruencies) involved with the organizing and playing of structured games. In no particular order, they are: (1) The playing of games is a serious business, precisely because it isn't. (2) The real winners at play probably lose most of the time. (3) The structures of most sports programs foster social war (which, by definition, precludes fair play), yet those who act most war-like (by circumventing the rules) are punished. (4) Educators, philosophers, and medical people espouse the values of stress-free play, as they related to retarding the onset of man's mental and physical malfunctions. But, our scholastic institutions actively organize, administer and promote games-playing programs that are likely to induce psychological distress. (5) Those who promote athletics as a worthy undertaking often cite character development as being an outcome of participation. However, the structure and rules of play don't provide a significant opportunity for participants to make and communicate honest judgments. (6) People strive to attain extrinsic rewards through serious sport, which is substantially devoid of positive social significance; yet, the only legitimate reward in life, even for socially relevant achievements, is intrinsic. (7) Health, physical education, and recreation professionals are charged with the responsibility for stimulating a lifetime of physical activity amongst the nation's populace. For most people, the maintenance of a physically active life almost certainly requires intrinsic motivation. Most current programs of physical activity, whether they involve games-playing or solitary exercise, are based on extrinsic inducements. (8) The organizational control of institutional play, which is usually a matter of self-determination on adult levels, and adult influence on youth levels, must be usurped from current adult majorities, so people may actually be afforded the inherent freedoms of playful thought and activity.

There is considerable controversy in the literature over the values of highly competitive sport. Many are of the opinion that such outcomes as character development, loyalty, fortitude, discipline, altruism, physical fitness, mental alertness, educational achievement, adjustment to success and failure experiences, and cooperative teamwork can be attributed to sports participation[5][10]. As reflected by sociologist David Reisman's statement that "the road to the board room leads through the locker room,"[24] participation in serious sport is almost factually believed to be a preparation for life. Even author James Michener, who exposes many of the negative aspects of athletic programs in the book *Sports in America*, concedes that competition allows one to meet a challenge, and that competition in life is virtually inescapable.[18]

Even though participation in highly competitive sport surely has its positive points, Edwards[5] could find no evidence of such. Furthermore, Bryant Cratty says, "There is no data which indicates that a child who is not willing to endure the physical rigors of sports is likely to fail in tasks involving intellectual or artistic persistence....".[2] In the major study of its kind, Ogilvie and Tutko exploded the commonly held myth that sports build character. They found that those who do well in life do so with or without sports participation, because they were initially talented. The character of the ideal athlete is not formed by sport; rather, it is the consequence of a natural selection process.[21]

Twenty years after they won the Little League World Series in 1954, members of the Schenectady, New York team were interviewed by Martin Ralbovsky. Most players said they gained neutral or negative results from the experience. Killer instincts, sore arms, and senses of having been used by adults were developed by some.[23] Further, researchers Nelson and Kagan have found American children to be competitive to irrational degrees. They apparently achieve senses of accomplishment and/or satisfaction by simply preventing others from positive attainment, although nothing is personally gained by those blocking the attainment. A competitive jealousy is formed.[20]

Sport, in itself, is a neutral entity. Whether or not the playing of a game becomes one of life's positive experiences depends on the circumstances within which one plays and the attitude one has towards play and other people.

Too many people view the playing of games as a serious concern, which it is, but not for the reasons typically envisioned. Games-playing is important for the recreative effect it can have on an individual. Psychologist William Menninger says, "Good mental health is directly related to the capacity and willingness of an individual to play".[17] But, what is the usual American approach? People scramble away from their jobs or studies to engage in what amounts to a "working at play".[33] Involvement in sports contests and programs that authenticate winners and losers tends to imprison people psychologically into a lifestyle that allows little room for the free choice of relaxation. How many times does the so-called "casual" sports participant force him/herself to practice an activity, out of a sense of obligation and worry, when he/she would really prefer (subconsciously, perhaps) doing something else? Just think of all the time, thought, and effort that people dissipate in practicing sports skills, just so they can defeat other people in essentially meaningless activities.

On the scoreboard, there are more losers in sport than winners, so most people's efforts to achieve goals are frequently blocked. The likely result is frustration, tension, anxiety, envy, and aggression—in other words, stress. Considerable evidence[31] points to emotional stresses as causing many of man's health problems. People who lead stressful lives are susceptible to disease, organic dysfunctions, insomnia, and shortened life spans. The renewal of the human spirit, which free play offers anyone who will grasp it, is too crucial to the well-being of an individual to consider it lightly and squander available opportunities to engage in it. Thus, this question seems appropriate: Since a major thrust of life should be the avoidance of stress, and since sports programs, which have as their basis the determination of champions, regularly stimulate social conflict and emotional distress, how does one justify the perpetration of such a potentially unhealthy enterprise as structured intramural athletics?

One of the major objectives of all educational sports programs is to foster lifetime participation in physical activity. Ironically, though, those programs which stimulate extrinsic motivations for play probably do participants a disservice, in that physical activity in later life may be discontinued or significantly reduced when extrinsic rewards are absent. Studies by Kleiber[13] and Wankel[35] offer indirect, supportive evidence of that possibility by conclud-

20

ing that intrinsic motivation results in more permanent learning than that which is achieved from external incentive, and intrinsic drive may actually be abated by continual exposure to extrinsic concerns. Also, people who experience the negative effects of serious sport, whether it be undue pressure to perform well, a "weeding out" process, or simply the embarrassing identification of bad players relative to good ones, may be permanently "turned off" to play. If the pursuit of championships and extrinsic rewards is *so* important that people hesitate to play in its absence, or withdraw because of previously bad experiences, then such pursuit is *too* important. A lifetime of play seems most probable when people play for the right reasons (fun, positive socialization, psychological diversion, physical fitness) and under favorable circumstances (free-play structure).

The motives for, and purposes of, play have been found to be complex.[14] As researchers[15 18 37] have found, most people endorse playful attitudes (fun, socialization), rather than professional ones (skill, winning). But, Moriarty and Holman observed that sports participants' behavior did not support their expressed attitudes. Emphases in skillful performance and winning came to the forefront of people's consciousness under highly competitive conditions.[19] Seemingly, the basic motivation of a serious player is to establish dominance over other players, which usually leads to social prestige and a feeding of one's ego. That is a disturbing reality, for several reasons.

The boosting of one's self-concept, a nearly instinctive human concern, although questionable in any event, is particularly illogical when applied to sport. If one is determined to spend much of his/her physical and mental energies toward the achievement of some goal, and accept plaudits upon successful completion, it seems reasonable to expect that goal to be socially relevant. Of what conceivable benefit to the rest of the world is one's successful performance in the playing of games? If one can agree that there is none, why should the successful games-player be revered, when such reverence is based on false values? Our heroes can very nicely be found in other quarters of life. And, the widely held belief, that the serious pursuit of victory in sport is a laudable, important, and meaningful aspect of life, need not be perpetuated in our educational systems. If one wants to do something important, he/she can help an old lady across the street.

Beyond the absence of social relevance, serious play has more direct, potentially negative effects on people. The basis for most sport is a confrontation between two opponents, which tends to result in an enemy relationship. Although hatred and human conflict, whether manifested or inwardly withheld; may be acceptable to a large part of our society, they are unjustifiable on moral/religious grounds. In fact, when the dust and fog clears from any debate on the merits and demerits of athletics, it usually boils down to the moral issue. Author James Michener asks this pertinent question about

21

serious competition: "If winning is important and, in some instances a matter of keeping one's job, and if in order to win consistently one must develop a hatred for one's opponent and be ruthless, for fear of extinction, how does one relate that to morality and religion?"[18] Even more penetrating and thought provoking is a Christian quote from the Gospel of Luke: "For whoever wishes to save his life shall lose it, but whoever loses his life for My sake, he is the one who will save it."[9] Where does the march toward an intramural basketball championship fit into those thoughts?

The New Games Foundation, an organization dedicated to the promotion of recreative play, operates under the slogan: *Play Hard. Play Fair. Nobody Hurt.* That middle statement relates to an aspect of play that tends to be regularly violated in the atmosphere spawned by structured sport. The existence of organization, rules, officials, scorekeeping, and the inevitable sanction and recognition of champions seems to influence many serious players to engage in forms of moral cheating.

Cheating, as described by Michener, regularly occurs in the Soap Box Derby. Cars are to be built by contestants (the kids, themselves) at a cost not exceeding $75.00. But, some overzealous parents covertly have cars engineered for $20,000[18]. Richardson[25] and Webb[37] found that the more one is involved in highly competitive forms of sport, the more likely sportsmanship would take a secondary role to the pursuit of victory. Similarly, Feldman demonstrated that athletes and spectators displayed less desirable sportsmanship traits than non-spectators[7].

In contrast, participants in recreative games tend to advocate whatever seems fair at the time. But, rules, and officials to enforce them, are an open invitation for players to search for loopholes and gain advantages over opponents. With the high visibility of professional, collegiate, and high school sports programs that throw honesty and integrity to the wind, there is a disturbing emphasis, throughout our games-playing world, on beating the system without getting caught. It is of little concern to the successful cheater that victory is attained unfairly, as long as it is sanctioned by the officials. Unfortunately, the process provides all too realistic preparation for the outside world, as George Leonard suggests in *The Ultimate Athlete*[15].

Any time a ball is rolled between two people, a degree of competition usually takes place. But, one must not confuse the simple competition of an impromptu or informal game with the more complex competition for championships, recognition, and social prestige. Both have their "...own rules, judges, moralities, codes of law, jurisprudence, and taken-for-granted understandings."[3] And, the consequences of each are largely disparate. Moriarty and Holman, in studying Little League baseball teams, found differences in behavior amongst people participating in highly competitive structures and those involved in a more recreational play. Relative to the recreational play, observed behaviors of competitive participants included higher frequencies of self-dissatisfaction; hostility of players, coaches, and spectators toward umpires and opponents; apathy; and unhappiness.[19] On the other hand, games that are spontaneously organized, are controlled by the players without officials, and are flexible with respect to rules enforcement seem to induce amongst players fairness in judgment, cooperation, concern for the welfare of others, and genuine enjoyment.[12] That situation probably reflects what Holman and Moriarty had in mind in recommending changes in program structure to elicit appropriate sociability.[19]

In advocating that sports play be cooperative rather than competitive, Leonard quotes his aikido "master" as saying, "Aikido's spirit is that of loving attack and that of peaceful reconciliation."[15] The significant, if subtle, point is that, within the framework of an intrinsically-oriented play philosophy, potential outcomes of sports participation, such as the development of group cooperation, composure under pressure, individual leadership, the mature acceptance of success and failure, and humanistic attitudes and behaviors, are achievable and need not be coupled with supposedly unavoidable outbreaks of selfishness, hatred, and verbal and physical violence. For a player to learn cooperative skills within a team setting, he/she need not be taught to regard the opposition as an enemy, even temporarily. And, with regard to assimilating people into society and teaching them societal survival skills through sport, there is nothing inherently sacred about serious competition; unless, of course, the goal is to produce a society of inconsiderate, intolerant, and merciless people. To an annoying degree, that circumstance currently exists.

Bill Harper, former director of The Play Factory at Emporia State University in Kansas, says, "Any time you have games in which the participants have less control than the organizers about how they play, who they play, when they play, then it is not really play."[11] The primary motives of kids' participation in sports are fun and sociability.[8] When let alone to play, youngsters conform and cooperate to make games work, because they eventually realize that the equality of the teams and the uncertain outcome of a game is what makes it fun. In the process, they learn to negotiate, arbitrate, and make decisions.[13] The adult-directed games, that are currently so pervasive in American life, destroy that process and diminish the values of play, because rewards and punishments are provided by adults, rather than peers.[4]

It seems reasonable to believe that standard American attitudes toward play, those which have been inculcated into children by adults, must be driven out of those who have been infected with them, and keep from those who have not. Essentially, a remaking of the sports establishment is in order, so the "children at play," regardless of age, may have returned to them the inherent freedoms of unhindered play. Toward that end, and within our immediate sphere of influence, as intramural directors, we should structure the intramural programs of our scholastic institutions so free play, rather than athletics, can take place. That means, awards, point systems, championships, and officials must be removed from sports programs. The function of the intramural director is to provide people with the circumstances (equipment, facilities, rules information, scheduling) within which they can play.

It is widely accepted that sport reflects the societal values within which it operates;[15] and, it "generates loyalty to, support for, and assimilation into established society."[30] Since American life is saturated with an athletic consciousness, it will be difficult to reverse the current situation. So, the big question is this: If the vehicles for change can be identified as being the physical education and intramural programs of our educational institutions, and such change must initially counter the popular will, can such change occur; can it be effective; and can it be justified?

This author would like to believe, naively perhaps, that all three parts of the question can be answered in the affirmative. Obviously, the political situation within which one must operate substantially determines the possibilities for change. If the possibility exists at all, those educators who see the need for change should at least attempt to implement it. The critical accomplishment is a breaking down of people's traditional thinking and natural resistance to change. Once that is achieved, progress is foreseeable.

Subsequently, one may consider two arenas for battle—the public/private and post-secondary schools. Supposedly, one must come to terms with each separately, because the populaces to which one is potentially accountable are different in each case. It may be that the public schools provide the most vulnerable point of attack.

The adult decision-makers or pressure groups in any particular community are usually far more concerned with a school's athletic program than its physical education and intramural programs. Therefore, changes in the intramural program can probably be made without too many eyebrows raised, as long as the athletic program, its attendant entertainment viability, and the reputation of the community are not adversely affected, immediately. Quite practically, progressive programs of play could be gradually implemented, with little or no student complaint, by starting with the lower grades, and maintaining those programs as the kids move through the higher grades. Such an approach should maximize the effectiveness of ideological assimilation, and minimize the possibility for ideological confrontation. Systematic subversion just might have a chance of changing athletic programs, eventually.

The situation in collegiate life is somewhat different. On many college campuses, students are given as much decision-making influence as administrators think they can allow. Utilization of the democratic process, and the incorporation of students into that process, are usually cited as reasons for permitting students to considerably control programs, such as intramurals, that are peripheral to academics. Although democratic decision-making is nice, the suspicion, here, is that intramurals is not regarded by school administrators as being significant enough to warrant the same authoritative attention as do academics and varsity athletics. Thus, intramurals, and similar programs, can be viewed as crumbs thrown to students in an attempt to satiate their desires for decision-making power. But, even in the area of play, an educational enterprise has an instructive responsibility to its students. Because of the benefits potentially gained and the lessons learned or confirmed from participation in a program of play, intramurals is play education. Play affects the quality of one's life as much as do programmed exercise, nutrition, and relaxation; and, each of these concerns is every bit as important, or more so, than any of the academic or varsity athletic pursuits available. Further, a school has the responsibility to uphold its integrity and credibility as an institution concerned with social improvement. So, a program of serious play, which precipitates social conflict, is out of line with the charge of improving the human condition. For those reasons alone, faculty control of play is as appropriate as faculty control of any other scholastic function.

What is being advocated is not such an abridgement of human democratic rights as it may seem. Simply stated, faculty should have the authority and sense of obligation to determine program objectives, philosophy, and the general framework within which participants should be permitted to make decisions on specific issues. The functions of the intramural staff are to monitor student decision-making and appropriately veto judgments that clearly violate program philosophy.

Whatever the decision-making process is, particularly in highly competitive intramural sports programs, it is generally accepted that those participants who violate certain standards of behavior will be disciplined, usually by a suspension from play for a designated period of time. The problem with that approach, however, is three-fold.

Firstly, because of the behavior models presented by those involved with professional, interscholastic, and youth athletics, participants expect similar standards of behavior to be tolerated in intramural programs. But, as indicated before, those standards do not meld with the behavior that should be associated with an educational establishment. Secondly, even when discipline *is* employed against social deviants, it doesn't really make much sense. Is it not just to structure a program that fosters human conflict, then punish those who act pugilistically? Surely, disciplinary measures against those who misbehave are justifiable in programs that promote peaceful play, because misbehavior then becomes incongruous with the purpose and tone of the program. Thirdly, the withholding of people from play runs counter to one of the primary tenets of intramurals — to actively involve as many people as possible in the program. Therefore, circumstances should be arranged so the probability of disciplinary action is lessened.

In conclusion, [games] "have become marred by destructive competition, destructive aggression, sadistic rivalry, dehumanization, fear of failure, feelings of rejection, cuts, drop-outs, wounded self-concepts, a lack of fun, and a loss of love for activity."[22] Any program that cultivates those outcomes lies somewhere beneath the theoretical dignity of a scholastic institution. People must be encouraged to realize that the most important aspect of a game (and life, for that matter) involves the human relationships that exist between the people who play it. Atmospheres of confrontation should be dissolved. Attitudes that spawn enemy relationships between people should be neutralized. Good programs of play absolve people from the worrisome concerns of winning, skillful performance, and social prestige. Those who play for the sake of play are the real winners, because "the prize is play itself."[15]

BIBLIOGRAPHY

[1]Barnett, L. A., "Current Thinking About Children's Play: Learning to Play or Playing to Learn?" Quest, 26:5-16, 1976.

[2]Cratty, Bryant, quote cited in Tutko and Burns (see listing number 34).

[3]Denzin, Norman K., "Child's Play and the Construction of Social Order." Quest, 26:48-55, 1976.

[4]Devereux, E. C., "Backyard Versus Little League Baseball: The Impoverishment of Children's Games," in D. M. Landers, Social Problems in Athletics. Chicago: University of Illinois Press, 1976.

[5]Edwards, Harry, Sociology of Sport. Homewood, Ill.: Dorsey, 1973.

[6]Ellis, M. J., Why People Play. Englewood Cliffs, N. J.: Prentice-Hall, Inc., 1973.

[7]Feldman, Michael, "Some Relationships Between Specified Values of Student Groups and Interscholastic Athletics in Selected High Schools." Unpublished Doctoral Dissertation, University of Massachusetts, 1969.

[8]Frost, Reuben B., "Motivation and Arousal," in Walter C. Schwank, Editor, The Winning Edge. Washington, D. C.: AAHPER Publications, 1974.

[9]Gospel of Luke, verse 24, New American Standard Bible (New Testament). South Holland, Ill.: The World Home Bible League, 1971.

[10]Hanford, George, "An Inquiry into the Need for and Feasibility of a National Study of Intercollegiate Athletics," cited in Michener (see listing number 18).

[11]Harper, Bill, "Play Factory: Confessions of a Diletante." Proceedings of the Second Central Regional Intramural Sports Conference. p. 1-7. Wichita State University Press, 1977.

[12]Hopkins, Peter D., "A Child's Model for Adult Games: A Viable Alternative." Proceedings of the National Intramural-Recreational Sports Association Conference, 28:124-135, 1977.

[13]Kleiber, Douglas A., "Playing to Learn," Quest, 26:68-74, 1976.

Philosophical and Historical Considerations

[14]Kneer, Marian E., "The Role of Student Satisfaction in Developing Play Skills and Attitudes." *Quest,* 26:102-108, 1976.

[15]Leonard, George, *The Ultimate Athlete.* New York: The Viking Press, Inc., 1975.

[16]Loy, John, Susan Birrell, and David Rose., "Attitudes held Toward Agonetic Activities as a Function of Selected Social Identities," *Quest,* 26:81-93, 1976.

[17]Menninger, William, quote cited in Michener (see listing number 18).

[18]Michener, James A., *Sports in America.* New York: Random House, 1976.

[19]Moriarty, Dick and Marge Holman. "Change Agent Research for Citizenship, Sportsmanship, and Manhood," *Eric Reports,* #ED104871, August, 1974.

[20]Nelson, L. L., and S. Kagan. "Competition: The Star-Spangled Scramble" *Psychology Today,* September, 1972.

[21]Ogilvie, Bruce C. and Thomas A. Tutko, "Sport: If You Want to Build Character, Try Something Else," *Psychology Today,* October: 60-63, 1971.

[22]Orlick, Terry. "Cooperative Games," *Journal of Physical Education and Recreation,* 48:33-35, September, 1977.

[23]Ralbovsky, Martin, "Destiny's Darlings: A World Championship Little League Team Twenty Years Later," cited in Michener (see listing number 18).

[24]Reisman, David, quote cited in Tutko and Bruns (see listing number 34).

[25]Richardson, Deane E. "Ethical Conduct in Sport Situations," *National College Physical Education Association for Men Proceedings,* 66:98-104, 1962.

[26]Rokosz, Francis M., "Thoughts on the Purpose and Existence of Intramural Sports Programs," *Proceedings of the National Intramural-Recreational Sports Association Conference,* 27:64-67, 1976.

[27]Rokosz, Francis M., "A Significant Connection Between Public School and Collegiate Intramural Programs," *Proceedings of the National Intramural-Recreational Sports Association Conference,* 27:67-70, 1976.

[28]Rokosz, Francis M., "Changing Sport, Changing Man," *Journal of the National Intramural-Recreational Sports Association,* 2:42-46, October, 1977.

[29]Rokosz, Francis M., "Looking Good," *Journal of Physical Education and Recreation,* 48:31, February, 1977.

[30]Schafer, Walter E., "Sport and Youth Counterculture: Contrasting Social Themes," Paper presented at the Conference on Sport and Social Deviancy. Brockport, New York, 1971.

[31]Scott, Jack, *The Athletic Revolution.* New York: Free Press, 1971.

[32]Selye, Hans, *The Stress of Life.* New York: McGraw-Hill, 1956.

[33]Stone, Gregory P., Editor, *Games, Sport and Power.* New Brunswick, N. J.: Transaction, 1972.

[34]Tutko, Thomas and William Bruns, *Winning is Everything and Other American Myths.* New York: MacMillan Publishing Co., Inc., 1976.

[35]Wankel, Leonard M., "The Effects of Awards on Competition," Department of Kinesiology, University of Waterloo, an address to the Kitchener-Waterloo Regional Sport Council, January 28, 1974, Waterloo, Ontario, cited in Hopkins (see listing number 12).

[36]Watson, Geoffrey C., "Social Conflict and Parental Involvement in Little League Baseball." *Quest,* 27:71-86, 1977.

[37]Webb, Harry, "Professionalization of Attitudes Toward Play Among Adolescents," in *Aspects of Contemporary Sport Sociology,* Gerald S. Kenyon, Editor. Chicago: Athletic Institute, pp. 161-187, 1969.

THE EVOLUTION OF AN INTRAMURAL-RECREATIONAL PROGRAM FROM ATHLETICS TO PHYSICAL EDUCATION TO STUDENT ACTIVITIES

By: McKinley Boston, Montclair State College

I believe most professional Intramural-Recreation administrators have faced at some time or other the same overriding issues that eventually led to my seeking a new administrative base for the recreation program at our institution. The recreation program in its original capacity was programmed as a dependent structure of the Department of Athletics. The organizational structure being used by the Department of Athletics could be described as a centralized system of programming.

James Murphy[1] defines centralized systems of programming as, "systems that frequently reflect too much bureaucratization and a desire to preserve the status quo." Murphy further states, "the centralized system typically has proved itself incapable of responding effectively to the diverse needs of the population utilizing the service." It was my observation that the theory being used in the implementation of leisure services was ineffective. A careful analysis and evaluation of the program revealed several issues that defined the overall ineffectiveness in programming and delivery of services. The issues as I viewed them were:

1) No system allowing for participant input into the program at any level. Niepoth and Brown[2] state, "that the participant is the essential factor in the provision of recreation and leisure services."

2) No stated purpose, goals, and objectives.

3) No administrative manual or handbook for daily and future program continuity.

4) Numerous facility scheduling inequities.

5) No mechanism for program evaluation.

6) Only general acceptance by the total college community (President, School Deans, students, faculty and Administrators).

The above issues were examined and discussed with the athletic administration in an attempt to resolve some of the problems immediately and to determine if a master plan could be developed to deal with various issues on an intermediate basis. If we were going to develop a unit and a program that was capable of providing the entities necessary to satisfy the social, physical, and psychological recreational needs of our clientele, let alone becoming an organizationally stable program unit with its own identity, then I felt we needed to deal with the issues immediately.

Yet, after weeks of continued dialogue with athletic administrators analyzing the issues, it was determined that the department wouldn't be able to effectively at this time resolve the identified areas of concerns. The department's failure to react to concerns identified eventually led to dialogue concerning the feasibility of a transfer of the Intramural-Recreation Program to the Physical Education Department. This discussion eventually led to a division approximately one year later.

During the investigation of the past program, I was able to conduct program and organizational research, sample other similar institutional recreation structures, and survey our students as to what they were expecting in the delivery of Recreational-Intramural Services. The information gathered tremendously aided the Physical Education Chairman and myself in the establishment of the new organizational structure (Table I). The theory and/or approach to programming was to be a decentralized leisure service organization which would bring service closer to the clientele and make provisions for direct clientele feedback.

It was determined that direct student input would be maximized if the Student Government Association (SGA) would charter a student organization and fund it directly. A series of meetings were held with SGA officers in an attempt to determine the best possible method of involving students in the program. Based on all the gathered data and new concerns of the students, it was decided that we should attempt to involve the students at all levels of the program. The areas for student inclusion would be program planning and analysis, budget preparation and management, program rules, program evaluation, training and scheduling referees, league supervisors and the daily implementation of activities.

After careful analysis and evaluation of all concerns, we felt that the participation input we were seeking would be guaranteed by the creation of a Student Intramural Leisure Council. This Council would not be simply a window dressing for student involvement, but rather a sound administrative mechanism that would allow for direct involvement at all levels of the program.

The SGA insisted that the funds allocated to the program from its resources be controlled by the Council's Executive Board and that the Intramural Director's involvement with those funds be that of an administrative advisor. The Council would have full authority for the management of those funds. However, no salaries or student compensation for work could be paid out of monies allocated to the Council.

My initial reaction was negative to the suggestion. At the time I didn't feel the students had the professional knowledge or maturity to effectively manage the budget year in and year out. I also felt that because of the annual turnover of Council members that the overall continuity to this administrative phase of the program would be lost. However, over the past three years I have come to believe that my original concerns were not valid. This change in philosophy is based upon the fact that during the past three years there have been no recognizable problems with this phase of budget management. I must say, also, that my role as teacher and advisor to the students in budget management allows for greater personal insight into the student I've worked with. The implementation of a decentralized system that allowed for participation input—administratively and facilitively—had an immediate and resounding effect on the program. The SGA immediately began marketing the total program to other students. With their assistance program participation tripled during the initial year of operation. The program identity and stability had now become a reality. The students and college administrators were viewing Intramurals and Leisure activities as an integral part of the total college's operation and mission.

My second annual evaluation of the program as constituted under the Department of Physical Education evidenced other problems, such as state funding parady with physical education. This became an area of concern because of the academic thrust of the department. The Dean and the Physical Education Department were having difficulty in justifying funds allocated for academics being expended on student activity related programs. Although the Dean and Physical Education Department Chairman strongly supported the program administratively, it was felt that the academic thrust would eventually have an adverse effect on the continuity of the program.

During this annual program evaluation, the Dean, Physical Education Department Chairman, and I discussed these concerns and the possible linkage of the Intramural and Leisure Activities Program with the College Student Activities Program. I had previously successfully coordinated two summer recreation programs under their administration. More discussion and evaluation followed, and it was determined that all the missing administrative links that we were looking for were very feasible if we were to become a part of the Student Activities Office.

The Dean of Students and School Dean discussed the problems that I had previously identified with the College administrators. They were, at this time, also looking to improve the overall student related program's continuity as well as college communicators. The Intramural and Leisure Activities Program became a part of Student Activities three years ago (see Table II).

The Student Activities Office is a division under the guidance of the Dean of Students, who is a member of the College President's Cabinet. The current Student Activities staff has a Student Center/Student Activities Director, three (3) Assistant Directors, an all campus facility Scheduling Director and myself. Each Assistant Director has his/her area of student activities expertise. There is an Assistant Director in charge of the campus radio station and Student Center communications, an Assistant Director in charge of Student Center Building Operations and the campus Scheduling Officer. Although each of these individuals have their own area of operations, the daily

Table I

Intramural Organization

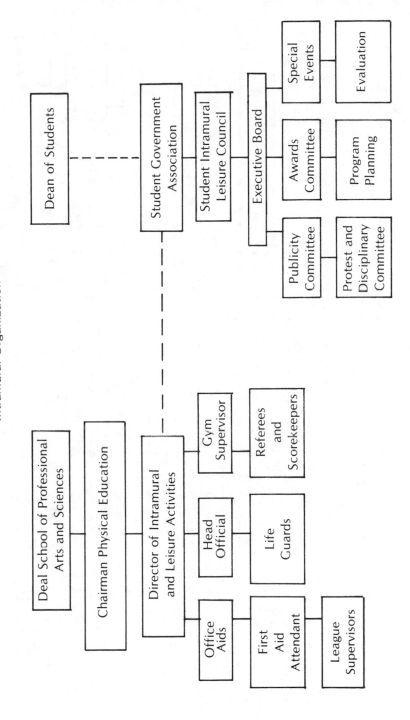

Table II

Intramural Organization

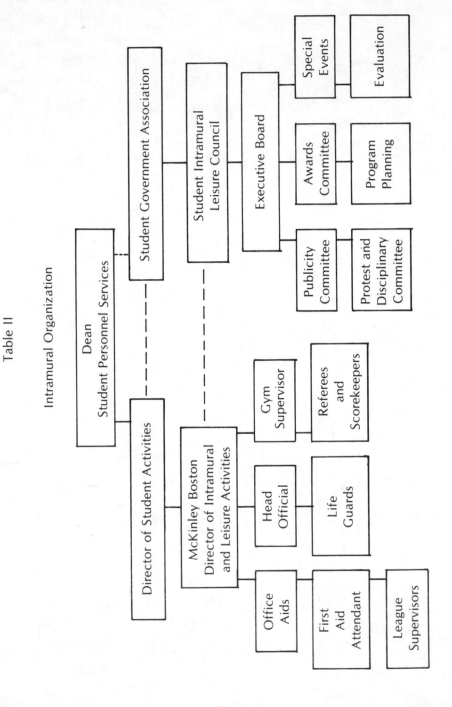

dialogue and Esprit de Corps has strengthened my total student services background immensely. Because of the variety of the Student Activities staff and the areas of the student population that we each are involved, the ability to now represent all the students and not just the traditional participating stereotypes is a reality. The direct communication with the Dean of Students has also opened a new line of communication to other college administrators, which is so important in the development of overall program continuity and growth.

Three years after the transfer, the financial assistance from the SGA has increased 50%; financial assistance from the College has increased 75%; program participation has expanded 300%, parity in scheduling of facilities has become a reality; we are represented on college committees; we have developed an active Student Intramural Leisure Council; an administrative handbook and Department manual has been produced; and most importantly, an administrative base has been established that allows for continued department growth and improved mechanisms for overall communication, program implementation, and participation diversity.

I strongly believe that Student Activities as an administrative base for Intramurals should be explored by other intramural professionals in NIRSA.

RESOURCES

Murphy, James F., Williams, John G., Niepoth, E. William and Brown, Paul D. *Leisure Service Delivery System: A Modern Perspective.* Philadelphia: Lea & Febiger, 1973, pp. 1, 18-19.

ADAM AND EVE WERE THE FIRST

Carolyn Bishop, Illinois State University

In any profession, and in this case as an intramural director, it is important to have a philosophy; a reason why one pursues certain goals within a program. A philosophy is the cornerstone of any idea put into practice. So it is with philosophy that I will begin my discusson on "Adam and Eve Were the First" — the original COED sport duo.

A typical philosophy of an intramural director might be to provide a quality intramural (competitive sports) program to meet the diverse recreational needs of all the students of an educational setting. Whatever is required to provide a quality program for all is planned and implemented, the net result being the creation of a men's and women's intramural program.

But what about the need for men and women to compete together? The increased interest in sport shown by today's woman has led her to seek opportunities to compete in sport together with men. One need only to take a look around; men and women are jogging together, playing tennis together, golfing together. The desire and need is evident. So within one's philosophy of an intramural program should lie the dutiful promise to implement a COED program. Not a program that receives only one-eighth of a staff member's attention, not a program that is administered by a student, not a program that is third in priority in terms of facilities, equipment, or funding, but a program that represents one-third of the entire intramural program.

One's approach to planning a COED program requires a sensitivity to the feelings men and women have towards sport and competition as they compete together as a team. Some may be very skilled or highly competitive while others may be of lesser competitive experience and wish merely to play in a sociable atmosphere. To accomodate these diverse needs, leagues of competition based on skill level could be devised, such as league A for the highly skilled athletes, league B for the average skilled athletes, and so on. Secondly, officiated and non-officiated team sport leagues could be provided. That is, in the officiated league trained, paid officials would be supplied by the intramural department to call the games, whereas in the non-officiated leagues the games would be called by the players or by volunteer officials from each team. To merely provide one type of competitive experience and not the other would be to turn one's back on providing a potentially *complete* COED program.

Now that it has been made evident that men and women wish to compete together with various intensities, how can an administrator facilitate channels of communication between the men and women in organizing teams? One method that has been successful at Illinois State University has been the "Co-Rec Pairing System." At the beginning of the school year the COED program director pairs male residence hall floors with female residence hall floors. Students, in comprising teams for certain sports, must play with their paired floor or floors. Each floor has a student Intramural Coordinator that is registered with the intramural office and acts as a liason between the students and the IM office, and it is through the coordinators from the paired floors contacting each other that teams are organized. Some off-campus living units could similarly be paired.

What types of sports could be offered in a COED program? Certainly the lifetime sports of golf, archery, bowling, tennis, and swimming should be included. However, the comradery of team sports shouldn't be overlooked. Softball, basketball, soccer, volleyball, and football should be considered. Yes, football. In any COED team sport, typical game rules may need to be modified in an attempt to equalize the competition and/or skill levels between men and women. This will enable participants to compete together with a minimal amount of danger in *any* sport.

Whatever the program—new activities, unusual activities, special interest activities—innovative programming is a must. So, why not try COED inner-tube water polo, water volleyball or basketball, a turkey trot, two on two basketball, or a track meet?

College students are ardent chess, checkers, backgammon, and card players. A COED tournament for these games could be a success. A particular activity may be of interest to a select group. For example, roller skating is extremely popular among the black student populace at Illinois State. Hence, a roller skating contest is included in our COED program.

Competitive COED sports can be initiated in conjunction with certain all-campus activities. At Illinois State, a section of the Informal Campus Recreation program deals with offering short classes in areas of interest to the students. One popular class was Disco Dance. At the conclusion of the unit, an intramural Disco Dance Contest was conducted.*

One can also look toward the media from time to time for new ideas. "Almost Anything Goes" and the "Superstar" competition as seen on television can make for exciting COED activities.

The same care could be taken to initiate a COED program or activity as one would use to introduce a men's or women's activity. To this end, all avenues of publicity should be sought. Use the school newspaper to the fullest as this may be the only means of communicating with the off-campus student. Utilize the student radio and television stations if they are existent at one's institution. Post activity information on bulletin boards in key student traffic areas. Alert student organizations, such as fraternities, sororities, minority student groups, etc., to the program. Establish an Intramural Coordinator system as mentioned earlier. One's school advertising department may be able to help in terms of planning a publicity program. The offering of quality programs whereby students encounter enjoyable competitive experiences tends to generate the best publicity possible—word of mouth.

Men and women competing together is a part of today's society. The interest is there. Thus, it is only fitting that as Intramural directors we offer a COED intramural program for our students. The quality of the program should be equal to or greater than that deemed acceptable for the men's or women's programs. After all, the first attempt at competitive sport was a COED activity with Adam and Eve being the first participants.

A NEED FOR A CLARIFICATION OF VALUES
FOR INTRAMURAL PARTICIPANTS

Connie Edmonson,   University of Kansas

INTRODUCTION

One of the major fundamental theoretical questions for the professional recreator is "Why do people play?" This question has been asked for centuries with many attempted answers, but there has been little questioning of these empirical answers in the field of research and practice. Ellis[4] stresses that "It is important for professionals dealing with the peoples of America to make serious attempts to understand the motives for the great variety of human leisure behavior."

Recreation and relaxation are generally regarded as necessities in the modern world. A goal of recreation is to provide opportunities for people to enhance the quality of their lives and their feelings of self-worth and satisfaction through leisure pursuits. Emphasis is placed upon the recreational experience and on what is happening to the individual's total development as a result of participating in recreation activities.[11] It has been said that the word "attitude" best identifies the recreative pursuits.[2] One's attitudes and values influence the choice and use of leisure, but the exercise of leisure may also reinforce, modify, or contradict one's attitudes and values.[5] One's sex and age can also cause variations in recreational sport values, preferences, and in the potential for attainment due to structural and functional characteristics.[8]

There is almost unanimity of opinion that mankind needs play and sport to enrich his life; but whether the enrichment is the actual experience of sport itself, or whether the enrichment is made-up of later resultants caused by the sports experience, still continues to be debated.[8] Interdisciplinary programs need to be initiated if recreation services is to keep pace with the "incessant demands" placed upon it by a growing population with diverse needs and interests. There has been a lack of standards against which performance has been measured to evaluate recreation services.[9] The lack of values associated with leisure has been in conflict with the increased quantity of discretionary time that is available to large numbers of people. Historically, recreation and leisure have been described as suffering from more value confusion than any other area of man's life.[3]

The physical activity of sport is one of the many dimensions of recreation. Sport provides an intriguing micro-analysis for the complex American culture and parallels the recognition of many behavior patterns within socie-

36

ty. Tandy and Taflin[15] describe the three dominant forces which have emerged in the sport society as: an individual search for identity, a search for emotional stimulation, and an attempt for achievement and status.

Alderman[1] revealed the influence of the sport society in the American culture when he stated:

> Life is a complex of physical, intellectual, emotional, and social developmental patterns, for a large number of people, especially children, sport and physical activity are integral parts of these patterns. Thus, an understanding of behavior in sport and physical activity will aid us in helping people to better fulfill their lives.

An "understanding of behavior in sport" may best be ascertained by determining the cultural values held by sport participants. At the National Intramural Association Conference in 1973, Susan Rohrer[13] made the following coment to recreation and intramural directors:

> It is not enough to justify our competitive activities or our values of standards of physical activity for students without the realization that man can grow when he finds value within himself first. We can certainly help him realize the methodology for search, but we cannot nor should not, impose our perceptions on him.

Research indicates that the college years are a crucial period in one's life. Students are searching for personal identity, and their attitudes and value systems are developed about their world. Much of the student's development of life values occurs during leisure time. Intramural sport has emerged as one of the most popular single undergraduate extracurricular activity today. Since sport and physical activity offer many opportunities for development of life values, there is a need for more attention to be given to the quality of the student's leisure experience that would lead them to take part in sport throughout their lives.[6][10][12]

Few people persist in the sport and physical activity domain of recreation for the physiological values alone. Other meaningful and significant benefits have kept them motivated. Once these other values are identified and systematically researched, a better understanding of people's involvement could result. The physiological benefits of physical activity are well established, but clarification of the psychological and sociological benefits is lacking.[5] Such a clarification would contribute to a better understanding of social reality and could be a primary prerequisite for the development of a sociopsychological theory of sport that would be an accurate assessment of the attitudes that various subgroups of people have toward physical activity.[7]

The goal of values clarification is to provide the time and space for one to deal with his own values. It is not a process by which one is expected to develop values, but rather to clarify existing values. The process involves knowing what one prizes, choosing those things which one cares for the most, and weaving those things into the "fabric" of daily living.[14] Values Clarification has been used in teaching, sexuality education, drug education, religious education, career planning, and leisure education.

Hence, a clarification of the college student's values toward intramural sports would grant the student a time and purpose to clarify his or her own values toward physical activity, and would also aid the recreation administrator in planning a diversified recreational program to meet the specific needs, interest, and values of the students.

PURPOSE

The purpose of the study was to clarify the values that college students held for the intramural sports in which they were interested. Most specifically, the study was designed to determine whether the attitudes toward physical activity of interested intramural participants at four different class levels of freshmen, sophomore, junior, and senior were 1) different between men and women, and 2) different between individual-oriented sport participants and team-oriented sport participants.

Individual-oriented sports are those in which only one player constitutes a team for singles play, or two players constitute a team for doubles play. Examples of individiual-oriented sports are tennis, racquetball, handball, squash, track, wrestling, table tennis, golf, and horseshoes.

Team-oriented sports are those in which three or more players constituted a team. Examples of team-oriented sports are football, volleyball, basketball, softball, and soccer.

METHODOLOGY

The study took place during the fall semester at the University of Kansas. The sample was composed of 349 students who were interested in participating in the intramural program under the Division of Recreation Services. Intramural managers, (who were students selected from their living group of dorm, sorority, or fraternity to be responsible for their group's intramural activities), assisted in administering the questionnaire to volunteer students from their living group who were interested in participating in the intramural program. The investigator administered the questionnaire to student volunteers living off-campus in apartments, homes, trailers, etc., at the intramural activity sites. Of the 452 subjects who received the questionnaire, the percentage of returned questionnaires was seventy-seven percent. The sample consisted of 70 freshmen, 79 sophomores, 88 juniors, and 112 seniors. There was a total of 192 males and 157 female subjects.

The information collected through the questionnaire was the student's class level (freshman, sophomore, junior, or senior), their favorite intramural sport, and Kenyon's Attitudes Towards Physical Activity Inventory, Form D. Kenyon's Inventory consisted of two forms, one for men and one for women, which determined the values held by interested intramural participants for their favorite intramural sport.

There are six subdomains of Kenyon's Inventory,[7] [8] including:

1. Physical activity as a social experience which is characterized by those activities whose primary purpose is to provide a medium for social intercourse.

2. Physical activity for health and fitness is justified primarily by its contribution to the improvement of one's health and fitness.

3. Physical activity as the pursuit of vertigo are those physical experiences providing, at some risk to the participant, an element of thrill through the medium of speed, acceleration, sudden change of direction, or exposure to dangerous situations, with the participant usually remaining in control.

4. Physical activity as an aesthetic experience are those activities conceived of as possessing beauty or certain artistic qualities.

5. Physical activity as catharsis are activities perceived as providing a release of tension precipitated by frustration through some vicarious means.

6. Physical activity as an ascetic experience required that the activity necessitates long, strenuous, and often painful training and stiff competition demanding a determent of many gratifications.

The statements on the inventory relating to the six subdomains had the possibility of scoring from one to seven on a seven-point Likent scale depending on whether the statement was positive or negatively stated. Separate mean scores were tallied for each of the six subdomains of Kenyon's Inventory.

A two-way analysis of variance was used to determine 1) whether there was a difference in the mean values held for intramural sports among the four class levels and between men and women, and 2) whether there was a difference in the mean values held for intramural sports among the four class levels and between students interested in participating in individual-oriented sports and those interested in participating in team-oriented sports. To those variables found to be significant, the student Newman Kuels Post Hoc Test was applied to determine the significant differences (at the .05 level), between the paired mean scores.

RESULTS AND DISCUSSION

Value Differences Among Class Levels

No significant differences were found among the four class levels for the subdomains of health and fitness, pursuit of vertigo, aesthetic experience, and catharsis. The four class levels were found to be significantly different at the .016 level for the social experience subdomain and at the .002 level for the ascetic experience subdomain.

In the social experience subdomain, the freshmen's mean attitudes were significantly different than the sophomore and junior's mean attitudes at the .05 level of significance. This result indicated that freshmen participants did not value participation in intramurals for social reasons as much as sophomore and junior participants. This may be attributed to the fact that college was a totally new experience for the freshmen. There was a decrease in the mean score of social values that senior participants placed upon intramurals as compared to the sophomore and junior participants; however, the mean scores were not significantly different. It appeared that sophomore and junior participants place higher values on intramurals for social reasons than the other class levels.

The results from the ascetic experience subdomain indicated that the freshmens' mean attitudes were significantly lower than the juniors' and seniors' mean attitudes at the .05 level of confidence. There was an increase in the mean attitudes from freshmen to sophomores, and from sophomores to juniors, but the differences were not significant. Junior and senior participants had similar mean attitudes. There appeared to be a trend that the higher class levels of junior and senior participants placed more value on intramurals for the "long, strenuous, and often painful training and stiff competition" aspect than the lower class levels of freshmen and sophomore participants. This was indicated by the results in that junior and senior participants were found to have significantly higher ascetic values than the freshmen participants. The investigator felt that possibly junior and senior participants concentrated more on skills and perfection in their favorite intramural sport than the lower class levels.

Value Differences Between Men and Women

No significant differences were found at the .05 level between the men and women mean values for the social experience and catharsis subdomains. Men were found to be significantly different than the women in the health and fitness and aesthetic experience subdomains at the .0001 and .001 levels respectively. The men obtained significantly higher mean scores on both of these subdomains. Women, however, were found to have significantly higher mean scores for the subdomains of pursuit of vertigo (at the .001 level of confidence) and ascetic experience (at the .0001 level of confidence).

A factor that may have influenced the women's values in the pursuit of vertigo and ascetic experience subdomains was that the surveys were administered during the major intramural fall sport of touch football. The women who volunteered to take the inventory from the intramural managers may have been those who were participating on the living group's intramural football team. Football has basically been considered a "new" intramural sport for women with few having much experience and background in the sport. It has become quite popular at the University of Kansas and the women are becoming more competitive. Many women's teams held regular practices in which learning the football skills may have been considered "long and strenuous training" (ascetic). Also, football has often been considered rough and possibly a risk (pursuit of vertigo) to the women.

On the other hand, there has been a change in society since the other studies were investigated. The influence of women's liberation and of Title IX may have socially influenced the values of women. The effect that Title IX over the last years has had in providing women competition in high school sports may have been carried over into their values in college. None of these facts were known to be definite causes of the results, but may be considered possibilities for the change of women's values.

The mean scores of the four class levels compared to the mean scores of the men and women were found to be significantly different at the .014 level in the pursuit of vertigo subdomain. Results denoted that freshmen and sophomore men and women participants held significantly different values for the vertigo domain than the junior and senior men and women participants. The junior and senior men and women participants all held similar values of vertigo. The freshmen and sophomore women participants valued risk activities extremely more than the freshmen and sophomore men participants. These results suggested that men and women value placed upon intramural sports for reasons of risk (vertigo) were significantly different in the lower class levels of freshmen and sophomores, but were quite similar in the upper class levels of juniors and seniors.

Value Differences Between Individual-oriented Sport Participants and Team-oriented Sport Participants

Within the assumptions and limitations of the study, there were no significant differences between the mean scores for students whose indicated favorite intramural sport was individual-oriented and those who were team-oriented. There also were no significant differences between the individual-oriented sport participants and the team-oriented sport participants when compared to the class levels. These results implied that there were neither significant differences in the student's values held for intramural individual-oriented sports and team-oriented sports, nor a significant difference in values as compared to the four class levels.

CONCLUSIONS

Within the scope and limitations of this study, the following conclusions have been drawn on the basis of the findings.

1. The four class levels of freshmen, sophomore, junior and senior held significant different social and ascetic values of intramural sports. Sophomore and junior participants valued intramurals significantly more for the social experience than the freshmen participants. Junior and senior participants valued intramurals for the "long, strenuous training" (ascetics) significantly more than the freshmen participants.

2. Men and women held significantly different values of intramural sports for reasons of health and fitness, pursuit of vertigo, aesthetic experience and ascetic experience. Men participants valued intramurals significantly more for reasons of health and fitness and for the "beauty of movement" or aesthetic experiences than the women. Women participants valued intramurals significantly more for reasons of "risk" or vertigo, and for the "long, strenuous training" (ascetics) than the men.

3. Men and women within the four class levels of freshmen, sophomore, junior and senior held significantly different values of intramural sports for reasons of vertigo.

4. There were no significant differences between the student values held for individual-oriented sports and team-oriented sports.

5. No significant differences of values held by the four class levels of freshmen, sophomore, junior and senior were determined by those students who prefer individual-oriented sports and those who prefer team-oriented sports.

RECOMMENDATIONS

After reviewing the results of this study, the following recommendations were made:

1. It was recommended that a longitudinal study be pursued over a period of at least four years in which the same subjects would be studied from their freshmen to senior year in college. This would determine how student values change through their college years.

2. It was recommended that other phases of the recreation program such as dance, sport clubs, and drop-in recreation be studied.

BIBLIOGRAPHY

[1]Alderman, Richard B., *Psychological Behavior in Sport,* Philadelphia: S. B. Saunders Company, 1974.

[2]Brightbill, Charles K., *The Challenge of Leisure,* Englewood Cliffs: Prentice-Hall, Inc., 1960.

[3]Davis, Joan, "Valuing: A Requisite for Education for Leisure," *Journal of Physical Education and Recreation,* Volume 47, Number 3 (March 1976), pp. 30-31.

[4]Ellis, M. J., "Play and Its Theories Re-examined," *Parks and Recreation,* Volume 6, Number 8 (August 1971), pp. 51-55, 89.

[5]Harris, Dorthy V., *Involvement in Sport: A Somatopsychic Rationale for Physical Activity,* Philadelphia: Lea and Febiger, 1973, pp. 1-52, 210-250.

[6]Hoge, Dean R. and Irvine E. Bender, "Factors Influencing Value Change Among College Graduates in Adult Life," *Journal of Personality and Social Psychology,* Volume 29, Number 4 (April 1974), pp. 572-585.

[7]Kenyon, Gerald S., "A Conceptual Model for Characterizing Physical Activity," *Sport, Culture, and Society,* eds., John W. Loy, Jr. and Gerald S. Kenyon, London: MacMillan Company, 1969, pp. 71-82.

[8]Lawther, John D., *Sport Psychology,* Englewood Cliffs: Prentice Hall, Inc., 1972, pp. 1-65.

[9]McClean, Christine, and Charles R. Spears, "Leisure Programs: Quandry or Quality," *Parks and Recreation,* Volume 10, Number 7 (July 1975), pp. 21-23, 42-45.

[10]Miller, Norm P., "Leisure Life Styles in the University Setting," *Journal of Health, Physical Education and Recreation,* Volume 45, Number 9 (November-December 1974), pp. 57-58.

[11]Mobley, Tony A., " . . . Philosophical Thought," *Parks and Recreation,* Volume 11, Number 7 (July 1976), pp. 16-17, 91-95.

[12]Mull, Rich, "Recreational Sport and the Future," *Twenty-sixth Annual Conference Proceedings of the National Intramural Recreational Sports Association,* Lubbock: The Texas Tech Press, 1975, pp. 103-112.

[13]Rohrer, Susan J., "Recreation in Intramurals," *Twenty-fourth Annual Conference Proceedings of the National Intramural Recreational Sports Association,* 1973, pp. 114-116.

[14]Simon, Sidney F., Leland W. Howe, and Howard Kirchenbaum, *Values Clarification: A Handbook of Practical Strategy for Teachers and Students,* New York: Hart Publishing Company, Inc., 1972.

[15]Tandy, Ruth E., and Joyce Laflin, "Aggression and Sport: Two Theories," *Journal of Health, Physical Education and Recreation,* Volume 44, Number 6 (June 1973), pp. 19-20.

CHAPTER II

Ideas For Programming

SPECIAL INTEREST RECREATION PROGRAMS

Ellen Gold, The University of Michigan

What are we speaking of when we use the term "special interest recreation?" Very often special interest programming becomes a catch-all, a term which encompasses everything other than competitive intramurals and sports clubs. Sometimes the term is used interchangeably with "informal recreation," appropriately or not. Special interest recreation is the melting pot for those programs which have trouble fitting into the sports club or intramural categories.

The Department of Recreational Sports at The Universtiy of Michigan has an extensive special interest recreation program design for special interest recreation that would allow people to understand the building base for our many programs offered. The result of much time, thought and discussion reads as follows:

> Special interest recreation is a concept of leisure service delivery which provides opportunities through programming for observation of, or participation in physical activity. For each offered opportunity, the structure-imposed programmatically, (i.e. time schedule, degree of supervision and degree of organization), is determined by the needs and choices of participants. The opportunities offered vary in degree of structure and cover a continuum allowing for little or no time schedule, supervision or organization to very highly supervised and organized activity at a scheduled time.

Keeping this concept in mind, I would like to introduce you to the many special interest programs offered by the Recreational Sports Department; programs which made the special interest recreation definition workable.

Disabled User Program

We are all aware of the fact that recreation should not be limited to any age, attitude or physical or mental condition. The Partner Program provides individuals (partners) for those disabled users on campus who would like someone to recreate with for whatever purpose that person needs served. Interested individuals are matched with volunteer partners who have similar interests and desire to participate in that selected activity and time slot.

Disabled users are also invited to participate in special events and clinics as well as intramurals, and are continuously provided with information concerning recreational opportunities. You might say that one of the Partner Program mottos is "There's something for everyone!"

Children's Sports-o-rama

The program goal is to provide the opportunity for children of students, staff and faculty to learn the true value and enjoyment of recreation on their own, with their families, and with their peer group.

By using this program goal as a building base, the Children's Sports-o-rama has successfully been developed and implemented. This program, designed for children ages 3-10, provides open recreation time and space on Saturday mornings for 10 weeks each semester in which structured, supervised recreational activities take place in the gym, track, exercise/gymnastics room and pool. Two sessions are held:

Session I	3-6 year olds	9-11 a.m.
Session II	7-10 year olds	11-1 p.m.

Approximately 75 children are registered in each session. The children are divided into 3 groups and rotate to all three activity areas each Saturday. There is a program fee and we do set limits on the number of children for each session since the program is extremely popular.

The program staff includes graduate and some undergraduate students in the fields of physical education and/or recreation and elementary education for the most part. They are responsible for planning the activities in their assigned area such as organized games, simple exercise, basic tumbling, and water activities, etc.

International Program

Members of the University community representing many countries and cultures gather weekly during the fall and winter terms to participate in recreational activities. While badminton and volleyball are most popular, other recreational opportunities are offered when requested by the group. The situation is informal; however, competition may be keen in various contests throughout the gym. Additionally, one family event is offered each term.

Sunday Funday Family Program

The Family Program, better known as "Sunday Funday" is designed so as to provide indoor open recreation time and space on Sunday afternoons between 2 p.m. and 5 p.m. for family use only at the North Campus Recreation Building. All activity areas are open including the track, gym, pool, paddleball and squash courts, exercise room and weight room. A program assistant is present each Sunday who acts as a facilitator, sets up nets, and provides a variety of equipment for use in the gym and exercise room for families to try out such items as utility balls, jump ropes, hula hoops and badminton racquets. This encourages people to come in and try out a variety of activities.

Another feature of this program is the structured family tournaments. Both husband/wife and parent/child recreative tournaments are held in table tennis, badminton, paddleball and racquetball with the main objectives being for all involved to have fun and get an opportunity to meet and recreate with other families.

Finally, the Department of Recreational Sports has introduced Operation Family Fitness, a physical fitness program for the entire family. One of the real advantages of a family fitness program is that there is a built-in buddy system in every family. To asssist the family in planning an adequate fitness program, the Department has designed an "Operation Family Fitness" booklet, which contains a detailed exercise program based on goal selection in the areas of bicycling, jogging, swimming and rope skipping. Further, family fitness clinics have been offered to assist families with their fitness programs.

Adolescent Program

Adolescents, ages 11-17, who are children of students, staff or faculty at The University of Michigan are being provided with the opportunity to recreate in a college setting along with their peers and university students by means of this first year program. Adolescents are paired up with University students who volunteer to serve as "Big Brothers/Big Sisters."

The program meets on specified Sundays from 11:30 a.m.-1:30 p.m. at the North Campus Recreation Building throughout the semester. Group games .such as floor hockey, soccer, basketball, as well as individual activity between pairs such as swimming, racquetball and jogging take place at this time.

A major objective of the program is to allow program participants to use recreational facilities without having to be accompanied by their parent. This is accomplished by allowing the adolescent and his/her "partner" to make arrangements to use the recreational facilities on a regular basis during any of the building's drop-in hours.

Self-Directed Fitness

The Self-Directed Fitness Program is designed to serve those individuals who wish to begin or augment their own fitness programs and increase their knowledge of such activities. "Run For Your Life," "Swim and Stay Fit," and "Presidential Sports Award" are the three types of programs from which to choose. Handouts are available pertaining to these programs as well as jogging guidelines, aquatic fitness, a calorie tally and much more. Progress charts are posted at all indoor tracks and swimming pools for those who wish to record their mileage. Mileage certificates are issued on an individual basis for every 10 miles swam or run. T-Shirts are awarded after the completion of 50 and 100 miles respectively.

Fitness-related films and clinics are offered on a monthly basis. Film and clinic topics include: bicycling, jogging, weight training, aquadynamics, cross country skiing, athletic injuries, conditioning for women and family fitness.

P.A.I.F.S.

For the individual who would like to receive qualified instruction or wishes to exercise with others performing the same activity, the Recreational Sports Department and the Department of Physical Education jointly offer PAIFS, Physical Activity Instruction for Faculty and Staff. Generally classes are offered for five and ten week sessions in such activities as tennis, swimming, jogging, weight training, fitness and paddleball/racquetball.

Instruction is presented by qualified personnel to allow both the novice and the skilled player or fitness enthusiast to gain valuable knowledge and experience. Instructors strive to develop and improve upon individual's skills and/or fitness program.

Unique Events

The unique event serves the Recreational Sports Department by showcasing what the Department is doing through novel and "out of the ordinary" recreational experiences. The unique event provides recreational opportunities to both the University and local communities and it serves to increase and stimulate social interaction among individual participants.

One example of a unique event we have held is an All-Nighter. A recreational facility is kept open all night with a variety of sports tournaments, sports club demonstrations, silly games, and drop-in activity. Special features include bands, movies and clown acts. Other unique events range from a New Games Festival to a bike rodeo.

Faculty Women's Club Sport Sections

The Faculty Women's Club, whose membership is composed of women faculty and staff as well as the wives of faculty and staff members, offers its members a wide range of special activity groups in which to participate. Four sport sections which meet in the Department of Recreational Sports facilities are available to members including badminton, tennis, racquetball/ paddleball and swimming.

Camp Adventure

The Department of Recreational Sports offers a summer day camp for children, ages 7-12. Camp Adventure has been in operation for one year and is designed to provide the opportunity for children to learn the true value and enjoyment of recreation, especially outdoor recreation, on their own and with their peer group through social interaction.

There are two sessions of camp offered, one being held in July and the second taking place in August. Both sessions meet Mondays through Fridays from 9:00 a.m. - noon, for a three week period. The camp is located in and around the North Campus Recreational Building.

Program activity areas include aquatics, organized games, crafts and nature experience, and "anything goes." The children are divided into three groups and travel with their group to every activity area daily. Two special event days and two field trips also take place within each camp session.

Each individual program within Special Interest Recreation provides a vital function. The ultimate goal in all areas focuses upon meeting the specific needs of specific populations within the total university community.

Several principles are viewed as important to the continued development of the special interest recreation program concept and they are as follows:

1. The program should be planned equally for both sexes.
2. The program should encourage family recreation.
3. The program should be planned for interaction among all ethnic groups and cultures.
4. The program should encourage cooperative behavior.
5. The program should provide for the total group and equal opportunity for everyone in it.

6. The program should provide opportunities at varying levels of participant proficiency and be adaptable to individual differences.

These six principles are especially important; however, they are not guarantees for success. They will provide a basic foundation to work from and hopefully positive results will follow.

"CLASS-IC CAPERS" SHORT COURSES IN RECREATIONAL ACTIVITIES

by Phyllis Glazier, Illinois State University

Massage, sailing, ballet, scuba diving, disco dance, and auto maintenance are just a few of the subjects taught in the Class-ic Capers program at Illinois State University. Class-ic Capers is a program composed of short, non-credit courses offered to students, faculty, staff, and the public to help enrich their recreation and leisure time. The courses meet once a week, for a one- to two-hour lesson, for a total of four- to six-weeks. The complete roster of courses is offered during each nine-week period of the university school year.

The program began on an experimental basis in 1976 with six different subjects being taught. A successful initial registration of 270 persons, encouraged continuation and expansion. Today the classes offered during each nine-week period include 15 to 20 different subjects.

Since the Class-ic Capers program does not receive university funding, all classes must be self-supporting. Because of this, class costs are predetermined and registration fees charged.

Although organizing a large number of classes each nine-weeks takes a great deal of time, through the diligent efforts of one well-organized, dependable student worker almost all of the work can be accomplished with only a small amount of aid from a recreation staff member.

Since it is usually too expensive and administratively time consuming to offer small special interest groups the programs they desire, Class-ic Capers has proven to be a good way to meet students' special interests.

If a student's interest in a Class-ic Capers subject becomes so intense that following the conclusion of a course he/she wishes to learn more, he/she can usually enroll in a college course the next semester or seek additional instruction elsewhere. Although Class-ic Capers is unable to meet the advanced interests of some persons, if it were not for the basic Class-ic Capers course the student may never have had the opportunity to pursue the activity.

A conference presentation on the short courses at a California university inspired the idea for Class-ic Capers. Unfortunately, a shortage of manpower in the recreation department delayed the program's start until the assistance of a graduate student in recreation was secured. With the added manpower, the program finally began on an experimental basis in January, 1976, with a core of six different subjects being taught. Today, the class offerings available each nine-weeks include 15 to 20 different subjects, with an average registration of over 350 students.

Budgetary Basis of Class-ic Capers

With budget limitations apparent in most campus recreation programs, the funding of new programs is usually of great interest. Class-ic Capers has no university funding so the classes must be self-supporting. Because of this, class registration fees are charged for participation in all classes. Despite the fact that this might be an ideal opportunity for producing income, this has never been a major goal of Class-ic Capers. In order to meet the primary goal of serving the special interests of the students, it is important to keep class registration fees reasonable to avoid discouraging students from enrolling in classes they want to take.

There are five basic factors which must be considered when setting the registration fee for each class. In short, these factors include the costs for instruction, advertising, class materials provided by campus recreation, rental fees for facilities and equipment, and the maximum number of students that can be accommodated in each class. Once the total cost for each course is calculated, the total is divided by the maximum number of students and the registration fee is set accordingly.

While it is not feasible to charge a different price for each course offered, some basic prices for similar types of classes are charged whenever possible. For example, a fee of $5 is charged for most physical activity courses that include five one-hour lessons. A fee of $6 is charged for most craft classes that include five two-hour lessons. Craft students usually have to purchase their own supplies as well, so enrollment costs are kept to a minimum.

There are some classes that have very special needs which result in extra costs. Consequently, these classes usually cost more than other similar classes. For example, expensive court rental fees for racquetball classes combined with a limited enrollment raises the total class cost so much that each student must be charged almost $4 per hour of instruction. In cases such as this, students usually understand the unavoidable costs of certain activities and appreciate the opportunity to take the specialized lessons.

As previously mentioned, making a profit is not a primary goal of Class-ic Capers. However, an average profit of $335 has been generated each session. During four nine-week sessions of the 1976-77 school year, a net profit of approximately $1500 was generated.

The profit is expended for three different things. First, the profit goes toward the purchase of equipment that may improve various classes. Second, free one-night clinics on topics of special interest are offered in an attempt to promote Class-ic Capers while also serving some special needs of the students. Finally, all remaining profit is applied to the salary of student help that is used to administer the Class-ic Capers program.

Class Planning Procedures

Organizing and planning classes for each new session must be started approximately five weeks in advance. Administrative staff for Class-ic Capers consists of one student director working approximately 20 hours per week under the direction of the Informal Recreation Director. The amount of direct planning needed by the Director depends on the capabilities of the student director.

Ideally, the student director should be a well-organized, dependable student who is good with details as well as with people. This student must enjoy assuming major responsibilities. The Informal Recreation Director should only serve in an advisory and supervisory role, leaving the routine organizational duties to the student director.

Prior to the organization of each Class-ic Capers session, the student director meets with the Director to discuss which classes will be offered in the upcoming session, possible instructors, class content, and dates for registration as well as which weeks classes can be scheduled.

Following this discussion, the student director begins work by preparing the worksheets that will serve as a major aid throughout the class planning. By carefully writing down details as they are discussed, class organization becomes much easier, and careless mistakes are avoided.

Once the worksheets are prepared, locating an instructor for each class becomes the first task of the student director. Previous instructors are rehired as much as possible if their previous classes have gone well. Locating new instructors often requires a great deal of time.

When a class instructor is contacted, the student director meets with the person to outline the details for the class, including:

1. The number of class lessons needed to present the subject adequately (usually 4 to 6 lessons).
2. The ideal length of each lesson (usually 1 to 2 hours).
3. The day and time the instructor prefers to teach (usually Monday through Thursday evenings).
.4. The number of students the instructor recommends for the class.
5. The type of room that is needed (depends on special seating needs, activity space needed, and the number of students).
6. The class supplies and equipment that will be needed.

Once this initial brainstorming and planning has been completed, the student director locates the required facilities. Once verbal approval has been received from the facility coordinator, a facility request form is completed and forwarded to the coordinator.

Next, the student director calculates prospective class costs to be sure that the class being planned is economically feasible. If any changes are needed, the student director must consult with the instructor to iron out problems. Once everything is agreed upon, the student director sends a confirmation letter to the instructor, clearly outlining class dates, times, and all other essential details.

As class planning progresses, it is important that the student director discuss plans with the Director so that potential problems can be identified and resolved before conflicts arise. The student director should freely discuss difficulties with the Director, as past programming experiences may reveal an immediate solution. There also may be times that the Director should make certain phone calls. The ease with which the two directors work together determines the success of Class-ic Capers.

Class Publicity

Once all classes have been planned, preparation of class publicity follows. Since poor publicity usually results in poor participation, it is essential that a thorough publicity program is done.

Publicity for each session consists of two full-page ads that include a small section on each class with specific details on class content, schedule, location, and cost. These ads are arranged in a pictorial display in the university newspaper. The cost of these ads is incorporated into the registration fee for each class and consequently paid without a major financial burden to any single class.

Other publicity sources used on a regular basis include:
1. Posting flyers and signs around campus on various bulletin boards in university buildings.
2. Submitting an announcement to the campus newspaper for inclusion in a special information section called "What's Happening."
3. Sending announcements to dormitories for broadcasting over the public address systems.
4. Sending announcements to radio stations.
5. Writing an article for inclusion in the city newspaper.
6. Submitting a class registration announcement for display on two lighted signs which flash public service announcements for the university's and community's information.

Program Registration

Two weeks before classes are scheduled to start, registration should begin. A basic enrollment form for each class is prepared, clearly indicating registration dates, enrollment fees, class dates and times, and the class location as well as additional details each class registrant should know.

Each form has space for 20 names, addresses, phone numbers, social security numbers, and acknowledgment of fee payment. If enrollment for a class is limited to less than 20, this is clearly indicated on the enrollment sheet and leftover space is used to compile a waiting list of names and phone numbers of persons who are still interested after the class is filled.

Student secretaries in the campus recreation office handle most of the class registration with some assistance by the student director. A hand-out sheet with all class details is also prepared for distribution to class registrants as one last attempt to insure that all students are aware of all details.

Once class registration is completed, enrollment in each class is examined and if the class is filled or has sufficient enrollment to be economically feasible, a class attendance sheet is prepared and everything is ready to go.

Occasionally, interest in a subject may be so low that only a few students enroll. In such a case, the student director does a cost study to see how much money will be lost if the class is offered. If the loss will exceed $20, the class will probably be cancelled. When a class must be cancelled, it is essential that the instructor and prospective students are called immediately and informed of the cancellation.

The first week of classes, the student director visits each class a few minutes to be sure that things get off to a good start. Attendance sheets are distributed to instructors at this time.

Program Evaluation Process

An important key to the continuing success and improvement of any program is a thorough and continuous evaluation system. For this reason, there are three different tools used to evaluate Class-ic Capers.

First, each student is asked to fill out an evaluation form on the classes he/she attended. Students are asked to rate the classes as excellent, good, fair, or poor in five categories:
1. time scheduling
2. class location
3. overall class organization
4. performance of the instructor
5. whether or not the class was worth the registration fee.

In addition to these straight ratings, space is provided for comments on each of these categories as well.

A second tool used to evaluate classes is the attendance sheets. It is helpful to know how many students attend most of the class lessons when evaluating class content. For example, if over half of the students in a class drop out after the first lesson, it is obvious that something is wrong. On the other hand, if over 75% attend classes through the last lession, it is obvious that the class is pretty much meeting the needs and interests of the students.

Finally, the third evaluation tool is a form prepared by the campus recreation office. On this form, the results from the student evaluations are summarized, and additional comments on the instructor and classes are noted after a discussion by the Director and the student director. At the bottom of this form is space for recommendations for improved instruction and rehiring the instructor, including recommendations for salary increases.

By using these tools regularly, classes are continually upgraded, keeping the quality of Class-ic Capers high.

Suggestions For Avoiding Problems

Through experience gained in the scheduling of over eight different nine-week sessions of Class-ic Capers, the following helpful hints cannot be discounted when discussing the scheduling and organizing of a short course program. To assist the student director in performing all job responsibilities without difficulty and confusion, a procedure manual should be written and constantly updated. This manual can then serve as a guide and reference tool for daily use by the student director as well as an essential tool for the easy training of new student directors.

Be sure that each class instructor realizes that while there is flexibility when planning a class, once a class is organized and publicized, details cannot be changed, especially if the details relate to the class schedule or budget.

Make sure that purchasing procedures are understood by class instructors who have been given a supply budget. Improper purchasing practices cause problems with the university purchasing department and such confrontations should be avoided.

Advise instructors ahead of time on what to do if an illness or other emergency is going to result in their absence from a class. Unannounced class cancellations cause problems for everyone.

Make sure all publicity is accurate and see that student secretaries are clearly informed. Poor communication in these two areas can result in a wide variety of problems.

ARTS AND CRAFTS: WHO NEEDS IT?

by Betty Montgomery and Alicia Cosky, Northern Illinois University

The term "campus recreation" is no longer synonymous with "intramurals" or "recreational sports." Campus recreation includes much more than the traditional local sports program. In striving for intellectual excellence, the college or university must also charge itself with creating programs for self-expression, and self-fulfillment during leisure time.

Although intramural sports *may* provide an opportunity for some to be creative, arts and crafts provides an outlet for personal expression as well. The new innovative campus recreation program recognizes the need for cultural programming and should therefore provide this opportunity.

Few activities "yield as direct, immediate, and lasting satisfaction to the individual as arts and crafts. Seeing an object take shape in one's own hands or transforming an idea into tangible forms gives a person a satisfying sense of achievement." (Butler, 1976, p. 313). According to Tillman, one of the most positive values of arts and crafts is that "making things puts your hands back on the steering wheel of your life." (Tillman, 1973, p. 154).

In answer to the question, "Who needs it?," it can be affirmed that anyone with a need for aesthetic expression needs it. At one time or another that probably includes everyone. There are countless media—the list is endless. For every individual interested in exploring this area, there is some means for obtaining a sense of personal accomplishment.

Determining the needs for an arts and crafts program and justifying its place in the total recreation program might be defined as dealing with the abstract, but developing the *real* program involves dealing with the concrete. Thus, our attention turns to questions such as where? and how much?

The multi-purpose arts and crafts facility is the dream of every craft-oriented recreation staff; however, a fancy, well-equipped building is not absolutely essential. Quite often a room with adequate lighting, a few tables, and chairs is all that is needed to offer simple crafts—macrame, weaving, jewelry-making, knitting, drawing, etc. If the convenience of a sink is added, painting and silk screening can also be included. For the more sophisticated crafts—woodworking, ceramics and pottery—special facilities *are* needed, in which case an arrangement for sharing with other departments might be possible.

"How much?", is a question asked in every aspect of programming, but it need not be a deterrent in developing this program. If available dollars are scarce, it is feasible to work toward *break even*. Charging a workshop fee adequate to cover the cost of the instructor and requiring each participant to purchase his/her own materials will help defray costs. Establishing a good business relationship with a local craft dealer is advisable. Often they will give a discount to workshop participants. Materials might also be purchased in bulk and sold to participants at cost.

Who teaches these workshops? Members of your community. Your campus has many qualified instructors—students, faculty, secretaries, the gardener, a custodian. Some may share their time for as little as a word of gratitude and others for a nominal fee. Regardless of budget size, tapping community resources for instructors is a wise investment.

Probably more than any other major category of recreation, arts and crafts lend themselves to adaptation for individuals at all levels of ability. This characteristic is particularly attractive when providing leisure time activity for special groups, i.e., hearing impaired and paraplegic.

IMPLEMENTING AN ARTS AND CRAFTS PROGRAM

Selection and Placement of Workshops

Once the decision is made to undertake an arts and crafts program, implementation should begin immediately. In attempting to plan a schedule, begin by "brainstorming" and list all the crafts conceivable. Ask fellow staff members to review the list and add what workshops they would like to see. Refer to craft magazines, confer with faculty from the departments of art and industry and technology and visit local craft stores in order to compile as extensive and thorough a list as possible. Consider next the availability of facilities; for example, scheduling a photography workshop is not feasible if a darkroom is not readily available for leisure time use. If the fortunate circumstance exists that a multi-purpose craftroom is at your disposal, half the battle is won! If not, look towards the art building for open times when specific classrooms or shops are not being used for academic purposes. But, it's often discovered that the art department is already booked and needs even more time and space for themselves! The search for space can be difficult, but don't overlook any possibilities. Let thoroughness and perseverance prevail. Perhaps there's an empty room in the student center, or how about all those dormitories? Secure permission to use such rooms and select your workshops accordingly.

When selecting a room, keep in mind these minimal requirements: adequate space, good ventilation, and proper lighting. No need to be concerned about fancy floor coverings or neatly painted walls because craft activities do not lend themselves to this type decor anyway. Make sure the door locks to insure the safe-keeping of equipment and supplies. Of course, one centrally located room would be ideal, but perhaps three or four varied locations could benefit the program even more.

Contract the room needed before advertising workshop locations. Not only will this verify use of the facility, but it can also serve as a reminder to the individual responsible for the room by listing dates, times, and the activity involved. Return to the original "brainstorming" list and modify it based on the facility secured and available equipment. In order to avoid duplication, take into consideration the workshops available through local craft stores or other organizations on campus which may provide similar services. Consider also the accessibility of instructors before making a final selection of workshops.

The nature of the workshop will dictate its longevity. Those ranging from one evening to six weeks will be more popular than those lasting longer. What little "free" time students have will not be committed for long periods of time. If planning more than one session a week, be sure to allow for a free day in between sessions. Due to the nature of campus activities, weekends are usually booked well in advance. Therefore, it would be wise to avoid scheduling sessions during that time. When arranging hours try not to conflict with dinner time or evening classes. Considerations of this nature increase the probability of sign-up. Noon hour workshops are particularly popular with faculty and staff members of the university community.

Advertising

The arts and crafts program will be as successful as the manner of advertisement undertaken. Plan the advertising approach well in advance and formulate set procedures which can be applicable for each workshop. Be consistent; people learn to look for information where they last found it! When preparing a schedule of workshops be sure to include a brief description of what each workshop entails; for example, one will not sign up for a dulcimer workshop if one doesn't know what a dulcimer is! It is beneficial to begin advertising at least two weeks in advance for maximum coverage.

Whether advertising the entire program or one workshop at a time there are some ideas worth considering. Discover all the possible media outlets on campus and take full advantage of them! Begin with the university newspaper by arranging ads and perhaps requesting a photographer for a few workshops. Inform the local radio stations and send them information on a regular basis to be aired. Run-off flyers giving the dates, times and location, usually a small illustration helps in making it more effective. Post these flyers in buildings throughout campus. Establish a line of communication with each of the dormitories and perhaps a bulletin board could be set aside for craft advertisements only. Randomly select names from the campus phone directory and mail flyers to these individuals, asking that they share this information with their friends and fellow employees. If possible, arrange to have the instructor demonstrate the craft a week prior to the actual workshop. This can be done both during the lunch hour outside the students' cafeteria and during the dinner hour in selected dormitories. Make sure the demonstration table has a poster stating exactly what is happening when and where. Have the sign-up sheet readily available instead of sending an interested individual somewhere else to register. Try to obtain a showcase in the student center in which articles from craft workshops could be displayed. This approach may be a little after the fact but it may increase awareness that an arts and crafts program exists on campus. Timing and location are probably the two most important elements when advertising a craft program. There is no guarantee that even with all of the suggestions previously discussed, every craft workshop will go, but effective advertising certainly increases the likelihood of it.

Securing Personnel

Instructors can be obtained from two different sources: the university or local help from craft stores. Using students as instructors allows them to make some extra spending money and offers an opportunity to teach on a small scale. Many take much pride in their efforts and often include it in their resume as a teaching experience. Usually a "help wanted" ad in the classified section of the university paper brings in more applicants than are actually needed. For example, "Crafts Instructor for woodworking, quill art, picture frame construction, rug weaving, apartment decorating, and batik, $3.00/hr. Apply at the Office of Campus Recreation, North Neptune, Ground Floor."

For a sample application refer to Table I. It also is helpful if the student lists his/her class schedule on the back of the application. This makes future contact with the person easier and aids in selecting the instructor since it shows which hours he/she is free and available to teach. If it is impossible to secure a student to instruct the workshop, then look to the local talent which may prove to be a little more expensive.

No later than two weeks prior to the workshop a letter of employment should be sent to the instructor arranging a meeting to discuss plans for the workshop.

It is imperative that the instructor is aware of all his/her responsibilities related to the workshop. Begin by issuing an employee identification card which the instructor should carry whenever teaching. This allows for easier access to a locked room in which the workshop is being held. Aside from actually teaching there is one other major responsibility and that is completion of the Daily Report Form (Table II). This form serves a two-fold purpose. First, it is used as a time card on which the instructor records time-in and time-out. Second, it functions as a means of communication between the instructor and the coordinator. If any accidents occur or more supplies are needed it can be noted on this form which should be in the office by the following morning.

Instructors should be required to formulate a class outline. This not only shows the coordinator the content of the workshop, but also serves as a future reference to the participant months after the workshop is over. Some workshops lend themselves very well to an outline while others don't, so use discretion in terms of what should be included in this outline. Usually the outline should list the necessary materials, a logical progression of steps, definitions or formulas and "tricks of the trades" if there are any. It should be written with the novice in mind unless otherwise stipulated. Make reference books readily available to the instructor for they often help in establishing an outline and can offer many different approaches.

Evaluation of the workshop is the last major responsibility of the instructor. During the final session evaluation forms should be distributed to each class member. These forms are reviewed by the coordinator in hopes of improving future programs.

Purchasing Supplies

Here again, there is a substantial amount of groundwork that needs to be done. The ultimate goal is to secure a better quality of materials at minimum cost. Try to contact the local craft stores either by phone or in person, the latter being more successful. Explain the craft program and request a discount on supplies bought for workshops. Attempt to reach an agreement by which a participant could purchase his own materials by presenting a discount card. With personal choice in materials it leaves the workshop open for more variety and creativity. Not all workshops lend themselves to this concept so at times supplies must be bought in bulk. If so, the discount should still apply. Leave a schedule of workshops with the dealer so the necessary materials may be ordered in advance to meet the program's demands.

Craft Assistant

The task of coordinating an arts and crafts program is not so difficult as it is time consuming. For professionals whose schedules do not permit the undertaking of such a program singlehandedly, it is strongly recommended an assistant be secured. Again, this individual should be a student, preferably with an art background, who is willing to commit ten hours per week toward the program. Once the groundwork is established, actual workshop maintenance as described in this article is not at all difficult. An interested coordinator and an energetic assistant is ample staff to administer a very versatile and respectable arts and crafts program.

Table I
OFFICE OF CAMPUS RECREATION
Application for Student Employment
ARTS and CRAFTS

NAME _____   _____
        Last   First   M.I.   Soc. Sec. No.

SCHOOL ADDRESS _____   School Phone (____)_____

HOME ADDRESS _____   Home Phone (____)_____
                Street   Apt.

                _____
                City   State   Zip Code

DATE OF BIRTH _____   MAJOR _____
                                    MINOR _____

YEAR IN SCHOOL (check one) Fr.____ Soph.____ Jr.____ Sr.____ Grad. ____

	Can Teach	Materials to Display
BASKETRY (coiled and reed weaving)		
WORKING WITH WOOD		
QUILL ART		
DULCIMCER CONSTRUCTION		
DROP SPINNING AND NATURAL DYEING		
PICTURE FRAME CONSTRUCTION		
RUG WEAVING		
APARTMENT DECORATING		
GETTING STARTED in BATIK		

Table II
ARTS & CRAFTS
Daily Report Form
Office of Campus Recreation
Neptune North, Ground Floor

Day of Week _____   Date _____   Building _____

Time In: _____   Time Out: _____

Craftroom Supervisor: _____   _____   _____

Craftroom Instructor: _____   _____   _____

1. Was room clean upon entering?   ____Yes   ____No

2. Was equipment in working condition?   ____Yes   ____No

   If not, what was broken? _____

3. Number of participants:_____

4. Did you leave the room in order?   ____Yes   ____No

5. Did any equipment break while you were there?   ____Yes   ____No

   If yes, explain what happened? _____

   _____

   Student responsible for breakage (if applicable):

   Name_____ Phone No._____ S.S.# _____

6. Accidents:
   Brief summary of any accidents (details on Accident Form)
   (Name — Injury — How Injured)

   _____

   _____

   _____

7. Comments: _____

   _____

NOTE: This report must be returned to the Office of Campus Recreation 10:00 a.m. the next school day.

Conclusion

The basic desires to create and express are present in all of us. These appetites must be satisfied. The mere fact that these desires do exist and must be served makes an arts and crafts program essential and places an obligation on the college or university to provide an opportunity for interested participants.

Arts and Crafts: Who Needs It? The college or university who wants to provide a well-balanced leisure time program for their entire community — that's who!

BIBLIOGRAPHY

Butler, George D. *Introduction to Community Recreation.* New York: McGraw Hill, 1976.

Kraus, Richard. *Therapeutic Recreation Service, Principles and Practices.* Philadelphia: W.B. Saunders Company, 1973.

Tillman, Albert. *The Program Book for Recreational Professionals.* Palo Alto, CA: National Press Books, 1973.

NASSAU HARNESS DRIVING CHAMPIONSHIP

Larry Dell Aquilla, Nassau Community College

With the cooperation of Roosevelt Raceway, Nassau Community College's (NCC) Intramural Program sponsored a NCC Night at the Races. Highlighted by the NCC Harness Driving Championship, on Friday, December 9, 1977, it was an event unparaled in the history of higher education.

The idea came from Larry Dell Aquila, Director of Intramurals and Recreation Program at NNC. The thought was to try to get total campus unity.

Five categories were set up to represent the entire campus (Civil Service-Faculty-Administration-Student, male-Student, female). For a period of three weeks, applications were available in the Intramural office and in the school newspaper. A lottery system was used for each category. Approximately 1500 people submitted their names to drive in the race. The drawing itself, with President George Chambers officiating and a horse and sulky overseeing, took place on November 10 during the half time of the Intramural Flag Football Championship game.

Students Cindy Jacowicz and Frank Guiliano, Director Dell Aquila, Robert Pepe-a printing supervisor, and James Cahill-Assistant Vice President, were selected to wear the silks for their respective departments.

Those selected as drivers started practicing under the supervision of Lou

Miller, the headmaster of the track's driver-trainer school. Miller later reported, diplomatically, that "they all showed interest and promise."

On December 6th at a luncheon sponsored by Roosevelt Raceway, the novice drivers drew horses and positions in a session highlighted by predictions of victory. On a blustery December 9th the race, on which, wisely, no bets were taken, was run before a cheering crowd that included over 1000 college fans, cheerleaders and band. President Chambers served as the official starter.

Although the posted time was probably "the slowest in the history of Roosevelt Raceway," it did not diminish the joy of the winner, Guiliano, who was followed in order by Del Aquila, Pepe, Cahill, and Jackowicz. The fourth and fifth place finishes by Cahill (the oldest driver) and Jackowicz (the youngest driver), who had drawn, respectively, the oldest and youngest horses, left unresolved any question about superiority of age or youth in such contests.

While disappointed by his second place finish, Dell Aquila is satisfied that the NCC Night at the Races was a success: "We got what we had planned — an evening of fun for everybody — students, faculty, staff. And judging by the coverage the event got in local and metropolitan area newspapers, television, and two national magazines, it appears that combining horse sense with education is a popular idea."

GUSSIED-UP GOLF AND LOW-BUDGET LACROSSE

By Nick Kovalakides, University of Maryland

Gussied-Up Golf:

For years, the annual fraternity golf tournament was a humdrum affair. It was played on a single-elimination basis with each match consisting of five individual 18-hole contests. Each house was to rate its golfers #1 through #5, with the #1's being the best. The #1's from each team were to play each other, as were the #2's and so on down the line.

The tournament format was not bad, that is, until some houses tried to finesse their way through by naming their best golfer as #3 hoping that their #2 could beat the other team's #1. While it was not illegal, the success of such a move brought about more ill will than praise.

The system also suffered when the golfers from each team could not all play on the same afternoon. Each pairing of fraternities was given 7 to 10 days to complete their five match-ups. This fostered a situation wherein, when one house would win the first three matches, the remaining two twosomes would never play as they knew that their scores could not affect the outcome of the match.

Another problem, which came up frequently, was many players' inability to find enough time to play 18 holes of golf virtually each week during the Fall semester.

In meeting with the fraternity representatives on the matter three years ago, the idea came up of patterning the fraternity golf tournament after those of the PGA (Professional Golf Association) tour. While not ready to take on the mammoth Thursday-through-Sunday format, it was decided to to it up right on *one* day.

The members of the Interfraternity Council were all for it and from there the forces and the resources for the "gussying-up" process began to materialize. The IFC Social Committee voted to add the "Greek Open," as the tournament has been named, to their calendar of major social events for each academic year.

The social aspect of the event comes in two parts—a semiformal (coats, ties and cocktail dresses) cocktail party for the golfers and their ladies/escorts the night before the tournament and a live-band, beer-blast type of get-together on Fraternity Row (a grassy area between the fraternities and sororities) on the night of the tournament.

All of the tournament trimmings, however, could not have been possible without the support of the IFC and an outside sponsor. It did not take long for students, who were campus representatives of national beer companies, to come to the forefront offering their firm support and their firm's support of the "Greek Open".

Among those invited as guests to join the festivities at the pre-tournament cocktail party are representatives of the sponsor's local distributorships and campus dignitaries, who are invited to play in the tournament in the "Guest" division. Naturally, by inviting such campus notables as the University President, Chancellor, Vice Chancellors and Deans, a great amount of good will and public relations is nurtured.

The university is fortunate to have an 18-hole, regulation, 6,400-yard golf course adjacent to the campus. It is very convenient and the Golf Course Director is very cooperative. He closes the entire course for the afternoon thus enabling a shot-gun start.

Rather than having a foursome tee off on the first hole, while another starts on the tenth hole, with the rest of the foursomes teeing off in turn (as in a PGA round), the shot-gun start allows for two foursomes to be placed on each of the eighteen tees (thus servicing a maximum of 144 players at one time) so that one of the two groups at each tee would all hit their drives at one time or at the firing of a "shot-gun" or similar noise maker. Once these players have hit their second shots toward their respective greens, the second foursomes tee off. This type of play enables everyone to start and finish their rounds of golf within minutes of each other rather than hours, as in a PGA round.

Each house entered fields a team of four golfers. The sororities have been invited to enter foursomes in the ladies competition, but, so far, only a few have accepted their invitations. Foursomes are set up so that no more than two golfers from the same house are in the same group. This not only helps to insure the honor system, but it fosters the making of new friendships. No handicap system is used and the house with the lowest four-player total wins.

Two mini-contests are held within the tournament as novelty items. They are the "Closest-to-the-Hole" contest held on one of the short par-3 holes and the "Longest Drive" contest conducted on one of the straight par-5 holes.

With regard to the financial arrangement with the Golf Course Director, the course was closed to all but this tournament for a guarantee of $300.00. Intramural golfers are required to pay their own greens fees. At least 100 golfers at the student rate of $3.00 on weekdays insures this guarantee.

The tournament has been held each year on the third or fourth Thursday in September. Thursdays are chosen for two reasons—one, it would have been too expensive to reserve the course on a weekend when most of the business is from faculty, staff and alumni play, and two, Thursday night has become the traditional party night on our campus thus lending itself to a successful post-tournament party. Teeing off at 12:30 pm causes a few participants to cut their afternoon classes, but they do not seem to mind and they also seem to to survive.

There are usually twenty fraternities entering foursomes, giving an immediate income of $240.00, the rest of the deficit is made up by allowing other fraternity members to play in the "Guest" division along with the campus officials, whose fees are paid for out of the IFC Social Account. If there are any spaces remaining in the field of 144, dormitory and commuting students are accepted into the "Guest" division. Naturally, the more golfers attracted, the more it pleases the Golf Course Director.

The tournament sponsors have been terrific. They have provided each golfer with a packet of favors, including a visor, a hand-towel, a ball marker, a golf ball and a package of tees. Last year, they provided, on their own volition, a magnificent golf bag, complete with head covers for four woods. It was presented to the low medalist.

The sponsors also provided their own beer truck, which was parked adjacent to the starter's hut between the first and tenth tees. In the first year, the sponsor felt the need to charge for its use. Consequently, a small fee per cup (25¢) was charged to help defray the cost of the truck. Last year, the truck was donated free, so the beer was free!

At the post-tournament party, everyone was invited and beer was sold to help defray the costs of the beer and band. It has been a money-maker for the IFC each time. Naturally, it was the sponsor's beer and they merely charged the IFC a nominal fee.

About halfway through the evening, the student-tournament director took over the microphone and presented the intramural awards to the winning and runnerup teams. A representative from the sponsor was on hand to award the golf bag to the low medalist.

In just two years, the "Greek Open" has become one of the annual bright spots — a far cry from when it used to be one of the dullest tournaments. The next step is to encourage the dormitory and commuting students to acquire some of this enthusiasm and industriousness. And, in case you did not notice, the Intramural Sports Department's involvement and expense in this entire affair was limited to hiring a student tournament director to handle the entries, govern play, such as interpreting rules, and compiling and announcing the results.

Low-Budget Lacrosse:

Since varsity lacrosse has been played in the United States, predominantly in the East, the University has fared quite well with highly-ranked teams each year and several national championships. This influence, plus the fact that many students come to the campus having played lacrosse in high school, has always provided the temptation of incorporating field lacrosse as an intramural sport.

Nevertheless, each year, the efforts become thwarted by the exorbitant costs of the equipment, not to even mention the problems of maintaining and storing it on an annual basis and issuing it on a daily basis. In order to play field lacrosse properly, that is, safely, each player should be equipped with a helmet and faceguard, shoulder and arm pads and padded gloves. Additional items, of course, include the lacrosse stick and balls and the goals with nets. Supporting field lacrosse would wipe out over half of the equipment budget!

Lacrosse equipment companies were very much aware of this problem and endeavored to do something about it. It was shortly thereafter that a game called "STXball" was investigated as a substitute.

The game is promoted as an indoor or outdoor activity. Any number can play on a side but four players per team on the floor at one time works best on basketball courts inside. It is called "Box Lacrosse" to take advantage of the flair that that sport had a few years ago on the professional level.

But that is where the similarity ends. This style of box lacrosse involves no body checking nor dangerous use of the stick. The stick, however, is made of a light, but durable, aluminum shaft with a flexible, molded rubber head, which allows for easy catching and throwing of the ball. These skills are learned quickly. The balls are soft rubber and painted bright orange for good visibility. The aluminum goals with nylon netting are 3' × 3' and rest on the floor without marring the surface.

It is estimated that the cost of the equipment is approximately 20% of that required by the field game. Since the molded sticks can be stored (hung) within each other—as in stacking paper cups— they take up very little room. Furthermore, the goals can be disassembled and hung on a wall peg next to the sticks. Footballs and basketballs use more storage space than do the new lacrosse items. The equipment has not been in use long enough to evaluate any maintenance problems, but with so few parts involved, no major repairs are anticipated.

The Head Lacrosse Coach, a former 3-time All-American himself, came over with his varsity players and put on a clinic using the rubber sticks and balls. The intramural athletes were quite impressed. The coach admitted that, while the body contact was missing, skill-wise and strategy-wise, the game was the same as the field game. After watching the varsity players going four-on-four with no body or stick checking and having fun at the same time, the over 150 intramural athletes in attendance at the clinic simply did the same when it became their turn to play.

In another effort to promote the newest sport, two of the better intramural teams put on a ten-minute exhibition during half-time of one of the varsity basketball games. With nearly 10,000 students among the 14,000 present, it was very effective in demonstrating the fun that they could have. It helped the entry count tremendously.

With regard to the rules of the game, the STX company have virtually left it up to each group or school. They simply recommend a few rules to insure the fun and safety aspects of the game. Besides no body and stick checking, they suggest that the ball be passed (not run) over the mid-court line and that there be at least two passes made before a shot may be attempted. More details have been added to the rules as the need was discovered for some refinements. A set of mechanics and guidelines for officials has been established.

The lacrosse needs of our student body have been met to a great degree. However, a glimmer of hope still exists that someday, the "real" game can be offered.

RUNNING TIME vs. STOP CLOCK TIME

Roy C. Easley, California State Polytechnic University

If intramural directors are to meet the primary objective of making in-tramurals fun, as it is supposed to be, there is a need to eliminate as many facets of the program as possible which create anxieties and frustrations. Remembering that intramurals can be one of a student's most memorable college experiences, directors need to pay attention to the many little things that afford the most comfortable atmosphere for the participants.

Since many intramural programs are, or have been, rather small one-man operations, directors of the programs must wear many hats. Therefore, time is not always available to tend to the many little things that create success. The descriptive definitive statement of an intramural director's role by Rokosz[1][9] is:

> At one time or another, and sometimes all at once, the intramural director is a philosopher, as he determines his general views of in-tramurals; a coordinator of activities and supporting tasks; a policymaker; an organizer and director of meets and contests; a scheduler; a supervisor of contests; a trainer of officials (official himself); a publicity man; a secretary; an arbitrator of disputes; a student relations man who seeks out feedback from participants in the program; an accountant and balancer of budgets; an expert in sports and sports rules; a purchaser and manager of equipment and supplies; a lawyer who must occasionally defend policies; a statistician; a handyman who designs and repairs special devices and equipment; an author of handbooks and informational materials; a mail carrier; an errand boy; and an office occupant who is constantly available to talk with anyone who might drop in.

One of the many little things easily overlooked or taken for granted, due to "more important areas of concern," came to the attention of the staff four years ago while putting together the 1974-75 basketball schedule. This item was a result of haunting comments by students involved in the Fall football program. Apparently most of the players were continually on edge with anxieties about the clock continuing to run in situations which normally would kill the clock in regulation type play. The questions raised about the practice of stopping of the clock during the last few minutes of play while running time was used during the major part of the contest were valid questions:

1. Are the last few minutes of a game more important than the first?
2. Why change the tempo of the game by stopping the clock?
3. How can your timers do a good job switching from running time to stop time the last few minutes?

4. Why use running time for any sport when clocks are available?

The particular question of "why running time is used when clocks are available" probed an investigation as to how running time originated. After many hours of searching and interviewing, historical data could not be located to successfully answer the question. It is hypothesized that several possible reasons could be considered:

1. To adhere to tightly regulated time schedules.
2. The lack of enough timing devices.
3. The lack of enough supervisory personnel to administer proper timing.
4. Tradition.

The amazing thing is that for quite a few years most programs have operated with a clock and a human timer on each game during the competition, with rules related to stopping the clock at certain prescribed times near the end of the games. So why is running time still in existence? Perhaps "tradition" best describes the staleness of a need for change. Or is it possible that this particular item is just another "little thing" that is taken for granted and ignored for most important functions?

The programs which require timing devices have been using the stop clock time for the past four years, and the staff unanimously agree that it has been a very successful and important change. A survey questionnaire administered to intramural basketball participants provided a good indication as to the positive addition it has been (Tables I-III).

There were many interesting comments, which appear on the questionnaire survey, but the response most often given was, "it gives us more playing time." This is a very interesting remark since all game schedules have not changed in length of time with the use of this timing technique. This change in attitude, that more playing time is allowed, is a positive indication that perhaps stop clock time can promote the growth of intramural sports objectives within the framework of our programs.

A most important objective of intramural-recreational sports programs is to establish an atmosphere where the participants can escape the hurry-up, rush-rush, daily routine things that are so prominent in the lives of a typical college student.

> Early to rise for morning classes—will the car start?—rush from building to building wtih short ten minute breaks—can't be late—hurry with lunch to make sure that afternoon job is covered—back to school finally for relaxation and recreation in the intramural program—"dammit!! the clock is running" so hurry up we can't afford to lose a second!

Are students relaxing as they should be in the intramural program or is it just another frustrating experience where more "hurry-up" pressures are surrounding them?

Table I

Questionnaires administered to 98 male basketball students who were involved in three different levels of competition in five-man basketball leagues during the initial year that stop clock time was introduced.

I. Student class status at the University:
   A. 12 Freshman   (12%)
   B. 20 Sophomores   (20%)
   C. 25 Juniors   (25%)
   D. 33 Seniors   (34%)
   E. 8 Graduates   (9%)

II. Have you participated in intramurals at Cal Poly during past years?
   A. 43 Yes   (45%)
   B. 54 No   (55%)

III. If you were in the program, was running time used?
   A. 42 Yes   (44%)
   B. 15 No   (16%)
   C. 37 No Answer   (38%)

IV. Do you think timing of games is an improvement?
   A. 75 Strongly agree   (76%)
   B. 15 Agree   (16%)
   C. 4 Makes no difference   (5%)
   D. 1 Favor running time   (1%)

V. Would you like other programs to use stop clock time?
   A. 62 Yes   (62%)
   B. 8 No   (9%)
   C. 7 Undecided   (8%)
   D. 20 No answer   (20%)

Table II

California College and University Intramural Director Replies, March 1974.

I. 40 questionnaires sent, 35 returned.

II. 32 of the 35 reporting indicated that they used running time (92%).
   A. Most related that clocks stopped during the last few minutes of the game (3-5 minutes).
   B. Some used maximum number of plays in football.

III. Question: Why is running time preferred? Four possible answers:
   A. Lack of timekeeper - 3   (9%)
   B. Meet time schedule - 31   (89%)
   C. Tradition - 2   (6%)
   D. Other - 2   (6%)
   89% of replies indicated reason for running time is to meet time schedule.

Table III

Comments:
On our campus, timed events are run on the following schedules:

I. Football
   A. 15 minute running time quarter requires approximately 1½ hours.
   B. 7 minute stop time requires about the same. 40 playing, 40 miscellaneous.

II. Basketball
   A. 20 minute running time half requires approximately 50 minutes.
   B. 12 minute stop time half requires approximately 50 minutes.

III. Water Polo
   A. 7 minute quarters running time quarter requires approximately 40 minutes.
   B. 5 minute stop time quarters require approximately 35 minutes.

Answer these questions, then ask yourself why your program is still in the dark ages of running time:

1. Do you normally have a timekeeper on each game?
2. Does the timekeeper know how to start, stop, and reset the clock?
3. How much actual playing time takes place during a ten minute quarter of a basketball game or a fifteen minute quarter of a football game where running time is used?
4. How many complaints have you had regarding running time during the past year?
5. Is there logical justification to stop the clock during the last few minutes of a game but at no other time?
6. Have you given careful consideration to meeting the needs of your participants in every feasible way?

DOWN WITH TRADITION!!!   DOWN WITH RUNNING CLOCK TIME!!!

BIBLIOGRAPHY
[1]Rokosz, Francis M. *Structured Intramurals,* Philadelphia W.B. Saunders Co., Philadelphia, 1975.

WAKO BALL—A NEW AGE ACTIVITY

By Patty Wade and Kathy Koch, Virginia Polytechnic Institute
and State University

If you are a badminton, handball, volleyball, or platform tennis enthusiast then try a combination of all these games by playing WAKO BALL! This new age activity challenges each participant's speed, agility, hand-eye coordination, and creativity. This fast moving version of an ancient Indian game has become increasingly popular since its first introduction as an intramural activity.

Wako Ball can easily be implemented in any activity program because equipment is minimal and inexpensive and the game can be adapted for use on any playing surface. The Wako Ball, which resembles an oversized shuttlecock, can be made from lightweight materials such as vinyl or leather, beans or styrofoam beads, and feathers. To contact the ball a play's hand and feet suffice as a racquet. The playing area, consisting of any available court or field space, will determine the game rules, number of players and nature of competition.

Wako Ball is played as a competitive individual/dual activity on a badminton court. Singles play utilizes the doubles long service court line and singles sidelines as boundaries. In doubles, the back baseline and doubles sidelines are the court boundaries. The net is set at 6½ feet. The service is delivered underhand from anywhere behind the short service court line. After the service, the Wako Ball may be hit in any manner using the hands or feet. Spiking and carries are illegal. Only the serving side can score. A side out occurs when the serving side commits a fault. Faults include: the Wako Ball landing out of bounds or within a player's own court; a player crossing the center line or touching the net; the ball touching the net on the serve, and the ball not crossing over the net. The best two out of three 15 point games constitute a match with each game being won by a margin of at least two points.

If badminton courts are not easily accessible perhaps the following ideas may help in adapting the game to a particular intramural situation: On a volleyball court, Wako Ball can be played as a competitive activity involving 4-9 players on each team. Twenty-one points constitute a game and volleyball rules govern play.

Wako Ball is played as an individual/dual activity on a platform tennis court. The net height is raised to 6½ feet and singles or doubles rules and court boundaries are used. The game is to 15 points.

On a handball or racquetball court, the Wako Ball is played over a ten foot neutral or dead space. The walls are considered out of bounds. A game consists of 15 points. The serve is executed from anywhere behind the neutral zone. A fault occurs when the Wako Ball lands in the dead space or hits the out-of-bounds walls.

The circle game may be played indoors or on outdoor field space. A circle 22 feet in diameeter with a 6 foot wide neutral or dead space is drawn. The Wako Ball is served from outside the circle. The game is to 15 points. Hitting the ball into the dead space or out-of-bounds is a fault.

Not all Wako Ball games are competitive in nature. A cooperative game can be played by individual, dual, or team players who attempt to keep the Wako Ball in play as long as possible. In addition, Wako Ball has become a favorite pastime among dynamic and versatile individuals who challenge their own skills and creativity in freestyle tricks, stunts, and contests of accuracy and distance. The Wako Ball freestyler lets the imagination set the rules and boundaries.

This new age activity offers the participant many obvious benefits. It contributes to physical fitness and conditioning, socialization, and hand-eye and foot-eye coordinating, ambidexterity and flexibility, and can be played by individuals of all ages. By inventing your own playing rules or using the ideas presented thus far, Wako Ball could become a popular addition to your recreational activity program. Take a whack at it!

FUNDAMENTAL TOOLS FOR A RECREATIONAL CROSS-COUNTRY SKI PROGRAM

by George Rader & Chuck Gormley, Northern Illinois University

PART I

"If You Can Walk-" A Collegiate Recreational Cross-Country Ski Program

Last year in order to increase participation in the program during the winter months, monies were allocated for the purchase of cross-country skis. This allowed for the purchase of 36 sets of skis. Whatever name it's called— ski touring, Nordic skiing, skinny skiing, or cross-country skiing—the activity has established itself as a very valuable addition to the recreation program and has made the winter months the busiest season of the year.

When the Office of Campus Recreation was created, one area which received special emphasis was the Outdoor Recreation Program. Several years earlier the student government had initiated a camping equipment check-out program, the equipment consisting of several tents, Coleman lanterns and stoves. The camping equipment check-out program proved to be very popular so that when the student government program was incorporated into the Office of Campus Recreation, the inventory of camping equipment was greatly expanded. But northern Illinois weather is not very conducive to year-round camping. The Outdoor Recreation Program was very successful during the warm weather months, but once snow covered the ground the only outdoor recreation activity offered the students was downhill ski trips.

There appear to be many reasons for the success of the cross-country ski program. One reason is that in order to go cross-country skiing it is not necessary to make an off-campus trip of at least 60 miles to an Alpine ski area. Student skiers would no longer have to stand with the other thousands in long lift lines or competing with other fashion conscious athletes who have each spent about $10 for a lift ticket. Rental for equipment would cost another $6 to $10 if one had not already made their own $200 to $300 investment for their own ski outfits. With cross-country skis you can ski anywhere there's snow, from scenic national forests and state parks to commercial touring centers or local parks and golf courses. Cross-country skiing can also be a very logical means of transportation on campus and downtown streets where other means of outdoor travel are nearly impossible due to inclement weather conditions.

The clothes a ski tourer wears can range from the bargains picked up at a local rummage sale to the latest ski fashions. The only thing that is important is that skiers are able to maintain a comfortable body temperature and have unrestrictive movement of their arms and legs.

Technique used in cross-country skiing is not difficult. It is often said that if you can walk, you can cross-country ski. Although this may be a slight over simplification, we have found that most students are able to learn enough basic skills by participating in the free one hour lessons offered by Recreational Sports to feel comfortable enough to go skiing on their own. Students who do not take any lessons seem to do fine, also, though it may take them a while longer to learn, as they usually use the trial and error method.

Many people who are concerned about the energy crisis and ecology have found Nordic skiing to be especially enjoyable. There are no power thirsty lifts needed to carry skiers to the top of hills or mountains. Cross-country skiing does not require the stripping of all trees and bushes off the side of a mountain for ski trails. Cross-country skiers do not go speeding by their surroundings. They glide down (or up) a hillside trail and are thereby able to better enjoy the beauty of the winter environment.

Another reason for the attractiveness of cross-country skiing is the current interest in physical fitness. Ski touring is cited by many doctors and physiologists as being superior to other physical activities since it requires muscles which are not used in other physical activities such as jogging, tennis, racquetball, or cycling. Nordic skiing can burn anywhere from 550 to over 1300 calories an hour, depending on the speed of skiing. Overweight skiers find this last statement especially enticing.

Equipment costs for cross-country skiing are quite a bit less than for downhill skiing. Whereas good quality downhill skis, bindings, boots and poles often cost more than $300, a comparable set of cross-country skis cost approximately $100 or less. Students who do not own their own cross-country ski equipment are able to rent a complete set of equipment from the Office of Campus Recreation for one dollar a day or two dollars for the weekend. Rates for faculty and staff of the university are double that of students since all equipment was purchased wtih monies from student activity fees.

In order to save money, the original purchase of skis was ordered with cable bindings. Cable bindings allow the skis to be used with any shoes or boots that have a sturdy sole, therefore, special ski boots were not necessary. Cable bindings are also adjustable, allowing a pair of skis to be worn regardless of the skiers shoe size. The idea of saving money backfired and all bindings have been converted to the standard three-pin Nordic Norm binding. The time it took to adjust cable bindings for each skier, the breakdowns, and the inefficiency of the cable bindings as compared to three pin bindings was dissuading many students from using the skis.

Providing ski boots was not nearly as great a problem as it was originally thought. Ski shops that rent cross-country skis indicated that between 1.5 to

2 pair of boots would be needed for every set of skis. A ratio of 1.3 pairs of boots to each set of skis allows the outfitting of most students without too great a difficulty.

Three times as many "no-wax" skis as waxable skis were ordered initially and subsequent orders have maintained this ratio of waxable skis to non-waxable skis. Future orders will specify only non-waxable skis. The only people who request waxable skis are members of the outing club who are going on club trips with experienced skiers. There is no doubt that a properly waxed ski will out perform a no-wax ski, and waxable costs less than a comparable no-wax ski. However, anybody who uses the waxable skis must provide their own wax, scraper, cork, and wax remover, making the cost of using waxable skis much higher than that of the no-wax skis.

There are a variety of "no-wax" ski bases available—fish scale, step and mohair bases. The mohair style seems to be the most efficient of the various styles. Mohair bases are also easiest to repair and if a mohair strip should become damaged or wear out, it is very easy to replace.

Cross-country skis are constructed of one of two different materials, wood or fiberglass. The fiberglass ski is a more responsive ski; however, the wood ski appears to be more suitable for the rental program. All Outdoor Recreation Program skis have synthetic bases rather than the traditional wood base. The synthetic bases require virtually no upkeep and when they do become scratched, they are much easier to repair than a ski with a wood base.

The addition of cross-country skiing to the Outdoor Recreation Program has greatly increased student participation in winter-time recreational activities. Now when the forecast for weekend weather includes snow warnings, students don't worry about suffering "cabin fever" while cooped up in their dorm rooms or at the local pub. Instead they are able to participate in an inexpensive activity that puts them in close contact with Mother Nature and provides a healthy release of pent-up energy.

PART II

Making It Work: A Step-by-step Guide to a Cross-country Ski Rental System

After it has been decided that a cross-country ski rental program should be established—after allocating monies, selecting models and suppliers, and after the receipt of the equipment—what next? What follows is a step-by-step guide for equipment preparation, inventory establishment, and a *"workable"* reservation/sign-out system. Undoubtedly there are other workable procedures.

I. Preparation of Skis for a Rental Program
    A. After delivery, all skis should be paired, as per manufacturer's serial

number on the side of the skis.
B. Inventory sheets should be filled out for skis, giving all pertinent information.
1. Name of item
2. Manufacturer
3. Model
4. Approximate replacement cost
5. A symbol to indicate if the ski has a "waxable" running surface as opposed to "wax-less" (mohair, step, fish scale) running surface
6. The length of the skis (in centimeters)
7. A number representing the particular pair of skis
C. Tools need to be gathered for the mounting of the bindings.
1. Felt tip marker
2. Hammer
3. Center punch
4. Drill
5. Pilot drill bit
6. Screw driver
7. Needle nose pliers
8. Short piece of 1" diameter pipe
9. File
10. Sandpaper
11. Templet (To be used as a jig for drill holes, if many pairs of bindings are to be mounted.)
D. The balance point of the ski should be marked.
1. Move ski up and down the pipe until it balances like a "teeter-totter."
E. The templet is centered over the balance point and the screw holes are marked.
F. A center punch is used to start screw holes.
1. A 2" × 4" block is used to support the ski, thus eliminating the gap in the center of the ski caused by camber of the ski.
G. Pilot holes are drilled to appropriate depth.
H. Rough surfaces caused by drilling of the pilot holes are filed flat.
I. Bindings are properly located and screwed to the ski.
J. Heel plates are nailed to the ski.
1. Estimate the average size boot used with a ski of the appropriate length.
2. Mount the boot on the binding.
3. Center the heel plate under the heel of the boot.
K. Top surface of skis is prepared for stenciling by sanding with fine grade sandpaper.

L. Skis are stenciled.
   1. Reusable acetate stencils are used.
   2. If appropriate, a symbol for "waxable" skis is placed near the tip of the ski.
   3. Next, the size of the ski is stenciled near the tip.
   4. Follow by the size in the skis individual inventory number.
   5. Thus * 200 - 14 indicates:
      * = "waxable" running surface
      200 = 200 centimeters in length
      14 = of all skis 200 centimeters in length this ski is number 14.
   6. Immediately in front of the bindings an "L" (left) or an "R" (right) is stenciled to indicate the foot (right, left to be used) for that particular skis binding.
   7. At the tail of the ski, the school's initials are stenciled.
M. Clear lacquer is sprayed over all stenciled material for protection.
N. The entire inventory number is burned into the ski with a common wood burning pencil. This is to further protect skis from theft or loss.
O. Old bicycle innertubes are cut into bands to hold skis together.

II. Preparation of Ski Poles for a Rental Program
   A. All poles should be paired by length and grouped by length.
   B. Ski poles, if constructed of bamboo, should be reinforced with nylon backed tape.
   C. Poles are color coded.
      1. All poles of the same length should have the same color and number of the tape bands.

III. Preparation of Cross-country Ski Boots for a Rental Program
   A. Inventory sheets should be filled out for boots, giving all pertinent information.
      1. Name of item
      2. Manufacturer
      3. Model
      Approximate replacement cost
      5. Size of boot
      6. A number representing the particular pair of boots
   B. Leather boots are marked with inventory number using a wood burning pencil.
   C. Leather boots are waterproofed.
   D. Synthetic leather boots do not require waterproofing.
   E. Inventory numbers are placed on all boots with an indelible marking pen.

IV. Construction and Use of an Inventory Board

A. Board is constructed from plywood or a bulletin board.

B. Using a system of color coded tags an equipment room attendant can view the entire ski equipment inventory status at a glance.

   1. Each inventory number (skis, boots) is assigned a peg (nail) on the board.

   2. If there is no tag covering a particular inventory number, it is assumed that that particular piece of equipment is available for reservation or sign-out.

   3. A black tag indicates a piece of equipment is lost, broken, or otherwise unavailable for sign-out.

   4. A red tag indicates a piece of equipment has been signed out.

   5. A yellow tag indicates a piece of equipment has been reserved for sign-out at a future date.

      a. To insure that a reserved piece of equipment will be available for sign-out on the prescribed date, that piece of equipment will not be allowed to be signed-out prior to the date it is reserved for.

V. The Reservation Process

A. Customer fills out pertinent information on a triplicate "Equipment Sign-out Request."

   1. Name

   2. Social security number

   3. Local address

   4. Telephone number

   5. Date

   6. Signature

B. Customer is asked to present two forms of identification one of which *must* be a current, valid, university I.D. card.

C. Equipment room attendant checks the request form to insure all information is recorded correctly and to compare signatures with those on the I.D.s.

D. Customer is asked if he or she wants "waxable" or "waxless" skis.

E. A centimeter scale painted on a nearby wall is used to determine the correct length of ski for the customer.

   1. The length from the floor to an upstretched wrist is about right.

   2. #1 above is a rule of thumb in actuality as much also depends on the customer's weight, the snow conditions, and the width of the skis.

F. The equipment room attendant reviews the inventory board to see if there is a pair of skis the necessary size available for reservation.

G. If equipment is available, a yellow (reserved) tag is placed on the appropriate peg covering the inventory number.

H. The inventory number is also recorded on the "Equipment Request Sheet."
I. The customer then is asked his or her shoe size.
J. The equipment room attendant uses a conversion chart to convert the American size to a European (centimeter) size.
K. He then reviews the inventory board to see if there is a pair of boots of the necessary size available for reservation.
L. If boots are available, the inventory number is covered with a yellow (reserved) tag.
M. The inventory number is recorded on the "Equipment Request."
N. If the customer is unsure of his or her shoe size a fitting may be necessary.
O. Equipment room attendant completes the necessary information on the equipment request.
   1. Fee charge per item
   2. Total fee charge
   3. Date due
   4. Pick-up date
P. The customer pays the maintenance fee.
Q. One of the triplicate "Equipment Request" forms is given to the customer as a receipt and "claim check" to pick-up skis.
R. One of the triplicate "Equipment Request" forms is sent to the accounting office along with all money collected.
S. One of the triplicate "Equipment Request" forms is retained in the "Reserved File" of the equipment room.
T. The customer presents his/her copy of the "Equipment Request" form on the day the skis are to be picked up.
U. The equipment room attendant locates his/her copy of the form.
V. The attendant completes the form by signing his/her initials.
W. For poles, the equipment room attendant estimates the length from the floor to the customer's arm pit and gives the customer a pair of poles of approximately that length.
X. Poles are not indicated on the equipment request forms. It is assumed that poles are part of the package unless otherwise noted.
Y. The customer then receives his/her equipment.
   1. Skis
   2. Boots
   3. Poles
   4. Receipt (Equipment Request Form)
   5. If skis are "waxable," a note is given that states that all wax must be removed from skis before returning.
Z. The appropriate yellow (reserved) tags are replaced with red (out) tags.

AA. The equipment request form is filed under "Out."
BB. If requested, a *Student Guide to Cross-Country Skiing* is given to the customer.
CC. Upon return of equipment the attendant locates the equipment request form filed under "Out."
DD. The form is reviewed to insure all equipment is returned and that it is returned on or before the "due date."
EE. All equipment is inspected for damage.
FF. "Waxable" skis are checked to insure all wax has been removed.
GG. The equipment room's and the customer's copy of the form is completed.
   1. Attendants initial "In"
   2. Date In
HH. The customer is given his/her receipt.
II. The other form is filed under "In."
JJ. The appropriate red (out) tags are removed from the inventory board.
KK. The equipment is returned to it's respective storage locations.

INTRAMURAL PROGRAMMING WITH LIMITED FUNDS

Eric L. Stein, University of Wisconsin-Milwaukee

At the National Intramural Recreation Sports Association convention last year in Boston, it became apparent that many of the new and innovative techniques and ideas were developed as a direct result of dollars. The film "Something for Everyone" involving recreation, intramurals and sport clubs at Oklahoma State University[1] was presented, and when it was stated that the film was developed professionally for a very reasonable price of approximately $3,000, several in the audience were surprised. The entire intramural/recreation budget at the College of Lake County in Grayslake, Illinois was less than Oklahoma State's promotional film.

It is important as NIRSA continues to grow, that intramural directors remain cognizant of the budgetary differences and program limitations between various programs. Ohio State's million dollar recreation budget certainly opens the doors to opportunities that smaller colleges such as the College of Lake County, Belleville Area College and Des Moines Area Community College may never dream possible. Individuals that don't have the large budget, must obtain the maximum mileage from the dollar through "stretching the buck." It is the purpose of the following information to present possible ideas for intramural programming with limited funds.

It is imperative that the intramural director faced with a limited budget, develop realistic goals and objectives and a priority expenditure order, so that the maximum amount of participation per dollar will result. As discussed by Mueller[3] an outline of budget items may include the following:

I. Personnel
   A. Full and/or part-time staff
   B. Student miscellaneous employees
      1. Game officials
      2. Area supervisors
      3. Office clerks and messengers
      4. Swimming lifeguards
      5. Publicity reporters-photographers

II. Equipment
   A. Sports equipment
   B. Office furniture
   C. Office machines

III. Supplies
   A. Office supplies
      1. Stencils, marking pens
      2. Stationary, envelopes
      3. Paper supplies
   B. Publicity
      1. Newsletters and posters
      2. Handbooks
      3. Orientation folders
      4. Photographic supplies
   C. Awards
      1. Individual and team trophies
      2. Medals, ribbons, certificates
      3. T-shirts, jackets, blankets

IV. Expenses
   A. Transportation
      1. Extramural participants travel
      2. National and regional meeting
   B. Professional literature and dues
   C. Insurance programs
   D. Telephone and telegraph
   E. Special events
   F. Contingency fund

Once the director has developed the priority expenditure order based upon budgetary considerations, the program implementation should begin.

Even though the intramural director may be faced with limited funds, the quality of the programs offered must always be high as each program adds to the overall picture and image of your program. Also, the director should attempt to involve as many sectors of the campus population as possible, thereby, implementing an intramural program based upon the motto that McGuire spoke upon when at Illinois "something for everyone."[2]

The College of Lake County developed a program that involved 20-30 various types of intramural tournaments, nine functioning sports clubs and a variety of special informal events. These programs resulted in numerous students, faculty and community members participating in the institutions first structured intramural/recreation program. These programs were developed with a total budget of less than $3,000, one full-time employee and a campus that was lacking a gymnasium or recreation faculty.

In developing the program with limited funds, it was necessary to promote our campus population whenever possible. Some of the most effective and yet inexpensive ways of developing the program included the following:

1. Student government leaders and other special interest groups and clubs speaking with physical education classes.
2. Organizational structure development.
3. Promotional booths at fall and spring registration.
4. Selection of male and female student directors
5. Development of space on campus for outdoor activity.
6. Rental of facilities (ex: gymnasium roller rink).
7. Strategic bulletin board placement.
8. Writing articles for student newspaper.
9. T-shirt awards.
10. Telephone recruitment.
11. Interest survey.
12. Extramurals.
13. Outdoor sports clubs.
14. Association of College Unions-International ACU-I Tournament involvement.
15. Self officiating.
16. Variety of activities and special events.
17. Open door for all suggestions.

Once the director has developed a soundly organized program based upon realistic goals and objectives that attempt to provide quality programs for everyone, the director may wish to attempt to secure additional funds for the program. These funds may be obtained through the assessment of fees that may include entry fees, forfeit fees, dues and admission to particular events. Additional methods of securing funds may be utilized through selling products such as fire extinguishers, smoke detectors, seat cushions, buttons, pizzas and other foods and magazines. Selling time through a work raffle, car wash or paper drive may be another method of obtaining additional funds for your program. It is important however, that the intramural director wtih limited funds keep the thought of generating additional funds in proper perspective, and thereby, concentrate on developing the best quality program possible with the situation at hand.

The intramural director who is in a position involving limited funds must keep a positive attitude about program potential. The intramural director must face the limited funds situation with an awareness that the program has the opportunity to develop in a unique direction based upon the specific monetary limitations. Through planning for the future with a positive attitude, intramural directors with limited funds will be ready to face their challenging and exciting positions.

BIBLIOGRAPHY

[1]Gonsoulin, Sid. "Something for Everyone," *Recreation Intramurals, Sports Clubs at Oklahoma State University,* Stillwater: Media Center, 1977.

[2]McGuire, R. J. "Imaginative and Innovative Informal Recreation," *NIRSA Proceedings,* 1975, pp. 52-53.

[3]Mueller, Pat. *Intramurals: Programming and Administration.* New York, Ronald Press Co., 1971, pp. 59-60.

INTRAMURAL PROGRAMMING WITH LIMITED FACILITIES

Michael C. Moore, Belleville Area College

There are certain problems that are unique to junior colleges, community colleges, and small commuter campuses. Intramural Directors at these institutions often face the problem of operating programs with limited funds, facilities, and personnel. Many larger colleges and universities can operate programs in enormous intramural/physical education buildings and have access to a wealth of outdoor facilities. It is important, therefore, to share ideas and experiences, so that Intramural Directors may overcome or work around these problems to provide student with well-rounded recreation and intramural programs.

The Inventory

The director must be aware of the total college environment. In order to establish a workable program, the director must take an inventory of:
1. Students—the type of students, their backgrounds, and the personality of the community in which they live.

2. Funds—the budget.
3. Personnel—the staff, whether professional or student, full time or part time.
4. Climate—the weather and geographical location of the college.
5. Facilities—The director must take stock of the available indoor and outdoor facilities.

Set Realistic Goals and Objectives

When faced with the problems of limited funds, facilities, and personnel, the director must develop realistic goals and objectives. In some instances, the traditional activities will not be functional. The director must look into alternative activities that will be operative in his particular environment.

Plan of Action

In making a plan of action, the five points listed under inventory will dictate the programming or at least greatly influence the program, and/or, the amount of "modification."

Recognize Available Facilities

It is imperative for the director to assess the current available facilities. Attempt to determine the number of intramural programming hours available through the use of existing facilities. Investigate the possibility of using facilities of various public and private organizations in the community.

After careful planning of the intramural program, the director needs to get into the actual programming of the activities. This section will deal with topics important to programming with limited facilities. Some instances of limited facility usage at Belleville Area College can provide examples. Belleville Area College is a community college in southern Illinois, located about 20 miles southeast of St. Louis, Missouri. The college now has a small gymnasium which has facilities marked for basketball, volleyball, and tennis. It also has a locker/shower room and weightlifting room. The only other indoor programming area is a small recreation room. The outdoor facilities are limited to some open space around campus, a varsity soccer field and recently constructed tennis courts. Two years ago the gym, tennis courts, and an even smaller recreation room did not exist.

Maximize Use of On-Campus Facilities

The limited space that may be available on campus must be utilized to its maximum potential. A lounge area may be used as space for table tennis and chess. Open outdoor space may have to be used for makeshift softball, football, or soccer fields. Campus parking lots may be used for temporary volleyball, basketball, tennis, and frisbee activities. Many parking lots are lighted which can benefit the director for longer programming hours.

Facility Rental

Facility rental is a necessary alternative when on-campus facilities are not available. Through the rental of bowling alleys, golf courses, horse stables, swimming pools, racquet clubs, trap clubs, and Y.M.C.A.'s, the director can obtain suitable facilities, often for a very reasonable fee. Through outside facility rental the director can add activities that will enhance the total intramural program.

Structured Intramural Activities

Experience has shown that the most popular intramural activities have been those with the best facilities. Students become active and interested when they are provided with quality equipment and facilities. For example, the flag football league on campus annually has had a small number of teams and a large number of forfeits. The field is rough, uneven, and overlaps with the varsity soccer field. Cold weather is not a factor with the small number of teams in the flag football league. A similar problem exists with the Spring softball league. The softball teams play on the same field as the football teams; therefore, the problem must relate to the facilities. Although the outdoor facilities are limited the needs of many students are met by offering structured football and softball activities. The basketball league, on the other hand, has been the mainstay of the intramural program. The new facility allows an overflow five-man league, three-man league, a one-on-one tournament, and a free throw tournament.

It is important to cooperate with other departments on campus when securing facilities. In this case intramurals cooperates with the Varsity Athletic Department in using the soccer field for football and softball activities. Besides facilities, valuable equipment and supplies can be borrowed from other departments. The Athletic Department, for example, donated an entire backstop for intramural use.

Tournaments

Many tournaments can be run, and facilities shared, through cooperation with the Physical Education Department. Judo, archery, golf, and tennis tournaments are conducted in conjunction with physical education classes. They help publicize the tournaments to their classes. Some instructors add it to their lesson plans as a competition day. The physical education classes are already paying for the facility rental.

Through cooperation with the Student Union at Belleville Area College, tournaments in billiards, chess, football, and table tennis have been developed. The Association of College Unions-International (ACU-I), holds regional recreation tournaments every year that eventually lead to the crowning of a national champion in each particular activity. The recreation room and a portion of the third floor lounge in the Student Union are available to operate campus tournaments, and the winners advance to the ACU-I regionals. Intramural Directors must be cognizant of the union's involvement in recreational tournaments. Intramural and union programs may prosper through a coordinated effort that results in efficient use of limited facilities and increased student involvement.

Special Events

Another campus organization that can help in facility sharing as well as promotion is the Student Activities Committee. In cooperation with the Student Activities Committee at Belleville Area College, the Intramural Program offers two special events, Freshmen Orientation, and May Day on the Mall. Freshmen Orientation is in the Fall and provides an opportunity to publicize the Intramural Program to incoming Freshmen. A small mall area in front of school is used for temporary grass volleyball courts, frisbee activities, and an area for an egg toss. A portion of the mall is used for a recreational equipment check-out station. The Student Activities Committee pays for a band and a cook-out luncheon. A similar event is held in the Spring called "May Day on the Mall." This joint programming makes maximum use of a small outdoor facility as well as to publicize the programs.

Other special intramural events with limited facilities are recreational trips. Intramurals sponsors a snow-ski trip, a canoe trip, and a horseback trail ride. There are no facilities on campus for these particular activities. A special travel package is scheduled or the facilities are rented at minimum cost. Students are able to take advantage of these activities in which they normally may not have the opportunity to participate.

Sports Clubs

Sports clubs were organized to give students with a higher degree of skill another avenue of competition. They have been organized for the student wtih a special interest who wishes to devote more time to that particular activity. A large number of sports clubs exist on campus regardless of the lack of facilities.

Clubs for Women's Flag Football, Women's Soccer, Jogging and Fitness, Judo, Men's Bowling, Chess, Women's Tennis, Ice-Hockey, Women's Softball, Women's Volleyball, Kung-Fu, Bicycling, and a Trap Club have been active on campus. Some of these clubs make use of the recreation room or the multi-purpose field. Most clubs, however, use off-campus facilities that can be rented. Clubs are entered in extramural leagues or tournaments, thereby, using the facilities of other colleges or community organizations.

It is important for directors to cooperate with the local Y.M.C.A. and Parks Department in facility sharing and programming. Women's Soccer, for example, was entered in the Y.M.C.A. league and used their facilities and officials. A reversal of this is the Women's Volleyball team. Interest for the intramural league was slight but there were enough girls for one team. The gym was idle Sunday night and the Belleville Recreation and Parks Department was looking for a gymnasium to run their league. The city was allowed to use the college facility and they included the women's team in their league without cost. They also provided officials and a gymnasium supervisor. If directors can establish a good rapport with community organizations, they can greatly enhance their programs by joint programming and facility sharing.

Community Programs

Another problem with facilities is the question of open play versus scheduled programs. To serve the entire community the gymnasium is open to students, faculty, and staff as well as the local taxpayers. With a small gymnasium, the problem of meeting the needs of varsity athletics, physical education, intramurals, and open recreation is magnified. Clift[2] recommended a ratio of one-third open use to two-thirds scheduled events. The community center was open 15 hours a week for open play, and people usually agreed they could set up a schedule to take advantage of the open use periods. Belleville Area College has open recreation 29 hours per week; however, intercollegiate and intramural games have priority if there is a conflict in scheduling.

Behrend recommends and explains the use of mobile recreation units. The units help wtih the problem of shortage of facilities but also provide a department with visibility, flexibility, and variety. The units can be scheduled day or night and may accommodate from 50 to 500 people. Many community organizations, such as Y.M.C.A.'s, hospitals, senior centers, play groups, churches, block associations, and museums are potential partners in sponsoring a mobile event. Twelve different types of units include: Arts and Crafts, Boxingmobile, Cinemobile, Puppet and Marionette vehicles, Playmobile, Showwagons, Sportsmobile, Tennismobile, Skatemobile, Zoomobile and the Swimmobile.

The Intramural Director in a college environment with limited facilities must keep a positive attitude about the program. Through sound and realistic planning an attractive program can occur even with a lack of facilities. In cooperating with various departments on campus and by establishing a good rapport with community organizations, the director can increase the number of facilities available to the program. With a little ingenuity, flexibility, and good public relations, the director will be able to establish a well-rounded intramural program. in spite of the limited facilities problem.

BIBLIOGRAPHY

[1]Behrend, Cathie. "Recreation at Your Doorstep." *Parks and Recreation Journal.* (June, 1977).

[2]Clift, Edward C. "The Public and Common Sense Programming." *Parks and Recreation Journal* (December, 1974).

[3]Stein, Eric L. "Sports Clubs with Limited Facilities." From a talk given for the National Workshop on Sports Clubs.

ADEQUATE PERSONNEL FOR SUCCESSFUL PROGRAMMING

By George Silberhorn, Des Moines Community College

Organizational structures for intramurals vary from campus to campus. Programs are supervised by part-time staff and by "complete" departments. An organizational pattern for a college campus with limited personnel for intramurals and campus recreation can operate simply and successfully.

A key to the successful operation of a quality program is the coordinator, part-time or full-time. The director will need to work closely with the part-time staff member. Organizational framework is a necessity if the programming is to be successful, but even more important are the personnel administering the program. Intramural programs succeed or fail directly in proportion to the actions and decisions of those administratively responsible for them. Within the framework of a small operation, the director and part-time coordinator may each find it necessary to play several roles in an effort to make the program successful. The director and coordinator may need to be facilities coordinator, secretary, equipment supervisor, maintenance man, referee, and public reporter.

Directors and coordinators of intramurals need to be genuinely interested in working in intramurals and campus recreation. They need to ensure that programs are well organized, creative and enjoyable for the participants.

A director's role or a coordinator's role varies. He forms policies, determines the program's direction, coordinates the activities, acts as the organizer, directs the events and tournaments, determines schedules, supervises where necessary, acts as an official where necessary, prepares publicity, researches previous events for improvements in the program, manages and maintains equipment.

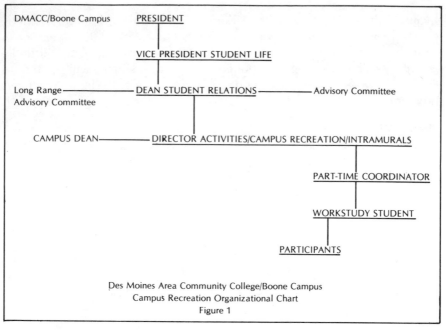

Des Moines Area Community College/Boone Campus
Campus Recreation Organizational Chart
Figure 1

A suggested plan for maintaining a successful program includes the following:

1. Appoint a coordinator who will work well in intramurals and campus recreation. The coordinator must plan to work a minimum of twelve hours per week at the rate of 2½ hours Monday through Thursday evenings for the program and ½ hour per day Monday through Thursday for minimal planning.

2. Utilize the services of work-study students when available. Most work-study students are allowed to work about 10 hours per week. V.A. work-study offers another valuable resource of student help, providing V.A. requirements are met. Practicum students from recreation and leisure services curricula are excellent assistants and generally offer valuable suggestions. Use students in classes in sports officiating. Classes such as Recreational Sports and Games provide an excellent source of student officials. Volunteers from earlier or later scheduled events can act as extra officials or assistants when needed.

3. Use department chairpersons and instructors in related areas.

An intramural program can be a success while being directed by only one person if that individual uses creativity in the use of part-time student help for programming and supervision. A ladder or challenge tournament requires no supervision, simply a daily check on the "ladder." Informal campus recreation, free time in an open gym, or an open lounge can each be supervised by one person. Checking out equipment such as horseshoes, frisbees, cards and checkers requires simple effort and no supervision.

A page in a campus newspaper sponsored for intramurals and campus recreation can accomplish much in making a program a successful endeavor and in helping its promotion. A daily record of intramural highlights and about ½ hour per week of writing by a part-time coordinator can mean the entire collegiate population can keep abreast of intramurals and campus recreation.

A handbook, well-written and complete with schedules and rules, can answer many questions and save a great deal of time for the part-time coordinator. The handbook can be prepared with minimum of effort and input. While preparing the handbook and schedules for the program, consider that beverage distributors are generally anxious to help with promotion materials like posters and schedules, thus saving valuable time for the coordinator. Following is an example of a schedule that might be implemented and supervised by a part-time coordinator:

EVENT	TYPE	ENTRIES CLOSE
Fall Softball	Co-Rec	Sept.-Mon. 2nd Week
Punt, Pass, Kick	Co-Rec, Men, Women	Oct.-Mon. 1st Week
Table Tennis I	Singles, Doubles	Oct.-Mon. 2nd Week
Pool/Billiards	Challenge	Nov.-Mon. 1st Week
Basketball	Men, Women	Nov.-Mon. 1st Week
Pinball	Co-Rec	Dec.-Mon. 3rd Week
Volleyball	Co-Rec	Jan.-Mon. 2nd Week
Table Tennis II	Singles, Doubles	Jan.-Mon. 4th Week
Football	Singles, Doubles	Feb.-Mon. 1st Week
Whiffleball	Co-Rec	Feb.-Mon. 3rd Week
Spring Softball	Co-Rec	Apr.-Mon. 1st Week
Tennis	Singles, Doubles, Challenge	Apr.-Mon. 4th Week
Frisbees	Co-Rec	May-Mon. 1st Week
Tug of War	Co-Rec	May-Mon. 2nd Week
Weightlifting	Open	
Table Games	Open	
Gym	Open	
Lounge	Open	
Tennis Courts	Open	
Softball Diamonds	Open	

BIBLIOGRAPHY

MOORE, Mike. "Directorship-Provincial Versus Progressive," National Intramural-Recreational Sports Association Proceedings, (1977), 31-32.

MUELLER, Pat. Intramurals: Programming and Administration. New York: Ronald Press Co., 1971, Chapter 3.

ROKOSZ, Francis M. Structured Intramurals. Philadelphia: W.B. Saunders Co., 1975, Chapter 1 and 7.

ALTERNATE INTRAMURALS

by Martin Hendy and Ian McGregor, Simon Fraser University

Until the Fall of 1977, SFU had what could be termed a traditional organization of its intramural leagues. People signed up for either the more skilled and more competitive A leagues or the less skilled and less competitive B leagues. The A leagues functioned effectively, and still do. But whilst B leagues seemed to be meeting the needs of most participants in them, there were occasions in some sports where non-registered players wanted to join in, and other occasions when defaults almost wiped out that session's games. So we decided to take a look at the B league structure and adopt an inclusive, not exclusive model. It seemed wrong to exclude people — the unregistered one who dropped in wanting to play — when some registered players were failing to show up. We accentuated only positive aspects (see flyer) and made it very easy for anyone to play. We hope thereby to attract into the new program, called Alternate, a larger percentage of the university community not already involved in A League intramurals. The model we developed draws from the experience of many, and is basically an adaptation of the Recreational league concept[1][2] and Hopkins' "Childs Model for Adult Sport"[3].

The activities selected were Ball Hockey, Indoor 5-a-side Soccer, Basketball, and Volleyball, all coed. B League activity in those sports was dropped but the gymnasium time retained for the new Alternate program. A league activity continues unchanged, as do the normal tournaments and special events.

The Alternate system depends upon sports managers who organize teams from participants who show up that day, offer instruction when required, and settle disputes if necessary. The manager does *not* referee (there are no referees).

There are major philosophical differences between Alternate and the old B league set-up. The two major objectives of the Alternate concept are to de-emphasize winning and to equalize competition. Clearly when two teams play a game, a competition occurs. But if the teams are variable, team affiliation becomes meaningless and so does the outcome of the competition. So winning is de-emphasized and other objectives highlighted by introduction of small modifications to the game situation. Thus, in soccer, ball hockey and basketball, when a team X player takes a breather, he joins the bench of team Y and comes on next for that team; in volleyball, rotation is under the net on to the other team (Figure 1).

This removal of team affiliation also has a secondary effect in equalizing competition as inevitably the more talented players play on both teams. But

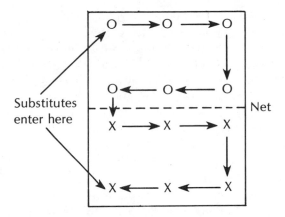

a more immediate move toward equalization occurs when in soccer or ball hockey, a goal scorer joins the other team. The team which has been scored on now has an extra player on the floor so should be able to score a goal, tie the score and equalize the players on the floor once more. This works in soccer and hockey where scoring rate is low and a stoppage in play occurs when a goal is scored. It doesn't work in basketball, because even with coloured pinnies, too much confusion results from the rapid scoring rate.

We have been delighted by the response to the Alternate program thus far, and have in fact expanded it to include innertube waterpolo. After one semester in action, we have made several general observations concerning the program.

Initially, the response to Alternate was slow due to its novelty and philosophical differences. However, participation picked up as the semester proceeded. In conjunction, we ran a very extensive advertising campaign.

We found that roughly half the former B league participants went into A league, and half joined Alternate. This caused some problems in A league. We have now adopted a tier structure in A league in an attempt to circumvent these problems and the response has been extremely positive despite the fact that the structure is basically similar to the old A and B league set up.

We found that some A league players were showing up to play Alternate. At the present time, we have banned all A league players from this program since we feel that their presence dissuades those whom we really want to attract to Alternate.

A certain amount of flexibility is needed to suit the situation. For example, we introduced a second serve in volleyball. Why not?

It appears that the concept of dropping in at any point in the semester is attractive to some. The percentage of new people showing up for the first time after week 5 (of a 10 week program) ranged from 10% in soccer to 31%

in floor hockey. We have also found that the participants are not merely the same people who keep coming back every week. On the average, for all Alternate activities, participants showed up four times per semester.

Participants themselves are enthusiastic about the program. Games are more relaxed and the general atmosphere is one of having fun.

The highlights of the Alternate program are as follows:

(a) Competitiveness is reduced;

(b) The terms 'winning' and 'losing' become meaningless;

(c) No referees, no points, and no standings are used;

(d) No sign up is necessary, just show up to play;

(e) No requirement (only encouragement) to show up every week. You may join in at any point in the semester;

(f) Emphasis is on FUN and playing the game for its own sake.

REFERENCES

[1]Hopkins, Peter, "Footballs have no feathers—do they?", *NIRSA Journal 1(1)*, 8, (1977).

[2]VanderWeele, Tom, "Recreational Leagues as a viable supplement to competitive Leagues in Intramurals," *NIRSA Proceedings XXVI*, 54 (1975).

[3]Hopkins, Peter, "A childs model for adult sport," *Recreation Canada Journal, 34(1)*, 29, (1976).

A WORKABLE FACULTY PHYSICAL FITNESS SELF-EVALUATION TEST

by Joseph Regna, University of Florida

For four years the Intramural Department tried, to no avail, to encourage the general faculty to participate in an organized program of some kind. Each dean either asked for a volunteer or selected a member of his faculty to act as a liaison between his individual college and the Intramural Department in order to help meet the individualized program needs of the various college faculties. At first it seemed as though the program would mushroom into something fantastic. However, this optimism soon proved just that—optimism. Interest waned. It became more and more difficult to communicate with the faculty representatives. Old representatives resigned and no new ones offered to take their places until finally there were no more. Even the deans seemed to lose interest. The Intramural Department took a new look and decided to reevaluate the program. Rigid programs as they related to scheduling and activities were eliminated completely and an informal type of program was initiated. This program allowed the faculty to participate in any activity they desired and on their own free time. The department's responsibility was to reserve the equipment and facilities, keep records, give awards, and provide publicity. Once again, this program was a flop. Other avenues were approached, such as age group competition, times offered, departmental competition and field days. Nothing seemed to work to stimulate significant participation. The only types of programs that held their own were the fitness related programs.

Three times weekly from 12 noon to 1:00 pm a weight room, including a universal gym and a qualified instructor, were made available to all male faculty. Individual programs were developed for each faculty member who attended, including a weight training program and a running program. All the running was done on an individual basis according to each faculty member's available time. Each faculty member kept up with his progress toward achieving his objectives and if necessary had his program revamped.

A similar program was offered to the women faculty two evenings a week. The program included a universal gym and a calisthenics type of exercise program with a qualified instructor conducting the exercises and instructing the women on the correct use of the weights. As with the men, the women were encouraged to run on their own.

The one thing that was missing from both of these programs was some method of testing the results in a scientific manner. Because of this, the current faculty physical fitness self-testing program was developed. The test included gathering the following data: personal history, strength, flexibility, body composition, and physical working capacity.

After each faculty member completed all of the tests, a personal interview with an expert in the field of exercise physiology was made available whereby each individual's results were analyzed and discussed privately. If requested, an exercise program suited to the needs of the individual was recommended and the faculty member was encouraged to follow through independently.

Pre-planning Phase

A test of this magnitude can only be successful with much cooperation from experts in the field of fitness and exercise physiology. In order to accomplish this, a meeting with the Chairperson of the Professional Physical Education program was arranged. The intended program was discussed in a general fashion, along with the rationale behind the test and the possible ramifications. I emphasized how this would really be a tremendous service to the University faculty which could only have a positive affect on the college.

The chairman saw the possibility of much favorable publicity for the college and instantly became my ally. I suggested he back me up by calling a meeting with two of his experts for the purpose of planning the content and date of the test. He agreed, and with his backing the first planning meeting was held. This meeting was held at the beginning of the Spring quarter which was approximately 7-8 weeks from the anticipated date of the test. A date was set with an alternate agreed upon in case of some unforseen event popping up. We brainstormed trying to establish objectives. Once the objectives were agreed upon, the tests to be used were discussed. Each member of the group agreed to take the responsibility of an area to be tested. We agreed upon four areas:

1. Strength
2. Flexibility
3. Body Composition
4. Physical Working Capacity (VO_2 Max)

Arrangements were made for the technicians necessary to run our individual tests and also to acquire the necessary equipment. Graduate students and test and measurements class students were used as technicians.

Publicity

Now it was time to inform the faculty of the test. A computer print-out of all the faculty with name and address was used to mail flyers describing the test to them. The flyer included a tear-off portion which was to be mailed to the Intramural Office, if the faculty member desired to participate in the test. As these forms were received by our office, each faculty member who returned the form was called and an appointment time was arranged. Because of the time necessary to complete this particular series of tests, only 25 people were scheduled each hour. Twenty-five were scheduled the first hour, then six every 15 minutes afterwards. This figure included a few extra names, because usually vacancies occur. A deadline date was established to more accurately plan the logistics of administering the test. An estimated 20-24 people could complete the test in an hour. From the numbers of forms returned we determined that it would require 4 to 5 hours to complete the test.

Administering The Test

The test consisted of 10 stations and required approximately 25 people to operate all the stations at once. This figure included the experts and the station leaders. Information and instruction were printed on posters and placed in appropriate locations throughout the test area.

Station 1 was the orientation area. The group was issued a record card (Appendix A) and was asked to provide: name, address, date of birth, sex, phone number, family doctor, and college or department. They were also asked to read and sign an informed-consent form before proceeding any further. The operation of the test was explained and questions were answered. This procedure was followed every 15 minutes after the initial group.

Each individual was to first go to station 2 and have his blood pressure read and recorded on the card. From this point on he/she was directed to any of the test areas that were open. Each group at Station 9 took approximately 12-15 minutes to complete the test.

As soon as all the tests were completed, the faculty member was directed to the table of experts (Station 10) for his/her personal interview and analysis of test scores. Interpretation of the scores and suggestions were given and the cards were collected.

This was a continuous process throughout the course of the evening. The test began at 6:00 pm and the last person finished at 10:20 pm.

The results of all tests were analyzed and norms were established for males and females of different age categories. These norms are based on the University of Florida faculty taking the test over the last three years. It would be quite safe to assume, that for the most part, the better fit group of faculty came to be tested. As a group, the faculty fared above average in most tests. We did have some norms to compare with, but the faculty was more interested in how they placed in relation to their own peers rather than from some other source. These norms were sent to all participants. They will be revised the next time the test is administered.

Description of Tests

1. *Body Composition* (Wilmore's fat test). This test was selected because of the importance of body composition as it relates to health and performance. Too much of a percentage of fat in the body is just plain unhealthy. Most people understand only what the scale tells them. The scale indicates the number of pounds we weigh. Unfortunately most people accept their weight and conveniently forget how much they weighed in earlier years. To determine body composition, the Wilmore test is used to determine the subject's percent of body fat. People do not react as much when they are told they weigh 200 pounds; however, tell them their body composition consists of 30% fat and 70% lean, then watch the reaction. Tell them that their "ideal" body weight should be 165 and even at 180 they are considered obese and that the extra 60 pounds is unnecessary. This most always results in a reaction.

The test is fairly simple, and requires only body weight and one skinfold measurement. The men are measured by a vertical abdominal fold and the women a vertical fold at the inferior angle of the scapula. Caution must be taken to acquire accurate measurements of skinfold. (Graduate students in exercise physiology are used to take the measurements).

Once the measurements have been taken, lean body weight (LBW) is determined by the following formula:

   Men LBW(lbs) = 22.62 + (.793) (Body Wt. lbs) − (.801) (Abdominal skin-
     fold measurement mm)

   Women LBW(lbs) = 20.20 + (.645) (Body Wt. lbs) − (.503) (Scapula skin-
     fold measurement mm)

When LBW is determined, the amount of body fat is simply body weight minus LBW. To get the body's percentage of fat, divide the body weight into the body fat and multiply by 100.

To determine "ideal" body weight, (assuming that men should have 15% fat and women 22.5% fat) take LBW/.85 for males and LBW/.775 for females. This predicted "ideal" or "allowable" body weight gives our faculty a goal to aim for in terms of weight control.

These fairly simple measures and calculations to determine LBW and percentage of body fat are valuable in predicting a person's body composition. This information is useful in judging health risks and weight control goals.

2. *Physical Working Capacity (Max VO_2 Predicted)* Physical working capacity (PWC) is a measurement of how much work a person can do before his or her heart rate reaches a certain level. In our case we use 150 beats/minute as the cut-off rate. We designated this as PWC 150. The units of work are Kilopound-meters (Kp-m). As we all know, work by definition is a product of force (the kilopound being the force exerted by a kilogram mass at sea level due to gravity) and distance (meters).

The tools required to undertake this test are few. All that is needed is a bicycle ergometer (we use the Monark Ergometer) from the exercise physiology labs and a clock with a second hand. (We used a timer). The only other requirement is a tester who can tell time and be able to determine a person's heart rate by palpation at the carotid.

We use a modified version of Astrand's test described in "Work Test with the Bicycle Ergometer" (Monark, Cresent, Varberg, Sweden.) The subject pedals at 50 rpm at a fixed workload (men 600 Kp-m and women 300 Kp-m). Every 60 second interval the heart rate is determined and recorded from a 10 second reading. The test terminates when the participant's heart rate reaches or surpasses 150 beats/minute. If this target rate is not reached after 6 minutes, the work load is increased. Some of our subjects were in such excellent condition that a 3rd level workload was required. The increases we used were:

   Men (1) 600 Kp-m (2) 900 Kp-m (3) 1200 Kp-m

   Women (1) 300 Kp-m (2) 450 Kp-m (3) 600 Kp-m

To determine an individual's physical working capacity (PWC), the workload at which he was pedalling when the heart rate reached the cut-off level (150 beats/min) was recorded. A relatively fit and strong person might have a PWC 150 of 1200 Kp-m/minute.

This number as such has very little meaning, however these PWC levels are extremely valuable because they may be used to predict Max VO_2. Maximum VO_2 is an excellent estimate of cardio-respiratory fitness. We can only make a *prediction* of Max VO_2, however this test (a sub maximal bicycle test) is quicker, less demanding, and definitely much safer than a maximum test.

To predict the Max VO_2 we study the heart rate determined during the 5th and 6th minutes of each workload which was completed. Tables in Astrand's text on work tests give VO_2 values in 1 O_2. These figures may be changed to ml O_2/kg. by dividing by the subject's weight. Age corrections are available for subjects over age 25 based on Swedish subjects which seem to show much better results than our faculty. The Swedish tables show an average of approximately 40 with a low figure of 34 and a high figure of 52. Our average is 35.8.

This test (Astrand bicycle test) is a single, safe and not too demanding way of measuring physical working capacity, and more importantly to predict Max VO_2. This prediction gives an estimate of cardio respiratory fitness which is a very important goal of our faculty fitness program.

3. *Flexibility*—We elected to measure 2 kinds of flexibility in this test. The first one was trunk flexibility. This test consisted of a platform with a scale attached in such a way that 0 was even with the platform with gradations of 1″ intervals in both directions. The numbers below 0 were plus numbers and the numbers above 0 were negative numbers. The subject stands on the platform with his feet together, one on each side of the scale and his toes to the front edge. He bends forward at the waist and stretches as far as he can, keeping his legs straight. The technician must be careful to check for any bend in the knee. The slightest bend invalidates the try. The subject then touches the face of the platform with fingers that have been covered with a chalky substance leaving a mark. If (a) the legs stay straight and (b) the subject holds the position for a minimum of 2 seconds, the results are recorded. The average score for males should be from 0 to −2 inches and for women from 0 to +1 inches. The results of our test showed our faculty to be above average in this test. (Table I)

The second flexibility test was conducted with a flexometer against a supporting column. The flexometer was attached to the upper arm of the subject and calibrated. The subject was then asked to rotate his arm as far as possible (the reading taken). This test was given for both shoulders and the results averaged. The norm for males should be between 250°-260° and for females 260°-270°. Our male faculty seemed to be a little low; however, the females were right on target. (Table II)

4. *Strength tests:* Three strength tests were used in our program. They

were back, leg, and grip.

Back lift: Before anyone was allowed to perform this test, the technician asked each subject if he had a history of lower back trouble. If he did, he was advised to omit this item. The test was performed with the use of a dynamometer. The subject stands on the base of the dynamometer with feet parallel and approximately 6" apart. The ankle joints are along side the base hook. The back is straight and the head is up. The arms are straight and the fingers extended downward along the front of the thighs. The technician holds the bar even with the subjects finger tips and connects the lower end of the chain to the base hook. The subject bends slightly forward with the knees straight and grasps the bar with a mixed grip. The action consists of a lift straight up with a steady and even extension of the *back only.* This effort should be maintained until a maximum exertion has been applied. The scale is read in pounds.

The test becomes invalid if (a) the knees bend, (b) the arms bend, (c) there is any sudden jerking action, or (d) the chain is allowed to slacken prior to the lift.

Leg lift: Before anyone was allowed to perform this test the technician asked the subjects if they had a history or predisposition to rupture. If so, they were asked to omit the left lift test. The starting position is the same as for that of the back lift except that the center of the bar is held, palm down, at the level of the pubic bone. At this point the safety lifting belt is attached to the subject. The subject is in a slight squat position (knees bent at an angle of 115 to 125° between the back of the thighs and the calf of the leg). The technician then connects the lower end of the chain to the base hook. The action occurs with a steady even extension of the knees. The subject should maintain a steady effort until maximum exertion has been applied. Any lifting with the back, sudden jerking action, or allowing the chain to slacken invalidates the test. The scale is read in pounds.

Grip strength: The last strength tests we used were grip strength measuring both the dominant and non-dominant hands. The only equipment needed for this test was a manuometer. The subject exerted maximum griping force first with one hand then the other and recorded the readings on the card. Most any movement is permitted with the exception of placing the fist against the body of any other object while exerting pressure. The measurement is recorded in kilograms.

Tests have been taken of over 100 faculty for three years and standards have been computed based on the cumulative information collected during this time. These figures are only representative of the faculty who have participated in the tests and consideration must be given when interpreting the results. In any event the test has provided our department and college with much positive feedback. The faculty use the same cards each year for com-

Table 1. Performance of University of Florida Faculty on physical fitness testing.

MALES

AGE	N	AVE. WT.	% FAT	VO$_2$	FLEXIBILITY		STRENGTH #		GRIP #	
					TRUNK	SHOULD.	BACK	LEG	NON DOM.	COM
20-24	2	168	14.0	44.0	+4.75	293°	375	770	57	55
25-29	9	172	19.0	37.1	+0.90	240°	378	710	61	56
30-34	41	161	19.2	38.9	+2.00	235°	307	610	55	49
35-39	30	168	19.5	34.5	-0.50	236°	335	661	56	50
40-44	21	173	21.7	35.1	-1.30	236°	351	662	60	55
45-49	21	166	20.1	33.1	-0.50	222°	345	757	57	52
50 & Up	31	177	22.2	27.1	-0.13	228°	337	642	49	48

FEMALES

AGE	N	AVE. WT.	% FAT	VO$_2$	FLEXIBILITY		STRENGTH #		GRIP #	
					TRUNK	SHOULD.	BACK	LEG	NON DOM	DOM
20-24	3	156	26.9	32.6	+	246°	191	446	32	29
25-29	9	117	26.0	44.0	0.00	240°	174	312	31	27
30-34	13	125	24.4	39.4	+	259°	195	238	31	30
35-39	6	124	25.5	35.8	+2.50	266°	200	303	34	31
40-44	5	133	29.7	32.5	+5.10	260°	267	513	38	36
45-49	5	126	27.5	34.7	+3.30	255°	205	451	37	33
50 & Up	5	131	24.3	32.6	+5.10	241°	189	501	28	27

parison. Most of them make an effort to improve their weaknesses and the results do show more improvements than regressions. Once again, in order for a test of this magnitude to be successful, one needs to plan well in advance. Arrange for considerable help, both learned and not so learned. Secure the equipment and facilities and above all be willing to spend a lot of time.

APPENDIX A

RECORD CARD

NAME_____ DATE OF BIRTH_____ SEX ____

ADDRESS_____ CAMPUS PHONE_____ COL. _____

FAMILY DR. _____ ADDRESS _____

Ht.____ins. Wt.____   #____   #____   #____

                    kg____ kg____ kg____

WILMORE'S FAT TEST				**STRENGTH**			
VARIABLE	1	2	3	**VARIABLE**	1	2	3
Skin Fold	____	____	____	Back	____	____	____
Fat %	____	____	____	Leg	____	____	____
Lean %	____	____	____	Dominant hand	____	____	____
Ideal Wt.	____	____	____	Non-dominant hand	____	____	____

FLEXIBILITY				**BLOOD PRESSURE**			
Trunk	____	____	____	Systolic	____	____	____
Shoulder	____	____	____	Diastolic	____	____	____
MAX VO$_2$ (Predicted) ml/kg/min	____	____	____	Pulse Pressure	____	____	____

AN INFORMAL ADULT FITNESS PROGRAM

By Donald Scherrer, University of Illinois-Chicago Circle

The Program

In our American society, it is not uncommon to see young men in their thirties and forties having a coronary heart attack, or possessing a diseased heart that requires coronary by-pass surgery. Also alarming is the fact that approximately half of all Americans die of coronary artery disease or other vascular related diseases. Research into the problem has revealed that there is no one single cause, but rather the problem stems from a combination of several factors. The longer an individual follows a pattern of living that includes these identifiable factors, the greater the danger of developing heart disease.

The factors have been categorized into "Prime Risk Factors" and "Secondary Risk Factors" depending upon the degree of relationship with heart disease. The Framingham Study and other epidemiological studies have determined that the 3 Primary Risk Factors are smoking, high levels of cholesterol in the blood, and high blood pressure. Possessing one of these risk factors, one has about an average chance of developing heart disease; possessing two risk factors, one's chances are about triple that of average for that age group; while if one has all 3, the chances increase more than 4 times greater than average. Other factors that have been found to be related to heart disease are obesity, inactivity, mental and emotional stress, the urban environment, heredity, one's sex, and age.

Many of these factors are related quite closely to one another. For instance, mental or emotional stress may cause one to smoke more, or eat more, and even develop hypertension. Individuals who are overweight and even obese will usually have an elevated cholesterol level and are generally sedentary individuals. The urban environment, where most of the population lives, exposes people to more stress and with less opportunity for physical activity. Of course there are those factors such as heredity, sex, and age which are beyond one's control, so special concern should be given to the other risk factors as one gets older, and if there is a family history of heart disease.

Controlling the Problem

Since the incidence of heart disease is directly related to risk factors, one must minimize or eliminate these factors in order to practice good preventive medicine. Fortunately controlling most of the risk factors is within every individual's capabilities.

It appears that incorporating physical activity into one's daily routine

103

reduces the threat of these risks. One's cholesterol level in the blood can be reduced for up to 48 hours as a result of a half hour cardiovascular workout. Also, exercise burns up calories for energy which might otherwise be stored as fat. If one utilizes more calories for energy than is taken in by diet, weight will be lost.

Physical exercise is also an excellent diversion from mental or emotional stress. The mind is diverted from its normal problems and involved with the enjoyment of the task of exercising. Also, blood pressure can be moderated after a single bout of exercise plus the body's muscular tension can be reduced.

Factual knowledge of the physiological effects of exercise is not sufficient to elicit a change in one's pattern of living. A common response to the question as to why don't you do more exercise, is, "I simply don't have the time." These individuals will generally not argue the fact that the exercise is not beneficial. Therefore, one of the major obstacles in getting people actively involved in a regular exercise program, is providing a convenient opportunity.

A second major consideration is motivation. In order to initially involve an individual into an exercise program, something about the exercise itself or the organization of the program must attract the individual to it. The program must be effectively promoted. In a college environment, publicizing an exercise program may include the effective use of bulletin boards, issuing of program T shirts, and sponsoring special events emphasizing physical fitness. However, there is no substitute for a properly administered exercise stress test. If individuals who take the test receive a positive experience which genuinely helps them become more aware of the importance of cardio-vascular fitness, details of the program will spread by word of mouth throughout the college community.

The Fitness Test

An exercise physiology laboratory is essential for implementing a fitness program that will allow for accurately assessing cardiovascular condition. An exercise treadmill is needed for the purpose of controlling the exercise intensity. Speed and incline can be changed according to a standard protocol. A monitoring system is necessary for the purpose of recording heart rate and ECG responses to the treadmill test. Also a sphygmonanometer is needed to measure blood pressure changes in response to changing intensities of exercise.

If one has not been physically active for a lengthy period of time, it is essential that a thorough physical examination be given prior the exercise stress test. The stress test should measure the important physiological responses to exercise of gradually increasing intensity by recording the electrocardiogram, and blood pressure response. The 3 primary purposes of the exercise stress are:

1. To identify symptoms of heart disease.
2. To assess the level of cardiovascular fitness
3. To measure changes in cardiovascular fitness in response to a training program

Other factors related to total physical fitness can be measured quite easily in a single visit to the laboratory. Body composition can be assessed by using a skinfold caliper. An accurate estimate of the per cent of one's weight which is fat tissue can be calculated based on the thickness of skin folds at various locations of the body.

Also, in order to offer a comprehensive fitness evaluation, an assessment of body strength and flexibility should be considered. Most texts in measurement and evaluation will include standardized tests for flexibility and strength. By including an assessment in this area possible deficiencies or weaknesses can be identified which can enable a program director to prescribe an exercise program based upon one's needs.

Getting Started

Certain educational environments, such as the commuter college campus, make arranging specified times for a class in physical fitness for faculty, staff, or other interested groups very difficult. People who include some form of physical activity in their daily routine tend to do so at various times of the day, at their own convenience. However many of these individuals do seek guidance concerning their personal fitness program and desire to be part of an organization that would help them in their activities. It was for the purpose of meeting this need that the informal fitness program was organized at the University of Illinois Chicago Circle.

The first step for joining the fitness program is to participate in the exercise stress test. If the individual is over 40 years of age, a copy of a recent physical exam needs to be on file. Also prior to taking the stress test, a personal consent form should be signed which described in detail the nature of the test. If the individual is under 40 and is asymptomatic, the test can proceed without a physician present. In all other situations a physician should be present during the test. Upon completion of the test, a consultation session follows, where principles and guidelines for an individualized exercise program are discussed. The individual is then on his own to participate in what should be a regular exercise program.

A program of this type would involve the combined efforts of the physical education department and the recreation department. The physical education department normally has the facilities and the expertise to conduct the stress test and to follow-up the test with the exercise prescription. The recreation department has the facilities and the faculty expertise to organize a systematic method for people to exercise regularly and to maintain records of the exercise sessions.

The primary objective of the adult fitness program is to improve cardiovascular fitness and minimize risk factors. Dr. Kenneth Cooper has developed a point system with which one can evaluate the relative value of any bout of exercise based upon the intensity and the duration of the activity. Estimates of "aerobic" points are made not only for jogging and swimming, but also for other activities such as tennis and racketball.

In order for one to monitor how many aerobic points are earned per workout or per week, a card must be designed to record the details of the workout. The card might very well be designed as follows:

```
Name _____
Date _____
Activity _____
Time _____
Distance _____
Aerobic Points _____
```

An ideal location for the cards and the card file would be at the intramural sports office or the recreation equipment checkout office. This office is usually located in a convenient area so that people can fill out the card as they leave the physical education or recreation facility. Also, many individuals may choose to exercise off campus, in which case they can simply call the intramural or recreation office and have the card filled out for them by a secretary.

For those who jog or swim, a progress chart can be posted where the total number of miles run or swum can be recorded. This chart serves as a motivational attraction for both the individual and for attracting the attention of others who might become interested in the program. The chart should keep track of each individual workout plus keep a record of the total number of miles run or swum since entering the program or from some other starting point.

Additional ideas can be implemented for the purpose of promoting the program or identifying those who are actively involved. "T" shirts with a logo of the program can be given to all who complete the exercise stress test. Additional "T" shirts can be awarded for jogging or swimming a designated number of miles. Also, a physical fitness bulletin board should be maintained where various recent articles can be posted. Photographs of various individuals in the program as they are going through their workouts also stimulate interest.

Special Events

Organizing special events periodically can stimulate interest among those in the program as well as the college community in general. These special events may be organized with each individual competing for himself, or they may be organized into a team competition event. Teams can be organized from different student organizations, college departments, and even groups outside the university if the program includes community groups. Listed below are a few ideas that have been conducted successfully.

1. 15 KM Handicap Run—Based on your age and sex, you are given a head start before an experienced marathon runner begins. These handicaps have been developed at the National Data Research Center by Kenneth Young.
2. Turkey Trot—Simply a distance race, conducted prior to Thanksgiving with turkeys being awarded to winners in various categories.
3. Ten Mile Marathon Medley—This is a team race where one runner covers 1 mile, a second goes 2 miles, a third runs 3 miles, and a fourth runs 4 miles.
4. Turf and Surf Race—This event is a combination run and swim. The participants begin by running a designated distance which ends up near a swimming pool where the runners take off their shoes, dive in the water, and complete the race. Recommended distances might be 3 miles for the run and 1000 yards or meters for the swim.
5. Couples Run—This is simply a male-female team, each running a pre-determined portion of the race.
6. Beat the Champ—As part of physical fitness day activities, various activities are planned where an expert in each activity will compete with all challengers. Suggested activities include racquetball, handball, 1 on 1 basketball, various swimming events, and track and field events. The activity combined with a scheduled teaching workshop adds interest to this event.

CHAPTER III

Intramural-Recreational Facilities

FACILITY PLANNING & JUSTIFICATION—
SURVEYING BENCHMARK UNIVERSITIES

Dr. Ronald W. Violette, Director of Campus Recreation-Intramurals
Memphis State University

There are probably as many strategies for planning and justifying a recreational intramural facility as there are colleges and universities. While there are a number of basic strategies (delineated very well by Gary Colburg[1] at last year's conference), it is important to remember that each institution is different. Every administrator who becomes involved in facility planning and justification would be well advised to examine his or her institution for special or unique avenues of attack.

At the University of Kentucky, we decided to explore one such avenue which we deemed to be rather specific to our institution. We were concerned in the Campus Recreation Department at Kentucky about the adequacy and maintenance of our recreational facilities both indoors and out. I am sure that most of you are currently facing some of these same kinds of problems. Physical education classes, intramurals, club sports, informal recreation, and in some cases varsity athletics place excessive demands on limited facilities. With these concerns in mind and with an eye to the future, we decided to survey those institutions designated as benchmark universities of the University of Kentucky. These benchmark institutions are chosen by the

Kentucky State Council on Higher Education. They are, by definition, those universities similar to the University of Kentucky and represent the major state and land grant institutions in states contiguous to Kentucky plus two North Carolina universities. These benchmark institutions are Illinois, Indiana, Missouri, North Carolina, North Carolina State, Ohio State, Purdue, Tennessee, Virginia, Virginia Tech, and West Virginia.

Why did we survey these particular institutions? At the University of Kentucky, President Otis Singletary continues to be very concerned about the salaries of faculty and professional staff as they compare to those paid at the eleven benchmark institutions. The goal is to be in the middle of this group of schools. Knowing full well the importance of these benchmark institutions to the administration at the University, we felt it would be valuable to find out as much as possible about the recreational facilities of these institutions. Ideally, we felt we should be in the middle of this group as far as recreational facilities and the maintenance of same were concerned.

In constructing the survey questionnaire we were concerned principally with brevity, encouraging complete responses and achieving a 100 percent response rate. The cover letter was designed to inform each institution of the selectiveness of the sample and, of course, to encourage a response from each of them. With the help of two follow-up phone calls we were able to achieve a 100 percent response rate from the institutions.

We found that the average enrollment at the institutions was 26,200 compared with an enrollment of 21,000 at the University of Kentucky. The findings should be viewed wtih these enrollment figures in mind.

It should be noted that, of the universities surveyed, seven reported that their facilities did not meet the needs of their programs. Three schools reported that there were definite plans for expansion of existing indoor facilities in the near future.

Generally, indoor, outdoor, and pool facilities were controlled by recreation-intramural programs after a certain time of the day. Physical education departments generally controlled the facility until somewhere between 3 and 5 P.M. in the afternoon. The same thing is true at Kentucky.

The average number of multi-use courts available for recreation-intramural use at the benchmark institutions was as follows:

	Mean	Range	UK
Basketball	10.6	3 to 24	6
Volleyball:	11.2	3 to 28	9
Badminton	15.3	4 to 45	8
Racquetball	10.9	5 to 20	4
Squash	5.6	2 to 12	4

The number of swimming pools at each institution ranged from 1 to 6 and averaged 2.4. At UK we have one very antiquated 25 yard indoor pool which is, of course, used very heavily.

Outdoor fields averaged 4.4 for soccer, 10.1 for flag football, and 13.9 for softball. The figures for UK are 2, 5, and 6 respectively.

Swimming	2.4	1 to 6	1
Flag Football	10.1	6 to 19	5
Softball	13.5	2 to 53	6

The recreation-intramural programs reported that they were open an average of 48.5 hours Monday through Friday (an average of 9.7 hours per day). Their facilities were open an average of 11.3 hours on Saturday and 9.4 hours on Sunday. Structured activities during these times were supervised by students at 10 of the 11 schools. Unstructured activities were supervised by students at five schools, by security personnel at two, by professional staff at one, and by no one at one institution.

The staff member in our department in charge of fields and facilities was very interested in the responsibilities for moving, setting-up, and maintenance of equipment as well as the lining of fields. Seven of the eleven schools surveyed indicated that in the first instance full-time building maintenance personnel were charged with this responsibility. Three schools indicated that students performed these tasks and one school reported that the athletic department took care of these functions. As for lining sports fields, the results were as follows:

Athletic Association	- 3 schools
Intramural Directors	- 2 schools
Physical Plant	- 2 schools
Students	- 2 schools
Physical Education Department	- 1 school

At the University of Kentucky, students perform both of these tasks and we are not completely satisfied with this arrangement.

Although not directly related to facilities, we were nevertheless interested in the remuneration of student supervisory personnel as well as student intramural officials. We averaged the highest reported salary at each school and found that the average pay for supervisory personnel was $2.80 per hour and for intramural officials, $2.56 per hour. At UK, the highest pay for both of these areas is $2.20 per hour.

After examination of the data, it is quite evident that the University of Kentucky is not on a par with its benchmark institutions in terms of recreational-intramural facilities. We had felt somewhat subjectively that this might be the case, but through the expenditure of a little time and effort, we were able to substantiate this contention with hard data. Now, we have a much more objective basis for these beliefs.

Again, it should be emphasized that each institution is different and that a strategy or strategies specific to each school may exist and need to be explored. This type of individual introspection coupled with Colberg's project planning guide[2] should stand the university recreation administrator in good stead in his battle to plan and justify additional recreational facilities.

FOOTNOTES

[1]Gary Colberg, "Facilities, The 'A' and 'B' Stages to Planning a Recreational Facility," *28th Annual Conference Proceedings of the National Intramural-Recreational Sports Association,* (Boston, Massachusetts, April 14-18, 1977), pp. 147-151.

[2]Ibid.

BIBLIOGRAPHY

Colberg, Gary, "Facilities, The 'A' and 'B' Stages to Planning a Recreational Facility," *28th Annual Conference Proceedings of the National Intramural-Recreational Sports Association,* Boston, Massachusetts, April 14-18, 1977, pp. 147-151.

PROVIDING THE FOUNDATION FOR SECURING NEW FACILITIES

Gary Miller, California State University, Northridge

Each year one of the topics of discussion heard on the formal program, as well as in informal discussions among individuals attending the conference, is facilities. Nearly every campus director expresses a desire and honest need for more facilities. California State University, Northridge is not an exception. The problem is how to secure these new facilities. The following program will supply you with a basis from which to better justify requests for additional facilities.

The initial step in the process of securing any new facility is defining the space requirements for your individual campus. Sapora and Kenny classified three different types of spaces used for physical education, recreation and athletics The breakdown is as follows:

Breakdown of Type A Space

Type A — Indoor Teaching Stations—Space Requirements: 8.5-9.5 sq. ft. per student (total undergraduate enrollment)
Including: a) Gym floors, mat areas, swimming pools, court areas, etc.
b) Adjacent to lockers and showers and within a ten minute walking distance of academic classrooms.

111

Uses: Physical Education class instruction, Varsity sports, Intramural sports, unorganized sports participation, student and faculty recreation, etc.

A1 . . . . . . Large gymnasium area with relatively high ceiling (22 ft. minimum) for basketball, badminton, gymnastics apparatus, volleyball, etc. (approximately 55% of Type A space).

A2 . . . . . . Activity areas with relatively low ceiling (12 ft. minimum) for combatives, therapeutic exercises, dancing, weight lifting, etc. (approximately 30% of Type A space).

A3 . . . . . . Indoor swimming and diving pools (approximately 15% of Type A space).

Breakdown of Type B Space

Type B — Outdoor Teaching Stations—Space Requirements:
Including: a) Sports fields of all types
b) Adjacent ot lockes and showers and within a ten minute walking distance of academic classrooms.
Uses: Physical Education class instruction, varsity sports, Intramural sports participation, student and faculty recreation, etc.

B1 . . . . . . Sodded areas for soccer, touch football, softball, etc. (approximately 60% of Type B space).

B2 . . . . . . Court type areas for tennis, volleyball, etc. (approximately 15% of Type B space).

B3 . . . . . . Specialized athletic areas for track and field, baseball, archery, varsity football, golf, camping demonstrations, etc. (approximately 25% of Type B space).

B4 . . . . . . Swimming pools (included in B3 approximation).

Breakdown of Type C Space

Type C — Sports Fields and Building, Intramural and General Outdoor Recreation Areas—Space Requirements:
120-140 sq. ft. per student (total undergraduate enrollment)
Including: Playing fields and athletic buildings of all types, softball diamonds, tennis courts, field houses, etc. Too far removed from student lockers, showers, living quarters and academic buildings for use as teaching stations.
Uses: Intramural sports, varsity sports, unorganized informal sports.

C1 . . . . . . Sodded areas for soccer, touch football, softball, etc. (approximately 40% of Type C space).

112

C2 ...... Court type areas for tennis, volleyball, etc, (approximately 10% of Type C space).

C3 ...... Specialized athletic area for track and field, baseball, archery, varsity football, golf, camping demonstrations, etc. (approximately 45% of Type C space).

C4 ...... Swimming pools (included in C3 approximation).

C5 ...... Sports and Intramural buildings providing lockers, showers, play space, office space, lounge rooms, etc. (approximately 5% of Type C space).[1]

These standards for space requirements are still currently accepted by the American Alliance for Health, Physical Education and Recreation. A study is now being conducted at the University of Southern California to update and improve these standards. However, it is not complete at this time.

In order to compare a campus with the accepted standards, five steps should be followed.

1. The first step involves the locating of existing and potential areas within the boundaries of the campus. This is done by physically canvassing the area and envisioning the potential of all areas. The initial phase of Step 1 should be the location and identification of all areas that are currently used by physical education, intramural sports, and athletics.

   The second phase is more difficult and requires more effort and imagination on the part of the observer. Potential areas of expansion are spaces (outdoor and indoor) that can be converted from whatever they are currently being used for to a usable recreation area. Cost of converting each area should be kept at a minimum to further enhance the attractiveness of securing new facilities. For example, the cost of converting a relatively small (50′ × 100′) grassy area to an outdoor volleyball area would only include the installation of two poles and a net. If further funds were available and the sport is popular, this area could further be converted to a sand or beach volleyball court at a small additional cost. Providing the alternatives or options also enhance the acceptability of the proposal.

   Space for conversion should meet the general criteria for Type A, B, or C space before that space is considered for alteration. For example, an indoor area with an eight foot ceiling should not be considered for conversion to gymnasium space; however, it could be converted to a dance studio or a karate practice room with the addition of mirrors and mats.

2. After *all* available and potential areas have been located, the next step requires the computations of the area in square feet. For indoor areas a tape measure is used; however, for large outdoor areas a cross country

measuring wheel is most effective.

When measuring any area, precaution should be taken to allow for a buffer zone of safety around any proposed playing area. An outdoor grassy area measuring 100 yards by 40 yards could theoretically accommodate an intramural football field, but if the boundaries are close to hazards such as chain link fence poles, trees, or buildings, this area should be considered for some other recreational purpose.

The same precaution applies to indoor space. Most areas considered will be fairly easy to measure. Normally, spaces are either rectangular or square in shape. Odd shaped areas should not be ignored and their areas should be estimated to the best of the measurer's ability while still allowing for the safety buffer zone. Odd shaped areas are also sometimes ignored because they do not fit the shape of a standard playing field. These areas may, however, accommodate a combination of two or more sports in that area, Any particular space should not be viewed as usable *only* for football or basketball but left over spaces could easily be used for a frisbee golf course or a single table tennis table.

The square footage for all areas considered should next be classified and totaled under one of the three types of spaces defined by Sapora and Kenny.[6] This total figure of space classified according to type can now be compared with the recommended amount of space. Recommended space is computed by taking current enrollment figures and multiplying them by the median figure in the range of each type of space. For example, a university with an enrollment of 15,000 students should have a recommended space requirement for Type A space of 135,000 square feet (15,000 × 9). The total amount of each type space is then compared with the actual amount to arrive at a figure illustrating the amount above or below recommended standards.

A further breakdown of space within each type into the twelve sub-classifications is required to determine the correct "mix" of facilities. This sub-classification of space enables the director to specifically locate areas of deficiency.

"When standards in terms of square feet per student are used as guides in college or university planning, it is natural to ask where the cut-off begins. Obviously, for a college of 200 students, nine square feet per student of indoor area for sports and athletics would be inadequate. It would not even provide one basketball court. A univeristy or college meeting the space standards for 1,500 students represents the minimum physical recreation space needs of any college institution. As a college or university increases in size, these standards are applicable regardless of enrollment."[2] Also, a ceiling effect applies to some sub-classifications of space.

In the beginning phases of planning for recreational facilities, area
, standards must be developed. A variety of standards relative to size,
location, and development of school and recreation areas and
facilities have been proposed over the years by School Administrators
and Facilities Planning conferences. The standards have been valid in-
sofar as they have been designed to provide space and facilities that
make possible a program which serves the basic needs of people for
physical education and recreation.

"The standards provide a useful guide; however standards can
seldom,if ever, be applied completely, or without modification.
Because a typical or ideal situation is seldom found, standards were
designed to indicate a basis for the intelligent development of local
plans."[2]

3. The third step involves a description of current and potential uses of
each area. A description of current uses should be done first. It should
include uses by physical education, recreation, intramural sports, and
"outside" departments. If a particular area is not being used for any
specific purpose, it should be so listed.

Potential uses should be as closely linked to the sub-classifications
as possible. It is in this phase of the process where the director must
make responsible choices as to the development of any given area.
One area must have the potential to be developed into several different types of space. The director must refer to the individual program needs and areas of deficiency to make informed decisions as to
the development of that particular area. Again, it is important to provide campus planners with options. However, the director should limit
the flexibility of the proposal to stay within the most urgent needs of
his particular program.

4. The next step is to determine the cost of converting an area from its
current use to its potential use. In some cases the cost of conversion
will be zero. This type of space should be accentuated in presenting
the proposal before any board involved with campus planning. Often
cooperation between two departments regarding scheduling can vast-
ly increase facilities available for recreational use at no cost to either
program.

Obtaining other costs of conversion generally involve requesting
estimates from the physical plant operations staff on campus or from
outside contractors. These estimates should be obtained prior to
presenting any proposal. Also the estimates should be tailored to the
amount of flexibility built into the proposal. That is to say, all options
should have their own separate estimate. This allows campus planning

115

boards to examine all suggestions of the proposal equally without regard to other suggestions in the proposal

5. Finally, the last step involves defining the availability for use by the major users. If facilities are shared by two or more users, the priority schedule for usage should also be listed. After all, a program may have access to a facility forty percent of the total time available but if those times are at undesirable hours, the facility is not meeting the needs of the program. If no consideration is given to the prime time needs of the students for recreational use, the percentage of availability may be misleading.

After completing the gathering of information, the supporting documents for the requesting of new facilities must be prepared. The proposal should contain five major parts.

The first part of the proposal should state clearly the objectives of the study. It should also list all areas and departments of the campus involved in conducting the study. Finally, it should include limitations or qualifications specific to the institution.

The second part should include brief historical developments of the sponsoring program from both a national and campus viewpoint.

The third section is a statement of the problem. In this section, all forces generating the study should be explained. All major problems affected by changing facility structures should be included and the majority of the information gathered in the aforementioned steps is included in this section. Listing the standards with the organizations using them will lend national support to the proposal. The relationship between the standard and enrollment is explained next. And, finally, the standards are applied to the specific campus in question. The comparison should emphasize those areas in which critical deficiencies exist because the largest deficiencies are not always the most critical ones. Section three should conclude with a summary of the work completed on the study and a restatement of those problem areas.

Section four contains recommendations for immediate action and long-term improvements. Flexibility (options) within the overall goal of the organization should be the guiding principle when preparing this section.

Finally, appendices should be prepared to support the proposal. Participation figures may be used in this section; however, the major part of this section should contain a map of the campus with all areas clearly marked. The map should be accompanied by a list of all buildings and rooms investigated. The most precise way of presenting existing and potential areas is according to the following seven point formula:

1. Location
2. Area (Structure Footage)

3. Type of Space
4. Current Uses
5. Potential Uses
6. Cost of Conversion
7. Percentage of Use

Each area should be listed and explained through this format.

In summary, the use of nationally accepted standards allows the director of a recreational program desiring additional facilities to support these requests with logically formulated documents. This system makes use of individual statistics from the campus in comparison with nationally accepted standards. No longer does the director merely rely on participation figures as justification for the need of additional facilities. The documents and the information contained herein are easy to prepare, easy to present, and convincing.

FOOTNOTES

[1] Sapora, Allan V., and Kenny, H. E. *A Study of the Present Status, Future Needs and Recommended Standards Regarding Space Used for Health, Physical Education, Physical Recreation and Athletics at the University of Illinois, Champaign;* Stipes Publishing Co., Champaign, Illinois, 1960.

[2] *Planning Areas and Facilities for Health, Physical Education and Recreation by Participants in the National Facilities Conference.* The Athletic Institute, Chicago, Illinois, 1966, p. 112.

[3] *Planning Areas and Facilities for Health, Physical Education and Recreation by Participants in the National Facilities Conference.* The Athletic Institute, Chicago, Illinois, 1966.

REFERENCES

[1] Athletic Institute, Inc. *Planning Facilities for Health, Physical Education and Recreation,* Chicago: The Athletic Institute, 1956.

[2] Athletic Institute, Inc. *Planning Areas and Facilities for Health, Physical Education, and Recreation,* Chicago: The Athletic Institute, 1966.

[3] Beeman, Harris F., *Intramural Sports,* Dubuque, Iowa: Wm. C. Brown Co., Inc., 1954.

[4] Bronzan, Robert T. "Game Plans for Getting the Facilities You Need," *National Intramural Association, 23rd Annual Conference Proceedings,* Champaign, Illinois, April, 1972.

[5] Gabrielson, M. A., and Miles, C. M. *Sports and Recreational Facilities for School and Community,* New York: Prentice Hall, Inc., 1958.

[6] Sapora, A. V. and Kenney, H. E. University of Illinois, College of Physical Education, Buildings and Fields Committee, *A Study of the Present Status, Future Needs, and Recommended Standards Regarding Space Used for Health, Physical Education, Physical Recreation, and Athletics,* Urbana, Illinois: Stipes Publishing Co., 1960.

[7] Scott, H. A. and Westkaemper, R. B. *From Program Facilities in Physical Education,* New York: Harper and Brothers, 1958.

THE USE AND RESERVATION OF PLAYING COURTS

Jack Eckdahl, University of Florida

At the University of Florida, we are fortunate to have twenty outdoor three-wall handball courts, as well as 12 four-wall courts. Sixteen of the three-wall courts are lighted. Racquetball has all but taken over use of the courts. Increased court use by women has also caused scheduling problems. At Gainesville, we have weather that is conducive all year for outdoor play. In spite of the good weather and many courts, we have the same scheduling problems as those situations with less courts, or with indoor courts.

Many people go out to play for recreation and exercise. When courts are not available, or hassles errupt over use of courts to the point that the frustrations outweigh the benefits, people will cut down on court use and perhaps change their leisure patterns completely. We have taken some steps to eliminate this situation and keep problems at a minimum.

Until three years ago, our courts were used on a first-come, first-serve basis. Even before this, when the courts were not crowded by the game of racquetball and the additional bodies, we had problems at peak hours when tennis players wanted to practice tennis strokes on our three-wall handball courts. Additional problems existed because of free play conflicting with scheduled classes and scheduled intramural tournaments interfering with free play. Some of these conflicts were eliminated by changing our class schedule to end at 3:00 pm instead of 4:00 pm, by posting schedules of intramural tournaments ahead of time, and by leaving some courts available for free play when not needed by classes or tournaments. It has also helped to post class schedules at all courts.

The biggest crunch on the use of handball courts came with the rapid growth of racquetball. Demands for court space increased many times. Prior to the development of racquetball here, women made little demand on court time. Very few women played handball, now they flood the courts. You can find men's games and women's games and mixed doubles in racquetball as well as in handball. Long waiting lines grow as a result. Potential players use all kinds of tricks to hold courts or to get ahead of others.

To keep individuals or groups from monopolizing the courts, we adopted a reservation and challenge system to attempt to accommodate all needs. This was instituted on 16 of our three-wall courts which are arranged in the following way and are in the same area. The eight courts on the south side were designated "challenge courts." They were for individuals who decided on spur of the moment to play, who did not have a chance to reserve a court, or who had no partner and wished to find one at the court.

The eight courts on the north side were designated for those who wanted a reservation. Since more people wished to play racquetball than handball

and because of the court layout, the east five courts were designated for racquetball and the west three for handball. If not used for the designated
sport, they were open for other use. Priority rules and reservation procedures
were posted on bulletin boards at the courts, and put on the outside of the
walls for reference. Painted signs designating court priority were put on top
of the walls for clear visibility and ready reference. We feel this system has
worked adequately. Reservations are made by calling the equipment room.
Arguments and complaints are few and there is a more systematic way of
obtaining a court. (Appendix A)

For tennis court control, we use a reservation system which does not require the hiring of personnel. This is necessary because we have courts at
various locations around campus. It would not be economically feasible to
employ enough people to control them. A large chalkboard placed at the
entrance with court diagram and numbers and with corresponding writing
space for names and times is used for reservation purposes. Players write
their names and the times started on the bulletin board at the court entrance. Players are then required to give up their court after a designated
period of time.

In setting up this system, it is important to make the signs as weather-
proof and vandal-proof as possible. Exterior plywood, painted with green or
black paint that can be used as a chalkboard seems to work well. The size of
the board is dependent on the number of courts to be served.

On weekdays, court reservations can be made from 7:30 am until 10:30
am by calling a designated number in the equipment room. All courts are
usually signed-up by 8:00 am. This can be done in person at the checkout
room. The phone line is so busy that it is best to do it in person. Student identification cards and current fee cards must be shown to pick up reservation
slips. These must be picked up in person even if the reservation was made by
phone. These can, however, be picked up at any open hour prior to playing.
Reservation slips must be taken to the courts and shown upon request.

Saturday and Sunday reservations have to be made on Fridays by 10:30
am, using the same system used for daily reservations. The slip must be picked up before 5:00 pm on Friday. A different color slip is used every day with
the date stamped on it to ensure that there is no misuse of old slips.

Time rotation of courts as used by Purdue University for their basketball
courts could also be used with automatic timers or hired personnel. This
might prove rather expensive in cases of disrupted courts, however.

Other adaptations of these systems to your particular situations could be
used for the advantage of the players. It is also suggested that if you put in a
system, advance notices should be posted and publicity put out that you are
adapting a particular system. Information about when it will become effective also should be disseminated.

APPENDIX A

MURPHREE AREA THREE-(3) WALL HANDBALL COURTS

CHALLENGE COURTS
Effective - Monday, 2-3-75

COURTS   Number 1-5. . . . . Racquetball
COURTS   Number 6-8. . . . . Handball

RULES FOR CHALLENGE

These rules apply when no courts are open. Classes have priority before 3:00 pm and intramural tournaments have first priority after 3:00 pm—Schedules will be posted.

1. Singles or cut-throat (round robin—3 players)
   Only one game of 21 points allowed—the two or three players involved must give up the court when the first player gets 21 points.
2. If all courts are taken, any two players may challenge the winners of any court on the challenge side. (South) A game consists of 21 points.
3. If a team wins twice in a row, they must relinquish the court for the next game. They may have automatic challenge of winners on that court if they want it.
4. Players coming from the reserved courts have to wait at least one game before they can challenge.

RESERVATION OF COURTS

COURTS # 9-13 are reserved for RACQUETBALL, and COURTS # 14-16 for HANDBALL.

Reservations can be made in the Intramural Check-Out Room located on the ground level—northeast corner of the Florida Gym from 7:30 am to 10:30 pm on the day desired. Saturday and Sunday, reservations can be made on Fridays from 7:30 am to 12:00 noon. All slips must be picked up in person prior to playing.

Either of the two sports may use any of the courts if not in use; however, they must yield immediately to the designated sport when needed. Challenge rules will apply when there is no reservation slip out on a court. All twelve of the four wall courts can be reserved the same way for handball or racquetball. Classes will have priority on the four wall courts only until 11:30 am.

OPENING A MAJOR URBAN MULTI-PURPOSE FACILITY

By Jeff Fries, University of Wisconsin-Milwaukee

Operating a large multi-purpose university facility today is indeed a complex and difficult task. I was recruited to the University of Wisconsin-Milwaukee in September of 1976 to begin to prepare for the opening of our new 100,000 square foot Physical Education/Recreation Building in September of 1977. The University of Wisconsin-Milwaukee is one of the largest urban universities in the country with almost 26,000 students and a faculty and staff of more than 3,000. The University is situated within a metropolitan area of one-million people. When I arrived in Milwaukee in September of 1976, the building was under construction but few things had been accomplished with regard to staffing, policies and procedures, operational budgets, supplies, etc. I began to gather as much information as possibly about the UW-Milwaukee campus and system. As we all know, each university is unique in itself, and to be able to function within the system one must know how to go about accomplishing various tasks.

One of the first things that I tried to do was talk to various people across the country wtih regard to their facilities and the problems they had with their openings. Many of the Recreational Directors and Facility Coordinators were very cooperative and extremely willing to help. I soon realized from all of them that the first year to two years would be extremely difficult and challenging. We also surveyed many universities and colleges as to the problems they had and were still having with their facilities.

One of the first things that I began to work on was the development of our policies and procedures for the operation of the new facility. These were quite complex and unique, as I am sure they are on all of the various campuses. Simultaneously as I began work on developing the policies and procedures, I began looking at calendar considerations; what I wanted to accomplish each month until we were open.

It is very important to have a logical sequence of projects to be completed and a check list when opening a large facility or you can become overwhelmed. I want to make it very clear that you cannot spend enough time in planning, projecting future problems, anticipating needs, etc., for a large multipurpose facility. Presently, we have almost 50,000 people per month utilizing our facility, and if we had not been extremely well organized the opening would have been very chaotic.

One of the more important problems that we began to look at very closely was staffing. Without good people an organization just does not run. So we began to look at the number of full-time people whom we would employ, and how many of these would be professional staff, clerical, and classified staff. We knew that we also would need many part-time employees. How many would be needed each day and projected costs were important considerations.

Once we began work on developing policies, procedures, and calendar, the next important consideration was the budget. How many positions would be available? What would be the budget that the university grants us for instruction? How much income revenue should we anticipate? Who pays for utilities? How is each system different with regard to budget category breakdown?

It is very difficult to summarize in a brief article all of the problems of operating a major facility. This brief outline plus our check lists and various surveys, I think, will be helpful.

Appendix A

Calendar Considerations

Jan. 1977
1. Have 1976-77 Budget squared around
2. Begin to advertise for graduate assistants
3. What is the legality for revenues production (who, what, from where)
4. Policy for families of faculty, staff, alumni, etc.
5. Begin screening secretarial help

Feb. 1977
1. Draw up contracts for various agencies
2. Finalize charges to Athletics, etc. . . .
3. Complete visitations to similar facilities
4. Finalize starting date for Administrative Secretary
5. Finalize starting date for Equipment Manager
6. Meet with Athletic Department on problems, etc.
7. Key problems and policies

March 1977
1. Begin facility articles in student newspapers on opening
2. Finalize starting date for Equipment Manager
3. Finalize hiring and starting dates for Maintenance Employees
4. Check on contract forms for events, etc....
5. Order towels
6. Check on all movable equipment

April 1977
1. Finalize all policies and procedures
2. Advertise for student help and part-time supervisors
3. Go over locker issuance procedures

May 1977
1. Check out lighting and heating
2. Inventory and set-up equipment in all areas
3. Check on vending machines service
4. Check on signs and additional signs necessary
5. Check on guarantee slips of equipment
6. Room-for-room (check) on equipment and layout
7. Check out sound system
8. Check on obstruction and safety hazards
9. Check on storage procedures
10. Make sure all equipment has been ordered (racquets, balls, etc.)
11. Contract with Payroll in regards to student work

June 1977
1. Finalize all procedures for security
2. Finalize all procedures for towels, locks, etc.
3. Order cards — I.D.'s (anything needed)

4. Work out locker problems for teams, daily use, community groups, physical education, athletics, etc....
5. Get all vending machines, etc, taken care of
6. Check to make sure we have all necessary forms in
7. Check on special provisions for handicapped and ageing
8. Order uniforms for facility staff
9. Make sure all necessary supplies are ordered for staff (custodial, office, etc.)

July 1, 1977
1. Finalize handling of all revenue sources (daily monies, etc.)
2. Finalize student workers policies (uniforms) payroll, etc.
3. Do we have locker arrangements made (daily use) visiting teams, special groups, etc.
4. Print guest passes and family I.D. cards
5. Finalize vending machines (security and service)
6. Finalize procedures for students and staff
7. Order keys for faculty members
8. Meeting for student workers
9. Check on cash register and safe

Aug. 1, 1977
1. Finalize schedule for the fall semester
2. Finalize with athletic depts.—schedule of events
3. Check out spectator accommodations and ground control
4. Check out concession procedures
5. Make sure handouts for students and staff are completed
6. Make up an "Information Sheet"—(New P.E.R.H.E. Building)
7. Meet with entire staff and go over final plans

Sept. 1, 1977
1. Make sure everything is set to go
2. Double check to make sure everyone is aware of what he/she is supposed to do
3. Enjoy the Labor Day holiday
4. The beginning of September I (1977-78) GOOD LUCK!!

Appendix B
Miscellaneous Problems

Phones

1. Who has access on weekends or evenings?
2. Do they have long distance capabilities?
3. Are phone locks needed?
4. Do you have a map for your weekend/evening employees showing the location for all phones, fire extinguishers, fire alarms, emergency doors, first aid equipment, and pool emergency equipment?
7. Is there an emergency phone in the pool area?
8. What about a phone at wheelchair height?
9. Do you have intercom capabilities from each major area?

Keys

1. Do you have key control cards?
2. Who'll make new keys for you?
3. What rationale will you use to justify key distribution, who gets masters, and how will you keep track of who has what keys?
4. How is the building being keyed? By zone? By floor? By activity area? By *one* master?

Opening & Closing

1. Who opens each morning? Do you just open the doors or do they also turn on the lights?
2. Where are the switches located? Are they key switches?

3. Who and how do they get your schedule?
4. Will the "last man out" system be used?

Main Office Operation

1. A "drop" safe is needed as is a cash register (multi-buttoned).
2. What is the cash register's operating procedure? Should you buy a multi-tray cash register? Will you need a cash register in the equipment room? (For collection of towel/locker fee/deposits.)
3. How does one "check-out" and/or change cashiers?
4. Who'll teach all your weekend/evening people the cash register operation?
5. The critical question is the location of the "Main Office." It must be near the turnstile for guest and ID purchase control. It must be secure and yet visible.
6. Where will the safe be located and who gets the combination?
7. How will ticket money be controlled?

Income Control

1. Will it be a cash only operation? Will you accept credit cards? Checks? If checks are accepted, what verification system does the University require?
2. Will all your money handlers have to be bonded?
3. When should the cash register be closed of money and the money deposited in the safe?
4. Do you have an alarm system, similar to a banks, to notify the authorities that a robbery is in process?
5. Will a billing system be used wherein an individual signs up now and pays later? What about faculty/staff paying through payroll deduction?
6. How do you close out on weekend nights? Who verifies the deposit and how? How do they "start up" the next morning with necessary money, cards, passes, etc.?
7. Where do you keep the weekend receipts? How?
8. Where is the money counted and deposited?
9. Do you clear the cash register with each new cashier?
10. Are refunds given? By who's authority?
11. Who'll set up your "books" to control/verify/audit your daily income by area? What about expenditure control? Your revolving account control?
12. What University regulations concerning cash handling must you be aware of? Have you asked the University Comptroller for help?

ID Cards-Sales

1. Who gets ID cards? Different colors for different groups?
2. Must certain University regulations be printed on them? What information do you need on the application card? Why?
3. What procedure will you establish for the sale of the ID cards? Can one buy a card via the mails?
4. How do you revalidate them from semester to semester?
5. Does the alumni sign up the same way as faculty/staff?
6. Undergraduate students get to use the center on the strength of their ID—but what about: grad students? part-time students? co-op students? continuing education students? professional students?

spouses/dependents of students? How old must a dependent be in order to use the facility without supervision?

7. Is the family rate higher if there are children? What defines dependent? family member? What about the married dependent?

8. Do students who drop out of school turn in their ID? How will you keep them out? What actions can you take against individuals who refuse to show their ID? What about the individual who forgets his/her ID card—must they return home or can you identify them as such?

9. Are there any freebies? Do PE and Athletics folks get free ID cards? What about the VIPs?

10. Are second semester undergraduate students allowed to use the center in the summer free of charge? What about other students?

11. Can one person buy an ID for another? What proof of identity must one show before purchase? Can one "pro-rate" the purchase price? Are ID cards transferable? Is there any charge for lost card replacement?

Lockers/Locker Rooms

1. What kind of locks should be used? Built-in combos, hanging combos, key, or key/combination?

2. Will the daily casual-use lockers be issued with the same locks as the permanent lockers? Will the small Athletics/VIP locker room have the same type?

3. Where will the master combo list be kept and who'll have access to it?

4. How will the lockers be distributed? What forms will have to be filled out?

5. What percent of lockers will go to classes? To Athletics? To recreational users on a permanent basis? To casual users?

6. Will non-UWM lockers be cut off? How and by whom?

7. How often will you clean and deodorize lockers?

8. If demand for permanent lockers exceeds availability, what system will you use to provide equality in future issues?

9. How long can one rent a locker for, where do you rent lockers, and at what price?

10. Is locker rental available for alumni? Spouses? Family members?

Miscellaneous

1. Who purchases equipment from who's budget? Even if the equipment is broken while another program is using it?

2. What are your emergency evacuating procedures for fire, bomb scares and power failures? Do your fire alarms ring locally (inside) or to the campus police/fire?

3. Location of first aid station, report forms? Do you have wheelchairs, stretchers, backboards, resuscitator, first aid and instruction booklets? Will your Supervisors receive CPR training?

4. What is the procedure for billing participants for lost, stolen, broken equipment and how do you determine the charges levied?

5. Lost and found area/procedure? Who's responsible?

6. Absent and substitute policy for part-time employees, job description, pay rate, pay days, time clock procedures?

7. Who has priority and what activity has priority during free play periods?

8. Turnstile procedures for individuals who have lost their ID, forgotten their ID, want to buy an ID, or are non-participating guests?
9. Guest policy, procedure, fee? Number allowed per visit? Number of visits per year? Less fee for children than adults? Who can sponsor guests? How do you control the system? What privileges do guests have? What if a guest breaks equipment? Guest pass sale procedure?
10. Can check-room equipment be removed from the building or stay out over night?
11. Proper pool operation re: chlorine control, PH levels, backwashing.
12. Lifeguard testing and manuals?
13. Location of water controls, emergency warning lights?
14. Who makes the decision to close the pool due to chemical imbalance, etc? Who secures the pool after each period, each night?

OPERATING A NEW URBAN MULTI-UNIT RECREATIONAL FACILITY

By Erick L. Stein, University of Wisconsin-Milwaukee

The operating of a new six million dollar multi-purpose recreational facility for a student population of 25,000 is a challenging and exciting opportunity. The facility opened September 7, 1978, and it is the purpose of this paper to consider and identify important ideas and techniques that we utilized at the University of Wisconsin-Milwaukee (UWM) to create a successful operation for our entire campus and surrounding community.

The facility was designed as a multi-purpose complex with our priority usage determined in the following chronological order:

1. Instruction
2. Campus Recreation
3. Athletics and Intramurals
4. Student Clubs officially recognized by the University
5. Alumni and Community Programs associated with the University
6. Community Groups

Priority usage order was established as a result of the manner in which the building was funded. Since the facility was funded through State fees allocated for educational development, instruction was the first priority, and the Physical Education Department received organizational control of the facility.

The understanding of your own particular administrative structure involving physical education, athletics and intramurals is instrumental in developing a successful operation. Our administrative structure at UWM involves a dichotomy between physical education and athletics. The Physical Education Department controls the usage of all the gymnasiums on campus (New Physical Education/Recreation Building, Baker Fieldhouse, Engleman Gym) and is funded through State fees. The Athletic Department controls all varsity sports, intramurals and sports clubs, and is funded through Student Senate allocations. Since these departments are separated and athletics is deisgned as non-instructional, the Athletic Department pays a rental fee to the Physical Education Department through a long term contract designated at the beginning of the year.

From the preceeding discussion, one can see that we have a complex administrative structure at UWM. This administrative structure has created the need for open communicatin and a commonality of purpose in providing quality physical activity programs for our entire campus and surrounding community. In the future, we hope that the Physical Education and Athletic Departments may be united, and thereby, remove some of the obvious barriers that the current administrative structure has created.

The staff relationships and "roll identification" are important considerations for successful building operations. The professionals, classified secretaries, students, custodial and maintenance workers all play an important part in operating our facility. Our professionals include our Facility Coordinator, Administrative Affairs Specialist, Program Specialist, Aquatics Specialist and Communication Specialist, and through a coordinated effort, we accomplish those designated tasks in our specific job descriptions. We have two full-time Secretaries whom the professionals utilize in accomplishing their responsibilities. Approximately forty-five student workers are coordinated through the Program Specialist in positions as I.D. Checkers, Arena and Weight Room Supervisors, Program Center Cashiers, Lifeguards, Equipment Room Workers and Secretaries. The eight Custodial and Maintenance Workers are coordinated through the Administrative Specialist and they are scheduled to work third shift so that the building is occupied at all times.

We emphasize the importance of each individual employee as the actions of everyone reflect the total building operation success. Through specific job descriptions, staff meetings, continual evaluations and social gatherings involving all our workers, we have developed a successful operation. It is definitely important that the staff relationships are solidly developed, and the importance of every individual is recognized as an integral part of the total operation.

The accumulation of statistial data involving budgetary matters, participation in specific areas as well as total building entry is extremely important. Since the budget for the first year was naturally determined prior to the grand opening, it is important that accurate records are kept for yearly accounting purposes as well as projections for future operational needs. Participation records kept by the student workers in the arena, natatorium, racquetball courts, and weight room are valuable in determining maximum and minimum usage times so that building programs may be more accurately developed. The building entry figure is important in determining total usage that your facility receives. Also, a building entrance survey determining student, faculty, alumni, guest, spouse, children under 16, children over 16, affiliate, sport club and other individuals percentage of entrance may serve as an instrumental figure in determining the population with which you are working.

We ran a building entrance survey at UWM during our first semester of operation because of a desire to know the actual percentage that various groups were utilizing the facility as well as dealing with student complaints that faculty and alumni were receiving a priority. We randomly selected a week during the first semester, and our survey produced the following percentages of usage and justified our program policies to the students.

Building Usage Auditing to Entrance Tabulations

Student -	79.4%	Children Under 16 -	0.8%
Faculty -	7.9%	Affiliate	- 0.25%
Alumni -	5.0%	Children Over 16	- 0.2%
Spouse -	3.0%	Sports Clubs	- 0.18%
Guest -	2.7%	Other	- 0.5%

The policies that are developed prior to the opening of the building will be continually evaluated by your building participants. Through the usage of sound statistical data, one may be better prepared for policy revisions. It is important that everyone who utilizes the facility has an opportunity to provide suggestions for the improvement of operations through our Bright Idea Board as our professional staff attempts to answer and deal with all suggestions that we receive. Through our commitment to "listen to the people," we have received numerous ideas that have improved the physical structure of certain areas, alerted us to dangerous situations as well as supplied us with thoughts concerning our operating policies.

The changing of any building policy must be communicated throughout the building staff so that everyone remains consistent in relating to the public. Since our facility involves a large population interested in a variety of activities, all policy revisions, special events, as well as holiday schedules must be communicated to everyone. Through a solid communication system, difficulties may be avoided and a program consistency may be developed.

The operating of a new urban multi-purpose recreational facility opens the door to unlimited program development. The Physical Education Department has developed new programs in the facility this year including the Open House, Handicapped in Sport, Family Swim, Adult Fitness, Fitness for Life, as well as a Community Night Recreation Program that opens the entire facility to anyone in Milwaukee for a nominal fee. Through our new programs, we have added another dimension to our overall operation.

The operating of a new urban multi-purpose recreational facility is a challenging and exciting position. Through the awareness of the administrative structure, staff relationships, accumulation of statistical data, policy revisions through continual building operation evaluations and suggestions, consistent communications as well as new program development, one may be on the road to developing a successful building operation. The challenge is ahead of us at the Universtiy of Wisconsin-Milwaukee, and we look forward to the potential affect of our new facility on the leisure time development of the entire campus and surrounding community.

CHAPTER IV

Public Relations and Publicity

REACHING OUT

by Tony Clements, Debra A. Kimme, Dave Garabedian, Dennis Gearou,
University of Illinois, Champaign-Urbana

Philosophy and Overview of Project

In an effort to reach out and increase personal relations among the Division of Campus Recreation (DCR) and the students and staff members that we serve, the DCR recently, throughout joint sponsorship with the Housing Office, developed another new program. This program, known as the Housing Recreation Project, established four graduate positions known as Recreation Graduate Assistants (RGA) in the residence halls and one graduate position, known as Orchard Apartments Recreational Programmer in the married student housing complex. This project has been in effect since last fall.

In the residence hall portion of this project, an RGA lives right with the people he/she serves, and is responsible not only for the coordinating of resident hall athletic chairpersons, and the production of recreational opportunities within his unit (i.e. ski trips, cookouts, football tournaments), but a large percentage of his/her time is spent in informing residents of upcoming deadlines and special events sponsored by the DCR.

The future of this position is seen as one which can aid the Division in the recruitment of officials and student workers; a position that can coordinate all athletic, recreation, or social chairpersons into a working unit for the development of recreational opportunities; and a position that is a personal face to face extension of the Division.

The residence halls were used to develop this position because of many reasons. For one, the rapport between the two staffs was of such a nature that it was assured that the proposal would be given adequate consideration. Secondly, the residence halls house about 9,000 students and it was determined that a direct contact with these students was to the Division's benefit. The residence halls, besides being the largest organized collection of people, also house a large percentage of freshmen and sophomores and thus allow contact with those people at the early stages of their University stay. This would then, in effect, give some connection with fraternities, sororities, and apartment complexes, because the members of these organizations would have in many cases been in contact with DCR when they lived in the residence halls.

The other part of the project is with the married student housing complex. This project allows a married graduate student assistant an opportunity to develop recreational opportunities for married students and their families.

Activities run through this married student's housing program include Halloween and Christmas movies, Saturday afternoon tobogganning, craft day, cartoon night, field trips, and a day camp. This program, which has met with a large degree of success, not only allows for the distribution of information, but also allows the programming of recreational opportunities in an area that has been neglected.

The recreation graduate assistants, coupled with the family housing position, gives a direct means of contact to over 10,000 people—ten thousand individuals who now receive, right at their door step, sport entry flyers, deadline information, and news of upcoming special events!

Developing and Coordinating the Project

After Housing and Campus Recreation settled all negotiations for this project, plans were immediately made for putting the project into operation. This initially entailed assigning one Campus Recreation staff member and one Housing staff member the task of jointly developing, coordinating, and supervising the project. It was agreed that these two staff members would only work with the residence hall portion of the project, not the married student housing portion. These two people pooled their efforts and resources and developed a comprehensive plan to organize this project. The plan consisted of developing an overall job description, a recruitment-selection process, a communications network, a training workshop, and the supervisory duties.

An overall description of the Recreation Graduate Assistant (RGA) position defined the purpose of the position, the responsibilities, the candidate's qualifications, and the remunerations. The purpose was to be more responsive to the recreational needs of residence hall students by establishing a comprehensive recreation program. The qualifications stipulated that the candidate must be pursuing a masters or doctorate degree in leisure studies, or a related field, must have a grade point average of 3.75 or above (on a 5.0 scale), and should have lived in a residence hall. The remunerations consisted of a single room, board, tuition and fees, and a stipend of $105 per month.

Recruiting and selecting individuals for these positions was very important to the project's success and continuation. It was imperative to select individuals who were capable of promoting and organizing a comprehensive recreation program for residence hall students.

Both Housing and Campus Recreation wanted to select individuals who had past experience living in a residence hall, who had past experience in intramural and recreation programming, and who were planning to pursue a higher education in the recreation field. This new position was advertised through the NIRSA Newsletter, AAPHER Journal, and school mailings.

During the summer, both divisions corresponded with our new R.G.A.'s. The purpose of the correspondence was to answer questions, to clear up uncertainties, and to inform them about the University, their position, their responsibilities, and their renumerations. To give them this pertinent information, printed materials were mailed to them and telephone conversations were conducted with them.

Also, over the summer, a workshop was designed with both Campus Recreation and Housing contributing to its content and organization. The workshop was held one week prior to new student week, the official opening of campus, and it lasted the entire week.

The purpose of the workshop was to orient the R.G.A.'s to the University and its policies, to the residence hall operations, to Campus Recreation and its programs, and to their new job. To properly train them in these areas, the workshop was divided into two portions. One portion dealt with University and residence hall information and was conducted by Housing while the other dealt with campus recreation and job responsibilities and was conducted by Campus Recreation. Both portions of the workshop were significant and were important to their total training.

Campus Recreation's portion was organized to provide the R.G.A.'s a thorough understanding of Campus Recreation, of their role with Housing and Campus Recreation, and of their job responsibilities. Knowledge of these three areas was vital to the RGA's job awareness and to their future performance. To effectively acquaint the RGA's in these subjects, two sessions were organized. One session consisted of a tour of all Campus Recreation's facilities and playing areas. The tour was accompanied by a description of the programs and activities held in the facilities and on the playing areas. This acquainted the recreation graduate assistants with the location of all activity areas and later helped them direct students to those ares. The second session concentrated on introducing the RGA's to Campus Recreation and its staff. Campus Recreation's structure, philosophies, and policies were discussed. Next, each staff member discussed his/her program responsibilities and program content. Finally, an in depth discussion on project purpose, project goals, responsibilities, and activity organizations was held. As a culmination of these sessions, each person practically applied their training experience by working for Campus Recreation during new student week. The entire workshop helped establish a foundation on which the RGA's could build and create recreation programs for residence hall students.

In developing the supervisory roles, the RGA's needed input from both Housing and Campus Recreation. A supervisor from both divisions was necessary. Both agencies agreed that the Housing representative would supervise and coordinate the resident advisor duties and that the Campus Recreation representative would supervise and coordinate the recreation duties. This arrangement allowed for equal input and for appropriate supervising expertise.

A problem which confronted Campus Recreation and not Housing was supervising these students while they lived and worked in their assigned residence hall. Definite physical barriers existed for Campus Recreation. And, these barriers tended to breakdown communications and thus, effectiveness. These barriers did not affect the Housing supervisor since he/she also lived and worked in the same residence hall. To compensate for the barrier, a communications system was established. This included bi-weekly meetings, frequent mailings and phone calls, and an office mailbox. The meetings, Campus Recreation programs were discussed, activities were planned for their residence hall, and problems solved. The mailings and phone calls helped to bridge the gap between meetings. Each person had an office mailbox which they checked often. Having an office mailbox encouraged them to come to the main building and interact with the staff and be more invovled with Campus Recreation happenings. These three methods of communications did help to tear down the barrier; however, they are not fool proof. Occasionally misinformation and misunderstandings occur.

Also, because of the physical barrier, it is impossible for the Campus Recreation supervisor to supervise the RGA's in their halls. As a result, the RGA's are pretty much on their own. That's why it is imperative to select highly competent and reliable people that have initiative and diligence to work on their own. Also, a good workshop is necessary so that they are

133

aware of their duties and are properly prepared.

So that Campus Recreation can "keep-tabs" on the RGA's, a program workbook is kept on each person. In this workbook, records are kept of all program ideas, program materials, program dates, and program places. This assists Campus Recreation in knowing exactly what is being planned, what activities are in progress, and which ones are completed. Also, this enables the Campus Recreation supervisor to check each person's work by attending one of his/her events unannounced.

This project is beneficial to Campus Recreation mainly because of the information about activities and policies that the RGA's transmit. Also, they act as a direct link between the Division and the students which has enhanced effectiveness and service.

Responsibilities of the Recreation Graduate Assistant

Having a graduate assistant actually living in an undergraduate residence hall and working with student-elect floor representatives not only has the advantage of providing Campus Recreation with a more personal and direct link to dorm residents, but also gives those residents some input in deciding what programs will be offered to them. The position was created to improve communication between the Division of Campus Recreation and the students in the undergraduate halls with the ultimate goal of increasing both the quality and level of participation by on-campus residents.

The Recreation Graduate Assistant (RGA) position is unique in that it is a joint effort between the Division of Campus Recreation and the Housing Division. In addition to responsibilities as an RGA, he/she serves as a Resident Advisor (or R.A.) on one of the undergraduate floors in the resident hall complex. This is a live-in, full time job which includes day-to-day administrative duties, counseling of students, and enforcing University Housing policies and regulations.

It provides the major portion of the student's remuneration: room and board, pius tuition and fees. The Recreation Graduate Assistant for the entire complex, which includes over 1500 undergraduate men and women in three separate buildings, has main responsibilities in four areas: (1) *programming* special recreation activities within the complex; (2) *supervising* the work of the 21 student-elected Recreation Representatives (one for each floor in the complex); (3) acting as a *resource person* for the Recreation Representatives and other students in the complex concerning the various events, activities, and services offered by Campus Recreation; and (4) providing *publicity* about them.

Meetings with the floor Recreation Representatives encourage input in the form of ideas for recreation programming in the complex with the emphasis on what the residents want to do. In-complex tag football, basketball, volleyball, and softball tournaments are a natural, but there has also been interest in setting up some bicycle trips to nearby state parks for picnics, overnight bicycle trips, canoe trips and camping trips. The possibilities are endless. There has been talk of organizing a bus or carpool trip to a major league baseball game this semester.

All of this programming costs money, of course, and although it remains to be seen whether Housing Division will be willing to give the Recreation Representatives control over even a small portion of the students' floor social fees for recreation programming, so far most floors have been *willing* to pay entry fees to cover the cost of awards, officials, and equipment out of their social fees. Association with Campus Recreation makes it easy to arrange for the reservation of fields and facilities, to obtain lists of available officials and supervisory help, and even to arrange for publicity. Campus Recreation will run off posters and flyers and even help with the design work.

Since most of the floor Recreation Representatives also serve as their floors' intramural chairmen (in charge of signing up teams and encouraging interested individuals to participate), the R.G.A. maintains a complete file of current schedules, rules and information in case any questions should come up. This is just an attempt to provide the Recreation Representatives with an alternative and more personal source for this kind of routine information, especially on evenings and weekends when the Intramural Office is closed. Campus Recreation has a mailbox in their office for each of the RGAs.

Campus Recreation also includes both the RGA and the floor Recreation Representatives on their mailing list of information on upcoming events and activities. Most of these are in the form of flyers and posters which the Recreation Representatives are asked to post on their floor bulletin boards. They are encouraged to enter as many teams as possible without forfeiting. Getting the word out to the residents with posters and flyers makes their jobs a little bit easier and insures that everyone in the residence halls at least has the *chance* to find out what's going on without having to *ask* someone first.

Working with the Resident Director of the complex enables the R.G.A. to clear the purchase of some recreation equipment; softballs, footballs, volleyballs, bats and table tennis equipment which can be checked out by students with an I.D. at the complex office.

Although the bulk of the work as an RGA comes in the form of programming, supervision of the floor intramural chairmen, and distribution of information on various sports and events, the R.G.A. spend a great deal of time publicizing some of the lesser known activities and services that Campus Recreation provides. For instance, few students are familiar with the procedures for reserving facilities on campus, and some may not be aware of the rules and regulations concerning their use. Campus Recreation also runs a camping equipment rental service and a self-directed jogging, bicycling, swimming, and wheelchair-pushing program on an informal basis. Much of this lesser-known publicity also comes in the way of posters and flyers, but connection with Housing gives access to students' mailboxes which enables contact with students on a more direct basis.

In addition to work in the residence halls, the RGA also has the opportunity to work directly with Campus Recreation on many of their special events such as All-Nighters and Quad Days. This helps to give the R.G.A. an inside perspective on what is involved in some of their large scale programming and some of the services that they can make available.

Probably the biggest problem faced by an RGA is motivating the floor Recreation Representatives, who are elected by their peers, to do their jobs well and to provide the input needed to run innovative programming and to provide some help in running the actual programs. There is a tendency for them to think only in terms of intramurals, sometimes at the expense of the other programs and activities Campus Recreation offers.

This RGA position represents a big effort on the part of both Housing and Campus Recreation to cooperate for their mutual benefit. Whether or not the presence of the R.G.A. in the residence halls has made a significant difference in the quality or quantity of participation by residents this year is hard to say. The position is a giant step in the right direction in terms of getting both Housing and Campus Recreation to work *together* to increase on-campus residents' awareness of the recreation opportunities available.

Married Student Housing Program

The Orchard Apartments position is very different form that of the Recreation Coordinators. Responsibilities are more in the area of programming and the actual conducting of programs. The major emphasis of the program is informal recreation rather than intramural sports.

Orchard Apartments is the University operated married student housing. It is located about 1½ miles off campus, and contains 780 living units. Of these 780 units, 516 are two bedroom apartments, and the other 264 are one bedroom apartments.

The total population of approximately 2100 residents comprises all age groups and many different nationalities. The residents also represent most levels of education, from undergraduate students to doctoral candidates, and of all families residing in Orchard Apartments about 70% are students on the graduate level.

Orchard Apartments is administered by the Housing Division. All major administrative decisions are made by the Director of the Housing Division. The Assistant Director of the Housing Division, the Orchard Apartments

Manager, and the Family Housing Council comprise the other administrative units.

The Recreation Coordinator's contacts are almost exclusively with the Family Housing Council. The Council is made up of interested residents of Orchard Apartments. They are given, each semester, funds from Housing to run various programs. They are not told how to spend this money and can use it as they see fit. In the past they have done such things as sponsoring the building of a community center and a children's playground. In addition to this, they sponsor activities such as nursery schools, English classes and a ladies exercise program. The Council also has a direct line to the Director of Housing and if any major problems occur in the complex they are free to contact him.

The Division of Campus Recreation, in the past, has had a very limited program in the Orchard Apartments complex. The main programming was the day camp, which is conducted every summer. In addition to this, the Informal Recreation Office sponsored some special events such as movies, puppet shows, and, in the winter, tobogganing.

From these limited offerings it was realized that there was virtually no recreational programming for this small university community. The turnouts at the Division of Campus Recreation sponsored activities indicated there was a definite interest, and need for a more extensive recreation program for the residents of Orchard Apartments. This realization was the deciding factor to develop the Recreation Programmer's position.

The Division of Campus Recreation felt that in order to get the "feel" of what types of recreation programming the residents want, it would be essential to have someone live in the Orchard Apartments complex. At this point Housing was approached with the idea and consented to provide an apartment for the Recreation Programmer.

The specific job title is the Orchard Apartments Recreational Programmer and Director, and the responsibilities are to develop, and administer, recreational programs for the families of Orchard Apartments. Five objectives were developed in order to provide a complete recreational program for the residents. These are:

1. To provide recreational programming in the following areas: family activities; adult activities; and children's activities.
2. To meet, and work in cooperation with, the various Orchard Apartments organizations, in order to prevent duplication of programming.
3. To promote unity among the Orchard Apartments residents, in order to provide a more enjoyable community in which to live.
4. To efficiently manage the existing facilities through recreational programming.
5. To create an awareness of the recreation program available to Orchard Apartments residents.

In developing a schedule of activities for the Orchard Apartments residents, many different sources were used to determine what types of programs would be successful. The list of activities was developed from questionnaires sent to the residents, suggestions by residents of Orchard Apartments, suggestions by Family Housing Council members and meetings with various Division of Campus Recreation staff members.

The final schedule of activities, for the first semester, included children's craft days, two movies, recreation night, international dinner, international dance night and a children's Christmas party. The success of these programs varied. It ranged from the children's craft days being very successful to no one showing up for the recreation night. Specifically, the children's activities were most successful.

For the second semester a different program was developed that emphasized one time events rather than continuing type programs. These activities included movies, a puppet show, field trips, workshops, a "mini" workshop, and a lecture series. These activities were decided on after discussions with some of the residents of Orchard Apartments at an open house at the community center and discussions with the Family Housing Council. At this point it is difficult to determine the success of these activities. The children's activities are very well attended, while there is less attendance at the adult activities. This semester's participation in the recreation program is up from last semester. The feedback received from the residents indicates that the remaining activities will be very well attended.

The Division of Campus Recreation came up with the following possibilities as to why some programs were not successful. First of all, there is somewhat of a language barrier. A large number of foreign students and their families live in Orchard Apartments. Within these families it is not uncommon for only one member to speak English, and not very good English at that. Also, since it is a new program, many of the signs of the success or the failure of the program will not surface for a couple of years. When programs were offered, many did not realize they were sponsored by the Division of Campus Recreation. It will take a while to get the word around to the residents that there is a recreation program available to them this year. Another possibility is that many of the residents have never seen snow before and have a hard time coping with the cold weather. They seem to lock themselves in their apartments at the first sign of cold weather until spring. The Orchard Apartments community has a majority of their apartments rented to families, as opposed to just couples without children. This causes another problem. In order to participate in some of the activities, the residents must find a babysitter, unless babysitting is provided. Many residents cannot afford to hire a babysitter, or it is too much of a hassle to get one. Finally, and probably most importantly, the residents are students, and they will only be temporary residents of Orchard Apartments. They are interested in finishing school and they put all their efforts towards this goal. Because of this, they feel they do not have time to get involved in the recreation programs we offer.

Feedback coming from most of the Orchard Apartments complex through the Family Housing Council will help determine what types of programs have a greater chance for success. In addition to this, the Family Housing Council is willing to co-sponsor some of the recreation activities. In the future this could be a very important source of funds for the recreation programmer.

Publicity for the activities is done in many different ways. The Housing Division sponsors a weekly newsletter which is received by all residents of Orchard Apartments. This newsletter encourages submission, for publication, any articles or advertisements that are pertinent to the Orchard Apartments community. The only restriction is they will not accept any commercial business advertisements that are associated with money-making activities. Currently the dates, times and descriptions of upcoming events are published. This could develop into a weekly recreation column. The Division of Campus Recreation's publicity office designs, and makes, posters which are displayed in the Orchard Apartments laundromats. Beyond this, dittos are run off with advertisements of different events, and these are handed out at other events. Last, but not least, word of mouth is used extensively. Every Family Housing Council meeting has time put aside for a recreation report, and this information is passed on by the Family Housing Council members to their friends.

What is the future of this program? This is a very big question. Feedback from the residents, and increasing attendance at the activities, seems to indicate that the Orchard Apartments community is very receptive to the programming continuing. With this in mind, there are some considerations which should be attempted in order to make the program even more successful. All undergraduate students in the Department Leisure Studies are required to do field work; and the Recreation Programmer at Orchard Apartments should utilize one of these students. They can be used to supplement the current programming, and to help the programmer with supervision and planning of activities. A recreation committee composed of Orchard Apartments residents should be organized. This committee can help to gain ideas from the different residents, and can help the Programmer to develop the best possible program for the residents. The residents themselves should be used as much as possible. Parents can help to supervise the children's activities, residents with certain expertise in different areas can be used to teach workshops and some of the residents can be asked to drive to different events on field trips. By considering these alternatives and looking at what is done now, the recreation program at Orchard Apartments can be a very successful program.

Some of the aforementioned considerations have been tried. A current field work student has definitely helped to make the program more successful. Also, two of the residents have taught workshops, which seemed to work out quite well. The fact the field work student and resident teachers worked out well indicates that these two considerations, and the others, should be expanded in the future.

Is this program beneficial? This question cannot be answered for three to five years. Only after this amount of time can a realistic evaluation be made of the success or failure of the program. At this point in time the word is finally getting around to all the residents that there is a Recreation Programmer and if they have any questions, ideas or suggestions, they can give the Division of Campus Recreation a call and some action will be taken. From all available feedback it appears that the program is beneficial and should be continued.

A MULTI-MEDIA APPROACH TO EFFECTIVE INTRAMURAL PUBLICITY

R. Wayne Edwards, Rose Mary Adkins, Manuel Martinez,
East Carolina University

In order to effectively sell one's program there must be an effective approach to publicity. How can the student population participate in an intramural program if they aren't aware of the opportunities provided? A comprehensive system of publicity should be structured to inform the students of the intramural and recreational sports programs and services.

The intramural department actually begins its publicity drive prior to the beginning of each school year. Throughout the summer months, the Student Affairs Office conducts a two-day freshman orientation session each week, and a 45-minute time period is devoted to the intramural and recreational sports program. To acquaint the entering students with the program, a synchronized slide-sound presentation is utilized as an opening. Following this, intramural handbooks, calendars and other program-related materials are made available, and a question-answer session completes the orientation presentation. Similar type orientation meetings are held with men and women's residence hall staffs, interfraternity and panhellinic councils and any other campus group upon request. Thus, the initial groundwork for the year's program has been laid prior to the official opening of the academic year.

The intramural handbook serves as one of the most important phases of the publicity drive. This publication outlines the program in detail. It contains rules and regulations governing the men's, women's, co-recreational and sports clubs programs and is updated annually. The handbook, printed by the university's print shop, is relatively expensive but in the long run proves to be a worthwhile expenditure.

The intramural calendar is a colorful one-page item, ideal for dorm walls and bulletin boards. Designed with the intramural logo, the calendar gives all entry dates and deadlines for activities and other pertinent information such as official clinics.

The "Intra-Action" hot line is one of the "hottest" lines of publicity communication and is leased from the telephone company on an annual basis. A three minute tape is used for announcing game schedules, upcoming events and facility operational hours, and is updated on a daily basis. A thirty second tape is used to inform participants of rained out games and postponements. Intra-Action is dialed on an average of 100-125 times daily and definitely saves a tremendous amount of secretarial time.

The intramural office employs a student journalist who's responsibility is to write and distribute the weekly *Intramural UPDATE*. The paper is typed and mimeographed by the secretarial staff and includes various items of interest of all intramural activities. Currently, approximately 700 copies are circulated each week. Another responsibility of the student journalist is to write the weekly intramural column for the campus newspaper. This column is a regular feature and enjoys a tremendous reading audience.

Each year the department hires an intramural graduate assistant whose primary responsibility is public relations in terms of publicity. This position requires a responsible person to coordinate radio and television publicity, as well as campus public relations. All of the local radio stations include announcements concerning upcoming registration dates as part of their free, public service announcements. Excellent cooperation is also received from the university radio station and the local television station provides occasional coverage of major events. Intramural bulletin boards, located within the lobbies of all residence halls, are updated weekly. Intramural drop-in centers are scheduled at strategic campus locations on a frequent basis.

Representatives from each of the participating organizations (fraternities, sororities, residence halls, clubs and independent groups) form the intramural council which meets monthly to discuss policies and procedures and to provide student input on future program directions for the intramural staff. These students carry back to their respective organizations all important program related information. In this way, a much needed avenue of communication is established between the intramural administration and the student participants.

Intramural events are scheduled as half-time features at several home basketball games each winter. The finals in the annual arm-wrestling tournament create a tremendous amount of excitement and enthusiasm. Preliminary championship and regular season games are scheduled prior to both men and women's intercollegiate basketball contests.

Key university administrative personnel are used for awards presentations which are held at the conclusion of each intramural activity. Involving such persons as the Chancellor, Dean of Men, Dean of Women and the Physical Education Department Chairperson has proven to be a meaningful experience. Such involvement has enhanced a better relationship between the students, intramural department and other departments on campus.

The success of any program depends upon the creation of student awareness. Effective publicity is the major key towards this success. The rapid growth of intramural and recreational sports programs is due in part to comprehensive and continual publicity efforts.

"PUBLIC RELATIONS EFFORTS THROUGH SANTA CLAUS TELEPHONE CALLS"

Steve Schlife & Warren Slebos

The University of Iowa has for the past two years conducted a public relations program of telephone calls to children of faculty/staff and students just prior to Christmas. These calls have been made by the most popular person at that time of the year, Mr. Santa Claus of the North Pole. Mr. Claus joins the Recreational Services staff at that time of the year on a temporary appointment.

Prior to the appointment period, parents of children who would like to receive calls must fill out a form with information requested by Mr. Claus and his student helpers. The student helpers at the University of Iowa have been members of the Intramural Official's Association. This is a service project for the Official's Association and the pay they receive goes to support their Association's functions. The information form is distributed to all married students residing in married student housing through "The Villager," a monthly married student newsletter. Faculty and staff receive the form through their weekly newsletter, the "FYI." These two media sources, which print the form free, have been able to produce a response of around three hundred information forms. The preschool gymnastic program conducted by the Division of Recreational Services is another fine source of interested parents.

The information form itself is very important since it enhances the believeability of the calls. The child on the other end of the line is much

142

more ready to believe that he or she is actually talking to Santa if certain information is released at points in the conversation. Information obtained on the form includes:

1. Child's full name, sex & age—This should be printed or typed since handwritten forms can at times be illegible. Sex is important since voice is often not an indication of sex at this age and Santa frequently asks if they have been a good boy or girl.

2. Names of brothers and sisters and their ages—This can be very useful during the conversation. A young brother or sister is frequently drawn into the conversation or a single call can be used to talk to two or more children.

3. Gifts received last year—A key to the authenticity of the call is contained in the fact that only Santa knows what the child received last year. This can mean success when a child is somewhat uncertain as to the identity of the caller.

4. Gifts to be received this year—Since Santa is aware of what the child is to receive this year, it is best to prepare him/her for their gifts. If the child asks for another gift, he or she will actually receive, however, Santa is quick not to promise a particular present and always adds that he knows the child will like whatever Santa brings.

5. Has a visit been made to Santa in person—Santa can be embarassed if he has forgotten an in-person visit and it can be very encouraging to the child if a visit is recalled by Santa.

6. Time call is desired—Most parents like to plan for the call for children's sleep periods and dinner. The calls are attempted within fifteen minutes of the requested time period and on the date requested. Early evening calls are the most popular.

Despite precautions which are taken, problems can occur. These can be minimized if they are anticipated. Some practice is needed for Santa's helpers. They should observe several calls before they try their hand at a call. Non-talkers will occur at times. Some children are so awed by the fact that they are talking to Santa that they freeze. The Santa Claus caller must be prepared to carry on a one-way conversation if necessary. Initial contact with the child can be a problem. If one parent has completed a form but the other parent answers the phone, an explanation may become necessary.

The Santa Claus Telephone Program as a Public Relation's Tool

The Santa Claus program has been one of the most effective public relations tool that we have ever undertaken. Besides being extremely popular for the children called, it is popular among their parents. Many of the parents will call us later to let us know they appreciate our thoughtfulness. The program also improves our image on campus. Many that participate in

143

the program do not take part in any of our other programs and this creates a positive image of our program. Many of the participants are children of University administrators and it certainly doesn't hurt to have them feel that we are providing a comprehensive, complete recreational program.

Radio coverage of the program has done a great deal to enhance our image. The University News Service heard about the program, interviewed us, and took excerpts from the calls. Local radio stations broadcasted the News Service program and also interviewed us. One station is interested in taping a "call of the day" during the holiday season next year. In short, this program has given us a lot of exposure to faculty, staff, students and community.

The Santa Claus program has been a great public relations tool. Perhaps the best selling point is that the program can be done for a very minimal cost. We use members of the Official's Association and give the Association some remuneration for their help. They in turn use the funds for their social functions. The program can be done with volunteers, however, reducing the cost even further. Most calls are only about 3-5 minutes in length and a single caller can contact many children.

The Santa Claus program falls during a generally slow time of the year for other Division of Recreational Services' activities. The program is therefore a minimal inconvenience. We suspect that this would be true for all collegiate recreational programs.

The program has also been beneficial in improving staff morale. Nearly all staff members become involved with the program and the enthusiasm of the children can't help but generate the Christmas spirit.

A METHOD OF SELLING INTRAMURAL-RECREATIONAL SPORTS TO HIGH SCHOOL ADMINISTRATORS

by William A. Thompson, Long Beach City College

Most secondary schools have strong, well-diversified interscholastic athletic programs for the physically skilled students. Conversely, the number of effective intramural-recreational sports programs for the rank and file student majority are limited.

The traditional approach of serving the gifted, often at the expense of the majority, continues. This condition is perpetuated out of a confidence that we can program well for the gifted and lack the knowledge and/or tools to provide for the balance of the student body.

Observing the needs and interests of this largest segment of students, it is apparent that a viable program to serve them can be organized and conducted. The planning effort includes a Joint Meeting of Principals to "sell" the concept. The concept calls for scheduling one man and one woman physical education staff member from 10AM-5PM daily.*

This concept allows for the provision of positive and constructive use of leisure time for those students not actively engaged in interscholastic athletics or working during the late afternoon. (3PM-5PM) The valuable experience of student exposure to a variety of leisure sports, concomitant learning and leadership involvement are definite inducements. Finally, pending success of events evidenced by student participation, specific events are introduced, expanded, modified or dropped through evaluative efforts.

Participation of adequate numbers of students should justify the department's commitment and support of the program to absorb more students to make the two instructors available at no extra cost to the district. It is felt that the inherent public relations value of such a program should enhance school district support.**

SCHEDULE FOR PROGRAM DIRECTORS

	Monday	Tuesday	Wednesday	Thursday	Friday
10	class	class	class	class	class
11	class	class	class	class	class
12					
1	class	class	class	class	class
2	class	class	class	class	class
3-5	coed event	boys' event girls' event	coed event	boys' event girls' event	evaluation and planning meeting

*Respective boys' and girls' departments must be supportive of the concept and willing to absorb an overload to cover the 8AM and 9AM classes of these two instructors.

**The result of parents shifting their attitudes concerning the school district taking an active interest in and making a legitimate attempt to serve "all" students.

CHAPTER V

Research

THE PROFESSIONALIZED ATTITUDE TOWARD PLAY
HELD BY INTRAMURAL PARTICIPANTS

Craig Edmonston, University of Kansas

INTRODUCTION

One of the many questions that should be asked by recreation administrators involved with intramurals is, "Does direct or indirect participation in intramural activities provide the individual with reinvorcement of a set of values which will allow him or her to move easily into the occupational segment of his/her adult role structure?" The empirical research dealing with the socialization potential of direct or indirect participation in physical activities and sport has been predominantly concerned with the relationship between involvement and the development of positive but intangible social values such as loyalty, fair play and sportsmanship.[1]

Little research attention has been directed to the potential of such participation for developing values which would be specific to, and advantageous for, effective involvement in major adult roles.[1] Webb[4] indicated that there was a close linkage between values emphasized in the economic sector and the orientations of male school students toward play from two rather related bases of thought.[4] It was from these two bases of thought, that he developed a theoretical concept of "professionalization of attitude toward play." By "professionalization" he meant the participant's substitution of "skill" for "fairness' as the paramount factor in the play activity, and an increasing importance of victory.

The first basis was to be found in those extreme cases where the importance of achievement in the play situation became so personally significant that the individual appeared to be superimposing the value structures of the work ethic into the domain of play and games. In the extreme manifestation of the work ethic, the individual sought a validation of his self-concept through evidence of his continuing ability to dominate others in his chosen profession or occupation. What became important were success over others and the demonstration of a high degree of skill with few other considerations being relevant in his evaluation of the situation. Accordingly, Webb, in developing the concept of the professionalization of attitude toward play, believed that the transposition of such value emphases into the world of play represented the intrustion of professional or occupational criteria into a domain of social life where they were not really necessary.[2][5]

The second basis of thought for Webb's choice of the term "professionalization of attitude toward play" may be illustrated by the significance of achievement in professional sports, where what were once play and game forms, have now developed into forms of work. The emphasis on the achievement criteria of success and the demonstration of skill, which is prevalent in professional sport, has increasingly been manifest at the lower levels of play. This has engendered a professionalization of attitude in the participants engaging in play activity, when the primary spirit should be associated with the development of the intrinsic satisfactions traditionally associated with play.[2][5]

Most of the research into professionalized play attitudes has been conducted on high school and university students, but little has been done on intramural participants. There is a need for research using intramural participants as subjects because intramurals is an extension of the athletic games learned in earlier life.

The leisure style displayed by students while at college reflects, to a major degree, their developing attitudes and values systems about the world they are about to inherit and the kind of life they want to live. Miller[3] described students as " . . . the leisure's mode of the future through the imagery and force of the student leadership tomorrow."[3]

PAST RESEARCH ON PROFESSIONALIZATION OF ATTITUDE TOWARD PLAY

Various studies have shown conclusively that males were considerably oriented to the use of achievement criteria in the evaluation of the key elements in the play situation, while the females were less likely to employ such criteria.[2] The studies found that it was essential for the male adolescent in this society to develop, through formal and informal socialization experiences, those values which were in keeping with the expected performance of his major adult role and which were in preparation for his participation as a member of an occupational group within the economic sector. The fact that these social values came to be associated with sport activities that were unrelated to occupational performance was an indication of the strength and significance of competitive sport preparation for these occupational experiences of the adult male.

It was apparent in the studies, not withstanding the activities of the Women's Liberation Movement, that there was little intrusion of achievement criteria into the evaluations of the female students toward play activity. Webb, according to Maloney and Petrie[2], hypothesized that such results were indicative of the fact that the predominant female adult role was associated with marriage and the selection of a husband as ascriptive standards. These results were interpreted to indicate a strong linkage between latent socialization experience in the milieu of the high school and in the direct or indirect association of the individual with athletic programs, or the development of value orientations concurrent with those emphasized in the female adult work role.[2]

Webb[5] believed that experiences in the high school setting promoted attitudes that were appropriate within the society by maintaining universalistic criteria for its major social institutions; however, experiences in the play sphere influences social attitude development as well. In turn, background factors such as religious orientation and father's occupation were found to become increasingly important in the development of these social attitudes as the student grows older. As play activities themselves became more rationalized with an increase in age, refined social standards were developed and an emphasis on success through skill replaced the equity factor for success. This was pronounced at earlier stages where the social standards did not operate in the same degree. A professionalized attitude of play was thus developed.[5]

PURPOSE

The purpose of the study was to determine the degree of professionalization of attitude toward play held by a select group of college students participating in intramurals. More specifically, this study has been designed to determine whether the degree of professionalization of attitude toward play of males and females are different among the intramural league divisions according to the competitiveness of the league entered.

Definitions

League Divisions—the league divisions are classified as "A", "B", and "C".

"A" *Division*—a highly competitive division for men and women designed to produce an ultimate victor. Rewards such as trophies, pictures, and certificates are given to the first and second place winners.

"B" *Division*—a less competitive division than the "A" Division for men and women. This division still produces an ultimate winner, but emphasizes participation by reducing the rewards for winning.

"C" *Division*—a recreational division for men and women with the only goals being to participate and have fun. There is no overall winner and win-lose records are not recorded.

Types of Leagues—types of leagues are classified as men's independent, women's independent, fraternity, sorority, and co-recreation.

Men's Independent League—a classification for men who compete in the intramural activities, but do not live in a fraternity house. The men reside in dormitories, or in off-campus housing. The league is divided into the following divisions: Independent Men "A", Independent Men "B", and Independent Men "C".

Women's Independent League—a classification for women who compete in the intramural activities, but do not live in a sorority house. The women reside in dormitories or in off-campus housing. The league is divided into the following divisions: Independent Women "A", Independent Women "B", and Independent Women "C".

Fraternity League—a men's league classification used by Recreation Services, taken from the college Greek system. League members must belong to a fraternity. The fraternity league is divided into the following divisions: Fraternity "A", Fraternity "B", and Fraternity "C".

Sorority League—a women's league classification used by Recreation Services, taken from the college Greek system. League members must belong to a sorority. The sorority league is divided into the following divisions: Sorority "A", Sorority "B", and Sorority "C".

Co-recreation League—a classification for men and women who compete jointly in the intramural activities. The league is divided into the following divisions: Co-recreation "A" and Co-recreation "B".

Webb's Play Scale—a scale which ranks the items important in a play activity. The items are: "play" meaning "to play the game as well as you are able," "beat" meaning "to beat your opponent," and "fair" meaning "to play the game fairly." The Play Scale is also referred to as the Professionalization Scale. After the items have been rank ordered, the degree of professionalization of attitude toward that activity can be scored from a set of six permutations ranked on a continuum of increasing support for the success item. (See appendix)

METHODOLOGY

The first study took place during the 1977 fall semester at the University of Kansas. The sample was composed of 225 students who participated in the intramural volleyball program. Twenty-five participants were randomly selected from each of the nine divisions; Fraternity "A", Fraternity "B", Independent Mens "A", Independent Mens "B", Independent Womens "A", Independent Womens "B", Sorority "A", Co-recreation "A", and Co-recreation "B". The investigator gave Webb's Play Scale (see appendix) to the participants before the start of each game during the third week of league play.

Webb's Table of Permutations (see appendix) was used to score the results of the Play Scale for both studies. The data from the Play Scale is translated into ordinal measures. This is done by arranging the six possible permutations in an order of professionalization ranging from low to high. The low end of the table is termed play orientation and the high end is termed professional orientation.

RESULTS AND DISCUSSION

The volleyball study results indicated that Fraternity "A" was the only league that had a professional orientation. On the Table of Permutations, this league scored a mean score of 4.2. All of the other leagues and divisions scored under 4, which puts them under the play orientation side of the table. Sorority "A" had the next highest mean score on the Table of Permutations, the highest play orientation score.

Several statements can be made about the results. The "A" divisions are more professionally oriented than the "B" divisions. Fraternity "A" was more professionally oriented than Independent "A". Co-recreation "A" was more professionally oriented than Co-recreation "B". Sorority "A" was more professionally oriented than Independent Women "A". Independent Women's "A" was more professionally orientated than Independent Women's "B". Fraternity "A" was more professionally oriented than Fraternity "B". Independent Men's "A" was more professionally oriented than Independent Men's "B". Fraternity "B" was more professionally oriented than Independent Men's "B".

As a player moved toward the professional attitude, victory became his main objective and fairness became a less important objective. As a player moved in the opposite direction toward a play orientation, he placed a high standard on fairness and placed the importance of victory last. He participated to have fun and to play fair.

APPENDIX B

		TABLE OF PERMUTATIONS			
	Play Orientation			Professional Orientation	
1	2	3	4	5	6
Fair	Fair	Play	Play	Beat	Beat
Play	Beat	Fair	Beat	Fair	Play
Beat	Play	Beat	Fair	Play	Fair

THE EFFECTS OF TITLE IX ON SELECTED CURRENT POLICIES GOVERNING THE INTRAMURAL SPORTS PROGRAMS OF THE CALIFORNIA STATE UNIVERSITIES AND COLLEGES

Keith G. Peters, California State University Long Beach

THE PROBLEM

The purpose of this study was to compile current information regarding policies pertaining to selected areas of the intramural sports programs of the California State Universities and Colleges. An attempt was made to identify and analyze any changes in selected intramural sports programs policies that may have been influenced by Title IX.

The following hypotheses were suggested as anticipated changes in policy that might be attributed to Title IX:

1. A majority of intramural sports programs reflect the trend towards consolidation of separate men's and women's departments into single units of administration.

2. Administrative responsibility has been transferred from men's and women's departments of physical education to other recreation related departments.

3. An increase in total fund allocations for combined intramural sports programs has accompanied administrative consolidation.

4. Budget allocations have been equitably divided among men's, women's, and coed intramural sports programs.

5. Rules governing facilities and equipment have been altered to provide for the needs and interests of women, as well as those of men.

The selected areas of intramural sports programs under examination were: organization and administration, finance, facilities and equipment, and publicity.

Research

IMPLICATIONS

The results of the studies using Webb's Play Scale may be used in many ways to aid the intramural director. After reviewing the results, the administrator could evaluate the league and division structure that was currently being used in his programs. This would enable the administrator to make changes that would aid in the decreasing or increasing of the professionalization of attitude toward play. Only the administrator can make the decision on which course to follow.

When an administrator must choose whether the degree of professionalization of attitude toward play must be decreased, increased, or left the same, he must consider more than just the structural changes necessary. The decision involves a philosophical question, "Should intramural programs be geared to compliment the competitive world or geared to let people of all degrees of professionalized play attitude participate?" Possibly administrators should do both.

BIBLIOGRAPHY

[1]Loy, John W., "The Nature of Sport: A Definitional Effort," *Sport, Culture,* and *Society,* eds. John W. Loy, Jr. and Gerald S. Kenyon, London: The MacMillan Company, 1969, pp. 56-71.

[2]Maloney, Lawrence T. and Brian M. Petrie, "Professionalization of Attitude Toward Play Among Canadian School Pupils as a Function of Sex, Grade, and Athletic Participation," *Journal of Leisure Research,* Volume 4, Number 3, (Summer 1972), pp. 184-195.

[3]Miller, Norman P., "Leisure Life Styles in the University Setting," *Journal of Health, Physical Education, and Recreation,* Volume 45, Number 9, (November-December), 1974, pp. 57-58.

[4]Vaz, Edmund W., "What Price Victory?;; *International Review of Sport Sociology,* Volume 9, Number 2, 1974, pp. 33-53.

[5]Webb, Henry, "Professionalization of Attitudes Toward Play Among Adolescents," *Sociology of Sport, Aspects of Contemporary Sport Sociology,* ed. Gerald S. Kenyon, Chicago: The

APPENDIX A

WEBB'S PLAY SCALE

What do you think is most important in playing the game? Rank the choices from 1 to 3. Put a one (1) beside the choice you think is most important, put a two (2) beside your second most important choice, and put a three (3) beside the choice you think is least important.

_____ To play it as well as you are able
_____ To play it as well as you are able
_____ To beat your opponent
_____ To play it fairly

RELATED STUDIES

A thorough review of literature relevant to the topic indicated that a study of this scope had not previously been conducted. Five years ago, current practices and policies of the men's intramural-recreational programs among the California State Universities and Colleges were surveyed (Ludwig, 1973), but it was assumed that progress has measurably altered those programs.

Maas, Mahan, and Hyatt, among others, have written about Title IX and offered theories regarding its impact; however, no mention of Title IX's impact on policies within California State University and College intramural sports program was discovered. Mahan (1977) and Hyatt (1977) expressed the need for research and documentation of the effects of Title IX on intramural sports programs.

PROCEDURES

The data for this study was collected by questionnaire. Twenty questionnaires were mailed to the intramural-recreational sports program directors of the nineteen schools in the California State University and College system (one program was known to have co-directors).

Nineteen of the twenty questionnaires (95%) were returned although one response indicated that an institution did not currently have an intramural sports program. The data generated by the eighteen responses to questions regarding selected current policies and possible effects of Title IX produced some interesting findings.

FINDINGS

General Information

1. The number of annual student program participants reported ranged from 101-250 men and 100 or less women, to a combined total of 25,000. Seven (38.9%) of the responses reported 1001-3000 male student participants while nine (50%) of the returns indicated that female student participation was less than 1000.

2. Six (33.3%) of the respondents were new to their job within the past year, and a large majority (77.8%) had held their position less than four years.

3. Physical education (61.1%) and recreation (11.1%) represented the majority of respondents' academic area of emphasis.

4. All respondents had earned a Bachelor's degree, seven (38.9%) had earned a Master's degree, five (27.8%) had continued their studies beyond a Master's degree, and two (11.1%) had achieved their doctorate.

Organization and Administration

1. Seventeen (94.4%) of the respondents indicated that the organizational structure of their intramural sports program reflected a single unit of administration. Two (11.1%) responses identified Title IX as the reason behind administrative consolidation.

2. A variety of departments were indicated to be at least partly responsible for the administration of intramural sports programs. Three (16.7%) autonomous intramural sports departments were identified. Six (33.3%) physical education departments participated in intramural sports administration. Seven (38.9%) student affairs/activities departments contributed administrative support. Two (11.1%) returns indicated that Title IX was responsible for the transfer of administrative responsibility.

3. Each of the seventeen intramural sports departments were guided by at least one director. Four programs (22.2%) indicated the existence of co-director situations. Intramural sports department staffs also included: assistant directors (44.4% of the time); faculty members (only 5.6% of the time); graduate students (55.6% of the time); undergraduate students (72.2% of the time); secretaries (55.6% of the time); and others (22.2% of the time). Two returns indicated that a change had occurred among intramural sports department staffs as a result of Title IX.

4. Of the intramural directors who identified their sex and responsibilities, twelve (66.7%) were male and three (16.7%) were female. Two (11.1%) returns indicated that Title IX had caused changes in the director's and/or assistant director's job responsibilities.

5. Fourteen (77.8%) responses indicated that activity coordinating responsibilities were assigned according to an individual's expertise in a particular area, regardless of sex. Four (22.2%) of the respondents indicated that coordinating responsibilities had been reevaluated and reassigned as a result of Title IX.

Finances

1. A variety of sources were identified as contributors to intramural sports program fiscal support. Fourteen (77.8%) of the responses identified student registration/activity fees as a source of support funds and for seven (38.9%) of the schools, this source provided 90-100% of the total financial support. Seven (38.9%) of the programs were provided funds by the department responsible for administration and two (11.1%) responses indicated that this was a major (90-100%) source of funds. Entry fees were mentioned six times (33.3%) and represented the major (90-100%) intramural sports program support base in one response.

2. Nine (50%) of the responses indicated that their budget had increased for the 1977-78 school year while two (11.1%) indicated that their budget

had decreased. Title IX was not identified as a reason for any of the budget changes.

3. In six instances (33.3%) men's activities received 34-50% of a department's operational budget. Women's activities were allocated 26-33% of the operational budget in five (27.8%) cases. The distribution of funds to coed activities runs the gamut from five (27.8%) reports of 10-25% fee distribution to five (27.8%) allocations of 50% of greater (including two reports of 100% of the operational budget being allocated for coed activities). In three (16.8%) responses Title IX was identified as having affected percentage amounts of fund allocations.

Facilities and Equipment

1. Fourteen (77.8%) of the returns indicated that the intramural sports departments were involved in scheduling facilities utilized by the intramural sports program. The other major participants in facility scheduling were nine (50%) physical education departments.

2. Response to a question regarding the purchase of intramural sports equipment generated data similar to that just presented in regard to facility scheduling.

3. Seven (38.9%) of the responses indicated that available facilities were inadequate to provide a broad program of organized and informal intramural sports activities for both men and women. Two (11.1%) returns claimed that positive action for providing additional facilities was a result of Title IX.

4. While nine (50%) of the responses identified the existence of plans for developing adequate facilities for future intramural sports program participants, two (11.1%) indicated that such a plan was a result of Title IX.

5. All eighteen (100%) returns indicated that opportunities for practice and games were provided to accomodate the intramural sports interests of both sexes equally, but two (11.1%) indicated that Title IX had caused a change in policy.

Publicity

All eighteen (100%) returns stated equal attention was given to the promotion of women's and coed activities, as well as men's activities, and again two (11.1%) attributed a change in policy to the impact of Title IX.

CONCLUSIONS

Evaluation of the hypotheses, and comparison of the findings of this study with those of a previous study (Ludwig, 1973), produced the following conclusions:

1. A great majority of respondents (94.4%) indicated that their intramural sports program represented a single unit of administration. Title IX was cited as the reason for administrative consolidation twice (11.1%).

2. Administrative responsibility had been transferred from men's and women's departments of physical education to other recreation related departments. Six (33.3%) physical education departments presently participated in intramural sports porgram administration compared to the fifteen programs administered by physical education departments in 1973 (Ludwig).

3. Total fund allocations are increased for intramural sports programs for the 1977-1978 school year in nine (50%) instances, but it could not be theorized that this was a result of administrative consolidation due to Title IX because Title IX was found to have little impact on organizational structure.

4. Budget allocations were found to be equitably divided among men's, women's, and coed intramural programs according to the expressed interests of the male and female program paticipants, rather than as a mandate of Title IX.

5. Rules governing facilities and equipment provided for the needs and interests of women, as well as those of men, and Title IX was rarely (11.1%) identified as the impetus for such policy.

6. Responses indicate that Title IX has not had a profound effect on the selected areas of California State University and College intramural sports programs examined in this study. Trends have been documented that were anticipated, but the stimulus for such trends was not Title IX and was otherwise not identified.

SELECTED BIBLIOGRAPHY

Berg, Otto. "Future trends in administration of intramural sports at the college level." *Proceedings of the 20th Annual National Intramural Association Conference.* Los Angeles, Ca.: 1969, 74-78.

Fidler, Merrie A. "Selected survey of the organization and administration of women's intramural programs." *Proceedings of the 24th Annual National Intramural Conference.* Tampa, Florida: 1973, 170-178.

Harms, Bill, and others. *Intramurals: Where Does it Belong? Physical Education or Student Affairs.* U.S., Educational Resources Information Center, ERIC Document ED 106 303, 1975.

Holmes, Peter E. *Memorandum to Chief State School Officers, Superintendents of Local Education Agencies, and College and University Presidents. Subject: Elimination of Sex Discrimination in Athletic Programs.* Washington: U.S. Department of Health, Education, and Welfare/Office for Civil Rights, September 1975.

Hyatt, Ronald W. *Intramural Sports: Organization and Administration.* St. Louis, MO., C.V. Mosby Co., 1977.

Ludwig, Donald F. *A Study of the Men's Intramural-Recreational Programs Among the California State Universities and Colleges.* Unpublished Master's thesis, California State University, Long Beach, 1973.

Maas, Gerry. "Merging men's and women's intramural sports programs." *Proceedings of the 27th Annual National Intramural-Recreational Sports Association Conference.* San Diego, CA.: 1976, 13-16.

Mahan, Mary Ellen. *Comprehension of Title IX Regulations by Intramural Administrators.* Unpublished Master's thesis, Southern Illinois University, Carbondale, 1977.

EMPLOYMENT STATUS OF MINORITY FULL-TIME PROFESSIONALS IN CAMPUS RECREATION-INTRAMURAL DEPARTMENTS

by Marianne Blodgett, University of Kentucky

The purpose of the study was to determine the employment status of minority, full-time professional personnel in campus recreation-intramural programs of colleges and universities in the United States which are member institutions of the National Intramural Recreational Sports Association (NIRSA). More specifically, the study attempted to determine the use of recruiting and hiring practices related to minority group employment, interviewing techniques employed, contracts offered, and career advancement policies in departments of campus recreation-intramurals. In addition, information was obtained in regard to the positions held, the level of education, and salaries commanded by minority group members.

Through the years attempts have been made through federal, state, and local laws to prohibit discrimination in the work force to include all groups without regard to race, color, sex, national origin, and more recently to include the physically disabled. The four federal laws which are most important in combatting employment inequities are: 1) Title VII of the Civil Rights Act of 1964; 2) Executive Order 11246; 3) The Equal Pay Act; 4) Title IX of the Civil Rights Act.

At the local level there are federal agencies which aid in the enforcement of laws related to discriminatory practices. However, there is a continuing need to ensure implementation of the intent of the law. This has been done through Affirmative Action programs which are federally mandated and designed to eliminate employment discrimination. Affirmative Action has established criteria for evaluating the success or failure of a programs' efforts to comply with equal employment legislation. Graham[2] stated in an article published in the NIRSA Conference Proceedings

> *Affirmative Action was enacted to provide a tool for tapping the wealth of human resources that either have not been utilized or have been underrepresented. Affirmative Action is a concept that allows for the development and implementation of programs designed to assist the entry of identified not utilized and under-*

*represented segments of the population into the employment
market, e.g. institutions. (p. 29)*

Graham in 1976 pointed out four areas of employment processes: recruitment and hiring, interviewing, contracts, and career advancement. Recognizing that these four areas are basic to who is and will be employed in campus
recreation-intramurals, these areas were used for developing the survey instrument.

Questionnaires were sent to the directors of all campus recreation-
intramural departments which were member institutions of NIRSA in 1977.
There were 298 institutions listed of which questionnaires were returned
from 210. Of the 210 returns, 181 were used in the analysis.

The sample was broken down into four groups for reporting purposes:
four year institutions with student enrollment of 10,000 and over and four
year institutions under 10,000, two year institutions with student enrollment
of 10,000 and over and two year institutions under 10,000. The first question
on the questionnaire dealt with whether or not the directors of campus
recreation-intramurals were aware of Affirmative Action and its purposes
and goals. Table 1 shows that the majority of directors (88.5%) have some
knowledge of Affirmative Action with those in four year institutions having
the greatest percentage. Table 2 shows that of the institutions where there is
an awareness of Affirmative Action, 87.6 percent have plans for implementation. Among all institutions, the four year schools under 10,000 and the
two year schools over 10,000 reflect the highest percentage those having no
plans for implementing Affirmative Action. Of the total sample, 87.6 percent
reported that an Affirmative Action program has been implemented, 7.1 percent reported they have no plans to implement an Affirmative Action program and 5.3 percent indicated that plans for implementation would be
underway in the next year to four years.

Another question asked if there was an office or agency within the institution which helped coordinate the hiring of racial and cultural minorities,
physically disabled, and women for professional positions within the campus recreation-intramural department. Of 179 responses, 78.2 percent
reported that there was an office or agency within the institution, while 21.8
percent reported there was no office or agency to provide assistance in hiring.

Federal Executive Order 11246 requires that employers advertise vacant
positions in conspicuous places to attract all possible candidates. Graham[2]
suggests that when vacant positions are available, employers should review
their existing programs and staff to determine if women or minorities are
under-represented. To determine recruitment and hiring practices,
respondents were asked whether or not their department had an established

policy for advertising vacant positions. Of the 177 respondents, 85.3 percent indicated that they had a policy for advertising vacant positions and the remaining 14.7 percent reported they had no established policy. Often the problem of under-representation of minorities and women is due to the deficiency of advertising in widely read sources. According to the responses (Table 4) the most popular source for advertising vacant positions was the *Chronicle of Higher Education* followed by the *NIRSA Journal, Journal of AAPHER, Journal of Higher Education* and *NIRSA Newsletter* in that order. The remaining four are not utilized as frequently as shown on Table 3. With lesser frequency, some institutions send their notices directly to selected colleges and universities or advertise their position vacancies in local or statewide newspapers. Still others reported that their personnel department handles the advertisement of vacant positions.

Respondents were asked what sources they used for seeking applicants for vacant positions. (Table 4) Professional colleagues were considered as the most important source with 76.8 percent, 63 percent reported that direct contact was important, 61.3 percent considered letters to universities, 44.2 percent utilized the job mart at national conferences, and 40.9 percent used newspapers as a source for seeking applicants.

It was determined that 98.2 percent of the total sample use interviews as part of the selection process. Of those that utilize interviews, 44.6 percent reported that their interviews were conducted using a definite format, while 51.2 percent indicated that the interviews were informal and did not follow a specific interview plan.

As stated earlier, Graham[2] pointed out that employers should review their present programs and staff to determine if women and minorities were under-represented. Respondents were asked on one item that, if a full-time professional position vacancy existed, which of two courses of action would they prefer to take in filling it? (Table 5) Of 165 responses, 37.9 percent prefer to hire within the department, 35.7 percent prefer to hire outside the department, while 36.4 percent indicated alternative preferences. Among the latter responses, 45 indicated that they would hire the best person or most qualified candidate, 12 responded with the answer that it makes no difference, while 8 reported that it would depend on the position or the candidate.

The questionnaire also attempted to identify those factors that appear most important to an employer when considering applicants for employment. The respondents were asked to rank in order of importance from a list of ten factors, those which they would consider when hiring for a full-time professional position, 1 being most important, 10 least important. (Table 6) Unfortunately, due to an obvious misunderstanding of the directions to the question, 71 of the responses had to be eliminated. Table 11 shows that in using the weighted mean and frequency of responses, experienced ranked as the most important factor with 45 respondents ranking it as number one. As the factors decrease in importance, noticeable is the spread of frequencies showing a diversity of opinion among directors. Significant as well is that personality is ranked higher than potential for professional growth and professional reputation.

Graham[2] discussed the significance of contracts and the importance of receiving equal contractual conditions without regard for sex, race, color, national origin, and physical disability. In campus recreation-intramural departments, only 71 percent of the institutions require any kind of contract and 92.5 percent are for one year.

Information was obtained in regard to the positions held, the level of education, and salaries earned by minority group members. Respondents were requested to list the staff positions within the department. From the data, it was decided to group administrative personnel in two categories: Level I and Level II. Level I pertains to directors of campus recreation or intramurals, Level II includes all other full-time professional faculty and staff. This category includes a diversity of subordinate staff with varying degrees of responsibility but was made necessary because of the difficulty in categorizing them according to unspecified roles and functions. There were 158 male Level I administrators, 88.6 percent of whom represented the White/Caucasian group, 5.1 percent Black/Negro, 1.9 percent Oriental, and .6 percent American Indian. There was one physically disabled person employed. (Table 7)

There were 20 female Level I administrators. In this group 90 percent were White/Caucasian and 10 percent were Black/Negro. Table 9 shows the minority group breakdown of four year and two year institutions by size of student enrollment.

Level II administrators refer to all other staff in the department. In this group there were 128 male employees, 79.7 percent of whom were White/Caucasian, 10.9 percent Black/Negro, 1.6 percent Oriental, 6.2 percent Spanish surnamed American, and 1.6 percent American Indian. (Tables 9 and 10).

There were 82 females employed as Level II administrators. The minority breakdown is as follows: 84.1 percent White/Caucasian, 12.2 percent Black/Negro, 2.4 percent Oriental, and 1.2 percent Spanish surnamed American.

As Table 7 indicates, potential employers ranked level of education as the third most important factor when considering applicants for full-time professional positions. Of 148 male Level I administrators, 12.8 percent had a doctorate degree, 78.4 percent a masters degree and 8.8 percent bachelor degree. For female Level I administrators, there were no doctoral degrees, while 75 percent had masters degrees, and 25 percent bachelors degrees. (Tables 11 and 12)

Referring to Level II male administrators, six percent of 127 had doctoral degrees, 65 percent had masters degrees, 26 percent had bachelor degrees, and 2 percent had no college degree. There was one female (1 percent) Level II administrator possessing a doctoral degree and of the rest, 66 percent had masters' degrees. 29 percent bachelor degrees, and 3.6 percent had no college degree. (Tables 13 and 14)

Average salaries of Level I administrators (Tables 15 and 16) are reported in relation to level of education. There were 132 male Level I administrators and 15 of them possessed doctoral degrees with a mean annual salary of $27,557. There were no Level I female administrators with doctoral degrees. Among Level I male administrators, 104 had the masters degree and earned an average annual salary of $17,228 compared to 10 females with an average annual salary of $16,264. Those with bachelors degrees included 13 males with an average annual salary of $16,653 and 4 females who averaged $9,716 annually.

Table 17 and 18 shows the mean salaries of Level II administrators. There were 111 male administrators among whom six had doctoral degrees earning an average annual salary of $18,340. There were no female administrators with doctoral degrees. Referring to masters degree, there were 74 males with a mean annual salary of $14,267 compared to 54 females making an average annual salary of $13,784. There were 29 males with bachelor degrees earning an average annual salary of $12,846, and 19 females with average annual salaries of $10,083. Two Level II male administrators had no college degrees and had an average annual salary of $10,250. By contrast, there were 3 females with no college degree making $9,500 annually.

Several conclusions can be drawn from the data as they have been analyzed to this point:

1. There tends to be a greater understanding of the purposes and goals of Affirmative Action among the directors of departments in four-year institutions and particularly among the larger (10,000 and over) institutions.

2. By virtue of that greater understanding, implementation of Affirmative Action plans has been effected to a greater degree by the larger four-year institutions than by the other three categories of schools.

3. The source most frequently used for advertising position vacancies is the *Chronicle of Higher Education*. This is a signal for those in the field seeking positions to refer to that source for the most comprehensive information available.

4. The most frequently used methods for seeking and identifying applicants are in order: professional colleagues, direct contact, letters to university departments, job marts at professional conferences, and newspaper advertising.

5. Four year institutions are more prone to hire without the department than two-year institutions which prefer to hire from within.

6. When ten factors are ranked in terms of importance, campus recreation-intramural directors rank experience as the single most important factor. Combined with the next two most important factors, professional knowledge and level of education, there is evidence that the employer is concerned with objective, measurable factors primarily. Grouped together in following order are three rather intangible qualities, an evaluation of which must be subjective: personality, potential for professional growth, and professional reputation. The last four factors: physical appearance, sex, race, and religion appear to be considerably less relevant to the applicant's potential for performance in the department.

7. Concerning minority group representation, it appears that Level I administrators are represented primarily by the White/Caucasian group in both the male and female groups.

8. Level II administrators have a broader representation of minority groups, with the White/Caucasian group again being the dominant group represented.

9. It appears that there are substantially fewer female Level I administrators as compared to men. However, the ratio of males and females becomes more balanced in relation to Level II administration.

10. The majority of Level I and Level II administrators have masters degrees for both male and female. However more males have attained the doctoral level of education in both Level I and Level II administration.

11. The average salaries in relation to level of education of Level I and Level II administrators appears to be higher for males than for females.

SELECTED REFERENCES

[1] Equal Employment Opportunity Commission. *Job Discrimination. Laws and Rules You Should Know.* 1975.

[2] *National Intramural Recreational Sports Association.* Twenty-Seventh Annual Conference Proceedings. San Diego, California, April 11-15, 1976.

[3] *National Intramural Recreational Sports Association.* Twenty-Sixth Annual Conference Proceedings. New Orleans, Louisiana, April 23-27, 1975.

[4] The President Committee on Employment of the Handicapped. *American Profile What States are Doing (and can do) To Hire the Handicapped.* 1975.

[5] United States Equal Employment Opportunity Commission. *Affirmative Action and Equal Employment, A Guidebook for Employees.* Volume I and II. January 1974.

[6] United States Department of Labor. Employment Standards Administration Women's Bureau. *Women Workers Today.* 1976.

Table 1

Knowledge of Affirmative Action Purposes and Goals by Directors of Campus Recreation-Intramural Departments

Institutions by size of student enroll-ment	N	Informed of A.A. purposes and goals		Not informed about A.A. purposes and goals	
		n	percent	n	percent
Four Year: 10,000 and over	65	59	90.8	6	9.2
Four Year: Under 10,000	80	71	88.8	9	11.2
Two Year: 10,000 and over	10	8	80.8	2	20.0
Two Year: Under 10,000	24	21	87.5	3	12.5
	179	159	88.5	20	11.2

Table 2
Status of Implementation of Affirmative Action Plans in Campus Recreation-Intramural Departments

Institutions by size of student enrollment	N	Plans Implemented		No Plans for Implementation		Plan to Implement	
		n	percent	n	percent	n	percent
Four Year: 10,000 and over	63	60	95.2	2	3.2	1	1.6
Four Year: Under 10,000	73	63	86.3	8	11.0	2	2.7
Two Year: 10,000 and over	10	8	80.0	1	10.0	1	10.0
Two Year: Under 10,000	23	17	73.9	1	4.4	5	21.7
	169	148	87.6	12	7.1	9	5.3

163

Table 3

Sources for Advertising Campus Recreation-Intramural Department Position Vacancies

Source	Institutions (n)	Percent of all Institutions (n = 181)
Chronicle of Higher Education	69	38.1
NIRSA Journal	51	28.2
Journal of AAHPER	44	24.3
Journal of Higher Education	34	18.8
NIRSA Newsletter	36	19.9
NRPA Bulletin	17	9.4
New York Times	13	7.2
NRPA Journal	10	5.5
AALR Reporter	1	.5
Other	76	42.0

Table 4

Sources for Seeking Applicants for Position Vacancies in Campus Recreation-Intramural Departments

Sources	Institutions (n)	Percent of all Institutions (n = 181)
Professional Colleagues	139	76.8
Conference (Job Mart)	80	44.2
Letters to Universities	111	61.3
Direct Contact	114	63.0
Newspaper Advertising	74	40.9
Other	26	14.4

Table 5

**Courses of Action Preferred for Filling Professional Position
Vacancies in Campus Recreation-Intramural Departments**

Institutions by size of student enrollment	N	Hire from Within		Hire from Without		Other	
		n	percent	n	percent	n	percent
Four Year: 10,000 and over	59	8	13.6	20	33.9	31	52.5
Four Year: Under 10,000	76	24	31.6	30	39.5	22	28.9
Two Year: 10,000 and over	9	6	66.7	2	22.2	1	11.1
Two Year: Under 10,000	21	8	38.1	7	33.3	6	28.6
	165	46	37.9	59	35.7	60	36.4

Table 6

**Ranking of Factors of Importance in Employing
Professionals in Campus Recreation-Intramural Departments**

Rank	Factor	N	Frequency of Response										Weighted Mean
			1	2	3	4	5	6	7	8	9	10	
1	Experience	104	45	30	15	10	1	1	0	0	0	2	2.12
2	Professional Knowledge	106	22	39	25	6	10	3	0	0	1	0	2.60
3	Level of Education	104	16	14	20	18	17	14	5	0	0	0	3.65
4	Personality	105	4	9	15	24	20	28	2	1	2	0	4.49
5	Potential for Professional Growth	105	8	4	16	19	23	20	12	2	1	0	4.79
6	Professional Reputation	103	7	7	13	15	15	24	20	2	2	0	5.56
7	Physical Appearance	110	1	0	2	9	17	15	57	5	2	2	6.32
8	Sex	95	1	2	0	2	0	3	5	58	18	6	7.91
9	Race	94	1	1	1	1	0	1	5	11	48	25	8.73
10	Religion	93	1	0	1	1	1	1	1	11	21	55	9.17

Table 7

Minority Group Representation of Level I Administrators in Campus Recreation-Intramural Departments

Institutions by size of student enrollment	N	W/C*		B/N		O		AI		SSA		PD	
		n	percent	n	percent	n	percent	n	percent	n	percent	n	percent
Male													
Four Year: 10,000 and over	56	53	94.6	1	1.8	—	—	—	—	2	3.6	—	—
Four Year: Under 10,000	69	61	88.4	4	5.8	1	1.45	1	1.45	2	2.9	1	1.4
Two Year: 10,000 and over	8	7	87.5	1	12.5	—	—	—	—	—	—	—	—
Two Year: Under 10,000	25	19	76.0	2	8.0	2	8.0	—	—	2	8.0	—	—
Female													
Four Year: 10,000 and over	6	6	100.0	—	—	—	—	—	—	—	—	—	—
Four Year: Under 10,000	7	7	100.0	—	—	—	—	—	—	—	—	—	—
Two Year: 10,000 and over	1	1	100.0	—	—	—	—	—	—	—	—	—	—
Two Year: Under 10,000	6	4	66.7	2	33.3	—	—	—	—	—	—	—	—

*W/C = White/Caucasian
B/N = Black/Negro
O = Oriental
SSA = Spanish Surnamed American
AI = American Indian
P/D = Physically Disabled

Table 9

Minority Group Representation of Level II Administrators in Campus Recreation-Intramural Departments

Institutions by size of student enrollment	N	W/C*		B/N		O		SSA		AI		P/D	
		n	percent	n	percent	n	percent	n	percent	n	percent	n	percent
Male													
Four Year: 10,000 and over	85	71	82.5	11	12.8	1	1.2	2	2.3	1	1.2	—	—
Four Year: Under 10,000	28	22	78.6	2	7.1	—	—	3	10.7	1	3.6	—	—
Two Year: 10,000 and over	7	4	57.1	1	14.3	—	—	2	28.6	—	—	—	—
Two Year: Under 10,000	7	5	71.4	—	—	1	14.3	1	14.3	—	—	—	—
Female													
Four Year: 10,000 and over	64	55	85.9	7	10.9	1	1.6	1	1.6	—	—	—	—
Four Year: Under 10,000	10	9	90.0	1	10.0	—	—	—	—	—	—	—	—
Two Year: 10,000 and over	4	2	50.0	1	25.0	1	25.0	—	—	—	—	—	—
Two Year: Under 10,000	4	3	75.0	1	25.0	—	—	—	—	—	—	—	—

*W/C = White/Caucasian
B/N = Black/Negro

O = Oriental
SSA = Spanish Surnamed American

AI = American Indian
P/D = Physically Disabled

Table 8

Total Male and Female Minority Group Representation of Level I Administrators

	N	W/C n	W/C percent	B/N n	B/N percent	O n	O percent	AI n	AI percent	SSA n	SSA percent	PD n	PD percent
Male	158	140	88.6	8	5.1	3	1.9	1	.6	6	3.8	1	.6
Female	20	18	90.0	2	10.0	—	—	—	—	—	—	—	—

Table 10

Total Male and Female Minority Group Representation of Level II Administrators

	N	W/C n	W/C percent	B/N n	B/N percent	O n	O percent	AI n	AI percent	SSA n	SSA percent	PD n	PD percent
Male	128	102	79.7	14	10.9	2	1.6	2	1.6	8	6.2	—	—
Female	82	69	84.1	10	12.2	2	2.4	—	—	1	1.2	—	—

Table 11

Education of Level I Administrators in Campus Recreation-Intramural Departments

Institutions by size of student enrollment	N	Doctorate		Masters		Bachelor	
		n	percent	n	percent	n	percent
Male							
Four Year: 10,000 and over	53	11	20.8	37	69.8	5	9.4
Four Year: Under 10,000	68	5	7.35	58	85.3	5	7.35
Two Year: 10,000 and over	8	—	—	8	100.0	—	—
Two Year: Under 10,000	19	3	15.8	13	68.4	3	15.8
Female							
Four Year: 10,000 and over	6	—	—	5	83.3	1	16.7
Four Year: Under 10,000	7	—	—	5	71.4	2	28.6
Two Year: 10,000 and over	1	—	—	1	100.0	—	—
Two Year: Under 10,000	2	—	—	1	50.0	1	50.0

Table 12

Education of Male and Female Level I Administrators

	N	Doctorate		Masters		Bachelor	
		n	percent	n	percent	n	percent
Male	148	19	12.8	116	78.4	13	8.8
Female	16	—	—	12	75.0	4	25.0

Table 14

Education of Male and Female Level II Administrators

	N	Doctorate		Masters		Bachelor		Other	
		n	percent	n	percent	n	percent	n	percent
Male	127	8	6.3	83	65.3	33	26.0	3	2.4
Female	83	1	1.2	55	66.2	24	28.9	3	3.6

Table 13

Education of Level II Administrators in Campus Recreation-Intramural Departments

Institutions by size of student enrollment	N	Level of Education							
		Doctorate		Masters		Bachelor		Other	
		n	percent	n	percent	n	percent	n	percent
Male									
Four Year: 10,000 and over	86	6	6.9	62	72.1	17	19.8	1 (H.S.)	1.2
Four Year: Under 10,000	27	1	3.7	14	51.9	11	40.7	1 (no degree)	3.7
Two Year: 10,000 and over	7	—	—	2	28.6	4	57.1	1 (H.S.)	14.3
Two Year: Under 10,000	7	1	14.3	5	71.4	1	14.3	—	—
Female									
Four Year: 10,000 and over	65	—	—	48	73.8	16	23.5	1 (2 yr)	1.5
Four Year: Under 10,000	10	1	10.0	3	30.0	5	50.0	1 (3 yr)	10.0
Two Year: 10,000 and over	4	—	—	2	50.0	2	50.0	—	—
Two Year: Under 10,000	4	—	—	2	50.0	1	25.0	1 (no degree)	25.0

Table 15

Salaries of Level I Administrators in Campus Recreation-Intramural Departments

Institutions by size of student enrollment	N	Doctorate		Salaries Masters		Bachelor		Total Mean Salary
		n	mean salary	n	mean salary	n	mean salary	
Male								
Four Year: 10,000 and over	51	10	24,423	36	17,282	5	19,240	20,035
Four Year: Under 10,000	60	4	17,250	51	14,868	5	13,388	15,259
Two Year: 10,000 and over	8	—	—	8	20,262	—	—	20,262
Two Year: Under 10,000	13	1	20,000	9	16,500	3	17,333	15,653
Female								
Four Year: 10,000 and over	6	—	—	5	17,957	1	10,000	16,647
Four Year: Under 10,000	5	—	—	3	13,100	2	10,150	11,920
Two Year: 10,000 and over	1	—	—	1	22,000	—	—	22,000
Two Year: Under 10,000	2	—	—	1	12,000	1	9,000	10,500

Table 16

Average Salaries of Male and Female Level I Administrators

	N	Doctorate		Salaries Masters		Bachelor	
		n	mean salary	n	mean salary	n	mean salary
Male	132	15	20,557	104	17,228	13	16,653
Female	14	—	—	10	16,264	4	9,716

Table 18

Average Salaries of Male and Female Level II Administrators

	N	Doctorate		Salaries Masters		Bachelor		Other	
		n	mean salary	n	mean salary	n	mean salary	n	mean salary
Male	111	6	18,340	74	14,267	29	12,846	2	10,250
Female	76	—	—	54	13,784	19	10,083	3	9,500

Table 17

Salaries of Level II Administrators in Campus Recreation-Intramural Departments

Institutions by size of student enrollment	N	Salaries								Total Mean Salaries
		Doctorate		Masters		Bachelor		Other		
		n	mean salaries	n	mean salaries	n	mean slaries	n	mean salaries	
Male										
Four Year: 10,000 and over	83	5	18,680	60	15,195	17	13,825	1	10,500 (H.S.)	15,057
Four Year: Under 10,000	18	1	18,000	10	14,175	7	11,311	—	—	13,027
Two Year: 10,000 and over	7	—	—	2	13,700	4	11,250	1	10,000 (H.S.)	11,771
Two Year: Under 10,000	3	—	—	2	14,000	1	15,000	—	—	14,333
Female										
Four Year: 10,000 and over	63	—	—	48	12,606	14	10,784	1	10,500 (2 yr. coll.)	12,364
Four Year: Under 10,000	7	—	—	3	11,533	3	9,266	1	10,800 (3 yr. coll.)	10,457
Two Year: 10,000 and over	4	—	—	2	20,000	2	10,200	—	—	15,100
Two Year: Under 10,000	2	—	—	1	11,000	—	—	—	7,200 (no degree)	9,100

STUDENT PERCEPTIONS OF THE INTRAMURAL PROGRAM

Gerry Maas, Iowa State University

Introduction

The purpose of this survey was to sample a portion of the Iowa State University student population concerning their perceptions of the intramural sports program open to all students on campus. The purpose of this type of an investigation is to identify how students feel about intramural programs and also indicate reasons why students participate. This information is important to gather as program modifications can be made to more accurately meet the needs of our student populace in view of the survey data.

Procedure

A two page questionnaire was constructed following a similar type of survey completed at Iowa State University.[1] The questionnaire consisted of two parts: 1) background information and 2) intramural sports. Some questions concerning intramurals were not related to students' perceptions or attitudes toward the program and were not included in this paper. The survey was distributed by two methods: 1) mailed to 1090 students (every 20th student on the Spring Quarter (1977) registration list) and 2) a table placed adjacent to the fee payment window so that students would stop while paying fees. The results were compiled by key punching the information on computer cards for analysis.

Results

The questionnaire was completed and returned by 539 students. This included 440 mailed questionnaires (1090 mailed) or 40.4%. Ninety-nine (99) questionnaires were completed at a table by the fee payment window as students paid fees for Spring Quarter, 1977. These included 317 men and 215 women. The breakdown of students by classes was as follows: 131 freshmen, 109 sophomores, 127 juniors, 119 seniors and 45 graduate students. The male-female and class breakdown was representative of the 1976-77 enrollment pattern for Iowa State University.

The data are listed in tabular form. Not all questions on the questionnaire were analyzed for this paper as they dealt with other aspects of the intramural program. Analyses of the data were done for the following groups and sub-groups: 1) all subjects 2) males 3) females 4) high school interschool athletic participants (henceforth referred to as athletes) 5) high school interschool athletic non-participants (henceforth referred to as non-athletes). The data are listed in per cent for each item.

Discussion

The data concerning intramural sports indicated some very interesting information. Table 1 indicates that a very high percentage of students (over 90% in most sub-groups) have heard about the intramural program. This is substantiated by previous research[1] which indicated the effectiveness of the program's publicity efforts.

Table 1

Question 1: Have you ever heard anything about the Intramural Program at Iowa State University?

Responses:	All Respondents N=539	Male N=317	Female N=215	H.S. Athlete N=382	Non-Athlete N=151
Yes	95.7%	95.9%	95.3%	97.4%	92.7%

Table 2 reflects the responses of respondents concerning whether or not they participate in the intramural program. Most groups showed 70%-80% participation figures except for the non-athlete at 61.6%. This compares with 84.0% for high school athletes. This would be expected as the high school athletes desire to continue their competitive sports careers while at the university. Approximately 10% more males participated in interschool athletics than females. This might be explained by more sports opportunities being open to males in the high school setting when compared with females.

Table 2

Question 2: Have you ever participated in organized (team/individual-dual) intramural sports?

Responses:	All Respondents N=539	Male N=317	Female N=215	H.S. Athlete N=382	Non-Athlete N=151
Yes	77.4%	81.1%	71.6%	84.0%	61.6%
No, would like to	13.0%	12.0%	14.4%	12.0%	14.6%
No interest	9.5%	10.2%	13.5%	4.2%	23.2%

Table 3 dealt with attitudes toward competition in the intramural program, asking if the respondent would participate (or participate more) if the program were less competitive. Approximately 60% of all respondents indicated they would *not* participate more if the program were less competitive. More males than females and more athletes than non-athletes favored competition in the program. Program participants also favored competition. The question of competition in intramurals and its associated problems has been debated in intramural circles for years. Rokosz[2] and Van Hoff[4] favor de-emphasis in competition by dropping elimination tournaments to determine "a champion." However, this survey indicates that participants are seeking the competitive experience which will be reinforced later in the survey.

Table 3

Question 3: Would you participate (or participate more) in intramural sports if the atmosphere were less competitive?

Responses:	All Respondents N=539	Male N=317	Female N=215	H.S. Athlete N=382	Non-Athlete N=151
Yes	29.9%	27.1%	34.9%	26.7%	39.1%
No	60.5%	63.4%	55.3%	63.1%	55.6%

Table 4 summarizes the high school interschool athletic participation of the respondents. It can readily be seen that 70.9% of all respondents were high school athletes. Also, 77% of respondents who participated in intramurals were high school athletes. More males than females had high school athletic backgrounds. These data point to a strong relationship between high school athletic participation and subsequent intramural participation. These data also indicate well developed high school athletic programs for both sexes in the state of Iowa.

Table 4

Question 4: Did you participate in interschool athletics in high school?

Responses:	All Respondents N=539	Male N=317	Female N=215
Yes	70.9%	75.4%	63.3%
No	29.1%	24.6%	36.7%

Table 5 dealt with co-educational intramural sports participation. More females (63.3%) participated in co-rec sports than did males (50.8%) with over one-half of all respondents participating in this facet of the program. High school athletes tended to participate more than non-athletes in the co-ed sports. Later survey questions will show that females place emphasis on social contacts as a reason for intramural participation and co-rec participation would increase contact with the opposite sex. Almost two-thirds of all intramural participants identified in this survey indicated participation in this phase of the intramural program. This can be substantiated by intramural participation records which show the co-rec division to be one of the fastest growing parts of the program.

Table 5

Question 5: Have you participated in organized co-rec intramural sports?

Responses:	All Respondents N=539	Male N=317	Female N=215	H.S. Athlete N=382	Non-Athlete N=151
Yes	56.0%	50.8%	63.3%	61.5%	43.7%
No	30.8%	37.5%	21.4%	31.7%	28.5%
No interest	12.2%	10.4%	14.9%	6.3%	27.8%

Table 6 summarizes terms that respondents felt described the Iowa State University Intramural Program as *they* perceived it. The terms most often circled were *fun, physical activity, recreation, competition. socialization, participation, emotional release, good, exciting* and *winning.* It was interesting to note that fun and physical activity were the two most common descriptive terms identified which are two of our stated objectives of the intramural program. Also of interest was the fact that females gave socialization a higher priority than other groups. Also, males put a high premium on competition—higher than any other group. This shows a difference in how males and females perceive the program and should be recognized in program planning.

Table 6

Question 6: Circle terms you feel describe the Iowa State University Intramural Program as you perceive it.

Responses:	All Respondents N = 539	Male N = 317	Female N = 215	H.S. Athlete N = 382	Non-Athlete N = 151
Competition	66.4%	72.2%	57.2%	69.9%	58.3%
Fun	80.0%	80.4%	79.1%	84.6%	68.9%
Emotional Release	41.9%	41.0%	42.3%	44.8%	35.8%
Winning	23.0%	27.8%	15.8%	25.4%	17.2%
Socialization	53.6%	46.1%	65.1%	52.4%	57.6%
Rigid	3.3%	4.4%	1.9%	3.7%	2.6%
Bad	1.5%	1.6%	1.4%	1.6%	1.3%
Exciting	24.9%	22.7%	26.5%	25.9%	21.9%
Innovative	9.5%	8.5%	11.2%	9.9%	8.6%
Physical Activity	79.8%	79.2%	80.5%	82.5%	74.2%
Recreation	71.8%	68.8%	76.7%	73.0%	69.5%
Frustration	7.6%	9.1%	5.6%	7.6%	8.0%
Participation	52.1%	50.2%	55.3%	53.7%	49.0%
Losing	5.6%	5.7%	5.1%	5.5%	6.0%
Flexible	10.2%	7.3%	14.4%	25.8%	10.6%
Good	38.4%	34.7%	43.7%	41.9%	31.1%
Indifferent	4.8%	5.0%	46.5%	2.1%	8.0%
Boring	2.0%	2.5%	1.4%	1.6%	3.3%
Repetitious	1.9%	2.8%	1.9%	1.6%	2.7%
Other					

Table 7 reflects reasons why respondents participated in intramurals. The most cited reason for all groups was *physical exercise* followed by *diversion from class/study* and *leisure time interest.* The next few reasons for participating exhibited some differences in the analyses groups. Almost twice as many males (46.7%) cited *competition* than did females (25.1%) and females cited *social contacts* as a reason for participating (49.3%) more often than the males (34.4%). As might be expected, high school athletes cited *competition* (47.1%) more than four times as often as high school non-athletes (13.8%). Males and high school athletes selected *display physical skill* at higher percentages (20.2%) and (19.4%) respectively than did females (8.4%) and non-athletes (6.0%). Males and ex-high school athletes also selected *to win* at higher percentages (26.8% and 25.4% respectively) than did females (12.1%) and non-athletes (9.9%). These data indicate that males and ex-high school athletes tend to compete more for *competition, display physical skill,* and *to win* when compared to females and non-athletes. This can be explained by males tending to be more competitive in sports than females[3] and that the high school athletes have the competitive experience which they desire to continue in the intramural program.

Table 7

Question 7: Circle reasons why you participate in intramurals.

Responses:	All Respondents N = 539	Male N = 317	Female N = 215	H.S. Athlete N = 382	Non-Athlete N = 151
Physical Exercise	74.2%	77.3%	69.3%	81.7%	56.3%
Competition	38.4%	46.7%	25.1%	47.1%	13.8%
Display Physical Skill	15.6%	20.2%	8.4%	19.4%	6.0%
Social Contacts	40.3%	34.4%	49.3%	42.2%	30.4%
To win	21.0%	26.8%	12.1%	25.4%	9.9%
To lose	1.9%	2.5%	0.5%	2.6%	0.0%
Diversion from class/study	52.5%	51.7%	53.0%	56.3%	43.7%
Leisure time interest	49.5%	49.5%	49.3%	55.5%	34.4%

Table 8 summarizes the respondents' judgement of the quality of Iowa State University intramural officiating. Most respondents indicated the officiating was *fair* with *good* being the next most frequent evaluation given. Females tended to rate officiating higher than did the males. This could be explained, in part, by the reduced stress on competition when compared to males as indicated in Table 7. Officiating was rated most often as *poor* by males (9.5%) and ex-high school athletes (10.0%). This could be explained by their earlier indicated goal of experiencing competition which would lead to higher expectations of intramural officiating in the competitive setting. When these higher expectations were not met by the intramural program, lower ratings of officials may have resulted. Also of the interest was the date on Table 9 which indicates that over 90% of all respondents had never officiated in the Iowa State University Intramural Program. Most respondents felt intramural officiating was fair-to-good but most were not interested in officiating.

Table 8

Question 8: What do you feel is the quality of intramural officiating at Iowa State University?

Respondents:	All Respondents N=539	Male N=317	Female N=215	H.S. Athlete N=382	Non-Athlete N=151
Bad	3.0%	3.5%	2.3%	3.1%	2.7%
Poor	8.2%	9.5%	6.5%	10.0%	3.3%
Fair	37.8%	42.3%	31.6%	39.8%	33.1%
Good	34.0%	29.0%	40.5%	34.6%	33.8%
Excellent	2.6%	3.2%	1.9%	2.9%	2.0%
0	14.5%	4.7%	4.7%	9.7%	25.2%

Two open-ended write-in questions were listed as the last two questions in the questionnaire. These questions were analyzed by hand. The first question asked how intramural at Iowa State could be best improved. The write-in response with the highest frequency (n = 61) related to improvement of officiating. Comments on this topic usually included indicating dissatisfaction with the proficiency of officials that officials needed more extensive training. The comment with the second highest frequency (n = 46) concerned publicity for intramural programs and scheduling information. Respondents indicated that more communication was needed so that they would be better informed concerning program operation. Other comments which appeared in this section included the following: de-emphasis on competition, no tournament games (n = 22), more games to play or more games before tournaments (n = 15), increased efforts to publicize and organize students living off-campus for intramural participation (n = 15), more facilities to reduce crowding (n = 14), better times to play games—too late at night (n = 12) and better scheduling—classification of teams, reduce forfeits (n = 10).

The second write-in question asked what new sports or activities the respondents would like to see added to the program. The sport listed most frequently was baseball (n = 6) with other responses ranging from boxing to rodeo bronc riding. Other than baseball, no other sport or activity was mentioned more than two or three times.

Conclusions

1. Most Iowa State University students have "heard something about" (95.7%) and/or participated in (77.4%) the Intramural Program.
2. Ex-high school athletes tend to participate at higher rates than ex-high school non-athletes.
3. The competitive intramural sports experience was sought by 60% of the survey respondents. More males than females and more ex-high school athletes than non-athletes desired the competitive experience.

4. A high percentage of survey respondents (70.9%) and intramural program participants took part in interschool athletics in high school. More males participated in high school athletics than did female respondents.
5. Over one-half of all respondents participated in co-rec sports. More females surveyed participated in co-rec sports than males.
6. Respondents perceive the Iowa State University Intramural Program as follows: (in descending order of frequency): fun, physical activity, recreation, competition, socialization, participation, emotional release, good, exciting, and winning.
7. Respondents indicated they particpated for the following reasons (listed in descending order of frequency): physical exercise, division from class/study, leisure-time interests, competition, social contracts, display physical skill and to win. Males and ex-high school athletes participated for the competition more often than females and ex-high school non-athletes respectively. Females participated for social contacts more frequently than males.
8. Most respondents felt intramural officiating was fair-good. Females rated officiating better than did males. Males and ex-high school athletes rated officiating as poor more often than other groups.
9. Most respondents had not officiated in the Intramural Program.
10. Most suggestions for program imnprovements written in identified the following areas of concern: officiating, better publicity-information dissemination, reduction of competitiveness, more information and organization for off-campus students, more games planned before tournaments, additional facilities needed, and games scheduled at more convenient times.

BIBLIOGRAPHY

[1]Maas, Gerry. Survey of Iowa State University Students Concerning Intramural Sports Related Interests. *NATIONAL INTRAMURAL ASSOCIATION CONFERENCE PROCEEDINGS*, 26:206-214.

[2]Rokosz, Francis M. Changing Sport, Changing Man. *NATIONAL INTRAMURAL RECREATIONAL SPORTS ASSOCIATION JOURNAL*, Vol. 2(1):42-46, 1977.

[3]Rokosz, Francis M and Louis Fabian. A Study of the Attitudes and Motivations for Play of Intramural Sports Participants. *NATIONAL INTRAMURAL-RECREATIONAL SPORTS ASSOCIATION JOURNAL*. Vol. 2(21):10-13, 1978.

[4]Van Hoff, Johannes, J. Creating an Atmosphere in Intramurals. *NATIONAL INTRAMURAL-RECREATIONAL SPORTS ASSOCIATION PROCEEDINGS*, 27:103-108, 1976.

Table 9

Question 9: Have you ever officiated in the Iowa State University Intramural Program?

	All Respondents N=539	Male N=317	Female N=215	H.S. Athlete N=382	Non-Athlete N=151
Responses:					
Yes	5.2%	4.7%	4.7%	6.8%	1.3%
No	92.6%	94.6%	96.7%	91.4%	96.0%

Table 10

Question 10: Write in questions—How can Iowa State intramurals be best improved?

	All Respondents N=539	Male N=317	Female N=215	H.S. Athlete N=382	Non-Athlete N=151
% comments	49.7%	53.3%	44.2%	54.5%	36.4%

Table 11

Question 11: Write in question—What new sports or activities would you like to see added to the Iowa State University Intramural Program?

	All Respondents N=539	Male N=317	Female N=215	H.S. Athlete N=382	NOn-Athlete N=151
% comments	28.9%	32.8%	23.3%	30.1%	26.5%

WHY DO THEY PARTICIPATE?
A Marketing Study of Intramurals

by Keith Mah, Ian McGregor, Robert G, Wyckham,
Simon Fraser University

INTRODUCTION

The problem of increasing the number of participants in an Intramurals program at a university or college is a familiar one to most Intramural administrators. The National Intramural-Recreational Sports Association (NIRSA) has addressed this problem at a number of their annual conferences, most recently, under such topics as 'Promoting Intramurals' (1972, 1973), 'Focus on Media in Intramurals' (1974), and 'Public Relations' (1976)[6]

Although many papers on the problems of increasing Intramural participation have been published, only one has shown the importance of applying the principles of marketing to the development and promotion of Intramurals. Peterson[1] described how marketing theory can help the Intramural administrator encourage participation in his programs. Using the framework developed by Kotler[3], Peterson[6] examined four broad areas of marketing management theory and the implications for the Intramural administrator. The areas are: conceptualizing marketing management; analyzing marketing opportunities; organizing for marketing; and planning the market program. Today, marketing theory is being applied in almost every field to develop and promote various products and services. The purpose of this paper is to demonstrate the practical application of marketing principles to the development and promotion of Intramurals by outlining a marketing study.

MARKETING INTRAMURALS

Marketing Intramurals is not simply selling Intramurals. Rather, it is a total concept incorporating, among other things (1) the analysis of the Intramurals market; (2) the organization for effective marketing of Intramurals; (3) the planning of the marketing program for Intramurals; and (4) the controlling of the marketing effort. Most importantly, marketing Intramurals requires a *participant orientation*. That is, the aim of marketing Intramurals is to analyze, organize, plan and control for the purpose of generating participant satisfaction. The successful marketing of Intramurals is particularly difficult because of the intangibility of what the participant "gets out" of participating. Intramurals are not products which can be put on a shelf and displayed, nor are they a service where someone performs some function to meet the customer's request. Intramurals are actually opportunities for the participant to experience; they provide for the active participation of the individual, rather than the passive consumption of products or services. The participant does not "receive" a floor hockey game, he engages in an experience, and receives excitement, physical exertion, or fun.

Therefore, analyzing the market to determine the underlying motives of participants is crucial to the development of an effective marketing plan for the promotion of Intramurals.

ANALYSIS OF THE INTRAMURALS MARKET

The analysis of the Intramurals market is essentially (1) defining the market; (2) gathering information on the market; and (3) segmenting the market.

1. Market Definition

The Intramurals market has been defined as all faculty, staff, and currently enrolled students, both undergraduate and graduate, who are actual or potential participants. Alumni are also included, but on a conditional basis, that is, they are permitted to participate only if space is available after currently enrolled students have had a chance to register. The immediate market totals almost 10,000; about 8,600 students, 520 faculty and almost 900 staff members. Participant rates for the Spring, 1977 semester are as follows: students 16.2%; faculty 8.3%; staff 17.4%; all males 24.4%; all females 4.9%; all participants 15.6%. [These are real participant figures, not participation figures, calculated by McGregor's computer method (1977)].

2. Data Collection

Gathering information on the market refers to the collection of data pertaining to participants and non-participants. As mentioned earlier, the central orientation in market theory is consumer satisfaction, or in this instance, participant satisfaction. In other words, the Department of Recreation can best achieve its goals by being cognizant of the needs and desires of the participants and potential participants and by developing programs with a view toward satisfying those needs and desires. Consequently, it is essential that information be gathered to allow a greater understanding of actual and potential participants. The Intramural market survey, which will be described in more detail below, was designed to gather the following information: the characteristics of participants and non-participants, sources of information used by participants and non-participants; the reasons why some participate and others do not; and, the attitudes of members of the university community toward Intramurals and related activities.

3. Market Segmentation

Market segmentation is a key feature of marketing planning. It facilitates the analysis of the market by grouping individuals sharing common characteristics into smaller, more comprehensible units. At the same time, it provides specific market targets for which Intramural activities can be designed and for which specific promotional campaigns can be tailored.

There are various ways to segment a market. For instance, the market can be segmented by demographic variables such as, faculty, staff, students, sex and age. Or by behavioural variables such as expressed reasons for participating, (to be with friends, to compete, or to have fun), or, by the expressed reasons for not participating (lack of skill, job, or intimidation). Another method of market segmentation is to use volume variables, such as heavy, medium, and light participation based on the number of activities played during the course of a semester, or the number of times a participant actually turns out to play. The method used to segment a market is dependent upon the characteristics of the market and the objectives of the study.

There are two distinct benefits of market segmentation. First, it provides a better perspective from which to identify marketing opportunities. That is, by examining the needs of each segment and comparing them to the needs that are currently being satisfied, the areas of the Intramurals program which can be developed to accommodate those segments which are not being satisfied adequately can be identified. Second, market segmentation allows finer adjustments to Intramural activities and promotional appeals. Rather than one promotional program aimed at everyone, separate programs can be created which can be tailored to meet the needs of the different segments.

INTRAMURAL MARKETING SURVEY

Objectives

The overall objective of the Intramural marketing survey was to gather specific information on participants and non-participants for the purpose of designing a marketing plan for Intramurals. Specific objectives were as follows:

(1) To determine the demographic characteristics of Intramural participants.

(2) To determine the sources of information used by participants and non-participants to learn of Intramural activities.

(3) To determine the reasons why individuals participate or do not participate in Intramurals.

(4) To determine the attitude of Intramural participants and non-participants toward:
   a) the value of physical activity and exercise;
   b) competition in Intramurals;
   c) skill level in Intramurals;
   d) Varsity athletes;
   e) the current administration and management of Intramurals; and
   f) a separate Intramurals program for faculty and staff.

(5) To determine the degree of satisfaction participants have with the current Intramurals program.

Survey Method

To gather the required data, a stratified random sample of 2,000 persons was taken from the University population. The list of potential respondents was compiled from undergraduate and graduate student listings and administration mailing lists of faculty and staff. A table of random numbers was used to generate the sample. Questionnaires were sent to 1,000 students, 375 faculty and 625 staff members.

The respondents selected were mailed a questionnaire entitled "Intramurals Survey" (Appdx. 1). The questionnaire contained two rank-order questions dealing with reasons why an individual may or may not participate in Intramurals; 21 rating-scale items dealing with attitudes toward physical activity, exercise, Intramurals in general, control of Intramurals, competition, skill level, and a separate faculty/staff program; and questions dealing with awareness of Intramural activities, sources of information and selected demographic characteristics.

The items for the rank-order and rating scale questions were developed from a pilot study conducted during the Summer Semester, 1977. The pilot study included an unstructured questionnaire, face-to-face interviews with selected individuals, and extensive discussions with administrative and management personnel in the Department of Recreation.

Most questions were structured (close-ended) to restrict the range of response and for ease of computer coding. One question dealing with weekend Intramurals was open-ended and space was provided for comments.

The questionnaires were mailed to the respondents' homes along with a covering letter outlining the purpose of the survey and an appeal for their cooperation. A return-addressed envelope with first class postage was included with the questionnaire. Questionnaires were mailed during the third week of November, 1977; the cut-off date for receipt was December 15, 1977.

SURVEY RESULTS

The present paper will discuss results in 3 areas; demographic characteristics; information sources; and reasons for participating and not participating.

(1) Demographic Characteristics

Four hundred and fifty-six usable questionnaires were received by the cut-off date, a response rate of 22.8%. It can be seen from Table 1 below that the sample is quite similar to the population in terms of proportions by sex. However, in the sample, students are greatly under-represented and faculty and staff are much over-represented. Age data on the university community are not available for comparison.

Table 1. Demographic Characteristics of the Sample and the Population

	Sample		Population	
Sex	#	%	#	%
Male	254	55.7	5606	56.1
Female	195	42.8	4380	43.8
No Data	7	1.5	— —	— —
	456	100%	9986	100%
Status				
Students	212	46.5	8586	85.9
Faculty	84	18.4	521	5.2
Staff	157	34.4	879	8.8
No Data	3	.7	— —	— —
	456	100%	9986	100%
Age				
24 yrs. & under	156	34.2	NA	NA
25-36 years	163	35.7	NA	NA
37 yrs. & older	137	30.0	NA	NA
	456	100%		

NA = not available

Intramural participation by the sample is outlined in Table 2. As one might expect, in view of the interest in the topic of the survey, a larger proportion of the sample, 33.8%, were Intramural participants than is reflected in the Spring, 1977 total participation rate, 15.6%[1]. Members of the sample who are classified as participants tended to be male, twenty-five years and older, students and staff. Non-participants were more likely to be female, younger and students.

Table 2. Participation of the Sample.

	Participants		Non-Participants	
Sex	#	%	#	%
Male	109	70.8	145	48.0
Female	42	27.3	153	50.6
No Data	3	1.9	4	1.3
	154	100%	302	100%
Status				
Students	58	37.7	154	50.9
Faculty	34	22.1	50	16.6
Staff	61	39.6	96	31.8
No Data	1	.6	2	.7
	154	100%	302	100%
Age				
24 yrs. & under	40	25.9	116	38.4
25-36 years	64	41.6	99	32.8
37 yrs. & older	50	32.5	87	28.8
	154	100%	302	100%

(2) Information Sources

Respondants were asked how they found out about Intramural activities at SFU. As is shown in Table 3 below, interpersonal communication is the most important intramural information source for participants. Most non-participants are apparently outside of the personal communication network which discusses Intramurals. Intramural booklets, describing up-coming activities, are the second most influential source of information for participants; only a minority of non-participants report these booklets as a usual way of finding out about Intramurals.

Non-participants were more likely than participants to learn about Intramurals from the *Peak*, the campus newspaper, or from the weekly administration newsletter, *SFU Week*.

The data in Table 3 suggest that the limited resources be applied to those media which appear to be most valuable. That is, Intramural booklets and posters for participants, and posters, the *Peak* and *SFU Week* for non-participants.

Table 3. Information Sources about Intramural Activities—All Respondents

Information Sources	Participants (%)	Non-Participants (%)	Statistically Significant Difference*
Friends	59.1	24.8	YES
Intramural Booklet	46.1	20.9	YES
Posters	38.3	41.7	ZNS
SFU Week	30.5	36.1	NS
Peak	27.9	41.4	YES
Bulletin Boards	27.3	27.2	NS
Recreation Booth	15.6	10.9	NS
Recreation Reports	14.3	7.3	YES
Intramurals Office	9.1	2.3	YES
CSFU Radio	2.6	1.0	NS
Other	0.6	1.7	NS
n =	154	320	

*Statistical Significance: Chi square test; YES = 0.5; NS = 0.5

Students.

For student participants, friends are a highly important information source as are the Intramural booklets. Compared to the total sample, posters and the campus newspaper are more important to students, but *SFU Week* is less important.

It appears that the best way to communicate to non-participating students is by means of posters, bulletin boards, and the *Peak* newspaper.

Table 4. Information Sources about Intramural Activities — Students

Information Sources	Participants (%)	Non-Participants (%)	Statistically Significant Difference*
Friends	65.5	30.5	YES
Intramural Booklets	65.5	19.5	YES
Posters	44.8	46.8	NS
Peak	36.2	45.5	NS
Bulletin Boards	32.8	29.9	NS
Reception Booth	24.1	18.8	NS
SFU Week	24.1	22.7	NS
Recreation Reports	12.1	0.6	YES
Intramurals Office	12.1	2.6	YES
CSFU Radio	1.7	1.9	NS
Other	— —	1.3	NS
n =	58	154	

*Statistical Significance: Chi square test; YES = 0.5; NS = 0.5

Faculty.

The top three information sources for faculty who participate are identical to those used by participating students. In addition, *SFU Week* is more important as a way to get to faculty.

SFU Week, posters and the *Peak* appear to be good media to reach non-participating faculty.

Table 5. Information Sources about Intramural Activities — Faculty

Information Sources	Participants (%)	Non-Participants (%)	Statistically Significant Difference*
Friends	55.9	14.0	YES
Intramural Booklets	38.2	10.0	YES
Posters	32.4	36.0	NS
SFU Week	29.4	40.0	NS
Bulletin Boards	17.6	18.0	NS
Peak	11.8	34.0	YES
Recreation Reports	5.9	2.0	NS
Intramurals Office	11.8	2.0	NS
Recreation Booth	5.9	2.0	NS
CSFU Radio	— —	— —	NS
Other	2.9	2.0	NS
n =	34	50	

*Statistical Significance: Chi square test; YES = 0.5; NS = 0.5

Staff.

As with the other sub-samples, personal communication with friends is the most important information source for staff who participate. *SFU Week* is a more important medium to staff than to faculty or students, while posters come third. The top three information sources for non-participating staff are *SFU Week,* the Peak, and posters.

Table 6. Information Sources about Intramural Activities— Staff

Information Sources	Participants (=)	Non-Participants (=)	Statistically Significant Difference*
Friends	55.7	21.9	YES
SFU Week	36.1	56.3	YES
Posters	34.4	36.5	NS
Intramural Booklets	32.8	29.2	NS
Peak	27.9	39.6	NS
Bulletin Boards	26.2	27.1	NS
Recreation Reports	21.3	20.8	NS
Recreation Booth	13.1	3.1	YES
Intramural Office	4.9	2.1	NS
CSFU Radio	4.9	— —	NS
Other	— —	2.1	NS
n =	50	87	

*Statistical Significance: Chi square test; YES = 0.5; NS = 0.5

Tables 3 through 6 indicate that the same set of media are most appropriate for communicating with the three market segments of participants, i.e., students, faculty and staff. However, some difference in emphasis is suggested. While the Intramural Booklets do a good job of reaching faculty and students, they are less useful for staff. *SFU Week* is a much more important vehicle to reach staff members and the *Peak* is better for speaking to students.

Posters and the *Peak* appear to be the best ways to communicate with all non-participants. Another good way to get information to non-participating students is bulletin boards. Non-participating staff and faculty can best be reached by *SFU Week.*

(3) Reasons for Intramural Participation

Respondents were asked to put eight possible reasons for intramural participation in order from most to least likely. As is shown in table 7 below, exercise, fun and friends are the primary reasons for participating. Learning new skills, competing and low costs are the least important reasons.

There are some interesting differences in the responses of participants and non-participants. Fun is number one in the minds of participants, while

188

exercise is the top reason for non-participants. Social reasons are more important for non-participants, i.e., getting together with friends and meeting people. Participants rank tension-release a good deal higher than non-participants. Both participants and non-participants agree on the three reasons ranked lowest.

Table 7. Hypothetical Reasons for Participating in Intramurals—All Respondents

Reasons	All respondents Rank Order	Participants Rank Order	Non-Participants Rank Order
To get some exercise	1	2	1
To have fun	2	1	2
To get together with friends	3	4	3
To release tension	4	3	5
To meet people	5	5	4
To learn new skills/games	6	6	6
To compete	7	7	7
Costs are low	8	8	8

Question: The following list contains 8 possible "reasons" why an individual may participate in Intramurals. Please rank these "reasons" from most likely to least likely.

Messages designed to attract participants to continue their intramural activity should likely stress different things than should communications designed to encourage non-participants to get involved. An enjoyable way to get exercise and release tension would seem the most appealing to participants. In addressing non-participants, it may be more important to put the fun and exercise in a social setting.

Low cost is given the lowest rating, indicating that the fee variable is not of great concern to either participants or non-participants.

The data suggest that consideration be given to the design and management of intramural activities for individual market segments. Activities developed specifically for the orientation of non-participants may be successful in broadening the market.

Students-Faculty-Staff.

Although there is a good deal of similarity, there are some interesting differences in the rank orders of reasons given by the three market segments. Among participants, faculty rank tension release lower than do students and staff; faculty surprisingly rank competition much higher than do students and staff; staff members give slightly higher priority to learning games skills than do faculty or students (Table 8).

Among non-participants, faculty rate tension release higher than do staff and students; students give a higher ranking to meeting people compared to staff and faculty.

189

The survey results suggest that further refinement of intramural activities should be investigated. For example, should more competitive based activities be offered to participating faculty? Should more socially oriented activities be developed for non-participating students and staff?

It seems wise to bear in mind the relative importance of the various reasons for participating when preparing communications for each of the market segments. For example, low cost and skill learning do not appear to be factors of great importance to any of the sub-markets.

Reasons for Non-Participation

The respondents were also asked to rank order of number of possible reasons for non-participation. For presentation in Table 9 below, data on two reasons were removed (part or full time job takes up spare time; must study and/or attend classes) because they seemed to relate almost exclusively to students.

Table 9. Hypothetical Reasons for Not Participating in Intramurals — All Respondents

Reasons	All Respondents Rank Order	Participants Rank Order	Non-Participants Rank Order
Would rather do other things	1	1	1
Lack of skill	2	2	3
Unfamiliar with Intramurals	3	4	2
Not competitive	4	3	4
Intimidated by people who frequent sports facilities	5	5	5
Poor scheduling of Intramurals	6	7	6
Not interested in exercise	7	6	7
Costs are high	8	8	8

Question: The following contains 10 possible "reasons" why an individual may not participate in Intramurals. Please rank these "reasons" from most likely to least likely.

For the whole sample, the reasons ranked highest were: rather do other things; lack of skill; unfamiliar with Intramurals. Lowest rated reasons were: poor scheduling; not interested in exercise; high costs.

It seems appropriate to pay attention to the reasons for non-participation given by those who are not involved in Intramurals. Participants and non-participants rank the same four reasons in the top four; however, non-participants rank lack of skill and non-competitive lower and unfamiliar with Intramurals higher.

Non-participants who prefer other activities are probably the least fruitful market to attempt to reach. However, those who are unfamiliar may be

Table 8. Hypothetical Reasons for Participating in Intramurals—Students, Faculty and Staff.

	STUDENTS		FACULTY		STAFF	
	Participants	Non-Participants	Participants	Non-Participants	Participants	Non-Participants
Reasons	Rank Order	Rank Order	Rank Order	Rank Order	Rank Order	Rank Order
To have fun	1	2	1	2	2	2
To get some exercise	2	1	2	1	1	1
To release tension	3	5	5	3	3	4
To get together with friends	4	4	5	4	4	5
To meet people	5	3	6	5	6	6
To learn new skills/ games	6	6	7	6	5	5
To compete	7	7	4	7	7	7
Costs are low	8	8	8	8	8	8

made familiar and those who perceive of themselves as lacking in skill or not oriented to competition may be shown that there are programs which do not require skills and are not competitive.

Students.

A commendable orientation to scholastic endeavours and work commitments are the two top ranked possible reasons for not participating identified by both participants and non-participants.

Although those with jobs may be beyond the reach of intramurals, the scholarly minded may not be. Demonstrations of increased study efficiency resulting from exercise may result in more Intramural participants.

Table 10. Hypothetical Reasons for Not Participating in Intramurals—Students

Reasons	Participants Rank Order	Non-Participants Rank Order
Must study and/or attend classes	1	1
Part or full-time job takes up spare time	2	2
Would rather do other things	3	5
Intimidated by the people who frequent sports facilities	4	6
Not competitive	5	7
Lack of skill	6	4
Unfamiliar with Intramurals	7	3
Poor scheduling of Intramurals	8	8
Not interested in exercise	9	10
Costs are high	10	9

Also, students who are unfamiliar with the program or those who see themselves as lacking in skill may be attracted. It is noteworthy that non-participating students give a low rank to not competitive and not interested in exercise.

Faculty and Staff.

Data in Table 11 below indicate considerable similarity in response from faculty and staff members. Some small differences, however, are evident: participating faculty rank unfamiliar with Intramurals lower, and not competitive and not interested in exercise higher than do staff members.

Non-participating staff and faculty rate not interested in exercise considerably lower as a reason for not participating than do their participating colleagues. Those active in Intramurals give slightly lower ranks to unfamiliar with Intramurals and intimidated by people who frequent the sports facilities.

Table 11. Hypothetical Reasons for Not Participating in Intramurals—Faculty/Staff

| | Faculty | | Staff | |
| | Participants | Non-Partic. | Participants | Non-Partic. |
Reasons	Rank Order	Rank Order	Rank Order	Rank Order
Would rather do other things	1	1	1	1
Lack of skill	2	2	2	3
Not competitive	3	3	4	4
Not interested in exercise	4	7	5	7
Unfamiliar with Intramurals	5	4	3	2
Intimidated by people who frequent sports facilities	6	5	7	5
Poor scheduling of Intramurals	7	6	6	6
Costs are high	8	8	8	8

What students of marketing call "product adjustment" was suggested earlier on the basis of the respondents' reasons for participating in Intramurals. Some refinement is also indicated on the basis of the reasons for not participating. Activities designed to be fun, provide exercise and which are perceived by non participants to require little or no skill and are not competitive should be examined. Perhaps in cooperation with the Kinesiology Department, it may be possible to develop demonstrations of increased study capability resulting from Intramural fun. Non-participants may be attracted to exercise through intellectual curiosity and motivation for higher grades.

Costs and scheduling do not appear to be critical in increasing market penetration.

Communication of Intramural activities should recognize the relative importance to the various sub-markets of reasons for not participating as well the reasons for participating. This is especially important for messages prepared for non-participants.

SUMMARY OF RESULTS

Information Sources:

1. For participants, communication through friends is the most powerful means of spreading Intramural information for students, faculty and staff. The second and third most effective methods are, in general, the Intramural Booklet and posters. The student newspaper is more effective for students, while the administration newsletter reaches more faculty and staff.

2. Non-participants are not reached through the buddy network, but rather through posters and the two campus publications—the student newspaper and the administration newsletter.

193

Reasons for Intramural Participation

1. Exercise, fun, and getting together with friends are the three primary reasons for participating in Intramurals; learning skills, competing and low costs are the least important reasons.

2. Participants rank fun as the number one reason for participating, ahead of exercise, while for non-participants, the order is reversed.

3. Social reasons for participating are more important for non-participants than participants, while tension release is less important.

4. Some interesting differences for participating exist between students, faculty and staff.

Reasons for Non-Participation

1. For the whole sample, the three main reasons for not participating are: rather do other things, lack of skill, and unfamiliar with Intramurals. Lowest rated reasons are poor scheduling, not interested in exercise, and high costs.

2. For students, the reasons studying/attending classes and working ranked ahead of the above three main reasons.

INTRAMURAL MARKETING STRATEGY

The major ingredient of the marketing concept is the consumer orientation. Applying marketing to Intramurals means that we do not measure success in terms of budgets, size of staff, numbers of programs, or quality of equipment but in the numbers of satisfied participants. A particularly meaningful refinement of this measure of success is share-of-market. That is, out of the total number of people in the university community, what proportion do we satisfactorily serve. The application of market segmentation, i.e., breaking the total university population into meaningful groups, adds to the value of this measure.

To apply marketing to Intramurals requires information about the market to be served. The survey results described above outline some of the data now available to be used in developing a marketing program for Intramurals at Simon Fraser University. Those responsible for Intramurals should analyze this data and additional information using the following marketing planning paradigm.

1. *Objectives*. For each of the market segments, set precise objectives to be reached by some particular date. For example, increase penetration of faculty by five percentage points by the end of the fall semester, 1978.

2. *Strategy*. Develop plans of action to reach the objectives identified above. Utilizing the data from the survey, and other information, analyze:

    a) Product: Evaluate each Intramural activity, and the program in total. Adjust the set of activities to better meet the needs of various segments of the market. For example, redesign co-ed volleyball placing greater emphasis on social aspects.

b) Fee Structure: No fees are currently charged for Intramurals; the participants' costs are for lockers, gymnasium membership, and gym strip only. Consideration might be given to small fees to fund activities more attractive to particular segments of the university community. For example, a modest fee might be charged for co-ed volleyball to pay for social events.

c) Place: Examine the various locations on campus where Intramural activity takes place. Where possible, on the basis on the survey responses from each market segment, adjust locations to make activities more attractive. In addition, give consideration to the need for any schedule changes. For example, design staff-oriented activities for the noon-hour and after 4:30 p.m. in the new multi-purpose area to be located near the administration building.

d) Promotion: On the basis of the needs of each market segment, design a communications mix including:

  i) media

  ii) message

  iii) frequency

For example, prepare a campaign to attract non-participating staff members utilizing *SFU Week*, the *Peak*, and posters. Design the message to portray Intramurals as a fun way to get exercise with your friends. Schedule the campaign to begin two weeks prior to the beginning of the fall semester, pushing the concept. Encourage staff registration just before the students return.

3. *Results.* Design a monitoring system to gather data on the results of the above strategies. The data to be collected by market segment.

4. *Planning Cycle.* Compare the results achieved with the objectives set. Set up a planning cycle to allow sufficient time to determine new objectives and strategies for the next time period.

BIBLIOGRAPHY

[1]Engel, J. F., D. T. Kollat, and R. D. Blackwell. *Consumer Behavior,* 2nd ed. New York: Holt, Rinehart and Winston, Inc., 1973.

[2]Engel, J. F., Hugh G. Wales, and Martin R. Warshaw. *Promotional Strategy,* 3rd ed. Homewood, Ill.: Richard D. Irwin, Inc., 1975.

[3]Kotler, Philip. *Marketing Management: Analysis, Planning, and Control,* 2nd ed., Englewood Cliffs, N.J.: Prentice-Hall, Inc., 1972.

[4]McGregor, I. *Computer Statistics and Records for Intramurals and Other Recreation Programs.* NIRSA Proceedings, 1977, pp. 286-300.

[5]Peterson, James A. *Marketing the Intramural Product: Tools and Techniques.* A paper presented at the annual meeting of AAHPER, Anaheim, California, March, 1974.

[6]Peterson, James A. "Marketing Theory: Implications for Intramural Administration". *Intramural Administration: Theory and Practice.* Peterson, James A., ed., Englewood Cliff, N.J.: Prentice-Hall, Inc., 1976.

[7]*Proceedings of the Annual NIRSA* (previously NIA) *Conferences.* 1972 through 1976.

[8]Zaltman, G. and P. C. Burger. *Marketing Research: Fundamentals and Dynamics.* Hinsdale, Ill.: The Dryden Press, 1975.

FOOTNOTES

[1]These two rates of participation are calculated differently. The rate for a semester includes only those who were active during that period. For purposes of the survey, a participant was defined as an individual who has participated in past semesters. Hence, one would expect the survey participation rate to be higher.

GROUP COMPATIBILITY AND PRODUCTIVITY IN COMPETITIVE TEAM SPORT GROUPS

by Rich Marcks, University of Kansas

Introduction

In the study of the organization and function of work groups, the factors of productivity, satisfaction, structure and compatibility are often identified as concepts which play a significant role in the description of such groups. Productivity is a factor of primary concern in industrial study as profit and loss command the attention of the economic sector. Satisfaction and compatibility appear in the human relations literature with an emphasis on people orientation and improving the quality of life. The concept of structure frequently appears in the literature of both areas, particularly when contingency analysis is present.

This study is concerned with the utilization of the body of knowledge concerning these concepts as they relate to a population of small groups that are not traditionally identified within the literature and theory of work groups. Sport groups, either recreational or professional teams have not been considered wtihin the literature probably due to a limited interpretation of the definition of "work." It is the purpose of this paper to address two basic questions:

1. Can sport groups such as recreational teams be considered in the same theoretical manner as industrial, cultural or social groups with respect to a contingency approach?
2. Can productivity (success) of recreational sport teams be predicted according to parameters of compatibility and cohesion, disregarding skill level?

In the attack on the concept of sport as a character building process, sport psychologists Ogilvie and Tutko[14] suggested that the personality of the athlete is not molded but rather comes out of a ruthless selection process that occurs at all levels of sport. The phenomenon of "selective mortality" identifies the traits of athletes who survive the high attrition as: 1) a great need for achievement and a tendency to set high but realistic goals; 2) highly organized, orderly, respectful of authority, and dominant; 3) a large capacity for trust, great psychological endurance, self-control, low resting levels of anxiety and a slightly greater ability to express aggression. Morgan's[10] review of the literature on Sport Psychology as an emerging discipline indicates that athletes differ from non-athletes in various ways and that high level competitors appear quite stable in their profiles. Morgan also reports that the evidence suggests most athletic groups are comprised of extroverts. It must be kept in mind that this review refers to "athletic" groups in terms of intercollegiate varsity or professional level. Dealing with a population with a broader background in physical education, Werner and Gottheil[20] examined personality profiles of 340 new cadets at the United States Military Academy, 116 of which were classified as non-participants in high school athletics. All cadets were required to participate in varsity or intramural sports in addition to extensive physical training. Testing all cadets on the Cattell 16 PF showed that the diversity in scores on entrance remained unchanged over four years at the Academy; that is, athletic participation did not have a "molding" effect.

Generally speaking, the literature suggests that there are identifiable differences that exist between athlete and non-athlete and that the demands of highly competitive sport facilitate a process of survival of the fittest. Perhaps these differences can be just as important to success in sport as motor skill.

These predispositions to competitive success may account in part for the variety of attitudes individuals hold toward physical activity. Webb[19] adds that background factors such as religious orientation and father's occupation become increasingly important in the development of those attitudes as students grow older, and that an emphasis on success through skill replaces the equity factor which is more noticeable at earlier stages. Among students, grades 3 to 12, Webb evaluated professionalization of attitudes toward play (Figure 1) according to value preferences for factors of skill, equity, and victory as they relate to playing a game. Also using Webb's instrument, Zeisner[21] found that full participants in a college Intramural program have higher professional orientation than the general student population. Zeisner intimated that many Intramural programs cater to individuals with "professional" orientations toward sport, suggesting a redirection of resources toward non-competitive programs. This comment more gently parallels Webb's charge that it is moronic to continue to insist upon the contribution of competitive sports to the development of "sweetheart" characteristics of honor and courage and the like.

FIGURE 1—Webb's Questionnaire of Professionalization[19]

> What do you think is most important in playing a game?
> Number of items below from 1 to 3, starting
> with the one you think is MOST important[1],
> and finishing with the one you think is
> LEAST important[3] . . .
>
> ____to play it as well as you are able
> ____to beat your opponent
> ____to play it fairly

FIGURE 2—Table of Permutations[19]

Play Orientation			Professional Orientation		
1	2	3	4	5	6
fair	fair	play	play	beat	beat
play	beat	fair	beat	fair	play
beat	play	beat	fair	play	fair

Kenyon[5] describes an attitude inventory with six dimensions for characterizing physical activity: social experience, health and fitness, pursuit of vertigo, aesthetic experience, catharsis, and to meet a physical challenge. These dimensions closely resemble the classification of games by Caillois[2] which distinguishes between competition, change, mimicry, and vertigo, each one having a range of intensity from diversion and free improvisation to a taste for gratuitous difficulty.

In a college environment it is not difficult for individuals to come into contact wiht a variety of ideas and attitudes. Newcomb[12] points out that, along with pre-college acquaintance and propinquinty of residence, similarity of attitudes is a factor of primary importance in the selection process of peer group formation. The importance to individuals of group supported attitudes leads to greater solidarity as the individual yields to the group's power over one's own attitudes. Libo refers to a characteristic similar to solidarity which he calls cohesiveness, defined as the attraction of a group for its members. He states that "the power of a group to induce change in its members, in fact, varies directly with the group attractiveness." Studying blue collar work groups at the Northern Electric London Plant in London, Ontario, Mikalachi[9] sought to identify the concept of Group Cohesion, the conditions that facilitate its development, and the effect it has on such values as tension, absenteeism, and level of productivity. Mikalachi identified:

1. Task Groups: focus of integration about the job goals for which the group was ostensibly formed.
2. Social Groups: focus of integration about a social goal.
3. Protective Task Groups: focus about a work goal so as to protect the group from undue influence by other groups.
4. Protective Social Groups: focus about non-work goals for distinction and perceived prestigious status.

Productivity in high cohesive groups was a function of the focus of integration. Task groups produced higher than social groups. In low cohesive groups productivity varied with the relationship between supervisors and group members. Compatible situations yielded higher productivity.

One now sees the introduction of another parameter that has been widely reported as influential over levels of productivity and satisfaction, that is, style of leadership. McGregor[8] promotes people oriented leadership styles as superior to task oriented styles. He accepts that effectiveness of authority as a means of control is dependent upon enforcement ability through punishment but that a limitation on effectiveness is the ability of alternative means of influence should authority fail. A more elaborate approach to leadership style is the description by Blake and Mouton[1] of a two dimensional scheme of managerial styles with the ordinate rising in concern for people and the abscissa rising in concern for production. The general nature of the presentation by Blake and Mouton is in favor of the style that seeks full utilization of human resources.

Returning to the concept of compatibility of groups, the hypothesis of Schutz[17] that if one is able to match individuals along the dimensions of three major need areas—affection, control and inclusion—the result will be compatibility which leads to more effective and thus more productive groups. Compatibility is achieved by matching two individuals who compliment each other. The lack of compatability in these areas can cause competition for position rather than devotion of time to ask requirements. Moos and Speisman[11], and Hewett, et al[4] offer studies in which subjects were assigned groups. Moos and Speisman formed groups according to control scores. Hewett matched individuals using Schutz's FIRO-B with the added dimension of person or task-oriented participatory leaders to groups. Both studies report that compatible groups had higher productivity than incompatible. But Hewett also indicates that it is necessary to take into account the way in which members are organized to complete the tasks.

Finally, two studies examine the effects of differing types of member compatibility, leadership styles and task structures upon productivity and member satisfaction in task oriented groups. Forming compatible overpersonal, compatible underpersonal and incompatible groups using FIRO-B, Larimer[6] found that all compatible groups did not produce higher than incompatible groups. Similarly, Downs and Pickett[3] obtained data contradictory to Schutz's theorem that "if the compatibility of one group, h, is greater than that of another group, m, then the productivity goal achievement of h will exceed that of m." The study viewed the interaction effectsof leadership style and groupings of people. The most productive group was that with the undesignated leader—compatible overpersonal profile. The results of these two studies suggests that a broader interpretatin of the term goal achievement is necessary. The low productivity levels of the compatible overpersonal groups seems to qualify them as a Social Group in the scheme of Mikalachi. The focus of integration was a goal about which they were not ostensibly organized. The satisfaction level of this group was the highest achieved in Downs and Pickett's study, indicating that Schutz's theorem is valid if satisfaction rather than productivity is identified as goal achievement.

With respect to sport groups and athletes, the terms stability, dominance and extrovert have been used to identify the high level competitor. Considering dominance and control desired as similar for the moment, one would suspect that a team composed of all typically high competition athletes would be incompatible. But with a professional orientation the measure of production must be considered as victory through beating one's opponent. Satisfaction is gained through victory and achievement. Thus a team with a professional orientation would be considered a Task Group by Mikalachi. At lower levels of competition, recreation teams could have either professional or play orientations to play. Each could have high levels of cohesion if the goal achievement were reached.

With respect to compatibility, one could hypothesize that, if skill levels were randomly distributed or reasonably homogeneous, then productivity could be predicted along the same contingencies of Downs and Pickett. The necessary predictive instruments would be a survey of team members on FIRO-B and identification of team leader and evaluation of leadership style. Productivity would be defined as the won-lost record for professionally oriented teams and cohesion for play oriented teams. Webb's instrument (Figure 1) would identify level of orientation according to the scale of Figure 2.

The Survey

The current study surveyed six Intramural teams participating in the 1976 University of Kansas Women's Volleyball League. Teams were randomly required to have the starting lineup (six players) complete two survey forms.
1. Group Cohesion. This questionnaire is patterned after the Seashore Scale[18] and scored in the same way. A high score is assumed to identify greater cohesion. Group Cohesion is the average of member scores.

2. FIRO-B This survey evaluates individuals along the dimensions of
the need areas of Control, Affection, and Inclusion.

Team Productivity was determined by a combined evaluation of Won-
Lost record and position reached in the Championship Tournament. The
team that advanced the furthest in the Tournament was determined most
productive. When discrimination by this measure was equivocal, the team
with the better Won-Lost record was determined to be more productive.

No attempt was made to identify group leaders or leadership styles nor an
attempt made to identify task orientation or level of skill for the teams.

Unlike previous laboratory studies, individuals were not assigned to compatible or incompatible groups, but were left in the natural setting. All
surveys were completed prior to the last match of the season. Each team had
completed three previous matches of three games per match. Four of
the six teams qualified for the Championship Tournament and played additional games until eliminated from the Tournament. Team B went on to
become the University of Kansas Intramural Champion.

Results

Table 1 presents the results of the data listed according to rank order of
Final Standing. Rank order correlations coefficients for each factor are listed
below each column.

Cohesion, affection and inclusion as predictors have not much more ability than chance. However, the control factor has a high predictive ability.
This could be related to Ogilvie and Tutko's description of dominance as a
requirement for survival in athletics. Suggesting that success is more likely
among teams whose members are collectively strong in desire for control.
Implications on other variables are not possible at this time.

TABLE 1

TEAM	FINAL STANDING (Productiv- ity Rank)	RECORD (Won-Lost)	RAW SCORES (RANK)			
			COHESION	CONTROL	AFFECT.	INC.
B	1	13-2	18.0 (1.5)	+14 (1)	76 (1)	94 (1)
E	2	9-5	15.0 (6)	+13 (2)	65 (4)	72 (2.5)
A	3	9-5	17.2 (3)	+1 (4)	64 (5)	69 (4.5)
F	4	8-6	18.0 (1.5)	+6 (3)	57 (6)	58 (6)
C	5	6-6	15.8 (5)	−3 (6)	70 (2)	72 (2.5)
D	6	5-7	16.8 (4)	−2 (5)	68 (3)	69 (4.5)
			r = .23	r = .89*	r = .14	r = .56

*significant at p = .01

Discussion

As a total package it does not seem difficult to incorporate the concept of sport into the contingency theory of organizational behavior. The major components of influence can be identified with a few minor extensions in the definition. Productivity can be defined in any number of ways according to the mountain of sport statistics, but the most logical method would be to consider competition as an assembly line operation on which workers are evaluated on a piecework criteria. Each game is a separate item on the line, and productivity is the total number or the percentage of games won. Satisfaction and Compatibility can be defined and measured in the same manner that current theory calls for. Task orientation could be enhanced by discriminating between Social and Task Groups. Goal achievement could then be presumed to vary from productivity for task groups to satisfaction for social groups. Cohesion may be a concept to consider as a measure of productivity or satisfaction. Style of leadership is perhaps the most difficult parameter to identify at this time primarily because of difficulty in determining the actual leader. Formal teams generally have two types of assigned leaders, the non-playing coach and the playing captain. In some cases the coach also plays. Among informal teams the role of coach and captain may merge into one individual who takes charge of the team. Or it may be that a leader neither is defined nor allowed to assume control.

The ultimate value of research in sport groups is to gain a better knowledge of the progress toward goal achievement. On the professional level, organizations constantly search for athletes who will increase the productivity of the team. Selection and recruitment is primarily guided by a search for the most skillful players. Adding the dimension of compatibility a sport organization may be able to utilize non-skill factors to discriminate between athletes of apparent equal skill level. Similarly the selection of a coaching staff could be the theoretical framework on the interaction of effects of leadership style and groupings of people.

On the recreational level, teams may have the same focus of integration as a professional team and obtain satisfaction through high competitive focus that the members seek to enhance through a sport experience. In this situation it would not be necessary to reward productivity in order to reach goal achievement. Considering these factors, the University of Kansas Intramural Basketball Program for 1977 had been designed to offer levels of competition that could be attractive to teams with either professional (task) orientation or play (social) orientation.

The entry procedure for teams provides a selection process by which the teams discriminate or identify themselves as task or social groups. Administration of the Webb questionnaire to a sample of teams in each league could test a hypothesis that teams with higher professional orientation toward play would choose a competitive league with the opportunity for rewards for success.

Several hypotheses could be made regarding this form of administration.

1. In the competitive leagues, productivity will be related to the expressed control.
2. In the competitive leagues, satisfaction will be a function of productivity.
3. In the recreation league, satisfaction will be unrelated to productivity. That is to say that, if the focus of integration is social, then satisfaction will not be related to a subordinate goal.

This study can only be considered as a pilot study. It remains to be seen in more defined and controlled research whether or not sport groups can be viewed within the theory of organizational behavior. Studies must be structured in more dimensions. Particular efforts must be made to identify leadership roles on sport teams. If knowledge can be advanced on the relationship between satisfaction and athletic participation in sport, perhaps recreation administrators can better design programs that would be attractive to broader population and not merely catered to the highly competitive.

BIBLIOGRAPHY

[1]Blake, Robert and Mouton, Jane, The Managerial Grid, Houston: Gulf Publishing Company, 1976.

[2]Caillois, R., "The Structure and Classification of Games," Sport, Culture and Society, London: The MacMillan Company, 1969, pp. 44-45.

[3]Downs, Cal W. and Pickett, Terry, "An Analysis of the Effects of Nine Leadership-Group Compatibility Contingencies Upon Productivity and Member Satisfaction," Unpublished Research Paper, University of Kansas, 1976.

[4]Hewett, T. T., O'Brien, G. E. and Hornik, J., "The Effects of Work Organization, Leadership Style and Member Compatibility Upon the Productivity of Small Groups Working on a Manipulation Task," Organizational Behavior and Human Performance, Vol. 11:283-301, 1974.

[5]Kenyon, G. S., "Six Scales for Assessing Attitude Toward Physical Activity," Research Quarterly, Vol. 39:566-574, 1968.

[6]Larimer, Michael W., Group Compatibility, Leadership Style, Task Structure and Their Relationship to Group Productivity and Member Satisfaction, Unpublished Ph.D. Dissertation, University of Kansas, 1973.

[7]Libo, L. M., Measuring Group Cohesion, Ann Arbor: The University of Michigan, 1953.

[8]McGregor, Douglas, The Human Side of Enterprise, New York: McGraw Hill Book Company, Inc. 1960.

[9]Mikalachi, A., Group Cohesion Reconsidered, School of Business Administration, The University of Western Ontario, London, Ontario, 1969.

[10]Morgan, Wm. P., "Sport Psychology," Psychomotor Domain: Movement Behavior, Lea and Febiger, 1971, pp. 193-22.

[11]Moos, R. H. and Speisman, J. C., "Group Compatibility and Productivity," Journal of Abnormal and Social Psychology, Vol. 65 (3):190-196, 1962.

[12]Newcomb, Theodore and Wilson, Everett K., *College Peer Groups,* Chicago: Aldine Publishing Company, 1966.

[13]O'Brien, G. E. and Ilgen, D., "Effects of Organizational Structure, Leadership Style and Member Compatibility Upon Small Group Creativity," *Proceedings of American Psychological Association,* 3:555-556, 1968.

[14]Ogilvie, Bruck and Tutko, Thomas, "Sport: If You Want to Build Character, Try Something Else," *Psychology Today,* Vol. 5:60-63, 1971.

[15]Ryan, E. D. and Foster, R. L., "Athletic Participation and Perceptual Augmentation and Reduction," *Journal of Personality and Social Psychology,* Vol. 6:472-476, 1967.

[16]Schacter, S., Ellerton, N., McBride, D. and Gregory, D., "An Experimental Study of Cohesiveness and Productivity," *Human Relations,* 4:228-238, 1951.

[17]Schutz, W. C., *The Interpersonal Underworld,* Palo Alto, California: Science and Behavior Books, 1958.

[18]Seashore, S. E., *Group Cohesiveness in the Industrial Work Group,* Ann Arbor: Survey Research Center, University of Michigan, 1964.

[19]Webb, Harry, "Professionalization of Attitudes Toward Play Among Adolescents, *Sociology of Sport,* Chicago: The Athletic Institute, 161-178, 1969.

[20]Werner, A. C., and Gottheil, E., "Personality Development and Participation in College Athletics," *Research Quarterly,* 37:126-131, 1966.

[21]Zeisner, Robert E., "The Attitudes and Motivations of Participants in an Intramural Sports Program," *Proceedings of the National Intramural-Recreational Sports Association,* 215-22, 1975.

THE NATURE AND SCOPE OF INTRAMURAL-RECREATIONAL GRADUATE ASSISTANT POSITIONS

by Steven Cohen, Nassau Community College

Introduction

Since the early formalization of intramural-recreational programs under faculty direction at the turn of the twentieth century, such programs have undergone constant growth and expansion. Substantial increases have been observed in staff numbers, programs, budgets, and facilities. Intramural-recreational programs have evolved into large-scale, professionally-staffed operations.

In discussing a proposed model for the professional preparation of intramural administrators, Preo[9] pointed to practical work experience as a crucial aspect of the model. Serving as a graduate assistant in an intramural-recreational program is viewed as a particularly invaluable form of professional preparation. In challenging active members of the intramural-recreational field to improve themselves and their profession, Preo stressed that, "We must attract graduate assistants who are interested in our field and then cultivate and mold these individuals to be our future leaders." (p. 18)

There is general agreement that the graduate assistant has become an integral part of many intramural-recreational programs[7]. Recognizing this, the concept was thought to have merited investigation in regard to prevalent practices and policies which have accrued to the position. The results of such a study were viewed as a potential benefit to those departments seeking information related to graduate assistantship programs, as well as a complement to the growing body of knowledge related to the intramural-recreational field.

It was felt that a study of this nature would also be useful to students, academic advisors, intramural-recreational personnel, and all others involved or interested in this area. Students, particularly those seeking graduate assistantships, could use the information generated to acquaint themselves with the nature and scope of graduate assistant positions. The information could also be of value to academic advisors when they confer with students interested in seeking graduate assistantships in this field. The study could give both the advisor and the student an indication of the role of graduate assistants in the surveyed institutions, as well as what the student might expect to find in institutions of comparable size and with similar modes of program administration. Intramural-recreational personnel could gauge and analyze their particular program in relation to other programs of similar size and degree of function. This information could be useful in terms of seeking additional budgetary expenditures to upgrade programs to the level and caliber of those found in similar categories.

Statement of the Problem

The purpose of this study was to determine the nature and scope of intramural-recreational graduate assistant positions at randomly-selected, four-year colleges and universities. More specifically, the study sought to ascertain what general areas of intramural-recreational programs were supervised and directed by graduate assistants, and what specific tasks and responsibilities were performed by intramural-recreational graduate assistants. In addition, this study sought to determine: (1) the number of intramural-recreational graduate assistantships applied for against the number available; (2) the number of male and female intramural-recreational graduate assistants currently employed; (3) the amount of stipends offered to graduate assistants, whether they were taxable, and how they compared to those offered by other university departments; (4) the tuition payments required or waived; (5) the availability of financial support for attendance at specified professional conventions; (6) the type of office or work space allotted; (7) the accessibility to secretarial and clerical personnel for work related to the intramural-recreational program; and (8) the average number of hours per week a graduate assistant is required to work as part of his or her responsibilities.

Procedures

The study involved 95 randomly-selected, four-year colleges and universities which conduct intramural-recreational programs and which also offer Master's degree programs in health, physical education, and/or recreation education. The institutions were divided into two groups: one consisting of 44 institutions with student enrollments below 12,500 and specified as Group I Schools, and the other consisting of 51 institutions with enrollments above that figure and specified as Group II Schools.

Two questionnaires were developed to collect the data sought for the study. One was intended for the directors of the selected intramural-recreational programs, and consisted of 11 questions dealing with the institutions' graduate assistantship programs. Among the areas covered were: the number of assistantships applied for against the number available, the amount of financial remuneration, and the particular benefits accruing to the positions. The other questionnaire was intended for each graduate assistant employed in the intramural-recreational program of each institution. It was designed to elicit information on the areas of program responsibility supervised and directed, and the specific tasks performed by graduate assistants.

The two questionnaires, both in one envelope, were mailed to each of the directors of the 95 intramural-recreational programs. With returns from the directors in 90 of the 95 institutions, a response rate of 95 percent was achieved. Of the 152 intramural-recreational graduate assistants employed in the 90 institutions, 135 responded to the questionnaire designed for them. for a response rate of 89 percent.

The data, presented in 17 tables, were tabulated in terms of frequency of responses, percentages, means, medians, and ranges. Results of the responses received from institutions with enrollments below 12,500 were compared to the results from those with enrollments above that figure. Additionally, the extent of male and female graduate assistant involvement in supervision and direction of intramural-recreational program areas, and performance of specific tasks, were analyzed. The final phase of the analysis of the data was to incorporate the information from all questionnaires, irrespective of the size of the institutions, in order to determine the nature and scope of intramural-recreational graduate assistant positions.

Conclusion

Based on the tabulation and analysis of the data, the following conclusions could be drawn:

Intramural-recreational graduate assistants are involved in the supervision and direction of 16 areas of program responsibility, but predominantly in: Men's Independent Intramurals, Women's Independent Intramurals, Fraternity Intramurals, Co-Recreational Intramurals, Men's Residence Hall Intramurals, Overall Supervision of Areas and Facilities, Sorority Intramurals, Women's Residence Hall Intramurals, and Faculty-Staff Intramurals.

Intramural-recreational gradute assistants perform a wide variety of specific tasks, but those which they are most frequently involved in performing are: planning, organizing, and helping to administer special events; attending staff meetings; conducting daily office hours; supervising undergraduate students employed in the program; drawing up and scheduling intramural tournaments; supervising (night or day) intramural-recreational facilities; dealing with protests of intramural contests; filling out and maintaining accident report forms; publicizing the intramural-recreational program; setting up intramural-recreational equipment for program activities; recruiting intramural sports officials; applying first aid to injured program participants; and scheduling intramural sports officials.

There are four applicants for each intramural-recreational graduate assistantship available.

There are, for all graduate assistants employed in intramural-recreational programs, approximately two males for every female.

The average stipend offered to an intramural-recreational graduate assistant amounts to $2,725 annually, is taxable, and is equal in amount to those awarded by other university departments.

Slightly more than half of all graduate assistantships do not involve a full wavier of tuition and fees, but most do involve a waiver of the out-of-state portion of tuition.

Institutions do not, as a policy, offer financial support to intramural-recreational graduate assistants for attendance at professional conventions.

As part of their assistantships, intramural-recreational graduate assistants are provided office space which is shared with either other graduate assistants, or members of the intramural-recreational staff.

Intramural-recreational graduate assistants have access to secretarial staff for work related to the intramural-recreational program.

Graduate assistants in intramural-recreational programs are required to work from 15 to 25 hours per week.

There are substantially few differences in the areas of program responsibility supervised and directed, and in the performance of specific tasks, for graduate assistants in Group I Schools as opposed to those in Group II Schools.

Despite the similarity in the nature and scope of areas of program responsibility, and performance of specific tasks, the size of the stipend offered to intramural-recreational graduate assistants in Group I Schools is considerably less than the stipend offered to graduate assistants in Group II Schools.

Schools in the Group II category employ twice as many intramural-recreational graduate assistants as schools in Group I.

Female intramural-recreational graduate assistants are involved most frequently in the supervision and direction of program areas dealing with participation by women.

In relation to performance of specific tasks, there is little differentiation that can be made in regard to the kind of tasks performed by males as opposed to females.

REFERENCES

[1] Good, Carter V., and Doublas E. Scates. *Methods of Research.* New York: Appleton-Century-Crofts, Inc., 1954.

[2] "HPER Directory of Professional Preparation Institutions," *Journal of Health, Physical Education and Recreation,* 45:37-47, September, 1974.

[3] Kerlinger, Fred N. *Foundations of Behavioral Research.* New York: Holt, Rinehart and Winston, Inc., 1964.

[4] Kleindienst, Viola, K., and Arthur Weston. *Intramural and Recreation Programs for Schools and Colleges.* New York: Meredith Publishing Company, 1964.

[5] Marciani, Louis, ed. *National Intramural Recreational Sports Directory for Colleges and Universities,* 1976-77. Hattiesburg, Ms.: National Intramural-Recreational Sports Association, 1976.

[6] Moser, C. A., and G. Kalton. *Survey Methods in Social Investigation.* New York: Basic Books, Inc., 1972.

[7] Mueller, Pat, and Elmer D. Mitchell. *Intramural Sports.* New York: The Ronald Press Company, 1960, pp. 41-42.

[8] Podolsky, Arthur, and Carolyn R. Smith, eds., *Education Directory: Colleges and Universities 1976-77,* National Center for Education Statistics, Washington: U.S. Department of Health, Education and Welfare, 1975.

[9] Preo, Lawrence S. "Professional Preparation of Administrators of Intramural and Physical Recreation Programs," *Intramural Administration: Theory and Practice,* ed. James A. Peterson. New Jersey: Prentice Hall, Inc., pp. 13-18.

[10] Weber, Jerome C., and David R. Lamb. *Statistics and Research in Physical Education.* St. Louis: The C. V. Mosby Company, 1970.

Table 1

Institutions Offering Intramural-Recreational Graduate Assistantships

Classification	n	Institutions Offering Graduate Assistantships		Institutions Not Offering Graduate Assistantships	
		Number	Percent	Number	Percent
Group I Schools	42	24	57.1	18	42.9
Group II Schools	48	25	52.1	23	47.9
Total Sample	90	49	54.4	41	45.6

Table 2

Number of Intramural-Recreational Graduate Assistantships Offered Annually

Classification	n	x	Median	Range
Group I Schools	24	2.2	2	1-7
Group II Schools	25	4.3	4	1-9
Total Sample	49	3.3	2	1-9

Table 3

Number of Applicants for Intramural-Recreational Graduate Assistantships Annually

Classification	n	x	Median	Range
Group I Schools	20	13.0	10	2-50
Group II Schools	25	13.7	11	2-35
Total Sample	45	13.4	11	2-50

Table 4

Number of Intramural-Recreational Graduate Assistants Currently Employed

Classification	n	Total Number Employed	x	Median	Range
Group I Schools	24	52	2.2	2	1-7
Group II Schools	25	100	4.0	3	1-9
Total Sample	49	152	3.1	2	1-9

Table 6

Amount of Annual Stipend Awarded to Intramural-Recreational Graduate Assistants[a]

Classification	n	x	Median	Range
Group I Schools	20	$2,229	$2,250	$ 450-3,750
Group II Schools	25	3,123	3,000	1,200-6,600
Total Sample	45	2,726	2,750	450-6,600

[a]Using .50 as a normal FTE for a graduate assistantship.

Table 7

Taxable and Non-Taxable Stipends Awarded Intramural-Recreational Graduate Assistants

Classification	n	Institutions with Taxable Stipends		Institutions with Non-Taxable Stipends	
		Number	Percent	Number	Percent
Group I Schools	24	19	79.2	5	20.8
Group II Schools	25	22	88.0	3	12.0
Total Sample	49	41	83.7	8	16.3

Table 9

Institutions Offering Full Tuition and Fee Waiver for
Intramural-Recreational Graduate Assistants

Classification	n	Full Waiver Offered		Full Waiver Not Offered	
		Number	Percent	Number	Percent
Group I Schools	24	9	37.5	15	62.5
Group II Schools	25	11	44.0	14	56.0
Total Sample	49	20	40.8	29	59.2

Table 10

Institutions Offering Out-of-State Tuition Waiver for
Intramural-Recreational Graduate Assistants

Classification	n	Out-of-State Tuition Waiver Offered		Out-of-State Tuition Waver Not Offered	
		Number	Percent	Number	Percent
Group I Schools	12	9	75.0	3	25.0
Group II Schools	14	12	85.7	2	14.3
Total Sample	26	21*	80.0	5	19.2

Table 11

Institutions Offering Financial Support to Intramural-Recreational
Graduate Assistants for Attendance at Professional Conventions

Classification	n	Financial Support Offered		Financial Support Not Offered	
		Number	Percent	Number	Percent
Group I Schools	23	6	26.1	17	73.9
Group II Schools	25	9	36.0	16	64.0
Total Sample	48	15	31.3	33	68.7

Table 8

Comparison of Intramural-Recreational Graduate Assistantship Stipends with Those Awarded in Other University Departments

Classification	n	Intramural-Recreational Stipends Higher		Intramural-Recreational Stipends Lower		Stipends Equal	
		Institutions	Percent	Institutions	Percent	Institutions	Percent
Group I Schools	24	2	8.3	3	12.5	19	79.2
Group II Schools	25	0	0.0	0	0.0	25	100.0
Total Sample	49	2	4.1	3	6.1	44	89.8

Table 5

Male/Female Data on Intramural-Recreational Graduate Assistants Currently Employed

Classification	n	Sex	Total Number Employed	Percent	x	Median	Range
Group I Schools	24	Male	31	59.6	1.30	1	1-3
		Female	21	40.4	.88	1	1-4
Group II Schools	25	Male	63	63.0	2.50	3	1-7
		Female	37	37.0	1.50	1	1-5
Total Sample	49	Male	94	61.8	1.90	2	1-7
		Female	58	38.2	1.20	1	1-5

211

Table 13

Number of Hours Per Week Intramural-Recreational Graduate Assistants Are Required To Work

Classification	na	0 - 10 Hours		10 - 15 Hours		15 - 20 Hours		20 - 25 Hours		Others	
		Number	Percent	Number	Percent	Number	Percent	Number	Percent	Number	Percent
Group I Schools	52	4	7.7	4	7.7	27	51.9	12	23.1	5	9.6
Group II Schools	100	3	3.0	16	16.0	43	43.0	33	33.0	5	5.0
Total Sample	152	7	4.6	20	13.2	70	46.0	45	29.6	10	6.6

an represents number of graduate assistants.

Table 12

Type of Office Space Provided for Intramural-Recreational Graduate Assistants

Classification	n	Each Has Own Office		Office Shared With Other Graduate Assistants		No Office Space Provided		Other	
		Institutions	Percent	Institutions	Percent	Institutions	Percent	Institutions	Percent
Group I Schools	24	5	20.8	9	37.5	1	4.2	9	37.5
Group II Schools	25	3	12.0	15	60.0	1	4.0	6	24.0
Total Sample	49	8	16.3	24	49.0	2	4.1	15	30.6

Table 14

Graduate Assistant Involvement in Supervision and Direction of Intramural-Recreational Program Areas

Program Area	Group I Schools (n=45)		Group II Schools (n=90)		Total Sample (n=135)	
	Number	Percent	Number	Percent	Number	Percent
Men's Independent Intramurals	28	62.2	54	60.0	82	60.7
Women's Independent Intramurals	26	57.8	47	52.2	73	54.1
Fraternity Intramurals	29	64.4	43	47.8	72	53.3
Co-Recreational Intramurals	28	62.2	43	47.8	71	52.6
Men's Residence Hall Intramurals	23	51.1	44	48.9	67	49.6
Overall Supervision of Areas and Facilities	24	53.3	42	46.7	66	48.9
Sorority Intramurals	25	55.6	38	42.2	63	46.7
Women's Residence Hall Intramurals	20	44.4	38	42.2	58	43.0
Faculty-Staff Intramurals	20	44.4	34	37.8	54	40.0
Aquatics Program	8	17.8	18	20.0	26	19.3
Outdoor Recreation Program	5	11.1	15	16.6	20	14.8
Club Sports	8	17.8	11	12.2	19	14.1
Other	11	24.4	20	22.2	31	23.0

213

CONTEMPORARY PROGRAM PHILOSOPHIES-PART II

by George W. Haniford, Purdue University; Paula J. Page, University
of Minnesota and Larry S. Preo, Marquette University

Good afternoon. Thank you for selecting our program to attend. Our presentation is titled "Contemporary Program Philosophies - Part II". Part I was given last year at the NIRSA Conference in Boston.

Paula Page of the University of Minnesota, Larry Preo of Marquette University and I, George Haniford of Purdue University are going to present to you some of the findings of a national study which we conducted to make an analysis of recreational sports professionals opinion of selected policies governing the intramural sports, informal recreational sports and sports clubs programs.

The information compiled in our study was obtained from 76 questionnaire returns. Questionnaires were originally mailed to a sample of 100 professional members of NIRSA. The returns came from 30 of the 40 men 40 + years of age; 34 of the 40 men 39 − years of age; and 12 of the 20 women. There were eleven additional questionnaire returns which were received too late to be included in the analysis.

We are fully cognizant that this is not a meeting of the Research Section; thus, we are not going to follow research oriented jargon in either the visual or verbal portions of our presentation. However, for those interested, we will at the close of the program distribute complete copies of the study which give the statistical treatment of the data and the hypotheses studied.

The time we have been allocated unfortunately does not permit us to examine with you the philosophical responses towards all 100 of the policies studied. Rather, we are limiting our report to 36−12 governing intramural sports, 12 governing informal recreational sports and 12 governing sports clubs. Two slide projectors will be used. Upon the screen to my right and your left the policy statement will be shown. It will also inform you of the number of schools reporting their use or non-use of the policy. We ask that you read the policy and then immediately determine your personal opinion of the policy. After a few brief moments we will upon the screen to my left and your right project the opinions of the policy as expressed by the three categories of respondents. Namely, the men 40 + years of age, the men 39 − years of age and the women. The number at the top in the yellow portion of each cube represents the number agreeing with the policy. The number at the bottom in the green portion of each cube represents the number disagreeing with the policy. The size of the cube merely reflects the difference in the number of respondents in each category.

Throughout the visual presentation Paula, Larry or I will attempt to call to your attention some of the more important aspects of the contemporary program philosophies being reported. Paula will lead off with the policies governing intramurals followed by Larry with the policies governing informal recreational sports. I will present the policies governing sports clubs. We suggest that you jot down any questions that you have. Hopefully at the end of the program there will be time for your verbal involvement. Now on with the show.

Closing summary. Contrary to what is in many instances popular belief—there are few philosophical differences of opinion toward recreational sports policies between male recreational sports professionals 40+ years of age and female recreational sports professionals or male professionals 39— and the women professionals or the men 40+ and men 39— years of age. Thank you for your attendance.

I. INTRAMURAL SPORTS

		Men 40+	Men 39—	Women
1.	To participate in any intramural contest, a student must have insurance protection. (17/58)	18/11	21/13	6/6
2.	Full-time staff members may not participate in undergraduate intramurals. (42/34)	24/6	22/12	6/6
3.	If a student wins a class B or lower championship, future play in that sport will require entry in a higher class. (15/60)	17/12	17/17	5/7
4.	Undergraduate students serving as counselors are not eligible to participate in residence halls intramurals. (5/70)	4/70	13/21	3/9
5.	Only one sports club member may participate per intramural team in his/her respective sport. (5/70)	14/15	17/17	7/5
6.	Once a default has been claimed, it may not be withdrawn. (48/28)	21/9	21/13	7/5
7.	League contests that have been postponed and not played or completed before the regular league schedule is concluded will count as a default. (30/45)	14/16	18/16	8/4

8. The intramural protest committee shall consist of students only. (30/46) 17/13 14/20 3/9
9. The team filing the protest must pay a protest submission fee. (20/56) 12/20 16/18 6/5
10. The intramural staff is not responsible for rescheduling postponed contests. (23/53) 11/19 14/20 5/7
11. An entry fee is required for intramural team events (26/50) 12/18 15/19 5/7
12. In some team events the number of entries is controlled. (24/48) 17/13 14/20 5/7

II. INFORMAL RECREATIONAL SPORTS

	Men 40+	Men 39−	Women
13. A student may sponsor a guest upon the payment of a guest fee. (29/44)	18/10	26/7	9Z/3
14. Guests of students may not reserve courts. (54/18)	26/1	26/7	11/1
15. Student spouses may use the facilities upon payment of a fee. (38/33)	18/9	25/8	11/1
16. Student children are not eligible to use the facilities except under "special programs". (51/22)	23/5	19/14	12/0
17. Staff members have the same usage privileges as students. (67/6)	23/5	29/4	12/0
18. A court reservation must be made on the day desired. (42/31)	20/8	25/8	8/4
19. A court reservation must be made in the names of at least two (2) eligible participants. (33/40)	21/7	25/8	8/4
20. No additional charges are made for court reservations. (60/13)	27/1	29/4	12/0
21. Participants are not charged for sports equipment which they break unless the breakage is determined to be deliberate. (54/19)	23/5	27/6	9/3
22. An advisory board assists in formulating policies. (49/24)	25/3	31/2	11/1
23. The department encourages participant input through the use of a suggestion box. (23/50)	24/ 4	25/8	10/2

24. A departmental appeal system exists for students and/or organizations to appeal fines or penalties. (25/47)   22/5   25/8   10/2

III. SPORTS CLUBS

		Men 40+	Men 39−	Women
25.	The University restricts membership in all student organizations to students and staff. (37/20)	23/3	23/5	5/4
26.	Departmental funding should be restricted to those sports clubs non-sedentary in nature. (17/39)	15/10	15/13	6/3
27.	Excluding safety equipment, travel is the number one budgetary priority. (26/30)	15/10	16/12	7/2
28.	Members over the age of majority must sign a release form. (20/35)	19/5	22/6	7/2
29.	Sports clubs are required to have a staff member accompany them on all out-of-town trips. (19/36)	20/5	15/12	4/5
30.	Sports clubs are required to have a staff member present at all home contests. (18/37)	17/ 8	15/12	4/5
31.	The staff member representing the university may not be the coach or a playing member of the team. (14/43)	17/9	12/16	2/7
32.	Members are provided special time blocks for academic scheduling. (15/42)	15/11	14/14	1/8
33.	If available a club must travel in University vehicles. (17/37)	17/8	18/9	8/4
34.	Before a person may be paid for officiating a home contest he/she must have a contract on file. (13/41)	15/9	16/11	4/5
35.	Contracts for sports clubs games must be signed by the Head of the department. (26/30)	16/9	23/5	6/3
36.	Expenses incurred for the treatment of an injury are the responsibility of the participant. (46/10)	22/4	21/7	8/1

CHAPTER VI

Intramural-Recreation Sports Personnel

MICHIGAN STATE UNIVERSITY PANEL PRESENTATION OF A GRADUATE INTRAMURAL ADMINISTRATION PROGRAM

by Frank Beeman, Carol Harding, Russ Rivet, Larry Sierra

Introduction

At Michigan State the Intramural Sports and Recreative Services Program is directly responsible to the Vice President of Student Affairs.

In all the facets of a comprehensive student recreative program, this administrative structure is the most appropriate. As our subject concerns the development of men and women into competent, tolerant intramural or recreation directors, there is no need to detail the advantages of this plan for the activity program.

The advantages of Student Affairs support for a graduate program include philosophical as well as direct considerations. Because Student Affairs touches all aspects of campus life, the intramural staff is automatically integrated throughout the University on an equal basis with other University administrators and academic officers. The following relationships and interactions are then more easily initiated and explained:

1. Education for leisure on an informal basis through student social and recreational group activities is widespread. It is the linkage of such activities to the fullfilment of the academic purposes of a university which requires emphasis and which makes necessary professional leadership and direction

to effect this integration.

2. Utilization of professional curricula in the University as a source for leadership for the recreative program, the utilization of the various colleges and specifically of the recreation program as a field work-laboratory experience in the professional preparation of recreation leaders, teachers, social and urban workers is enhanced.

3. Organization of, representation on and/or leadership in various University committees and boards for the purpose of improving the coordination and effectiveness of campus cultural and recreation activities. These include: Union Board, Natural Resource Quality Water Research Program, Lecture Concert Series and various campus building committees.

4. Evaluation of campus and recreative programs and services for administrative and planning purposes. Active liaison with the several key departments on campus whose activities and concerns are either similar or are complementary to the objective of effective coordination of campus recreation and cultural affairs. These include: Intercollegiate Athletics, the Athletic Council, Physical Education, University Relations, Campus Parks and Planning, Associated Students, Foreign Students Office, Student Activities Office, Housing Office, Continuing Education, The Alumni Association, Faculty Club, and Student Publications. (chart #1)

5. Students from a variety of disciplines such as College Personnel, College of Urban Development, Hotel and Restaurant Management, interact with our staff in informal and formal arrangements in the form of seminars and practicums.

MSU style is obviously not the only style in which to prepare IM Administrators. We do think it is appropriate for use because we see the position of an IM Administrator as providing a service to the student body. The reason we initiated this type of program in 1969 was because of the expressed and growing interest from the field, and the pressures from students wanting more background in the administration of Intramural-Recreative Programs. Because we provide services to the students in this phase of university life, we feel comfortable as an administrative division of the Vice President for Student Affairs and Services. As a matter of fact, the closer I can get to the Vice Presidents and Presidents, the more comfortable I feel.

We, and I mean all of the Directors, because the entire staff is involved in this area, see two main skills in administering intramural-recreative programs. One consists of mechanical, tangible skills such as scheduling facilities, club sports, teams and individual sports, — hiring, training, pay and scheduling student and regular employees, — all the tangible skills and very important skills necessary to the operation of any program. We think we can teach these skills to anyone who is capable of enrolling in Graduate School.

The other area involves not only skill but art — intangible perceptions, insights and modes of response. This is a much more difficult and perhaps more important area of administration if that administration is to be successful—particularly if successful in terms of the participant. We think it is how the participant ultimately feels about his or her recreative experience—his or her reception at Reservation Desks, Supply Rooms and Director's Offices—determines the success of the program.

This means not only should the leagues and tournaments and leisure time be well organized, but that every student has equal opportunities to participate enjoyably in the activity of their choice be they handicapped or able bodied,—black or white, yellow or brown,—skilled or unskilled,—rich or poor.

It means that the administrator must have the skills of communication—to be able to communicate with all of these participants—mostly this means the ability to listen perceptively. If you do not hear people, you cannot serve people.

It means the administrator must realize that time spent with students is probably more important than time spent with administrative duties. It means that the administrator must accept that people are more important than things.

It means that the administrator must have enough confidence not to feel he or she is being challenged, because they are being questioned; that the important thing is the problem the person has, and that to resolve that problem you attack it, not the person with the problem.

These skills in human relations, in addition to the mechanical skills, are what we strive to imbue in each graduate student in our IM administrative master's program.

We pursue this hopefully, through our staff example, our internships and formally through our interdisciplinary courses in management, sociology and psychology.

We hope to bring this to you more specifically through the panel presentation.

A component of progression toward the advanced degree in Intramural Administration is that of curriculum development. In order to meet the needs of each graduate student, the curriculum is designed to allow students to build their own individual expertise.

Generally, three phases of experience is structured by the students. The first, not listed by importance, is that of actual course work, both elective and required. The beginning takes place by the planning of a personalized course outline under the supervision of the Director, Dr. Beeman. During this phase of education, each student is expected to gain knowledge, theory and understanding in the pursuance of the M.A. degree. A constant reevaluation of the elective courses is conducted by either some of the professional staff taking these potential courses or critiques from graduate students on how these courses might relate to the area of Intramural Sports and Recreative Services.

The elective program concentrates in the area of sociology and management since interpersonal relations is an integral part of Michigan State Intramural's philosophical base. Some sociology courses offered are:

Behavior of Youth

Racial & Ethnic Inequality

Modern American Society

Social Organization & Administration

In addition, a few of the management courses offered are:

Human Relations in Business

Organization & Administration

Personnel Management

Human Relations

These courses emphasize the Individual's place in society, the organization and administrative structure.

The most recently added elective courses which may prove very interesting are a History of Sports and a Bio-Mechanics course, the latter dealing with the recognition and maintenance of injuries as a result of athletic contest trauma.

The remaining two experiences are actually a blend of each other. Allow me to explain. Separately, we will call them the internship and practical involvement to learning, not to be confused with the earn to learn concept.

During the internship each student is required to work on two phases of the Intramural program and develop these areas into a mini thesis. This is a 6-9 credit block which allows the students to use their competences in a selected area such as sports clubs, officiating, facility co-ordination or related areas which the director feels will enhance and challenge their knowledge. Each internship proposal asks for an introduction, comprehensive review of the literature, procedures of operation and, of course, an accurate bibliography.

The experience from this proposal is blended with further practical learning when the graduate student seeks professional interaction in such areas as the competitive program, equipment supply area, main office, business and payroll exploration, just to mention a few. This self-motivated, on-the-job type training, in my opinion, is the most interesting and exposing. The tools which are experienced at this time are the ones which will be utilized most frequently on the job.

Two additional areas of growth must also be mentioned which reward the graduate with valuable experience:

The independent study usually varies from 1 to 16 credits and encompasses work which will benefit both the student and department. Examples might be short surveys on the reservation system or participation time desired in a particular area such as the paddleball court areas. Reservation length and availability frequently are surveyed. These studies usually are always directed so the graduate will have interaction with the participant and thus have some sensitivity concerning the desires of the student-faculty-staff participant.

Allowing the graduate student this type of involvement usually receives the greatest amount of input when the grad finally moves on to a professional setting.

One last directed learning experience is that of the graduate Intramural seminar which is conducted specifically to expose the Intramural graduate to high level administrative personnel, such as the Vice President for Student Affairs, Director of the Placement Bureau, Associate Dean and Director of the School for Advanced Studies, Director of Intercollegiate Athletics, Director of Women's Athletics, Dean of the College of Urban Development, Director of Women's Programs, Director of Legal Aid for ASMSU, just to mention a few.

The designed curriculum of learning should take about 3-6 terms and 45 credits to complete.

In closing, we would like to emphasize that one major point is stressed at Michigan State and that is the program we have described is not the only way to run a comprehensive Intramural program in higher education, but just one way. Situations, philosophies and programs change and vary at other institutions.

Preparing an Administrator via Earning and Learning

Historically, the graduate assistant or teaching assistant has been a very important position to be sought by a graduate student in all academic and administrative areas. These positions have enabled outstanding students to join the faculty, gain administrative or teaching experience and have an opportunity to make a departmental contribution on a very different level than the regularly enrolled graduate student.

In the last six years more and more capable graduate students have enrolled in the IM administration Master's program. Almost all students now come with some background experience in IM and it is much more common that the student's IM experience is more than just having been a participant. Certainly their interest and motivation in gaining administrative opportunities is at an optimal level.

As graduates come to East Lansing from universities and colleges, their IM experience has had increasing depth. We fully recognize this is due to the improved delivery and emphasis on recreational services on so many campuses.

Our main concern has been to do our best in working with these people. Also, our awareness was increased gradually to note what we were missing if the student was not effectively "plugged in" to the system of administration so definitive contributions could be made.

The graduate student has the opportunity at Michigan State to be employed at a wage ranging from $2.65 to $4.05 per hour for work in twenty-five sport and building related positions in the recreational delivery system. Depending on the student, financial need and need for specific work experience an individual work profile can be developed to best serve the graduate student. We each advise students and attempt to assist them in gaining what experience they need to develop competency and confidence. Also, of course, the student has an understanding of strengths and weaknesses by way of the follow up evaluation and plan for the next term of employment. No one is locked into one work category. The strength is in the variation available. One term the student may be a Sports Supervisor for 690 teams and the next term work with co-rec with 78 teams or work as a building or equipment supervisor. The actual hourly pay could be comparable to the stipend for the graduate assistantships. A working, active relationship can be formed with each member of the faculty—directors and assistants.

There is no question that the graduate student brings to the IM a mature view, appropriate philosophy and a dedication that is valuable for the other undergraduate employees to be exposed to and emulate. The contribution of all student employees at State has been remarkable and the graduate students have created an even more superior work environment and better service for all people.

Priority is given to IM graduates in employment.

It does seem that the actual work for pay situation is valuable because the work responsibility is real, the responsibility assumed, completed and evaluated. Students seem more than happy with the parameters for employment. Also, the actual work experience parallels the academic work load to allow the formal curriculum offerings to contribute to the actual work. Our interest and work is to make the students successful in their academic, line and management experience. We work alone and collectively as a team with the individual and this is a particular advantage to the graduate person and a strength of the program.

Graduate students are selected primarily from graduates of undergraduate programs in Physical Education and Recreation. The program is also open to graduates of other academic disciplines. Students make direct application to the program director. They may be referred to the director by Intramural Staff or colleagues from other academic disciplines. The primary consideration for acceptance is the demonstrated and potential ability and willingness of the applicant to work equally well with participants from a wide range of backgrounds, including economic status, race and sex.

The assessment of the student's academic record, knowledge of intramurals, leisure education, lifelong education, ability in planning, managing and administering intramural sports and recreative services programs or any component in the program is made by the director. From this information, a prescription is made outlining the student's participation in the three components within Phase 1.

Phase 1 of the program consists of the required courses and electives in the curriculum outline (Appendix 1), direct contact and work with intramural staff members and on the job direct work experience within the intramural program. The student will proceed through this phase of the program taking each component or part of a component, in order, to the extent warranted by results of the individual assessment and prescription.

Students develop a course outline under the supervision of the director. Through this course work the students will gain the knowledge, theory and understanding necessary as a foundation upon which can be built all the requisite skills for implementation of these concepts into an ongoing intramural sports and recreative services program.

The student learns a broad base of techniques and skills necessary in administering the various facets of an Intramural Sports and Recreative Services Program. The student meets with each member of the intramural staff on a one-to-one basis to achieve the necessary competencies in each particular area of staff responsibility. In addition special projects may be arranged through staff members for a student on an elective credit basis.

The student actually works as an Intramural Student Employee. Through the prescription and feedback mechanism the director and student decide on job placement. This allows the student an opportunity for practical application of course work and skill techniques in a setting of field experience.

Through Phase 1 of the program the student achieves competence in the three components contained therein. The student now works with the director and the Intramural Staff in the assessment and prescription of the components of Phase 2 of the program. This assessment will be based on these results and the student's interest in the available options.

The student enrolls for six to nine credit hours in course HPR 879 Internship (Appendix 1). In the internship phase, the student uses his/her acquired competencies to work in the intramural programs in a supervisory or administrative capacity. This component calls upon the student's initiative, skill, knowledge, and creativity in the development and completion of an Internship Proposal in partial fulfillment of the requirement for the degree of Master of Arts.

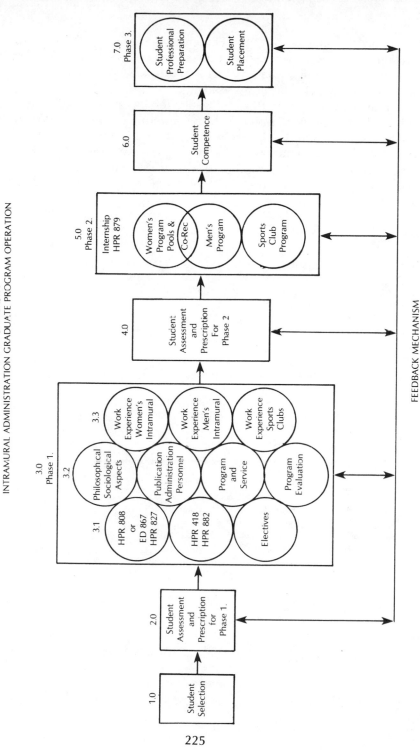

MICHIGAN STATE UNIVERSITY
INTRAMURAL ADMINISTRATION GRADUATE PROGRAM OPERATION

1.0
Student Selection

2.0
Student Assessment and Prescription for Phase 1.

3.0
Phase 1.

3.1 — HPR 808 or ED 867 HPR 827 — HPR 418 HPR 882 — Electives

3.2 — Philosophical Sociological Aspects — Publication Administration Personnel — Program and Service — Program Evaluation

3.3 — Work Experience Women's Intramural — Work Experience Men's Intramural — Work Experience Sports Clubs

4.0
Student Assessment and Prescription For Phase 2

5.0
Phase 2.
Internship HPR 879 — Women's Program Pools & Co-Rec — Men's Program — Sports Club Program

6.0
Student Competence

7.0
Phase 3.
Student Professional Preparation — Student Placement

FEEDBACK MECHANISM

Figure 1

225

Through experience gained in Phase 1 and Phase 2 of this program, the student will have achieved the necessary competencies to plan, develop, manage and administer an Intramural Sports and Recreative Services Program in College and University settings.

The student works with the director and the Intramural Staff to construct a resume. The student works with the Intramural Staff and the Student Placement Center in developing skills for position application and the conduct necessary for a successful interview. Personal contracts are made by the members of the Intramural Staff with professional colleagues and prospective employees in support of the employment of the Intramural Administration graduate.

APPENDIX 1

INTRAMURAL ADMINISTRATION GRADUATE PROGRAM

A combination of the courses below will satisfy the student's particular interest within the field of Intramurals. Forty-five required credits.

Required by				Credits
Department	HPR	808	Research Techniques or	5
	ED	867	Educ. Research Meth.	3
	HPR	827	Seminar	1
Advisor	HPR	418	Intramural Athletics (winter term)	3
	HPR	879	Internship	6-9
	HPR	882	Seminar	2

Electives

HPR	401	Organization & Administration of Com. Recreation	3
	404	Facility Planning & Construction	4
	418	Intramural Sports	3
	422	Theory & Philosophy of Recreation	3
	803	Current Problems in Recreation	3
	806	Sports & Society	3
	829	Supervision of Physical Education	3
	860	Admin. of Phys. Education in Schools & Colleges	3
SOC	332	Behavior of Youth	3
	333	Racial & Ethnic Inequality	4
	429	Urban Society	4
	471	Modern American Society	4
	473	Culture & Personality	4
	868	Social Organization & Administration	3
LIR	826	Organizational Development	4

MGT	414	Human Relations in Business	4
	806	Organization & Administration	4
	808	Seminar in Management Organization & Administration	4
	810	Personnel Management	4
	813	Human Relations	4
ED	815C	Student Personnel	3
	822A	Community Colleges	3
	822	Seminar—Budget and Finance	3
PSY	356	Psych. of Human Relations in a Work Setting	3
	436	Psych. of Communication & Percussion	3
HPR	342	Teaching Techniques Team Sports	4
	344	Teaching Techniques Individual Sports	2
HST	403	History of Sport in America	3
ED	882	Sem. Adm. Ath. Hlth. or BIM 880 Ath. Med. Sys.	3

Dr. Harris F. Beeman, Professor and Director of Intramural Sports, serves as academic advisor to all graduate students taking the Intramural Administration emphasis and teaches two formal courses, HPR-418 and HPR-882. Intramural staff members, Carol Harding, Assistant Professor and Director of Women's Intramural Sports, Larry Sierra, Assistant Professor and Director of Men's Intramural Sports and Russ Rivet, Assistant Professor and Director of Sports Clubs, work directly with the students for the intern program, special projects and serve on graduate committees. The administration internship involves direct work experience and parallel seminars with the following content:

1. Philosophical and sociological aspects of sport participation for men and women
   A. cultural view
   B. actual sport experience
   C. projected view of sport participation
   D. problems in sport participation involving minority participants
   E. importance of people in relation to things (program, schedules, equipment)
2. Administrative techniques and procedures
   A. allocation of facilities
   B. reservations and scheduling
   C. supervision of employees
   D. communications

  E. injuries and liability
  F. specific job classifications and responsibilities
  G. finance
  H. equipment—inventory and ordering
 3. Personnel—hiring and training
  A. Intramural supervisors (reservation and information desk, office and building)
  B. pool guards
  C. sport supervisors
  D. officials
  E. security workers
 4. Publications
  A. printed material available to faculty, staff and students
  B. published handbooks for men and women
  C. professional contributions
 5. Program and Services
  A. sport workshops
  B. orientation sessions
  C. drop-in recreation
  D. competitive sport
  E. special community events—volunteer and community agencies
 6. Professional placement
  A. construction of resume
  B. interview conduct
  C. personal contacts with employers
 7. Evaluation
  A. internal procedures
  B. external in relation to actual work experience
  C. long range—retain interest and involvement in intern experience

Because of the employment potential as well as the competency of the present Intramural staff, a natural expansion is occurring with an increasing number of students applying for admission each year.

The content of the Intramural Administration emphasis in the Physical Education curriculum follows:

> Each masters degree candidate is expected to select an area of emphasis for their graduate program. The core of courses listed under each area is highly recommended but not required. The student and their advisor must determine the specific program of study that will best meet the student's individual needs.

Intramural Programs

This area is designed to prepare students to develop and conduct intramural leisure-time activities in educational institutions. Special consideration is given to the study of interpersonal relationships involved in the administration of competitive and recreative programs. Participation in various phases of the university intramural program is an integral part of the total experience.

CERTIFICATION OF INTRAMURAL-RECREATIONAL SPORTS PERSONNEL: IS IT NEEDED?

by Peter J. Graham, Northeastern University

The time has come to seriously examine the question of professional certification of intramural-recreational sports personnel. The concept of professional certification (or registration) is a positive one and should be approached by the profession without trepidation. For many individuals, however, the mere mention of such a proposal brings certain questions to mind: What does certification entail? What are its ramifications? How will it effect me?

Simply stated, professional certification can be described as a competency based assessment of individuals aspiring to enter into or practice within a profession or occupation. Its prime purpose is to identify and evaluate an individual's professional abilities; it is a process of determining whether an individual has acquired the level of skills and knowledges deemed necessary by peers. From another perspective, certification might be called a "rite of passage" or referred to as a process of being admitted into the "club." Nonetheless, it is a professional competency assessment process and as such is constructed, evaluated, and revised by professional peers.

Another question often posed is one which can usually be divided into two segments: Why is professional certification needed? Is professional certification really necessary in the field of intramural-recreational sports? In response, it should be noted that certification is needed in all professions and is probably long overdue within the intramural-recreational sports profession.

Intramural-recreational sports is a rapidly growing profession. It is a profession which has as its main focus — people. It is a profession which must deal with a microcosm of the society in which it exists. Intramural-recreational sports professionals must deal with both the positive as well as the negative aspects of society. All of the problems associated with contemporary society are mirrored by the various collegiate communities throughout the nation.

Individuals participating in the various phases of a campus intramural-recreational sports program are representative of the myriad segments of the general society. To insure that intramural-recreational sports personnel are competent to successfully confront the many challenges posed by such complex collegiate communities, minimal professional standards must be developed and either met or surpassed by those individuals wishing to pursue careers as intramural-recreational sports directors, assistant directors, supervisors, activity leaders, and so forth.

The establishment and implementation of a professional certification process represents a unique opportunity for upgrading the profession; upgrading in terms of currently employed personnel, upgrading in terms of those individuals seeking entry into the profession, and upgrading in terms of the status accorded the profession by those engaged in other areas of professional pursuit.

Furthermore, the introduction of a professional certification process may create additional employment opportunities for those holding such status. Over the years, many fine, reputable, competent individuals have been associated with the administration and management of campus intramural-recreational sports programs. During this same period, however, numerous individuals have gained entry into the profession not because of their expertise in the field or personal vocational interest but, rather, because campus administrators have traditionally viewed intramural-recreational sports as an area in which they could conveniently place personnel once their effectiveness in their primary employment role had expired. The common practice of assigning individuals relieved of coaching responsibilities to the intramural-recreational sports program is a classic example of this point.

Although many of those who entered the intramural-recreational sports profession through the "back door" have proven to be fine persons and assets to the profession, the continuation of such entry modes can no longer be tolerated. Given the complexities and extensive responsibilities associated with today's campus intramural-recreational sports programs, we can no longer allow access to the profession without requiring the candidate to present some evidence of professional competency.

In this writer's opinion, intramural-recreational sports is at a professional crossroad. If that which we refer to as the profession of intramural-recreational sports is to be truly representative of a profession, then we must institute a system designed to insure that all those allowed to practice within the boundaries of the profession are certified to do so. If we fail to develop and institute such an assessment process, then we will be reinforcing the concept that anyone and everyone is capable of practicing within this occupational area. In essence, if we fail to establish a certification process, then we should relinquish any pretense or claim to being "professionals."

Most intramural-recreational sports personnel interact with academic colleagues on a daily basis. Yet, in many instances, intramural-recreational sports personnel tend to be stereotyped by their academic associates as "jocks." It is unfortunate that such a perception exists for although most intramural-recreational sports personnel possess the positive attributes associated with the "jock" image they do not exhibit the negative characteristics commonly related to this stereotype. To the contrary, Intramural-recreational sports personnel frequently possess the necessary skills, knowledges, and experiences to successfully interact with their academic colleagues in a variety of interest areas, whether it be education, music, physics, art, business administration, history, chemistry, engineering, physical education, or recreation and leisure studies.

Thus, the concept of professional competency assessment should not be viewed as a threat by members of the intramural-recreational sports profession. Rather, the introduction of a certification process should be received as a positive and beneficial event, one which at the very least can only serve to enhance the image of both the profession and those pursuing careers within it.

Throughout the world of work, there exists a host of professional or quasi-professional occupations for which an individual must receive certification prior to engaging in the "art." As shown in Figure 1, numerous and varied occupations require certification (or registration) as a prerequisite for employment. It is interesting to note that in the area of public school education, the only personnel not required to possess professional certification have historically been coaches and athletic directors. In recent years, however, this inconsistency has been the target of legislation designed to require both coaches and athletic directors to possess certification as a condition of employment.

Thus, as one looks at the various professions, it rapidly becomes apparent that certification is a rather common concept. As a matter of fact, most people would be quite concerned and uncomfrotable if their suppliers of professional services, such as physicians, electricians, and lawyers, had not successfully complied with the certification standards associated with their particular occupations. In a similar vein, the provisions of intramural-recreational sports services should also be required to meet competency standards to insure consumers of their services that they are competent to function in their professional roles.

How might a certification process for intramural-recreational sports personnel work? A logical approach would be to divide the profession into several certification catagories. For example, an individual might apply for certification as an elementary school (grades K-6), secondary schools (grades 7-12), or collegiate intramural-recreational sports specialist. The creation of different certification categories has merit. The types and depth of competencies would vary according to the specialist category. To illustrate the point, an individual working with and providing programs for youngsters of elementary school age must deal with a different set of physiological, sociological, and psychological criteria than does an individual focusing upon a collegiate community. Subsequently, it only seems reasonable to assess such individuals in terms of those skills and knowledges related to the elementary school area of professional pursuit. Needless to say, there would be substantial overlapping in each of the areas of certification.

Within the collegiate catagory, it is possible to further refine the certification process by developing sub-catagories. For instance, certification standards could be developed for co-recreational, club sports, men's, women's, general recreation, and outdoor activity programming. Moreover, certification criteria could be developed for leadership roles, such as directors, assistant directors, supervisors, activity leaders, and so forth.

What types of skills and knowledges should be included in the competency assessment? Although not inclusive, Figure 2 lists a variety of assessment areas. Most, if not all, of these areas would be germane to each certification catagory — in differing degrees, of course.

How should such a certification program be developed? It is the writer's recommendation that the National Intramural-Recreational Sports Association assume the leadership role in developing a professional certification program. Moreover, in an effort to capitalize upon the expertise of other professionals and to enhance the image of our profession in their eyes, it is suggested that outside consultants be engaged to assist in the development of this certification process, i.e., experts in the areas of psychology, computer technology, business administration, and so forth. Their individual and collective expertise could provide decisive in the success or failure of the certification program. It is also suggested that this certification development committee design an instrument to evaluate the effectiveness of the certification process and that the committee serve as supervisors of both the certification process and its evaluation. Furthermore, when evidence indicates a need for change or alteration in the certification process, it is suggested that the committee assume responsibility for the development and implementation of those corrective actions deemed necessary.

To allay the fears of certain segments of the profession, the writer also suggests that a grandfather clause be attached to the certification proposal. Such a clause would exempt those individuals currently employed in the profession from having to secure certification. However, in the event that an exempted individual sought a new position at a different institute or sought

Figure 1 CERTIFIED PROFESSIONS

PHYSICIANS
DENTISTS
LAWYERS
REAL ESTATE BROKERS
STOCK BROKERS
PHYSIOTHERAPISTS
NURSES
RECREATIONAL PERSONNEL
DRIVER EDUCATION PERSONNEL
AUTOMOTIVE DRIVERS
AIRLINE PILOTS
PSYCHIATRISTS
CERTIFIED PUBLIC ACCOUNTANTS
BARBERS
HAIRDRESSERS
INSURANCE ADJUSTERS
INVESTMENT COUNSELORS
SOCIAL WORKERS
DIETICIANS
PLUMBERS
ELECTRICIANS
REAL ESTATE ASSESSORS

Figure 2 AREAS OF COMPETENCE

TOURNAMENTS
SCHEDULING
EQUIPMENT AND FACILITIES
LAW
PUBLIC RELATIONS SKILLS
MARKETING SKILLS
COMMUNICATION SKILLS
HUMAN RELATIONS SKILLS
PERSONNEL RELATIONS
DECISION-MAKING SKILLS
RESEARCH SKILLS
ACTIVITY/SPORT KNOWLEDGES
BUDGET AND FINANCE SKILLS
GRANTSMANSHIP
PSYCHOLOGY OF SPORT
PHILOSOPHY OF SPORT
SOCIOLOGY OF SPORT
COMPUTER AND WORD PROCESSING SKILLS

a promotion within his/her current department, certification for the new role would be required. This certification exemption should under no circumstances be construed to imply that currently employed intramural-recreational sports personnel are prohibited or discouraged from seeking certification. To the contrary.

Once the criteria and process for certification have been developed and are ready for implementation, it is recommended that the National Intramural-Recreational Sports Association create and disseminate information about the certification program. All informational releases should seek to delineate the value of certified personnel and should encourage potential employers to give preference to candidates who possess professional certification for the position sought.

In summary, it is this writer's opinion that the certification of intramural-recreational sports personnel is not only needed, it is long overdue. Only after successfully fulfilling the requirements of a certification process can those employed in intramural-recreational sports programs (or for that matter any other occupation) truly be considered as "professionals." As the leading representative of those associated with intramurals and recreational sports, the National Intramural-Recreational Sports Association should grasp at the opportunity to become the guiding force behind the establishment and adoption of this critical professional certification process.

GUIDELINES FOR STUDENTS SEEKIING AN
INTRAMURAL-RECREATIONAL SPORTS POSITION

by Dennis M. Carey, Northeastern University

Finding a job in the Intramural-Recreational Sports profession is not an easy task. This presentation will attempt to give tips on resumes, letter writting, interviews, and seeking job opportunities.

Perhaps the most important reality of any job search is that a college degree or degrees does not guarantee a job. Both part-time and full-time experiences are now a prerequisite for employment. Employers look closely at outside the classroom experience for a professional position.

A second reality of this field deals with employment oportunities for women. Fortunately, the stigma attached to women's participation in recreation and sport is behind us. Simple supply and demands tells us that more opportunities for employment are now available to women. The increased women's participation has demanded increased numbers of female professionals.

Another noteworthy reality is Affirmative Action. In essence, Affirmative Action means sound hiring practice because it attempts to tap the resources of qualified women and minorities through advertising job vacancies in such a way so as to make these groups aware of the vacancy. Some institutions adhere quite strictly to these guidelines, some interpret them to mean that they must or will only hire a minority, while others don't advertise at all and simply recruit by personal contacts.

Job hunting involves a great number of variables including luck. However, there are some things which can be controlled such as resume content, letters of application, and preparation for an interview.

THE RESUME

Generally, an employer's first exposure to a candidate is through a resume and some form of cover letter. An important point to remember is that a resume is always accompanied by some type of cover letter.

Virtually all selections for interviews for a position are based upon the qualifications which are apparent from a candidate's resume. While resume formats are numerous it is important that the format you ultimately choose provide the following information:

1) The resume tells who you are
2) The resume tells what you know
3) The resume tells what you have done
4) The resume tells what you would like to do

In order to assume that your resume adequately covers the aforementioned areas, I would suggest the inclusion of the following categories for your resume:

Name, address, and telephone number. This immediately informs the employer who you are and how and where you can be contacted.

Personal Data. Age, citizenship, and health status are sufficient. How much information you choose to include is strictly a matter of personal preference. It has been said that the more information you provide, the more potential you give the employer to discriminate against you.

Employment Objective. Be specific only if you are limiting your job search to a specific position. Otherwise, show some creativity in your employment objective and be specific enough to at least indicate you're seeking an Intramural-Recreational Sports related position.

Education. List both college and high school education. List most recent degree first. Include institution attended, date of graduation, and degree obtained. Don't abbreviate your degree. If you received a Bachelor of

Science degree write it out that way, not as a B.S. degree. Grade point averages and course emphasis are optional.

Employment Experience. Position should be listed in reverse chronological order with your most recent position first. Job title, duties performed, and dates of employment are essential. If you did something special while employed, make note of it in your description of the position where this special accomplishment occurred. If you have a large number of work experiences you may want to divide the work into a number of categories. This works especially well if you have experiences in several distinct areas.

Additional Competencies. The point of such a category is to cover other abilities which you may not have been able to include in your educational and/or work experiences. Certifications, teaching abilities, or any number of things may be included here. The point is, present what you can do in a complete, yet concise manner.

References. Try to list at least four people and try to have these references be from a variety of areas. Two important things to remember when listing references are:

1) Be sure you ask the people you wish to have as references before using their names.
2) List the person's title, address, and telephone number. Make sure that this information is totally correct and accurate.

Optional Categories. There are other areas you may wish to include such as Professional Affiliations, Honors and Awards, or Publications. Much of this depends on the extent of your accomplishment and/or involvement. Again, the rule of thumb is completeness, yet conciseness.

Reproduction of the Resume

After you have put together your resume, you will need to duplicate it. Please don't cut corners when you get to this point. Many people with quality credentials are eliminated because they sent out either poorly reproduced resumes or resumes that contained errors. I believe that spending a few extra dollars for photo-offset or actual type-set printing of your resume is a worthwhile investment. The quality of paper and the total appearance of your resume will be far superior to that of Xerox copies.

There is no rule that requires the use of white paper for resumes. Put some color into your personal portfolio not only with the words you choose, but with the paper you put them on.

SEEKING JOB VACANCIES

After completing your resume you are now prepared to pursue job vacancies. One thing you will discover is that finding job vacancies is difficult.

Common sense tells you that the greater number of job openings you become aware of and eventually apply for, the greater chance you have to get a job. Here is a list of some resources that can be utilized to find job vacancies:

> *The Chronicle of Higher Education*
> *Journal of Health, Physical Education, and Recreation*
> Vacancy Bulletins from your College or University Placement Services
> *National Intramural-Recreational Sports Journal*
> The Intramural Office at your School
> Previous graduate of your school, particularly if your school has an academic program in Intramural Administration or related area
> *The National Recreation and Parks Association Job Bulletin*
> Rejection letters, if they happen to list the name and former institution of the newly hired person

Another way which you can seek job vacancies is by sending out a letter of inquiry along with a copy of your resume. This allows you to pursue locational preferences should you have any, as well as getting your name into circulation. From these letters you may learn of a vacancy at the school you wrote to or perhaps learn of a vacancy in the immediate area.

LETTERS OF APPLICATION

Once you learn of a job vacancy you have to go about applying for it. This is where the letter of application comes in. Again, its importance cannot be stated enough. The letter of application, like the resume, is a reflection of you. Misspelled words, poor grammar, and general sloppiness are intolerable.

A typical letter of application should have three to four paragraphs which are broken down in the following manner:

1st Paragraph: Indicate you are aplying for the position. Be sure to use the *exact* postion title that appears on the job announcement. Refer the reader to an enclosed resume.

2nd Paragraph: Describe your experiences using the *same* words that appear in the job description. If the description says experience in programming, supervision, and evaluation, try to relate your experiences in that context. Try to cover all the areas which are listed under experiences required or responsibilities that the job would entail.

3rd Paragraph: Use this paragraph to break up the monotony of a long drawn out paragraph. This paragraph may be combined with the second paragraph if things are short and concise. If the second paragraph is getting long, find a natural breaking point and continue to cover your background in this paragraph.

4th Paragraph: Reiterate your interest in the position and request an interview. Don't be shy because if you don't get an interview you won't get the job. Thank them for their consideration of your application and tell the employer that you are looking forward to hearing from him/her.

Generally, the most important thing in these letters is to be positive about yourself. Be creative in the way you express your thoughts and don't sound mechanical. All letters of application should be neatly typed. The use of a form letter is totally unacceptable.

THE INTERVIEW

After you have received a few rejection letters or perhaps when you least expect it, you will receive a call inviting you for an interview. A trend seems to be developing where applicants are being required to cover travel expenses incurred while traveling to and from an interview. This is another reality you must be aware of.

The resume and letter of application have done your talking up to this point. Now with an interview opportunity you must be able to verbalize your qualification to the number of people who will interview you.

To properly prepare for an interview you should make sure that you thoroughly know yourself and can speak truthfully and concisely about the experiences which you have listed on your resume. You should try to learn as much about the school and the Intramural-Recreational program it offers prior to going to the interview. Anticipating possible questions and thinking out possible answers to these questions is another good way to prepare yourself.

Once in the interview the best advice is to be yourself. It's easier said than done, but don't try to be someone you aren't. After all, it was you who got yourself this far, so why not stick with yourself the rest of the way. Be confident, but not cocky. Pay attention and be enthusiastic. Stress what you can do for the program and its participants, not what they can do for you. Maintain eye contact at all times with the person(s) that are interviewing you. Ask relevant questions and try to find out exactly what expectations would be placed upon you should you be hired for the position. If at all possible try to avoid philosophical discussions.

Upon completion of the interview, a short note of thanks for the interview opportunity is very appropriate. This is an often overlooked courtesy and beside this, it helps keep your name fresh in the minds of those making the employment decision.

CONCLUSION

This presentation certainly does not offer all the answers. If anything, I hope that it has shown that finding a job is a job in itself. The job hunt can be very frustrating because the process involves people which makes it a subjective, rather than objective experience. Despite this fact, I sincerely believe that if you have worked to prepare yourself for a position in this field and are persistent in your job search, you will be rewarded with a job in a very challenging, exciting, and rewarding profession.

STUDENT LEADERSHIP DEVELOPMENT AND HUMAN RELATIONS TRAINING WORKSHOPS

by Kathryn G. Bayless, Indiana University

Introduction

The use of workshops for student leadership development and human relations training has been in effect within the recreational sports program at Indiana University for three years. The idea of tapping the potential of workshops as an avenue for leadership and human relations training was shared by colleagues from residence life and from student activities.

Currently, the Division of Recreational Sports conducts separate workshops in the Fall for intramural unit managers, club sport officers, intramural sport officials, intramural sport supervisors, and informal sport supervisors. The focus of the workshops has been on a variety of topics such as communications skills, cooperation, problem-solving and decision-making, impact of leadership styles, personal leadership assessment, conflict resolution, assertiveness, and role clarification.

Although the focus and format for workshops vary, there are similar planning steps and principles which can apply equally to any program and any student organization. Following is a listing of planning steps that are intended to be chronological, but it is recognized that the steps can occur differently.[1]

Identify the Workshop Planning Committee

The size of the workshop planning committee is a determination that must be made first. A workable group should be identified that represents as many aspects of recreational sports as possible. Among the variables to consider are class standing, leadership experience, sex, and race. Six to ten individuals should provide enough variety of thought so that effective decisions regarding a workshop can be made.

Other student leaders should be involved in decision making, and staff advisors should be able to make intelligent contributions. Input from representatives or workshop target populations can be very valuable and a commitment to the workshop experience can be established. If possible, the planning committee should be convened about two months before a target date for the workshop.

Identify the Workshop Participants

The first decision for a planning committee concerns the make-up of the target population. It should be noted that goals for the workshop will be dependent upon the nature of the target group. Possible participants include: intramural officials, intramural supervisors, informal sport supervisors, lifeguards, unit managers, club sport officers, governing board members, and other identified student leaders.

Projections must be made regarding the expected level of response from these invited so the size of the participating group can be anticipated. The level of response can, of course, be influenced by the manner in which the invitation is expressed.

Identify the Skills, Abilities, Needs, and Experiences of the Target Group

After the target group has been identified, the planning committee should address itself to an assessment of that group. The committee may be able to complete this task independently based on its own familiarity with the target group. This has been the most commonly used means of target group assessment.

Whatever assessment method is chosen, it is important to give the potential participants feedback on the assessment before the workshop begins.

Identify Goals for the Workshop; Involve Target Group

As the identification of the skills, abilities, needs, and experiences of the target group is completed, the process for the establishment of goals for the retreat should begin. The development of goals should reflect the participants's needs as well as the desired outcomes that the committee identifies.

To help participants perceive workshop goals to be their own, the planning committee should be prepared to negotiate those goals with them. Effective ways to approach this task include asking the target group to prioritize a list of suggested goals (making additions if they wish), to initiating a brainstorming session in which participants and planners generate goals. It is essential to provide feedback regarding the final product to the potential participants.

It should be remembered that goals must be able to be refined into specific objectives.

Communication and Publicity

The type(s) of publicity and communication used will depend largely upon the composition of the target group. If the group consists only of select people, personalized letters and meeting announcements are probably sufficient. However, if the workshop is open to a large group, the following suggestions may be employed: letter to representatives, meeting announcements, flyers and posters, P. A. announcements, and articles in the school paper. Regardless, the importance of one-to-one communications should not be overlooked. Members of the planning committee and other interested people should be directed to contact people and explain the workshop personally. All communications should contain information regarding the purpose and objectives of the workshop, tentative agenda, location, cost, and participants' responsibilities. They should also be eye-catching and might include pictures, cartoons, color, etc.

Identify Support Personnel

Outside facilitators should be used when:
a. the skills required are beyond that available with the planning group,
b. there is a desire to introduce the outside person to the group,
c. the facilitator's role for the particular exercise or series of exercises is seen as inconsistent with the ongoing relationship between the participants and the conference leader, and/or
d. it is desired to capitalize on the perceived aura or objectivity of an outside expert.

Prior to contacting a facilitator, workshop planners should have thought through the five steps discussed in previous sections. Once a facilitator has been selected, he/she should be as actively involved in the program planning process as possible. When more than one outside facilitator is scheduled, it is important to coordinate the structured experiences and debriefing techniques they are planning to use. A general meeting of all outside facilitators prior to the workshop can add a feeling of continuity and flow to the program. If the outside facilitators are not remaining with the conference group throughout the workshop, it may be necessary to bring the individual up-to-date with the feelings of the group at the time he/she arrives at the workshop site. Due to the frequent use of the limited number of support personnel, it is recommended that the planning group contact prospective facilitators a minimum of one month in advance of the scheduled program.

Choosing a Location

There are a number of factors that need to be considered in determining a location for a workshop or retreat. Planners need to keep in mind the following factors:

1. Size of the group
2. Amount of money available to spend
3. Type of setting desired (rustic vs. modern; scheduled vs. convenient, etc.)
4. Food plans (meals provided for the group or preparing meals yourself)
5. Sleeping arrangements desired (large, dormitory arrangement or several smaller rooms)
6. Recreational facilities desired (while a variety of recreational facilities/ equipment is nice, keep in mind that unless facilitators establish some ground rules, this can serve as a distraction)
7. Type of meeting facilities desired
8. Type of transportation available

Funding

Before seeking funding, it is necessary to have a maximum cost estimate which should include prices for the following: food, lodging, transportation, materials, advertising, equipment and utensils, insurance (if applicable), speaker's fees, and entertainment. It has been found that charging participants a percentage of the total cost not only helps to defray expenses but also increased probability of other funding and increases their commitment to the experience.

Division of Responsibilities Regarding
Physical Accommodations

Groups can save themselves considerable time and trouble if they assign participants some "housekeeping" responsibilities ahead of time. An assignment sheet should be posted in a strategic location at the beginning of the retreat listing persons responsible for each meal preparation, meal clean-up, fire building, set-up, and any other tasks that planners feel are appropriate. In addition, various end-of-retreat clean-up assignments should also be included.

Determine Time Parameters for the Workshop

Time periods for successful workshop and/or retreats have ranged from 3 hour workshops to full weekend experiences. The University calendar should be consulted to avoid scheduling in conflict with campus athletic or major social events. The use of extended time can be very advantageous. That is, it is better to schedule less content into a weekend experience and use weekly meetings of target groups to facilitate leadership development with structured exercises than to ignore extended time opportunities and try to pack a weekend with too much content.

Establish Workshop Content

After the workshop goals have been refined into specific objectives and the time parameters for the workshop or retreat have been established, specific content can be identified. Following are some points to keep in mind in making decisions about content.

a. The content should be able to be *conceptualized* and experienced. Sessions should provide theoretical information on group process as well as an opportunity to practice application of new skills or techniques. It is assumed that behavior more likely will be affected if both dimensions are included.

b. One of the benefits resulting from any workshop, whether intended or not, is that participants will learn more about each other and will probably feel more comfortable when working together. However, to insure that this is not simply a haphazard process, facilitators need to designate an appropriate length of time at the beginning of the workshop, or even before the workshop begins, to provide some structured experiences that will help participants learn more about each other—hopefully more than simply name, hometown, and major. This will build some trust among participants which will pay dividends during later sessions.

c. As facilitators select structured experiences for a workshop, they should try to avoid those that will be repetitive for participants. This sometimes can be accomplished by simply revising exercises that may be familiar to some participants. If there are exercises being used which several participants have experienced previously, and if their participation in them might dull the effects, one may wish to have them serve as co-facilitators and/or observers. So, planners should keep a file of past workshops which indicates which exercises were used and who attended.

d. Complimentary exercises should be used. Exercises should be chosen which build on one another to achieve the ultimate goals of the workshop. It is important to start with exercises which teach basic skills and which do not tend to be personally threatening. As the workshop progresses, exercises requiring fundamental knowledge of terms and analysis may be chosen as well as those requiring self-analysis and criticism. Complimentary selection also requires that exercises be chosen which reinforce one another through debriefing and the use of previously learned skills. Finally, the presentation and exercise models should be varied to stimulate enthusiasm and learning potential. Concensus building exercises, role playing, situation simulation games, paper/pencil exercises, individual, small and large group experiences are a few examples of varied presentation methods.

e. Pacing is important—Free time should be constructed and sequentially building content should be used. Allow time for debriefing. The use of sequentially building content was discussed in the previous paragraph. Debriefing, however, is one of the most essential elements of an effective workshop. Sufficient time must be allowed for a thorough explanation of the purposes of the exercise, the concepts which should have been learned, and the applicability of this learning to the group's current situation. Attention should also be paid to the individuals' personal feelings especially where the exercise could be seen as threatening or critical. In planning for the debriefing of exercises, be certain that the presenter is familiar with the group and is knowledgable in the concepts to be discussed. It is also wise to allow at least fifteen minutes more than the estimated time for presentation for questions and individual attention. Free time is essential for maintaining the enthusiasm and freshness of the group. It also allows for individual questions and discussion. Free time can also be structured to reinforce some of the concepts learned in previous exercises: teamwork, cooperation, group decision making, creativity, and informal group interaction.

f. Know the skills and limitations of facilitative personnel. Provide facilitators with progress reports and assessments of the group. If goals of the workshop have been established prior to seeking consultants, it is possible to identify outside resource personnel with the specific abilities needed. When meeting with potential facilitators, explore with them their ability to prepare a learning experience adapted to the needs of your group. It is appropriate to ask the facilitator for a written proposal outlining the methods or techniques he/she would use in the presentation. If the selected facilitators cannot remain with the group throughout the workshop, it is important to update them with information regarding the group and its interactions when they arrive at the workshop. Facilitators may often be able to adapt their exercises to meet emerging attitudes or concerns which have developed since the workshop began.

g. Determine what exercises can be applied to the roles and needs of the group. Participants might be allowed to opt from a number of specific exercises. The uniqueness of the target group must be considered.

It should be remembered that whatever workshop content is chosen, it must be relevant to the target group. If simulations are used, time should be spent after those exercises discussing their applicability to the mission of the group. Facilitators should always be prepared to discuss the objectives of exercises and the application of those objectives to the purposes of the workshop.

There is a massive supply of workshop-type exercises, and it may become quite difficult to make decisions about the selection of appropriate ones. In dealing with this difficulty, some organizers prefer to offer a number of exercises at the same time, so participants can choose to attend those which seem most attractive to them.

h. Observe the group dynamics and be flexible enough to respond to those dynamics. Efforts should be made to assess the attitudes and feelings of the group throughout the workshop. Facilitators should encourage and remain receptive to feedback regarding the content of the retreat. One may find that there may be some needs that should be met through techniques other than those provided by pre-arranged exercises. Some content might have to be eliminated, and some might have to be added. Facilitators might come prepared with energizing exercises or those involving more play and fun than work.

i. Be able to follow up and assess the impact of exercises and the workshop in general. An important part of every workshop experience is the evaluation. Not only does the evaluation allow the participants to express their feelings about the workshop, it provides the planning team with feedback on their effectiveness.

Several methods of evaluation are available: (1) Following each exercise or activity, participants may be asked to give brief verbal or written feedback. (2) As a final segment of the workshop, participants can be given time to fill in a workshop evaluation, rating and commenting on their experiences. (3) Days, weeks, or even months after the workshop, participants should be polled to assess the long-term reaction to their experience. (4) If all or part of the workshop was content-oriented it may be appropriate to administer a post test, permitting participants and facilitators to discover how much they've learned.

Whatever methods of evaluation you, as planners, choose, remember there are two components to be assessed: (1) The participants' reactions to or feelings about the experience and (2) The level of skill or learning achieved by the participants.

j. Certainly completing an evaluation helps to reinforce the retreat experience in the minds of the participants. However, the retreat will seem more "real" (and will be remembered longer) if participants are provided with some tangible evidence of their experience. This "evidence" should serve to refresh their memories of workshop learnings as well as rekindle the interest and energy generated during the workshop.

The planning team may wish to distribute handouts which reiterate or elaborate the material covered. It's particularly effective to "package" handouts in an attractive folder or packet—this makes them more valuable to the participants and they are less likely to lose or forget about them. In addition, participants should leave the retreat with some record of what they personally thought and/or learned. Allow space for note-taking and encourage participants to develop personal or group action plans *in writing*. When participants brainstorm for ideas, develop new plans by consensus, or participate in group discussions. Record their sharings for publication and distribution following the workshop. Thus it becomes obvious that a significant part of planning involves reproducing materials, purchasing supplies and visual aids, securing audio visual equipment, and so on. Below is a checklist of helpful workshop aids:

newsprint	microphone	paper clips
butcher paper	writing paper	stapler
pencils (sharpened!)	index cards	thumbtacks
felt markers	clock	pencil sharpener
masking tape	clear tape	folders or manila
name tags	chalkboard/chalk	envelopes
hole punch	easels	record player
tape recorder	projector	...you get the idea...

Monitor Impact—Arrange for Follow-Up and Evaluation

a. Expectations should be set in advance and monitored during the workshop.

Workshop facilitators should have in mind specific desired outcomes for each individual workshop program as well as for an entire retreat as a whole. Expectations should be continually assessed during a retreat. Again, facilitators should retain enough flexibility so that intelligent responses to reactions to workshop and/or retreat content can be made.

b. Outcomes of the workshop should be followed up from the workshop. Successful workshops end with participants retaining good feelings about the experience, each other, and their roles as student leaders. It is one of the responsibilities of organizers to monitor those feelings and make efforts to remind participants of them afterwards. If goal and objective exercises are conducted, the results of them should be shared with participants at a later date. Generally, all efforts should be made to retain the community spirit and work attitudes that are evidenced in the workshop setting.

c. Evaluations should be processed and shared with participants.
A workshop evaluation should be used to solicit feedback from participants for organizers to use for future references. It is probably more useful to have each exercise evaluated separately. The summarized results of evaluations should be shared with participants, so that each individual can assess the way in which his/her attitudes regarding the workshop correlate to those of the total target group.

d. Relationships with non-participants should be monitored afterward.
Usually there are a number of members from target groups who do not attend the workshop. Efforts should be made to educate those individuals regarding the workshop objectives, content, and outcomes as perceived by facilitators and planners. They should be up-dated as much as possible. Their relationships with the workshop participants should be monitored to determine that problems of cliqueishness and ostracization do not occur, in either direction.

Workshop/Retreat Content

Selection of content for workshops/retreats affords the planning committee the opportunity to creatively prepare a format to accomplish its stated goals and objectives. This section has attempted to organize some basic workshop/retreat components into 18 categories, indicating possible objectives and potential outcomes, as an overview for the newcomer to workshop/retreat planning.

a. Awareness and Use of Resources
These exercises are designed to provide retreat participants with some knowledge of their work setting. They attempt to provide participants with an awareness of administrative and student government structure and personnel and they reflect the appropriate use of resources.

b. Communication Skills
Included here are a variety of exercises that help participants become aware of the need for good communication as well as to develop the skills necessary to communicate effectively with others. Included are the following areas: listening skills, non-verbal communication, precision in written communication, and one-way vs. two-way communication.

c. Community Building
Community building as an objective is often used in workshops to create a sense of belonging and a realization of the elements which pertain to an effectively functioning group of people. Relating to either large or small groupings and dealing with the varying levels of formality required is possible with exercises of this type.

d. Creativity

Exercises in this category usually provide opportunities for participants to express themselves in ways that are particular to their personalities and abilities. They may focus on individual traits that are ordinarily associated with creative people such as sensitivity, flexibility, independence, tolerance for ambiguity, and ability to abstract and synthesize. They may also stress impediments to creativity such as lack of self-confidence, resistance to change, and conformity. Similar approaches may be used to deal with creativity in groups. These exercises are often used as introductory experiences for other exercises which attempt to focus on specific aspects of creativity.

e. Decision Making, Problem Solving, and Change Analysis

Exercises in this area provide participants with experiences in group process. They can involve providing participants with a problem to which there is one appropriate response, or they can relate to decision-making only, where there may be no single correct answer or response. Many of these exercises, specifically those of an exclusively decision-making nature, involve a value identification component. Problem-solving exercises usually demonstrate to participants the benefits of a group rather than individual approach to a task. Facilitators and participants can be provided with decision-making or problem-solving models to provide a logical approach to performing a task. It is often most useful in facilitating these exercises to provide the group with a non-participating process observer to give feedback to the group regarding their operations.

f. Goal Identification and Follow-Up

Prior to any selection of a particular direction to take, it is usually proper for a group (organization) to identify priorities and goals. That done, energies become more focused and coherent. Activities within this framework would be expected to be a vehicle for such identification. As it is imperative to determine the adequacy of goals, there is necessarily a place for a follow-up examination. This should provide essential feedback and the opportunity to alter goals as it becomes prudent to do so. It is often useful to supplement these exercises with an opportunity for participants to be assigned to specific goals to enhance their potential for realization.

g. Group Dynamics and Task and Process Roles in Groups

Exercises within this category attempt to experientially demonstrate basic concepts of group dynamics such as task and process dimensions of organizations, functional roles performed within any group setting, "hidden agendas," power and influence, etc. Through the debriefing, particular concepts can be identified and emphasized to direct the experience toward the learning desired.

h. Impacts of Leadership Styles
    Exercises in this area are designed to provide participants with a working
    knowledge of the variety of leadership techniques and the subsequent
    impact of those techniques on group process. Often these exercises in-
    volve role playing where participants are given specific directions re-
    garding a particular leadership approach that is to be adopted. Many
    times an extended debriefing of Personal Leadership Assessment exer-
    cises may realize some of the goals of these kinds of exercises. Debrief-
    ing of these exercises involves a discussion of the leaders' impact on the
    group including group efficiency, morale, decision-making and in-
    dividual group participants' feelings about the group leader.
i. Introductions and Relaxation
    Exercises here are primarily designed to provide an atmosphere conduc-
    tive to initial interpersonal interaction where at least a large proportion
    of the participants are acquainted with each other or know each other
    only superficially. The object of introductory experiences is to "break
    the ice" by having people communicate and share with each other.
    Commonly, participants will learn names of people and possibly a few
    of their interests. Relaxation exercises are those oriented toward allow-
    ing participants to feel more at ease or in touch with their bodies or im-
    mediate environment.
j. Negotiation, Trust, and Compromise
    Exercises within this category usually provide problems for participants
    to resolve or tasks to be completed. Through negotiation with other par-
    ticipants, compromises are usually reached which may solve the prob-
    lem or accomplish the task. Many of the exercises used for this pur-
    pose can create an atmosphere of competitiveness and distrust that will
    thwart the efforts of the participants. Debriefing is usually built around
    the importance of trust and compromise in the group setting. Most exer-
    cises are long and require some expert debriefing skills.
k. Personal Growth
    These exercises provide participants with the opportunity to learn about
    themselves through self-awareness and appreciation. Some measure of
    personal growth will hopefully be achieved by any retreat component,
    but exercises in this area are designed for that purpose only. There is
    usually a relatively strong values clarification component in most of
    these exercises. Exercises in this area are most effective when the par-
    ticipating group, or sub-group, is limited to twenty or fewer participants.
l. Personal Leadership Assessment
    Experiences or exercises categorized as personal leadership assessment
    focus attention on the individual as a leader. Through the use of such
    exercises, program participants evaluate themselves on their ability to

provide direction to others in a task group. Related topics which are likely to be discussed during the debriefing are leadership styles, the impact of the leader on the group, and the responsibilities of leadership.

m. Position Role Assessment

In this category are those exercises or experiences which assist individuals to examine their roles as members of a task group. Further definition of job responsibilities and an evaluation of the degree to which these have been met are basic components of such exercises. Related topics which are likely to be discussed in the debriefing include purpose and goals of the organization, individual goals of members, and possibly the restructuring of the division of labor within a group.

n. Revitalizing

Purposefully energizing a group's movement, information flow, or introducing a new approach to problem resolution are the major thrusts of these exercises. Accordingly, a judicious use of exercises of this type is needed since their effectiveness needs to be coupled with a sense of timing for maximum value.

o. Specific Group Assessment

Activities designed to bring about specific group assessment are scheduled to cause an evaluation of the group's purpose, goals, and current status on any of several group dynamics dimensions (level of trust, sense of loyalty or belonging, adequacy of communication within the group, etc.). These activities typically generate considerable data which will need to be dealt with both in debriefing as well as the work setting when the group returns to its day-to-day operation. Related topics which are likely to be considered include program planning, problem solving, and knowledge and use of available resources to accomplish group goals.

p. Trust Building

Exercises in this area are designed to simulate a trust relationship between an individual and a group or between several individuals. They are usually designed to be facilitated in small groups. A trust simulation often involves an actual physical dependence on a group or individual. It is important that these exercises be monitored closely to insure their success, otherwise participants might learn not to trust each other.

q. Values Clarification

These are exercises that help participants to clarify their own values and, in some cases, to understand how their value systems might influence the decisions they make when confronted with several alternative solutions to a problem. They also may afford an opportunity for participants to compare their value systems with others and with society.

250

Conclusion

The use of workshops in student leadership development and human relations training has been very well received by employee, volunteer, and staff personnel in the recreational sports program.

Although workshops/retreats provide a practical medium for enhancing group cohesion and improving job performance, perhaps the greatest benefit lies in their potential as avenues for specialized training and mainstreaming of minority and women into leadership positions. The increasing availability of resources on leadership·development, human relations training, and minority concerns open the door to creativity and flexibility in tailoring workshop/retreat formats that best suit particular group needs. The determining variable in the provision of effective workshop/retreats rests with the degree of commitment of the administrative staff toward the concept.

PARTIAL BIBLIOGRAPHY OF RESOURCES

Amiott, William K., *Grouping for Solutions,* Sigma Nu Educational Foundation, 1971.

Amiott, William K., *Honor, An Ideal in Practice,* Sigma Nu Educational Foundation, 1969.

Gibbs, G. S. (ed.), *Handbook of Games and Simulation Exercises,* Beverly Hills, California: Sage Publications.

Lawson, John D., et. al., *Leadership is Everybody's Business,* San Luis Obispo: Impact Publishers, Inc., 1977.

Maier, Norman, et, al., *The Role Play Technique,* La Jolla, California: University Associates, Inc., 1975.

Nylen, O., Mitchell, J. R., and Stout, A., *Handbook of Staff Development and Human Relations Training: Materials Developed for Use in Africa,* Washington, D.C., 1976.

Otto, H. A., *Group Methods Designed to Actualize Human Potential: A Handbook* (3rd ed.), Chicago: Achievement Motivation System, 1968.

Pfeiffer, J. William, and Heslin, Richard, *Instrumentation in Human Relations Training,* La Jolla, California: University Associates Publishers, Inc.

Pfeiffer, J. William, and Jones, John E., *A Handbook of Structured Experiences in Human Relations Training,* La Jolla, California: University Associates Publishers, Inc., vols. 1-7, 1969-1977.

Pfeiffer, J. William, and Jones, John E., *Annual Handbook for Group Facilitators,* La Jolla, California: Associates Publishers, Inc., #1-6, 1972-1977.

Stadsklev, Ron, *Handbook of Simulation Gaming in Social Education,* University of Alabama, 1974.

[1]Material adapted from *Perspectives on Residence Education: A Resource For Leadership Workshop Planners and Facilitators;* eds. Bustello, Hennessey, Lorenz, McKaig, McPheron, Miller, Rowe, Shipton; Department of Residence Life, Division of Student Affairs; Indiana University, August 1977.

ASSERTIVE BEHAVIOR: A TOOL FOR THE EFFECTIVE ADMINISTRATOR

by Sally Meyers, Miami University

Have you ever been intimidated by a rigid athletic director or an uninformed physical education department chairperson; reluctant to negotiate salary increases, changes in job title, or job function, concerned about dealing with colleagues who make sexist, racist, or condescending remarks, nervous about presenting yourself at a committee meeting where others ignore, discount, or put down your ideas, uncertain about having to confront a staff member or employee for not performing in his position, or afraid to talk back when your intramural recreation program or actions are unjustly criticized? If you have, or if any of these situations have relevancy to you, then learning about assertive behavior may be important to you.

I have entitled my presentation, "Assertive Behavior: A Tool for the Effective Administrator," and will speak to you from a personal as well as professional perspective. I want to make it clear from the begining that I am not an expert in the field of assertiveness training, nor am I am an expert in the field of administration. I feel comfortable speaking on the two topics simply because I perceive assertiveness as a real asset to administrative effectiveness. When I could find no other author who had advocated this relationship, I felt that what ideas and thoughts I would share with you might be meaningful.

Since becoming a bonafide "administrator" just two short years ago, and in eight previous years as a college instructor, I have been continuously dismayed, frustrated, and annoyed by the ineffectiveness of many administrators with whom I have worked and observed. When I became an administrator myself, I soon realized that I, too, was often ineffective, and I began to appreciate the difficulty of dealing with situations that involved the terms authority, management, adjustment, conflict, controversy, supervision, and goal setting which characterize, in part, the role of all administrators. My past educational training had not prepared me to competently handle the administrator's role. Like me, many administrators reach their position by being promoted through the ranks, rather than taking specific training aimed at developing administrative competencies. Thus, it should not be too surprising that most administrators are simply unaware of certain skills, tools, and behaviors that would increase their effectiveness. As the Dean of the School of Education at the University of Chicago wrote, "Education administration is an emerging, not an established, profession. Its practice varies, by whatever criteria one may employ, from excellence to failure." (6:16)

It was with this awareness of administrative incompetency in mind that I became interested in the procedure of assertiveness training which, despite its impressive recent history and wide popularity, is still a very young and developing procedure. While the term "assertive" has provided a field day for would-be semanticists. I have found the most useful definition of the term to be the one you see on the overhead. Assertive behavior is an honest and direct approach to interpersonal interaction that allows an individual to stand up for and express needs, opinions, and appropriate feelings in a way that properly regards and respects the rights, opinions, feelings of the other interacting individuals. (3:Chapter 2)

While this definition is intended to be comprehensive, it is recognized that any adequate definition of assertive behavior must consider several dimensions. Such dimensions might include four areas:

A. Intent: behavior classified as assertive is not intended by its author to be hurtful of others.

B. Behavior: behavior classified as assertive would be evaluated by the objective observer as itself honest, direct, expressive, and non-destructive of others.

C. Effects: behavior classified as assertive has the effect upon the receiver of a direct and non-destructive message, by which a "reasonable person" would not be hurt.

D. Socio-cultural Context: behavior classified as assertive is appropriate to the environment and culture in which it is exhibited, and may not be considered "assertive" in a different socio-cultural environment.

Because the term assertive is frequently confused with other types of behavior, it is important at this point to clarify the differences among certain types of behavior. The three general types of behavior which I will discuss with you include assertive behavior, non-assertive behavior, and aggressive behavior.

The basic message in assertion is: This is what I think. This is what I feel. This is how I see the situation. This message expresses "who the person is" and is said without dominating, humiliating, or degrading the other person, but assertion involves more.

Assertion involves respect—not deference. Deference is acting in a subservient manner as though the other person is right, or better, simply because the other person is older, more powerful, experienced, or knowledgeable or is of a different sex or race. Deference is present when people express themselves in ways that are self-effacing, appeasing, or overly apologetic.

Two types of respect are involved in assertion: respect for oneself, that is, expressing one's needs and defending one's rights, as well as respect for the other person's needs and rights. An example will help to clarify the kind of respect involved in assertive behavior.

Bill Johnson is an intramural recreation director at a large, midwestern university in Indiana. He is a very busy man and trys to manage his time so that he can accomplish most of his numerous tasks while at the office. A faculty member, Mr. K., "drops in for a chat" usually two or three times a week. Usually Bill enjoys these visits, but in the past month they have occurred almost daily, and he has become somewhat annoyed. Moreover, the loss of time has begun to interfere with the accomplishment of certain tasks. Still, Bill doesn't want to hurt his friend's feelings. As he sees Mr. K. entering his office door this morning, Bill chooses to be assertive.

Bill smiles but remains firm, saying, "John, I just can't visit with you today. We've spent a good deal of time talking this week, and although I've enjoyed it, I just can't afford any more time. I must get a lot of paper work done today. In fact, I'd like to set up a sort of 'limit' on our visits — I get carried away and I do need to discipline myself to work."

The goal of assertion then is communication and "mutuality"; that is, to get and give respect, to ask for fair play, and to leave room for compromise when the needs and right of two people conflict. In such compromises neither person sacrifices basic integrity and both get some of their needs satisfied. (2:357-360)

It is most important, however, to recognize that assertion is not simply a way to get what one wants. This type of viewpoint emphasizes success in attaining goals. Thus, it can cause people to become upset or discouraged when they believe that acting assertively will get them what they want. Second, this view concentrates only on the asserter's rights and not on the personal rights of both parties. Such an attitude increases the chances of people using aggressive or manipulative methods to get what they want. Third, it may lead to irresponsible behavior in which assertion is used to take advantage of other people. When used irresponsibly, an assertive person can assertively ask for favors and think that it's just too bad that the other person is not strong enough to refuse their requests. It is interesting to note, however, that a byproduct of responsible assertion is that people often do get what they want because most people become cooperative when they are approached in a way which is both respectful of self and respectful of others.

The term nonassertion involves violating one's own rights by failing to express honest feelings, thoughts, and beliefs and consequently permitting others to violate oneself, or expressing one's thoughts and feelings in such an apologetic, diffident, self-effacing manner that others can easily disregard them. In this latter type of nonassertion, the total message which is communicated is: I don't count — you can take advantage of me. My feelings don't matter — only yours do. My thoughts aren't important — yours are the only ones worth listening to. I'm inferior — you are superior.

Nonassertion shows a lack of respect for one's own needs. It also sometimes shows a subtle lack of respect for the other person's ability to take disappointments, to shoulder some responsibility, to handle his own problems, etc. The goal of nonassertion is to appease others and to avoid conflict at any cost. (3:Chapter 2)

The term aggression involves directly standing up for personal rights and expressing thoughts, feelings, and beliefs in a way which is often dishonest, usually inappropriate, and always violates the rights of others. Aggression is often confused with assertion by the general public, but a simple example should make the difference apparent.

Marilyn is a community recreation director in a large city. In her busy job, Marilyn handles a variety of responsibilities and her superiors feel she does an excellent job. Her staff, however, sees her very differently. The "queen bee" they call her — an office tyrant who runs her office with an iron pen. Her secretaries are confronted with Marilyn's attacking, "put-down" style of criticism frequently. "Joan," she would scream, "can't you ever get those schedules in correct form? What the hell is wrong with you anyway?" Marilyn is acting as if the only way to gain the respect and cooperation of her staff is to browbeat them into obedience. This style of relating to others is labeled aggressive. Although Marilyn usually gets her way, she does so at the expense of others, and in the process, she loses their esteem.

Marilyn's employees would work as hard, maybe harder, and respect her more if she treated them assertively with respect. She could have said, "Joan, you have not prepared these schedules correctly. They must be done over again." That simple statement, in a firm but non-hostile tone, would give the message clearly without attacking the secretary personally.

The usual goal of aggression is domination and winning, forcing the other person to lose. Winning is insured by humiliating, degrading, belittling, or overpowering other people so that they become weaker and less able to express and defend their needs and rights. The basic message is: This is what I think — you're stupid for believing differently. This is what I want — what you want isn't important. This is what I feel — your feelings don't count.

This table should help to identify some very important differences between these three types of behavior:

A COMPARISON OF NONASSERTIVE, ASSERTIVE, AND AGGRESSIVE BEHAVIOR*

ITEM	nonassertive	assertive	aggressive
Characteristic of the behavior	Emotional dishonest indirect, self-denying, inhibited.	(Appropriately) emotionally honest direct, self-enhancing, expressive	(Inappropriately) emotionally honest, direct, self-enhancing at expense of another, expressive
Your feelings when you engage in this behavior.	Hurt, anxious at the time and possibly angry later.	Confident, self-respecting at the time and later.	Righteous, superior, deprecatory at the time and possible guilt later.

255

The other person's feelings about herself when you engage in this behavior.	Guilty or superior	Valued, respected	Hurt, humiliated
The other person's feelings toward you when you engage in this behavior	Irritation, pity disgust	Generally respect	Angry, vengeful

*Modified from Albert and Emmons (1970)

Clearly assertive behavior as I have just discussed is called for in nearly all areas of interpersonal relationships. For the administrator in intramurals and recreation these relationships on the job might include staff members, peers, colleagues, parents, students, bosses, employees, salespersons, and the general public. Let me identify some of the characteristics of the assertive administrator.

The assertive administrator is fully in charge of himself in interpersonal relationships, he feels confident and capable without cockiness or hostility, he is basically spontaneous in the expression of feelings and emotions, and is generally looked up to by others. For some professionals, such feelings are already present, at least to a certain degree or in specific situations. But in truth, there are very few of us who have developed an adequate repertoire of assertive behaviors so that we may choose an appropriate and self-fulfilling response in the variety of situations in which we are placed. Consider with me as I delineate a variety of administrative situations which could be appropriately handled by assertive behavior. When a situation has meaning in your own life, try to think how you have handled the situation in the past and how you felt about the way it was handled:

1. Being the target of unwarranted backbiting by the physical education department or athletic department.
2. Being unable to get your ideas regarding staff increases, budget increases or program expansion accepted in meetings with your superior's.
3. Being rejected or simply not considered for faculty rank.
4. Being pressured for more time when you are already working beyond your capacity and responsibilities.
5. Having a strong superior shift undue responsibility on your shoulders.

Such situations often develop into a conflict situation in which it seems that one party will win and the other will lose. It may surprise some of you that a great deal of work has been accomplished in recent years to develop effective methods of conflict resolution in organizational settings. It is possible for all parties to win—at least in part—and no one need lose. Conflict which has reached a point of strong angry feelings can be resolved only if those feelings are expressed honestly and openly. An assertive, "I'm really angry about your unwillingness to see my point of view" can be the beginning of a constructive dialogue. A non-assertive, "Let's forget it" avoidance of the problem or an aggressive "You stubborn S.O.B." is certain to leave both sides frustrated and unsatisfied. (3:105)

Assertiveness training says, go ahead, get angry but develop a positive, honest, assertive style for expressing it. One must always keep in mind the four components of an assertive response:

1. A knowledge of what your feelings, needs, opinions, beliefs are.
2. A commitment to extend the right to others to have and express their own feelings, needs, etc.
3. An understanding exactly what that the conflict is between components 1 and 2 above.
4. Practice and exercise the right you have to express your needs, feelings, beliefs, etc. in working out a solution that is acceptable.

Assertiveness training endorses without qualification the concept of the equality of human beings. Each individual has the same fundamental human rights as the other person in an interpersonal relationship, roles and titles notwithstanding. It is most important in learning to be assertive that one becomes aware of his/her own personal rights. Different people may allow themselves different rights, but an individual must also realize that all rights carry with them certain responsibilities and limitations.

An example of a framework of rights for an administrator might include the following:

1. An administrator has the right to set attainable and realistic objectives and goals for his program and to set parameters for achieving these objectives and goals.
   a. Responsibilities: To provide the staff, or means, to achieve the objectives in striving for the goals; To secure approval from his superiors regarding the goals which are set.
   b. Limit: One should not arbitrarily change the objectives and goals that have been set without considering the inconvenience, confusion, and responsibility which may be involved.
2. An administrator has the right to settle conflicts and controversies.
   a. Responsibilities: To attempt to have both sides work out a solution that is acceptable to both parties; To recognize that other persons may have ideas and feelings totally different from yours; To be sure all concerned parties have the same information about the problem.
   b. Limit: One does not have the right to be unfair or disrespectful in dealing with conflict situations.
3. An administrator has the right to be wrong
   a. Responsibilities: To recognize and accept when you are wrong without downgrading yourself.

      b. Limit: One does not have the right to be negligent or careless in situations which could jeopardize other individuals' rights.
4. An administrator has the right to exercise leadership and authority in creating policies and procedures.
      a. Responsibilities: To seek as wide a public as possible to participate in the formulation of all policies and procedures: To abide by and enforce the policies once they are adopted; To change policies and procedures when there is a need for change.
      b. Limit: One cannot expect others to uphold policies that are violated or not enforced by the administrator.

One of the first steps toward developing assertive behavior is to assess your own level of self-assertiveness. I have chosen a short series of questions, applicable to common administrative situations. Be honest with yourself in answering these questions. How "well" you do depends upon your own standards. The real question is: How do you feel about the way you handle these situations?

1. Do you generally express what you feel?
2. Do you find it difficult to make decisions?
3. Are you openly critical of other's ideas, opinions, behaviors?
4. Are you prone to "fly off the handle"?
5. When a company representative makes an effort, do you find it difficult to say no even though the product is not really what you want?
6. Are you reluctant to speak up in a discussion or debate?
7. Do you often step in and make decisions for others?
8. Do you think you always have the right answer?
9. When you differ with a person you respect, are you able to speak up for your own viewpoint?
10. Do you have a difficult time complimenting or praising others or accepting the same?
11. Do you shout or speak very loudly to get others to do as you wish?
12. At staff meetings do you control the conversations? (3:25-27)

The key to this type of inventory is choice. There is no single way that one must act in a particular situation. The goal is that you can simply choose for yourself how you will act, and not be manipulated by circumstances or people. In choosing how you will behave consider these questions:

1. How important is this situation to me?
2. How am I likely to feel afterwards if I don't assert myself in the situation?
3. How much will it cost me to assert myself in this situation?
4. Will the assertive behavior, which I feel morally obligated to make, make any difference in actuality?

The decision to assert oneself involves a sense of what is appropriate in a given situation. (7:64)

If you are now asking yourself the question, "Why should I change?" consider with me for a few moments, the consequences of your present behavior. If you are, at times, or most often, a non-assertive administrator the following situations may have developed:

1. You may come across to others as selfless, subservient, generally agreeable, and as one who does not cause problems for other people. In other words, an administrating marshmallow.
2. Staff members needing direction and/or discipline do not look to you for leadership or guidance.
3. You may be criticized by your colleagues for indecisiveness.
4. Your peers recognize that you avoid the issue and do not express opinions.
5. Students may have discovered that you can be persuaded or manipulated into agreeing with all their demands regardless of your own feelings or ideas.

Any of these consequences of non-assertiveness is bound to produce personal anguish, disappointment, perhaps self-recimination. In general, the non-assertive administrator fails to utilize the talents and powers of his superiors. In the long run, a person who is frequently non-assertive feels a growing loss of self-esteem and an increasing sense of hurt and anger. Even more internal tension may then result. When this tension is constantly suppressed, somatic problems may develop such as headaches, depression, stomach aches, or backaches. Finally, although other people may initially feel sorry for the nonassertive person, their pity often turns into irritation, and finally disgust and lack of respect.[2]

It is often more difficult for the aggressive administrator to acknowledge a need for help, since he/she is accustomed to controlling the environment to suit his/her needs. If aggressiveness is your style, you may wish to consider that your present relationships may become worse unless you seek change. Consider these questions:

1. Do you most always take the lead in staff meetings?
2. Do other colleagues, such as physical education chairpersons or athletic directors, seldom engage you in conversation willingly?
3. Are you invariably the "winner" in arguments?
4. Are you the "ruler" of your subordinates on the job?
5. Do you vehemently expound your feelings and opinions?

In general, the aggressive administrator fails to utilize and develop the talents and skills of his subordinates. Since behavior, is more easily influenced by immediate consequences, it is unfortunate that the most immediate consequences of aggression are usually positive, while the long-run consequences are negative. Immediate positive results include emotional release, a sense of power, and getting goals and needs met without experiencing direct negative reactions from others.

259

The long-term negative consequences include losing or failing to establish close relationships and feeling one has to be constantly vigilent against attack from others. You may be thinking that you might become more vulnerable and lose control over other people. It's like believing, "I can only survive if I'm invulnerable and able to control people." The myth of this belief is, I believe, overlooked by many administrators. When people apparently acquiesce under aggression, often they simply have gone underground and subtly sabotage the aggressor's control. Highly aggressive behavior may eventually cause individuals to lose jobs and promotions, get high blood pressure, become alienated from their staff, get into frequent arguments, and eventually feel deeply misunderstood, unloved, and unlovable. In addition, when one is aggressive, other people may retaliate in direct or indirect ways by causing work slowdowns, backbiting, or through doing things that are subtly irritating.

As you have been reading, perhaps, you have become aware of assertion, non-assertion, and aggression in yourself and in others. The concepts of assertiveness are basic enough so that you can teach yourself and others these concepts. As you become familiar with good eye contact, proper use of voice, appropriate ways to speak your feelings, and other methods that are suggested, you will find yourself recognizing the good and bad approaches which others use in dealing with people. Such awareness can be the beginning of helping yourself and others to be more assertive.

The main method, however, which is used to teach assertion is through assertive training groups. The process of assertive behavior development may be very effectively applied in a group setting. The key to the success of such groups often depends upon the skill of the group leaders or facilitators. These persons are usually counseling psychologists, counselors, or persons specifically trained in teaching others to develop assertive behavior. At Miami University in Oxford, Ohio assertiveness training classes have been conducted by the University's psychology department and by a husband-wife team of counselors sponsored by the community crisis-intervention center. If your community does not offer such opportunities, much can be learned from reading the books recommended in the attached bibliography.

An important caution to those of you who decide to try to develop more assertive behavior is that there are going to be failures in your attempts at assertion. At times the other person may be unreasonable or unyielding, and your best assertions would not move him/her. Although you want your assertions to work, and you want to achieve your goals, assertion procedures will not turn you into an instant 100% success in all your relationships with others. Remember that the greatest value of self-assertion is the good feeling of having expressed yourself. To know that you are a person of value who has a perfect right to self-expression and to feel free to go ahead and say what you're feeling as long as you don't infringe on the rights of others, and to do it are the most important benefits of all. Assertiveness training cannot be all things to all people — for you the administrator it is one tool for helping you to become the person you want to be. Such an accomplishment may prove to be the key to achievement of most of your goals in life.

BIBLIOGRAPHY

[1]Alberti, R. E. and Emmons, M. L. *Your Perfect Right: A Guide to Assertive Behavior.* San Luis Obispo: Impact Publishers, Inc., 1970, 1974.

[2]Albert, Robert E. (ed.) *Assertiveness: Innovations, Applications, Issues,* San Luis Opispo, California: Impact Publishers, Inc., 1977.

[3]Alberti, Robert E. and Michael L. Emmons, *Stand Up, Speak Out, Talk Back,* New York: Pocket Books, 1975.

[4]Bach, G. and Wyden, P. *The Intimate Enemy: How to Fight Fair in Love and Marriage.* New York: William Morrow & Co., Inc., 1968.

[5]Dawley, Harold H. and W.W. Wenrich, *Achieving Assertive Behavior: A Guide to Assertive Training,* Monterey, California: Brooks/Cole Publishing Co., 1976.

[6]Halpin, Andrew W. (ed.) *Administrative Theory in Education,* London: The MacMillan Co., 1958.

[7]Lange, Arthur J. and Patricia Jakubowski, *Responsible Assertive Behavior,* Champaign, Illinois: Research Press, 1976.

[8]Moriarity, T. "A Nation of Willing Victims," in *Psychology Today,* April, 1975.

[9]Phelps, S. and Austin, N. *The Assertive Woman.* San Luis Obispo: Impact Publishers, Inc., 1975.

[10]Rogers, C. R. *On Becoming a Person.* New York: Houghton Mifflin Co., Inc., 1961.

[11]Salter, A. *Conditioned Reflex Therapy.* New York: Farrar, Straus, 1949.

OUTDOOR COORDINATOR TRAINING PROGRAM

Jim Rogers, Illinois State University

Before discussing Outdoor Coordinator Training, the term outdoor coordinator must be defined. Then it can be determined if outdoor coordinators would be beneficial to a program and, if so, what responsibilities and duties would they have.

An outdoor coordinator is a program volunteer who is knowledgeable in one or more outdoor recreational activities and who uses his or her knowledge to help organize and participate in program-sponsored outdoor trips.

The first criterion for determining a program's need for outdoor coordinators is the sponsorship of outdoor trips. The Outdoor Progam sponsors approximately 60 outdoor trips each year and has found outdoor coordinators to be very beneficial.

If outdoor trips are presently being sponsored, the following questions should be considered when determining coordinator need:

1. Is outdoor trip liability a major concern to the program and the educational institution?
2. Is the outdoor program presently paying for trip leadership and supervision?
3. Is the program concerned with the safety of its trip participants?
4. Do sponsored outdoor trips use program-owned or state-owned vehicles?
5. Are there program or institutional policies and regulations that must be adhered to by the participants on outdoor trips?
6. Is there a need for a close working relationship between the trip participants and the outdoor program?
7. Does the program presently lack skilled outdoor instructors?

If one or more of the preceding questions was answered yes, then an Outdoor Coordinator Training Program would most likely be very beneficial.

The responsibilities and duties of an outdoor coordinator can vary to meet the needs of a variety of outdoor programs. Outdoor coordinators have a broad spectrum of responsibilities and duties. They are responsible for all records, policies, and procedures related to outdoor program transportation. It is also their duty to serve as the coordinator of equipment, people, food, time, and University policy related to the trips in which they participate. The program also requires its outdoor coordinators to instruct various outdoor workshops and to participate in various committees and boards related to the Outdoor Program.

At this point, it must be understood that once a group has reached their trip destination, the outdoor coordinator possesses no program designated leadership over the other trip participants. All outdoor trips are "Common Adventures" which require all participants to take an active roll in decision-making. The outdoor coordinators can make suggestions as can the other group participants; however, all suggestions and decisions are ultimately determined by the entire group.

Where can one find people who are so willing to dedicate their free time to a program? Each institution will have its special population of dedicated outdoor enthusiasts which can be used as its resource pool. Outdoor coordinators can come from a variety of academic departments.

During the first week of every fall semester, the Outdoor Program advertises in the school paper for volunteer men and women. The response to the ads has always been excellent, with at least 75 to 125 persons applying for the position.

At this point it is very important to have a set of tools developed which will aid in the selection of the right individuals for the job. It is very important to choose individuals who are dependable, loyal, knowledgeable, experienced, energetic, out-going, sincere, and who are interested in the program and seeing that others have good outdoor experiences.

The following set of tools will make the selection process much easier and more efficient.

1. *Outdoor Coordinator Summary*—This summary should include all responsibilities, duties, requirements, benefits, dismissal policies, and an estimated time commitment required of a coordinator. The summary should be given to all prospective applicants. It will eliminate many individuals who may not want to accept the responsibility or who may not want to make the time commitment required by the program.

2. *Outdoor Coordinator Application*—This application should include questions which will tell which individuals possess the characteristics that are required for outdoor coordinators. The application should only be given to those individuals who are willing to accept all requirements which were stated in the Outdoor Coordinator Summary.

3. *Coordinator Outdoor Skill Tests*—These tests should include questions on the basic principles and safety procedures related to the various outdoor trips being sponsored. Many individuals will have extensive outdoor experience, but only a small portion of these people actually understand the basic principles behind a particular outdoor activity.

4. *Personal Interviews*—These interviews are generally used to help clarify answers on applications which are not completely understood. It is a good tool for determining whether a particular individual possesses the appropriate personality which is needed for the position.

During the selection process it will be discovered that many individuals only possess the basic knowledge of one or possibly two of the outdoor skill areas in which outdoor coordinators are needed. Individuals tend to choose their favorite activity and excel in that area. Compensation for this fact can be made by only accepting coordinators into the program under one skill area, which should be that individual's area of expertise. Consequently, the program will have specialists in backpacking and specialists in canoeing. This will require individual tests in each skill area. It will require extra time and effort, but will ultimately improve the quality of the program. The above process has enabled the Outdoor Program at Illinois State University to choose the more specialized and consequently, the more knowledgeable individuals in the different outdoor skill areas.

The number of outdoor coordinators needed by a program will be determined by the number and variety of different outdoor activities offered. The University sponsors approximately 60 trips a year in four different outdoor skill areas and uses 24 outdoor coordinators. Each of the coordinators is required to coordinate 2 or 3 trips a semester. Since the program sponsors more canoeing and backpacking trips, the number of coordinators accepted into those areas is higher.

Outdoor coordinator training begins the second weekend of the Fall semester. All individuals who have been selected are required to attend a three day workshop which has been developed specifically for them. The purpose of the workshop is not to teach skills, but rather to teach and discuss group trip planning, program and coordinator responsibilities and duties, trip problem solving, transportation policies and procedures, trip safety, equipment usage, wilderness manners, program liability, and their importance and position in the program.

The workshop is held at a nearby Boy Scout camp in an outdoor setting, offering indoor accommodations which help prevent the loss of valuable time that would otherwise be needed for setting up camp and cleaning pots and pans. The weekend workshop is designed to give the coordinators extensive training, and at the same time it enables and encourages them to become acquainted with each other and the staff of the Outdoor Program. It is very important to develop a very close and open working relationship with the coordinators if the program is going to be successful.

The remainder of the outdoor coordinators' training is completed over a two to three year period. It includes mandatory outdoor workshops, outdoor reading requirements, teaching and aiding in the instruction of outdoor activity workshops, and direct experience in their particular skill area.

Each outdoor skill area, such as backpacking and canoeing, is divided into three distinct coordinator achievement levels. Each skill area and each achievement level has its own educational requirements. The first level of achievement is titled Trip Coordinator. Before a coordinator achieves this level, he or she must attend specific workshops which will enable them to increase their knowledge in their particular skill area. They must also read a required book list given to them by the outdoor program. Each coordinator is tested over each workshop and book. All must pass written and practical exams with a score of 85%.

The second achievement level under each skill area is that of Junior Coordinator. To achieve this level, the coordinator must first attain the level of Trip Coordinator. Then he or she must attend specified instructor workshops, read additional books, and successfully pass written examinations by 85%. They must also have the experience of coordinating two to four outdoor trips, depending on their particular skill area. The final requirement for this position is to aid in the instruction of specified workshops which have been designated by the program. At this point the coordinators are aiding the director in the instruction of workshops which they previously attended.

The third level of achievement is the Senior Coordinator rating. Once this level has been achieved, the individual has attained the highest position under his or her particular skill area. To attain this level, a Junior Coordinator must have been head coordinator on two to five trips, and must personally instruct a given number of specified workshops which are directly related to his or her chosen skill area. All workshops are per-arranged by the outdoor program.

There is one achievement level higher than that of Senior Coordinator and that is Coordinator Specialist. This level can only be reached by individuals who have attained the rank of Senior Coordinator in more than one skill area. Although coordinators are only accepted by the program into one skill area, they are encouraged to work on the educational requirements of other skill areas at the same time. This helps provide the program with more well-rounded and experienced coordinators.

This training program makes it possible to select the top individuals, slowly broaden their knowledge through various workshops and books, supply additional outdoor experience, provide teaching opportunities, and produces, for the program, a very knowledgeable corp of outdoor coordinators.

Each coordinator has made a time committment to the program and in turn, the program must make a commitment to them. It serves no purpose to set educational requirements for the coordinators and not make available the means to complete them. It is important to schedule the required workshops, purchase the required reading material, and provide outdoor workshops that they can teach. Each coordinator will set his or her own program goals, but the program must always encourage, stimulate, and provide the stepping stones for their success.

The outdoor program can take several steps which will stimulate, motivate, and keep its coordinators striving toward their final goals. One very important step is to strive to make the outdoor coordinator position well known and respected at the institution. Another step is the presentation of Achievement Awards. Outdoor Program shirts, emblems, jackets, and certificates are awarded to coordinators who have taken the step up to higher achievement levels. The cost of the awards are minimal compared to the benefits the program will derive from them.

It is also important to keep the coordinators involved in the program and in each other as much as possible. This can be accomplished through program mailers or letters, special coordinator events, and through their involvement in committees which deal with the future of the program. All these suggestions can make the coordinators feel more important and more a part of the total program. With very careful planning and programming, the seed of program pride will be planted and hopefully both will grow with it.

WOMEN IN INTRAMURAL OFFICIATING

by Charles Espinosa, New Mexico State University

Today, women are entering professions and avocations which were previously considered male domains. There are increases in the numbers of female business executives, governors, lawyers, and astronauts. The emergence of women as officials in intramural competitive sports is no exception. The number of women willing to work at this thankless art seem to be on the increase. They are out there calling contests for men as well as women.

It is really no surprise to observe accounts of striped-shirted women on the fields, courts and diamonds of our programs if one is cognizant of today's current issues of feminism and the Equal Rights Amendment. It is a sign of the times for women to work at jobs which seem to refute the traditional "female role" stereotype. However, the more thought that is given to these accounts of women officiating men's as well as women's competitive sports, the more profound these observations become.

Women officiate contests in the women's, men's and co-rec programs. They are scheduled for game assignments along with men. All the women officials have an equal opportunity to be selected for the higher paid post season play-off games.

From all indications, more and more women are entering the officiating ranks of the competitive sports program. An attempt to understand this more active role that women are taking in the competitive sports program must be left to conjecture since this area is yet void of research. For now, perhaps, we can speculate about this trend by asking some intriguing questions.

1. Why would a woman be willing to take on a task which has been described as "the most difficult job related to sports?"[1]
2. Why would a woman enter an area of work in which leading predictors of success were found to be "previous officiating and participation experience?"[2]
3. Why would an individual of the female gender be attracted to a job that requires one to render decisions in rather technical matters of sports, within an atmosphere charged with prejudice and emotion?

Perhaps through research, it will be found that women, like men, are attracted to intramural officiating for the modest financial gain. It may be that the women officials who call competitive sports for men and women are those more "active and potent" females in our society who are willing to accept or ignore the possible social consequences of refusing to adopt to the traditional female role.[3]

"Too long the 'masculine' and 'feminine' mystique has determined how one must behave and what one must do if one wishes to 'fit in' to society as it has been predetermined."[4] Intramural-recreational sports programs should be responsive to women and recruit them to participate in all aspects of sports. I would hope that women will continue to enter this most important facet of intramural recreational sports programs. A woman official can be just as dedicated, dependable, and competent as the male official.

Officials should be actively recruited from all segments of the campus population, especially the women's. It certainly seems that women are willing to come out to take on these jobs. Let's hire them!

BIBLIOGRAPHY

[1]Bunn, John, W. THE ART OF OFFICIATING SPORTS, Prentice-Hall, Inc., Englewood Cliffs, N. J., 1968.

[2]Fratze, Mel, R., "Personality Traits of Intramural Basketball Officials," NATIONAL INTRAMURAL ASSOCIATION-25th ANNUAL CONFERENCE PROCEEDINGS, National Intramural Association, 1974, pp. 114-116.

[3]Griffin, Patricia, S., "What's a Nice Girl like You Doing in a Profession Like This?", QUEST, 19 (January 1973): 96-101.

[4]Varner, Hazel. "Sexism, Discrimination, and the Laws", NATIONAL INTRAMURAL RECREATIONAL SPORTS ASSOCIATION 1975 26th ANNUAL CONFERENCE PROCEEDINGS, National Intramural Recreational Sports Association, 1975, pp. 262-268.

THE INTRAMURAL OFFICIAL: A "PROFESSIONAL" APPROACH

by J. Michael Dunn & Jon Allen, Marquette University

The purpose of this presentation is not to downplay any program currently being practiced in the training of Intramural Officials. Instead we hope to successfully demonstrate to you a few techniques that you may wish to incorporate into your present program.

The Marquette University approach to the Intramural Officials is as follows:
1. Recruitment
2. Training
3. Evaluation
4. Compensation/Satisfaction
5. Retention

This five step approach to developing a "professional Intramural Official" consists of a number of thoroughly planned objectives that should be met within each area.

Recruitment

1. Flyers and posters well-placed on campus meet some needs.
2. Returning officials are encouraged to let others know of this Intramural opportunity.
3. The campus newspaper and most notably, its weekly Intramural Page, announces training meetings and prints interviews with experienced officials in an effort to revive campus interest in officiating.
4. Men and women from all walks of campus life are encouraged to become involved in the phase of the intramural program that suits their needs. Men may work in the women's program and women in the men's. Faculty-Staff are even encouraged to sign-up.
5. "No prior training necessary" publicity is emphasized.
6. Existing game situations and managers' meetings are used to encourage chronic complainers to "come out and solve the ills of the program."
7. Athletic organizations on campus are informed of program needs.
8. Although "no prior training necessary" is emphasized, every effort is made to recruit the fully qualified officials.

Training

1. A 3 day training clinic is offered and is mandatory for all new officials.
2. Excellent officials from previous years who return to their roles as officials are required to attend only one meeting (rules discussion).
3. Each clinic training day consists of a 1½ hour session.
   a. Day #1 deals with handling administrative details, beginning the rules discussion and encouraging a non-academic growing experience for each person persent.
   b. Day #2 includes an introduction to the Marquette University Athletic Officials' Association, a slide and film show, and a discussion on proper positioning and mechanics.
   c. Day #3 ties together all loose ends, re-emphasizes major points, and ends with the written and practical examinations.
4. A mid-season clinic and pre-tournament meetings are also required of all officials.
5. A pre-season Officials' Classic Basketball Tournament (single elimination) is conducted to allow supervisors to provide on the court advice for the officials selected to work.
6. A training cycle of officials for the entire season is as follows:
   Early season — Rookies are paired off with the best veteran officials.
   Mid season — Rookies are paired off with others of similar or less ability.

      Late season   — Selected rookies and veterans work together.
      Tournament — Officials are assigned to games on the basis of their ever growing skills.

7. Throughout the season officials are selected on the basis of their talents and encouraged to seek state certification.

Evaluation

1. The supervisors rate every official during each evening's work on a departmental form. Feedback is both written and oral. Stressed are strong and weak points.
2. Certain areas of development are keyed upon:
   a. Knowledge of the rules
   b. Control of the game
   c. Proper positioning and mechanics
   d. Hustle
3. The Marquette University Athletic Officials' Association also rates their member officials whenever requested to do so by the individual official. Pay raises may come about as a result of this rating.
4. Officials rated excellent by their student associations receive many added benefits.

Compensation/Satisfaction

1. Officials are paid a basic rate with a nickel increase for each additional year of experience in the program.
2. Excellent ratings result in nickel pay raises and greater selection of games.
3. Excellent officials are scheduled purposely to work the more difficult games. Good performances may result in double time pay.
4. State certification or registered officials receive a nickel raise.
5. The better officials are often "farmed-out" to local and community programs. Our Intramural Offices serve as a clearing-house for many of these requests.
6. "Honor Games" are assigned to the better officials.
7. Excellent officials are given additional responsibilities (eg., key committee assignments, hearing boards, etc.)
8. The better officials may advance through the ranks to become supervisors, office assistants, and administrative personnel.

Retention

1. Professional attitudes and performance are encouraged through departmental evaluations, Association evaluations and constant peer ratings.

2. A realistic approach is used with each individual. We attempt to implant the seeds of pride and professionalism.
3. Supervisors and program administrators play-out their own "professional" roles.
4. Faithful, critical, and periodic evaluation is made of the entire program by the officials and supervisors. Lines of communication are maintained between all areas.
5. When an official takes the floor his/her fellow officials, supervisors and program administrators totally support his/her performance.
6. Veteran officials are asked to return the following season with a positive attitude and a friend who might also like to officiate.

With this final step we have travelled the entire cycle. For certain, many gimmicks and a variety of ideas are used each year. The secret is that—We search for quality through quantity, quality through training and development, but most important we practice quality through the requirement of a totally "professional" approach. We owe this much to ourselves, our supervisors, our officials, and our participants.

RECREATION AND INTRAMURAL SAFETY

Nissis Miholson and Jo Ann DeSantis, Loyola University New Orleans

Among those assembled today are students interested in pursuing the field of Recreation and Intramurals, others that arecurrently assisting professionals and finally professionals themselves. The number of people that are
The number of people who are highly knowledgeable about the causes and extent of injuries in different sports, as well as the general procedures for prevention that may be taken, is probably very limited. The knowledge of this subject matter will have a great influence on the safety of participants.

The search to pinpoint the cause of the many sporting accidents in the world seems to be never ending. Accidents and injuries are so varied in their extenuating circumstances that no single factor can be expected to stick out prominently. There is one inherent truth—at the root of any accident, lies human factors; whether they be physiological, psychological or social.

Human Factors

Physiological. Some of the factors that affect a participant's physiological ability in direct conjunction with accident probability include: sex, age, emotivity, fatigability, visual function, perception, attention, alcoholism and drug use.

Psychological. All phases of psychology apply to the accident experiences in sports. Basic human responses to stimuli such as reaction time, spatial relationships and depth perception are examples. Emotional disturbances either of chemical or organic origin can cause problems too. Adrenalization is caused by excitement which is sometimes as difficult to control as is aggression.

Social. People join in and play sports for gregarian reasons. They not only want to be with people but they want to test themselves. The social conquest can very easily get out of hand. Pressures to perform from peers and coaches can influence the athlete, even to the point of getting into an accident to escape these pressures.

Factors giving rise to these reflect untrained or poorly trained officials, participants who are untrained as far as the physical demands of the sport, inept coaching and overcrowding of facilities. Too often in recreational sports, activities are dropped because they are deemed dangerous. By merely learning to recognize these hazards, removing them or controlling those that cannot be removed, staff should be able to continue offering valuable activities. There are five major areas of concern the Recreation-Intramural specialist must be cognizant of. These are:

Hazardous Playing Areas—

Facilities, whether they be indoor or outdoor, should be inspected regularly and systematically. Padding should encompass any pole or standards in the vicinity of the playing area. Floors should be inspected and checked for traction, and playing fields should be level and free of any holes. Finally, areas should be sufficiently large so that teams are not required to play in crowded situations.

Inadequate Equipment—

Equipment checks are a very necessary item in accident prevention. Quality playing equipment and its maintenance fall in the laps of the Intramural staff. One of the specific duties of student directors is that of equipment maintenance, repairs and inventory. The student director is also assisted by several work-study personnel where additional help is often needed, and specifically on bicycle repairs.

Administration and Supervision—

Activity or game supervisors should be in attendance at all scheduled Intramural contests. Supervisors should be trained in first aid procedures, remembering of course that first aid is just immediate treatment. A training room or facility should be made available and emergency procedures should be posted and made to be common knowledge among all personnel of the Recreational and Intramural staff. In addition to activity supervisors the department utilizes floor supervisors who patrol the playing areas during the recreation facilities' hours of operation. The floor supervisors remove any obstacles that may create a hazard, help to maintain traffic circulation within the building, and act as a security force in terms of proper usage of apparatus, equipment and playing areas.

Most of the injuries these supervisors encounter will be referred immediately to the Student Health Center. In the event a participant cannot be moved, either a Student Health Assistant or nurse, both of whom are on duty 24 hours a day, are summoned to the scene of the accident. If an injury occurs on a playing field some distance from the school, then a two way communication system is put into use.

Game Officials—

Injury prevention and the quality of officiating are directly related. Game officials must be made aware of their role in controlling injuries. It has been an age old battle with most school officials in terms of rigidity versus wishywashiness. Officiating must be strict enough to reduce the number of injuries due to unnecessary roughness yet not so strict so as to remove the enjoyment from the game. The fine line between the two can be met by thoroughly schooled officials. Administrators should remember that the rules of the games may also be modified to eliminate potentially injurious situations.

Coupled with the abilities of the game officials is the implementation by the officials and staff members of the overall departmental philosophy. The adherence to this philosophy by all parties concerned, will create a much easier task for the student official and, at the same time encourage and increase participation. The philosophy of the Recreation and Intramural Sports Department reads like this—

> "The Department of Recreation and Intramural Sports is designed to provide opportunities for students, staff and faculty to participate in competitive and non-competitive, organized and informal sporting activities. It is the Department's express purpose to meet the diverse recreational needs of the University Community with a broad based comprehensive program, through the formal intramural program, informal recreation and the various sports clubs."

Finally, the last major point of concern.

Levels of Competition—

The grouping of participants according to skill level is at times a necessary administrative control. A skilled person can use his body much more efficiently and effectively than an unskilled person. In contact sports, pitting the skilled against the unskilled can pose a serious safety problem. Therefore the student participant should be given his option as to which level of competition he feels most comfortable competing within.

Legal Liability

The possibility of being sued by injured Intramural participants for an act of contributory negligence should be a concern of all staff members.

The key to liability as recreation specialists will be in regard to that aspect of the law related to negligence. The University Recreation and Intramural Sports Department and its personnel owe the participants the legal duty, of exercising care to prevent injuries. Negligence results from the breach of this duty. "Negligence is the failure to act as a reasonably prudent person would act under the particular circumstances."

Consider the full meaning of this principle of law. First of all, negligence can consist of inaction as well as action. If someone fails to do something expected of him by the law, he can be considered negligent. In the same sense, actively doing something contrary to what the law expects can also be negligence. "A reasonably prudent person . . .", is a mythical person established by the law; "foresight" is his major characteristic. As a recreation specialist, and administrator, you would be considered as being a person of ordinary prudence. If an instance arises where you could have, or should have, forseen the harmful consequences of a participant's behavior, it is negligence on your part if you do not take the necessary steps to prevent such consequences. A liability lawsuit poses this critical question: could or should the staff member, in the exercise of reasonable prudence and foresight, have anticipated danger or hurt to another, under the particular circumstances? Finally, the specific facts in a case are all-important in the determination of negligence. Negligence is a question of fact for the jury to decide.

Assumption of Risk—

The assumption of risk clause is one of the most obvious legal defenses that applies to Intramural sports. This is merely a statement that says when individuals voluntarily engage in activities, they take upon themselves the risks involved in such participation. Both players and spectators assume the normal risks involved in participating in or witnessing athletic contests. Several other defenses we have open to us in order that we may avoid losing a suite of tort are:

273

Proximate Cause of Injury.

The negligent behavior must be what is known as "the proximate cause of the injury", before a jury will sustain a damage suit. This means the negligent action of the Recreation-Intramural staff person was the direct and immediate cause of the injury.

Contributory Negligence.

If the injured participant failed to act as a reasonably prudent individual should have acted under the circumstance and, if this negligence contributed to the accident, any negligent conduct on the part of the staff member is cancelled.

An Act of God.

When an uncontrollable act of the elements occurs and there is an injury, no liability is attached to the Recreation-Intramural employee, even though he might have been negligent.

It becomes quite apparent that accident prevention in Recreation and Intramural Sports must include due consideration for legal liability. The most frequent litigation among athletic coaches and Recreation-Intramural Directors today, seems to evolve from alleged lack of supervision. See to it that contests, activities and games are well supervised and efficiently operated. Remember, injuries aren't in the budget.

Safety Education in the Department

At the start of each semester a first aid seminar is conducted. Those in attendance at these seminars include the Director of Recreation and Intramurals, the graduate assistants, the student directors and all activity supervisors. You may want to have all your student staff present, (i.e. officials, door checkers, equipment managers, gym leaders.)

At this seminar cover the 5 basic types of injury, their causes and how to care for them. Review the steps of mouth-to-mouth resuscitation and Cardio Pulmonary Resucitation (CPR); how to care for shock and what to do in an emergency. Discuss a Standard Operating Procedure (SOP).

The standard operating procedure should include diagnosis of extent of injury, when to call in health services, when to go directly to the hospital, how much first aid to administer, cases where the injured should or should not be moved and which hospital to go to.

Distribute the phone numbers of all the health assistants and their call hours, the hours of the health service facility, the nurses and the hours of their duty.

Go over all proceedures for filling out injury report forms, injury logs and follow up procedures.

These meeting may be adopted in any way you see fit.

Safety techniques presently employed include

(1) Safety lectures for the staff
(2) Have a direct tie to one of the nearby neighborhood hospitals.
(3) Work very closely with the Health Center and the health assistants.
(4) Have completely stocked training kits. For outdoor activities take the kits to the fields and place one on each field. For indoor activities have a kit on each court, plus the complete use of the athletic training room. During open recreation keep the training kits in the central equipment room and the training room ready for use.
(5) At all scheduled IM activities or specially planned recreation activities have a competent staff member on duty. This staff member should have the basics in first aid and/or athletic training.
(6) Have two sign-in forms. One is used at the initial time of injury—for us to record the extent of the injury, the care taken and referral. The second is used as a running log to help keep track of the progress of the injury. Sign the first injury report form as to whether the person was signed over to the Health Service Nurse or Assistant. If the injured was sent to the hospital record the hospital's diagnosis.
(7) Have a whirlpool report form to keep track of the progress of severe injuries.
(8) Print a sheet with all basic first aid techniques discussed and ways to care for them. This is distributed to all people in attendance at the meeting.
(9) Anytime there is a serious injury or doubt in one's mind as to the extent of the injury, tell the staff not to hestitate in referring the injured to the health services for treatment or further referral.

Safety Equipment Available

(1) Have air splints, crutches, a stretcher and blankets available for serious injuries.
(2) Have accessibility to 2 whirlpools and a foot bath available for those in need of rehabilitative care.
(3) Furnish a lower body and an upper body weight pulley system which is available for those in need of rehabilitative care.
(4) Have 2 completely equipped training kits and a training cabinet.
(5) Retain on file the Cramer book—"Athletic Training in the Seventies", along with their illustrated posters and monthly bulletin. Post these flyers around the training room and file the bulletins with the important info underlined in red. These are used both for reference and for the injured participant to gain a bearing on his injury.

Safety Precautions

An athletic trainer or person proficient in first aid should be at each scheduled IM activity or specially scheduled recreation activity.

The lines of communication between the recreation-intramural office and the Health Services Building should always be open. The students working in the control room in the recreation center should have a complete view of the facility. If they see an injury they call the main office. As the injured is cared for, students are informed as to whether or not we need them to contact the health center.

Two injury report forms can be used. One is used at the initial time of the injury and the second is used for any type of follow up treatment. Have a whirlpool sign in form to keep a record of those who use the whirlpool. Keep these contained in a book in the training room which can be personally updated every week.

Follow-up for any basic first aid administered to an injured participant of Recreation or IM's carried on within a 24-48 hour period. The injured person shall be contacted by phone and asked as to the general progress of the injury.

If it was a serious injury (such as a break or dislocation) the injured participant is requested to obtain from the Health Services Center a schedule of available rehabilitative care that is made at the Recreation Center. Two whirlpools and a weight pulley machines are used in conjunction with the program of rehabilitative exercises.

Have a policy concerning the return to activity of an injured participant which states:

> "The Recreation and Intramural Staff will not allow any student who has had to go to the hospital or the Health Services Center for medical treatment, regardless of the extent of the injury, to rejoin their team in any competition until a doctor's note is secured.
> This doctor's note must clearly state the extent of the injury, the length of time required for rehabilitation or inactivity, and any other restrictions to be placed upon that student in the future. This note is to be brought to the Health Center and a xeroxed copy will be forwarded to the Recreation Center. This policy will now take precedence over a former policy of leaving the decision of whether a player can rejoin his team, up to the team captain."

APPENDIX A
ITEMS CONTAINED IN AN ATHLETIC TRAINING KIT

1. Nitrotan
2. Cinder suds
3. Gauze, 4 x 4 and 3 x 3
4. Elbow Sling
5. Cold packs, plastic ice bags and ties
6. Tongue depressors
7. Inhalents, ammonia capsules
8. Strawberry Ointment
9. Rubbing Alcohol
10. Scissors for zip cuts
11. Oral screw
12. Zonas or porous white tape
13. Conform or Elastikon tape
14. Bandaids
15. Aspirin; not to be distributed before or after a game
16. Atomic Bomb, mild
17. Atomic Liniment
18. Ace bandages—Four inch, three inch and two inch
19. Felt and foam
20. Cold spray
21. Ice Packs
22. Foot Powder
23. Fungo Spray
24. Skin Lube
25. Black Glare
26. Butterflies, medium and large
27. Q-tips
28. Esophogeal Airway—only to be carried if user is proficient in its use

CHAPTER VII

Students Assistants in Recreational Sports

STUDENT ASSISTANT ASSISTANCE FOR RECREATIONAL SPORTS

Karen Olsen & Pat Mueller, University of Minnesota

Recreational Sports programs exist because of students, but students do not exist because of Recreational Sports programs. From this priority concept evolves the purpose of "serving universtiy and college communities through sports", by "providing them with mind-body sports experiences." To effectively accomplish this, policies must be established, scheduling completed, programs promoted, funds raised, officials recruited and trained, equipment maintained, and many other tasks completed on very tight timetables.

At a school such as the University of Minnesota, these essential chores could easily become an overhelming task for 18 full-time staff members, requiring many hours of overtime to keep the program going on a day-to-day basis, let alone time for the very important work of developing new and innovative programs. Fortunately, the Recreational Sports Director, as well as the other staff members, realize they hold their positions because students want a Recreational Sports program and that students are the focus of the entire program. Students are very clearly the folks that make the concept of extracurricular sports feasible for the 35,000 plus participants annually. Minnesota staff members serve as facilitators, providing continuity and guidance, while students set the tempo and flavor. Students determine quantity, as well as the quality of positive mind-body sports experiences, through participation in the program as teammates, lifeguards, referees, equipment managers, umpires, team managers, Sports Club officers, schedulers, clinic coordinators, instructors, office supervisors, special events administrators, and fund raisers.

This presentation identifies methods and benefits of student assistant utilization in Intramurals, Sports Clubs, self-service activities and in some non-traditional roles.

Intramurals

The oldest phase of Recreational Sports, Intramurals, at the University of Minnesota is the area which best utilizes the student assistant concept. During the 1878-79 school year, men competed in loosely organized baseball and football games. One hundred years later, how has the scene changed? More than 1100 softballs are used annually, 4200 towels are laundered each week, and 82 games played in a single sport on a single day. More officials are used in a single year than students graduating during the first decade of this century. With 18 full-time staff members for all phases of Rec Sports, who administers the important multi-interrelated details for Intramural programs offering more than 35 sports each year? The option chosen at Minnesota was to utilize students to the maximum.

One of the biggest hurdles in almost all programs is scheduling. To deal with this, student assistants to the Intramural Coordinator are hired. They are provided with team names, facility availibility schedules, officials lists, an eraser and a pat on the back. During Fall Quarter of 1977, five assistants successfully scheduled 3,258 games in 12 sports. This involved finding times for 11,229 people to participate. This was not the end of their task. They also carried most of the responsibility for the use, maintenance, and storage of equipment. These assistants supervised playing areas for their sports, making certain fields were chalked and first aid kits were filled, among countless other duties. Although they did not always personally perform the tasks, they followed up to be sure they were completed by those responsible for them. Training and recruiting of officials, for the most part, was also arranged by student assistants. And most importantly for the players, student assistants were knowledgeable enough to arbitrate disputes fairly.

Each of these areas, from start to finish, was the result of student conceptualization. They received advice from the coordinators of Intramurals, but at no time were they told "we've always done it this way". The result was a tightly run, yet highly creative set of tournaments.

How is it known that participants were satisfied? The repeat participation record speaks for itself. Many students participate in two team sports each quarter. It is highly improbable that Intramurals would be as successful or as popular today, if it were not for student input. Because these student assistants are also participants, they are able to provide the type of sports experience expected from the "other side of the fence." It is sometimes difficult to understand players' reactions regarding a particular rule, official, or facility, until the problem is seen from a player's perspective.

Sports Clubs

In 1957, Judo enthusiasts formed the first Sports Club at the University of Minnesota. In 1978, Sports Clubs number more than 50, each having an average membership of twenty-five. How did this growth pattern develop? Who was responsible for its success? What is involved in maintaining this type of program? These and other questions are best answered by those responsible for Sports Clubs — students. The following chronological review of the framework of how students "made to happen" also provides the blueprint for the continuance of this medium for making sports experience a reality for more than 1200 of their peers.

In 1974, the Director of Recreational Sports made a commitment to upgrade the existing Sports Clubs' program. A few students were contacted and presented with some ideas, as well as a full-time staff member to assist them. The program mushroomed. A student assistant to the full-time staff person began making changes. First, clubs were given one set of guidelines to follow. A uniform bookkeeping system, requirements for receiving funds, policies and procedures for use of University vehicles and methods of reserving facilities for games and practices were among these guidelines. The result was a decrease in confusion and misunderstandings. No longer were there irate phone calls from the auditor's office, nasty notes from the vehicle rental division, nor arguments with other users of facilities.

After establishing uniformity in practices and the first student assistant graduated, momentum did not decline. Instead, a snowballing effect resulted. More students joined existing clubs and others began to establish new clubs, reflecting the varied recreational interests of students on a campus of 50,000. Student assistants rose to this challenge. Subsequently, a newsletter was established to insure that clubs received the exact information at the same time. The practice of drawing up constitutions for each club was begun, adding cohesiveness to the program. And guidelines for establishing new clubs removed the difficulty for students to create something of their own. Each of these activities was supervised by a student assistant who received advice from the full-time staff member.

It is interesting to note that, while student assistants implemented these new policies, they were also advising clubs on long range policy matters, resolving disputes within and between clubs, helping club officers with day-to-day administrative tasks, and also serving as correspondents for the

Sports Club program. The overall effect of student assistants on the program was one of continuity. These individuals developed considerable expertise about Sports Clubs. Any member of any club could turn to them for advice. If they didn't have the answer, club members were referred to the proper source. They knew how to keep a club going, even after the president left, or following a potential rift in the club. They were willing and able to help their replacements learn the sports programming patterns.

What has been gained through utilization of student assistants? By the time they completed their stint as an assistant, they were well versed in administrative techniques and headaches. They also learned diplomacy. They acquired some skills which might not be expected, such as editing newsletters, accounting and bookkeeping, a bit about every sport in the program and how to draw up long and short range plans following an accurate timetable. These are the kinds of extra skills needed when applying for jobs, giving them advantages over other applicants. There is simply no way the total sum of these experiences can be found in a classroom on any campus. It adds to the concept that Sports Clubs are truly self-programmed by the students, for the students.

Self-Service Sports

Free-time activities have taken on as many different meanings as there are students on campus. In increasing numbers, however, students have begun to utilize their breaks by going to gymnasiums, swimming pools and tracks. To promote this beneficial form of recreation, many schools have developed self-service programs, which allow participants to use facilities without participating in organized competition. The concept of free-play time is one of the most important facets of positive mind-body sports experiences. However, there is a danger this time will not be developed to its fullest potential. Through careful scheduling of facilities, disseminating information, and programming design, participants can receive greater benefit from their free hours than just a couple of laps in the pool or a few bench presses in the weight room.

As in all other phases of the total Recreational Sports program, student assistants can make the difference between mediocrity and acceptability or excellence. To be more effective, this time should be scheduled when the maximum number of participants can benefit from it. A full-time staff member usually has more responsibilities than just bartering for facility time. An aggressive student can be the key to gaining the most usable self-service times, rather than just hours left over after varsity teams have finished practicing.

Once the facilities are available, it's important students know these times have been set aside for them. Several ways of distributing information like this are by posters, newspaper ads and informational talks. The success of any of these methods pivots on two important questions, where and when? Student assistants are the people who walk across campus each day. It's their peer group these informational items need to reach. With this in mind, it seems only appropriate that the student assistant help coordinate the publicity for this program.

Currently, the University of Minnesota offers three programs which have made a significant contribution to the over-all Rec Sports program. Each of these has been designed to encourage students, staff, and faculty members to recreate on an informal, self-directed basis, individually or with others.

The first of these requires that participants set goals and target dates for reaching those goals. Included are activities such as "Swim and Stay Fit" and "Run For Your Life". Utilizing student assistants as coordinators of these activities maximizes output of work by freeing the overall coordinator of the self-service program for items demanding immediate attention. Major tasks in this area would be to help participants set realistic goals and keep track of their achievements.

Secondly, a student assistant can help to meet the needs and serve the interests of the participants by designing and presenting self-improvement clinics. Minnesota's clinics on cross-country skiing, diet and nutrition, and bicycling have been extremely well received. Usually one day or less in length, these clinics give students a chance to share knowledge they've learned with others, as well as giving the student body an opportunity to hear speakers give tips on improving their side-stroke or accuracy in volleyball serving. A high quality clinic can be designed by a student assistant in a short period of time. With this use of personnel, these popular programs can be offered frequently.

Finally, many Recreational Sports offices find they are being called upon often to act as a referral service for participants looking for a jogging partner, a short-time swimming instructor to improve a backstroke, or even a sparing partner. This area provides one of the most unique and useful ways in which student assistants can encourage participation. Through a file system, individuals can be matched with a partner or a helper. This system may require some recruiting, but many students would enjoy teaching another the fundamentals of weight lifting or how to get the most out of running.

Each of these concepts are relatively easy to implement and require only minimal maintenance. However, the benefits to participants are immeasurable. The week spent by a student assistant preparing a clinic, designing a goal oriented program, or finding a tennis player for a novice, not only teaches that student skills in administration, but teaches participants knowledge that will always remain a part of their sports-for-life philosophy.

Another function of student assistants in self-service sports involves *Federal 504 Regulations,* which prohibit discrimination against disabled students. It's important to recognize that conditions must allow disabled students to participate in their fullest ability, unobstructed by facility barriers. To accomplish this on a department-wide basis, it's essential that this be the prime focus of one person. Student assistants can devote complete attention to the complexities of accessibility. Hopefully, in time and with the aid of the full-time staff member they can help the department meet the guidelines of 504 Regulations keeping in mind that the department exists to serve *ALL* of the students.

Non-Traditional Roles

In every department or unit, there are innumerable tasks which would add to the program, but aren't critical for day-to-day operations, so they remain, sometimes for years, on the proverbial "drawing board." Unfortunately, because of the overwhelming tasks of day-to-day administration, it's difficult to look at one of these drawing board ideas and see that it could cut-back or eliminate a daily red-tape blockage, or that it could refocus a lagging portion of the program. In Recreational Sports, there are a few areas which habitually remain in the idea stage, unless a specific effort is made to follow thru with them.

In January of 1976, the Universtiy of Minnesota's Recreational Sports Department decided to employ a "student assistant to the director" on an experimental basis, to take up the slack on some existing programs and to begin work on some projects left in the idea stage. Since that time, the position has evolved to include piloting new projects, previewing materials, investigating proposals, and providing student viewpoints when program policies were reviewed. This position had never been considered as a possibility anywhere on campus. Undergraduate students had always been thought of as test-tube washers, grounds-crew workers, and library aides. This thought pattern on the part of administrators was challenged when a student was given responsibilities that many of these same bureaucrats would not trust to their secretarial staff such as bidding on departmental publications, seeking outside funding sources, or preliminarily interviewing of prospective employees. What has been the result of such responsibilities being given to a student? Most of the projects have met with success. There have been a few which are classic examples of first degree failure. But these become the source of great humor, as well as hard, cold learning experiences.

There are four areas in which student assistants have the potential for making the greatest contributions. First, there is piloting of new projects.

One example alluded to earlier is finding ways in which the program can become more accessible to handicapped students. This requires seeking out disabled students to determine their needs. Sometimes, it may only be necessary to find a place for the blind to keep their guide dogs while swimming, or rigging up a ramp system for wheelchair students to get into the basketball courts.

From concern about the handicapped students at the University of Minnesota a second thought surfaced. Whan happens when someone has a heart attack during participation? The idea of teaching cardio-pulmonary resuscitation to all area supervisers was researched. Even though playing areas were within 5 or 10 minutes of some of the finest medical facilities available, those first 5 or 10 minutes are the difference between severe brain damage and a few weeks in the hospital before returning to work. Fortunately, supervisor CPR skills have not been utilized but they are available.

Another new project is the use of video tape. The student assistant to the director introduced this concept during Fall of 1977. Rec Sports video tapes are shown between classes on closed-circuit televisions. Categories include recognizing outstanding teams, promoting upcoming events, and generally spreading the Rec Sports world, without relying on the student press.

A second area which has been a great timesaver for the director is previewing materials. Having a student assistant highlight or outline materials enables the director to keep abreast with the latest developments on Title IX, conference proceedings and regulations on the handicapped. They do not have to read publications completely, but instead can skim the highlights or synopsis prepared by the student assistant; subsequently, the information can be completely read at their convenience.

This is essentially the same way in which the third area works. The director may consider the feasibility of a new project by having his student assistant investigate all options and proposals. Examples are the possibility of finding outside funding sources. It's highly unlikely the director would have time to wade through sources on foundation grants or to do the leg work for reviewing the possibility of selling sports equipment items. Researching these projects before giving serious thought to them reduces the guess work in proposal planning and implementation.

The final and perhaps most important role student assistants can play is that of student advocate at staff meetings. Eligibility rules, priorities in scheduling, and guest policies are based on students needs and desires. relative to the departments' ability to provide such services. Occasionally, it's easier to consider staff convenience over student needs. At this point the student assistant must be diplomatically vocal and assertive to insure the best possible arrangements.

The end result of a student assistant to the director is a two-way street.

The student learns research skills not usually acquired at the undergraduate level. They learn new and varied ways of dealing with administrative entanglements. Of course, they learn the fine art of getting their own way. The director has more time free from the paper and leg work. Proposals that had been tucked away for so long are finally implemented. And the entire department is assured of a "student conscience" when considering changes or reviewing previous decisions.

SO YOU WOULD LIKE AN ASSISTANTSHIP

By Jo Ann De Santis, Loyola University

The first step in obtaining an assistantship is to positively decide that you would like to further your education. This is where your biggest decision may come to pass. The next decision you will make is in reference to which area or region of the country you would least enjoy living in while furthering your education. If you are mainly or normally a warm climated person, do not even begin to consider schools in a cold climate area, unless you feel you can adequately prepare for it. Decide your area limitations and concentrate on the areas you would like to attend. Once this is done you can begin to write to schools in your favored areas to solicit needed information.

In writing to your favored area schools you should request information as to the type or types of assistantships available, the appropriate amount of money available, the length of the assistantship, whether or not that time can be lengthened or shortened, and if there is a need for you to attend summer sessions to meet that time requirement. Ascertain the length of time required to work on your masters, approximately what the assistantship covers, the types of available housing (undergraduate dorm, graduate dorm, off-campus housing) and their costs, general cost of area living, and requirements to be accepted at the school.

Once all this information is gathered, you have a base of reference. This reference may prove very valuable when you start to narrow your choices or cannot decide between two highly favored schools.

None of the above preparation should ever stop you or interfere with your going to as many interviews as possible. These personal and formal interviews are extremely important and should be experienced. You will find with the more interviews you go to, the more relaxed you will become and the more questions you will have. But to go to an interview such as these, you must be prepared.

To be prepared for an interview consists of many things such as an up to date resume, having some specific questions pertaining to your role or future duties and knowing exactly what it is you want from your masters degree.

Do not be afraid to ask questions, especially of an existing graduate student at the university of your interest.

Find out from these graduate students the exact nature and definition of your role. Ask about the positions entailing responsibilities, the housing situation, grading standards and proceedures in the graduate school, and most of all the school or community's social life.

At Loyola Universtiy, a private institution of 5,000 fulltime students, we are fortunate enough to have two graduate students. Stuart Johnson and I share all responsibilities of the Recreation and Intramural programs. He cares for the recruitment, training, ranking, scheduling and paying of all of our referees and officials. I handle all first aid and training responsibilities. This includes running the training-rehabilitation medicine room, seminars on first aid techniques and proceedures, caring for all game injuries, and the subsequent follow up care or treatment of anyone who was injured in our games. Stu schedules all teams as to time and place of all their games up until the playoffs. He prints a complete seasonal schedule for each league and posts it. This seasonal schedule includes dates, times, court number and opponents. He handles all game postponements and their rescheduling. I handle all publicity, sport introductory flyers, sign-up deadlines, manager's meetings, official's clinic information, scores of games or matches, league standings, playoff dates and times, divisional winners, and overall champions. We also publicize modified building hours, early or special closing hours, all postponed games and their rescheduled times, and forfeits. We are also lucky enough to have a very good rapport with our school newspaper. Each week they print for us entry deadlines, the past week's scores, the upcoming week's games and any special information we might think necessary.

Both Stu and I handle any type of game protest, all clinics for new and club sports. We each have specific nights when we are on duty at the recreation building, to act as overall activity supervisors of ongoing intramural games. As supervisors we make sure all games go as smooth as possible, all officials have shown or made other arrangements and all injuries are cared for properly. This is not to say that either of us does not do the other's job or assume the other's responsibilities occasionally.

We have very little discrimination of job duty. Because there are two of us we do not specify as to whom is the mens', women', or co-rec intramural coordinator. We are simply the intramural coordinators. We each handle what we are most proficient in. Stu handles football and basketball, while I take care of volleyball.

Neither of us handles the programming for the recreational facility on campus, but work in very close conjunction with the Director of Recreation and Intramurals and his recreational facility supervisors who do the programming for the facility. We keep them informed as to the times and number of courts we need weekly for either recreational or intramural activities presently being run. This is broken down into daily schedules and court set-ups, specific to each sport, number of teams and facility requirements.

As far as recreational activity is concerned, we plan many special activities throughout the year. Each year we hold an all-night activity. This year we added a men's class vs. class basketball tournament, a womens' powder-puff football game and live entertainment. We also run introductory sport clinics and clubs.

The most imoprtant thing that an incoming assistant should remember and keep in the proper perspective is to make yourself available. Be open to whatever comes along. Yet, never lose sight of your own personal needs and goals. You should always keep your main area of interest in focus, regardless of the area your assistantship covers. While doing this do not close yourself off from other programs that you may encounter and which may benefit you later on in your career.

Monetary considerations should include a monthly stipend and full tuition expenses. This stipend covers rent, food and some social expenses.

If at all within your means, try to visit the school of your final decision prior to moving there. This will give you a chance to check out rents, neighborhoods and expenses firsthand. Check out the dormitory situation and graduate housing facilities.

Go to your new position with some money in the bank that may be used for unexpected expenses or just to allow you some freedom of choice in housing and furnishings until you get really settled in. Try to go a few days prior to your expected starting date. This gives you a chance to get the feel of things, straighten out any last minute problems you might encounter and take care of a lot of personal needs.

Give the school, job, area and your associates a chance. They all have to get used to you as much as you do to them. Do not be easily upset or start to be ultra sensitive. It is just a matter of time until you all begin to get used to one another. Remember, it is just as trying on them as it is on you. Never compare past schools, jobs, bosses facilities or coworkers. It is a very easy thing to do, but once you start it is very hard to stop and only tends to make you feel alienated. Get involved in things around the school and at work as soon as possible. Do not sit in your room or apartment and wait for things to come to you. Go out and look for them. Most of all, do not get easily discouraged.

In summary, remember, this is a stepping stone into the profession. Anyone seriously considering a career in this profession should look long and hard at an assistantship. The role of a graduate assistant has taken on an increasingly important meaning. No longer will educational (book) training suffice. It now needs to be suplemented by the practical experience gained through an assistantship.

CHAPTER VIII

Sports Clubs

SPORTS CLUB FINANCING

Larry Cooney, Iowa State University

There are many definitions and philosophy statements concerning sports club programs. However, one thing in common is that Sports Club Programs provide many educational experiences for participants which will aid them throughout their life. Though Sports Club Programs are generally not conducted as traditional, formal education, they are a form of education and should receive funding from university sources to subsidize club programs.

Many different funding practices for sports clubs are used throughout the country.

In a sports club survey by Palmasteer[1], it was found that 27 out of 33 universities surveyed had club programs receiving some funding. He found that the larger the institution enrollment, the larger the number of clubs offered; however as enrollment and number of clubs offered increased, there was not necessarily a corresponding increase in funds offered. The average level of funding of those providing funds was $10,705.00 ($8,655.00 not counting one institution which provides funding at the $64,000.00 level).

Phelps[2] found in his study that all but one institution surveyed favored sports club funding from general student fees and departmental funds. Responses concerning funding of clubs by gate receipts and fund raising projects were not favorably accepted.

Sliger[3], surveyed 80 schools concerning sports clubs programs. Relating to sources of funds for sports clubs, 36% surveyed said student fees were the major source of revenue, 19% indicated a combination of student fees and general university funds received, 17% from club dues, 12% from general university funds, and 5% received funds from the Athletic Department.

The sports club program at Iowa State University started in 1961 with one club receiving $90.00 from the Government of the Student Body (GSB). The number of clubs has grown to 34 (1977) with a GSB block allocation of $36,000.00. It was not until a sports club council was developed in 1970, plus formulation of general philosophy and purpose statements of the sports club program (1972), that club funding by GSB increased. Before that time, there was an annual "free for all" by individual clubs at budget time. The clubs did not present a united purpose or budget plan. Therefore, GSB was always confused and negative as to the purpose of funding sports clubs.

Also in 1972 the university provided funds for a Sports Club Coordinator plus sports club office operating expenses.

The following information concerns a basic introduction, purpose, and philosophy of the sports club program. These statements were developed by Sports Club Council.

The Sports Club program is designed to serve individual interests in different sports club activities and is studnet oriented in every respect. It could be stated that the program is for the students and by the students under the supervision of the Sports Club Coordinator and Sports Club Council (SCC).

A sports club usually develops when several students express a desire to participate in particular sport activities. Each club has officers, a constitution, keeps miscellaneous records, charges dues, may receive GSB funds as per requirement, has regular meetings, and usually has practice sessions or special events. Each club elects one person to be a representative to Sports Club Council. The council deals primarily with budget decisions, promotion, policy and scheduling issues.

The following statements may help to define sports clubs and their philosophy:

1) Sports Clubs are voluntary in nature.
2) Sports Clubs are non-profit in nature. The members must assume most of the financial responsibilities according to their interest.
3) Sports Clubs adhere to certain regulations governing travel, budget practices, and records filed with the coordinator's office.
4) Sports Clubs offer members a chance to develop their knowledge and skill to greater degrees by organizing special clinics or programs directed by interested and knowledgeable individuals. These individuals usually help on a voluntary basis depending on the uniqueness of the club.
5) Most Sports Club members have a chance to exhibit their skills in competitive situations by traveling off campus or to other univer-

sities. The extent of their road game schedule is limited by their operating budget. Certain clubs are not interested in the competitive aspect of sport, but would rather combine efforts with other college clubs for activities of a social, educational, special event, or informal recreation nature. '

6) Club members do not emphasize strict training rules of conference regulations as with varsity competition.

7) Sports Clubs do not emphasize recruiting practices, financial aids, scholarships, letters of intent, profits, or expanded road trips.

8) Emphasis is placed on student leadership and the most successful clubs are the ones with outstanding student leaders. The club survives and thrives only by means of active student involvement and participation.

9) Sport is defined here as activity requiring more or less vigorous bodily exertion and carried on according to a traditional form or set of rules; sometimes termed large muscle activity (individual, dual, or team).

10) Sports Clubs do not discriminate on the basis of race, color, religion, sex, national origin, age or handicap.

It was not until 1975 that a block funding plan was developed by Sports Club Council and GSB. This plan was approved by the GSB Senate and resulted in the development of a Sports Club Budget Allocation Procedures Guide.

The following information relates to the Sports Club Council/GSB budget request and allocation procedures guide packet:[4]

HOW A BUDGET REQUEST TRAVELS

Sports Clubs Develop Budget

Sports Club Council Reviews Every Club Budget
Request With GSB Advisors

A Block Allocation Budget Request is Developed by SCC

University Recreation Committee Reviews Sports Club
Council's Block Allocation Recommendations

GSB Student Finance Committee Evaluates the Block Allocation

GSB Senate Votes to Fund the Block Allocation

SAFR Board Indicates Final Approval
(Students and Administration)

Sports Club Council Distributes Funds to Individual Clubs

Clubs Submit Final Budget Plans for the Year.

REGULAR ALLOCATION REQUEST

Each sports club develops its own budget request. Sports clubs that wish to have their operation subsidized by student fees must apply for such funding to Sports Club Council by the deadline publicized each winter quarter. Clubs requesting funds should follow the procedures and format outlined by Sports Club Council and GSB.[4]

Procedure

Each club requesting funding should submit eight (8) copies of their allocation request packet to the Campus Recreation Office at least two weeks before the scheduled budget hearings in the Sports Club Council (SCC). Representatives of the club should bring thirty-two (32) copies of the request packet with them to the budget hearings. The SCC will not consider a request unless each SCC member has a legible copy. The Sports Club Council will make any changes in individual budgets which it feels necessary before passing an aggregate request to the Student Finance Committee (SFC). The SFC will recommend to the GSB Senate, in the form of a bill, an allocation for the Sports Club Council. If the Senate accepts this recommendation, funds will be deposited in the SCC account for distribution to individual clubs. If the Senate rejects the SFC's recommendation, then the Senate may either do nothing, in which case the allocation dies and the SCC receives nothing, or the Senate may return the recommendation to the Student Finance Committee with instructions as to what to change before resubmittal. This last step may be repeated until the Senate accepts the SFC's recommendation.

Format

Each club should include the following statements in the allocation request packet so that the Sports Club Council and the Student Finance Committee advisors have all of the necessary information.

1. *Cover Sheet:* The cover sheet (Figure 1) should include the name of the club, the purpose of the packet, the year during which the information contained in the packet will be current, the signature of the President and Faculty Advisor, and the date the request was approved by the club. The cover sheet should not include any other information.

2. *Budget Request:* The budget request (Figure 2) is the budget which the club will follow during the next fiscal year (July 1-June 30) and includes projected income, projected expenses, and the requested GSB allocation.

Income: Income is a list of all the revenues which a club will realize durjected expenses, and the requested GSB allocation.

Income: Income is a list of all the revenues which a club will realize during its operation. In Figure 2, income consists of dues of $3 per quarter for 65 members, and a donation of $15. Professional fees for instruction and income from social events would be specified under "other."

Expenses: Expenses is a list of all the expenditures which a club will realize during its operations. Expenses can be divided into operating and capital expenses.

Operating Expenses: Operating expenses are those expenses which will benefit the club for a period of less than three years. Telephone, office supplies, dues, travel, and competition are all operating expenses.

Capital Expenses: Capital expenses are those expenses which will benefit the club for a period longer than three years. Equipment purchases are the only capital expenses a sports club should have.

GSB Request: The difference between the projected expenses and the projected revenues of the club is the allocation request.

Travel and Competition Breakdowns (Figure 3): All travel for which funding is requested must be broken down into its component parts of mileage, food, and lodging. Mileage is fundable at $.07 per 5-person car. Food is fundable at $3 per day per person. Lodging is fundable at $5 per night per person. The breakdown must include the destination, the number of people going, and the number of days and nights they will be gone.

3. *Current and Estimated Income and Expense Statement*

The Current and Estimated Income and Expense Statement (CEIES) (Figure 4) indicates how much of the budget items a club has used for operations to date and how much the club expects to spend during the remainder of the year. All line items on a club's CEIES should also appear on the approved budget.

Column 1: Column one is a list by budget line items of all the income and expense which a club has incurred from July 1 to December 31 of the current fiscal year.

Figure 1

The Sport Club Budget and Allocation Request 1978-1979
PRESIDENT _____
FACULTY ADVISOR _____
DATE CLUB VOTED ON BUDGET _____

Figure 2

The Sports Club Budget Request 1978-79			
Line Item			
Income			
Dues 65 @ $3/quarter		$585.00	
Donations		15.00	
Other		0.00	
Total Income			$ 600.00
Expenses			
Phone: local $108.00			
toll...... 72.00		$ 180.00	
Office Needs:			
Postage...................... $13.00			
Printing (budgets, etc.) 25.00			
Supplies (paper clips, etc.) 22.00		60.00	
Dues: regional........ $25.00			
national........ 40.00		65.00	
Publicity: Advertising................. $50.00			
Posters 10.00			
Flyers 5.00		65.00	
Travel (see breakdown)		35.00	
Competition (see breakdown)		1040.00	
Total Expenses			$1,445.00
Less Total Income			− 600.00
G.S.B. Request			$ 845.00

Column 2: Column two is a list of the income and expenses which the club expects to incur from January 1 to June 30 of the current fiscal year.

Column 3: Column three should be the sum of each line item in columns 1 and 2.

Column 4: Column four is a copy by budget line items of the GSB approved budget.

Net Income: Net Income is the difference between total expenses and total income for column three.

4. *GSB Approved Budget*

Each Sport Club recieved a GSB allocation based on a GSB approved budget (Figures 5 and 6) for the current year. A copy of this budget should be included in the allocation packet by each sport club. The club should also include a list of all competition and travel broken down into mileage, food and lodging, and copies of any budget changes which affect the approved budget.

Figure 3

Budget Request 1978-1979			
Travel and Competition Breakdown			
Travel:			
Convention (Mason City)			
December 15, 1978			
2 people, 2 days, 1 night			
186 mi. x $.07 x 1	$ 13.00		
2 x $3.00 x 2	12.00		
2 x $5.00 x 1	10.00	$ 35.00	
Total Travel			$ 35.00
Competition:			
Kansas City, Missouri, Oct, 30, 1978			
20 people, 3 days, 2 nights			
460 mi. x $.07 x 4	$128.80		
20 x $3.00 x 3	180.00		
20 x $5.00 x 2	200.00	508.80	
Lawrence, Kansas, Feb. 3, 1979			
20 people, 3 days, 2 nights			
540 mi., $.07 x 4	151.20		
20 x $3.00 x 3	180.00		
20 x $5.00 x 2	200.00	531.20	
Total Competition			$1,040.00

5. Balance Sheet

The Student Finance Committee and Sports Club Council requires all sports clubs to include a balance sheet (figure 7) for the previous June 30 and an estimated balance sheet for the June 30 of the current year. A list of club assets will normally comprise a club's balance sheet.

Cash: The cash balance on the Campus Organization Auditor's report should be entered under cash for the previous June. This cash balance plus the net income from current operations will equal the cash balance for June 30 of the current year.

Equipment: A list of all equipment owned by the club comprises the equipment entry of the balance sheet. All equipment should be entered at cost unless it is being depreciated in which case an entry for the repairs and replacement account should be made.

Repair and Replacement (R/R): The entry for the R/R account should include the account number, the balance on June 30 of the previous year, and the expected balance on June 30 of the current year.

Liabilities: No sport club should have outstanding debts. If the club has ordered a piece of equipment, etc., and has not yet been billed, then an en-

Figure 4

	July 1-Dec. 31 (Actual)	Jan. 1-June 30 (Estimated)	June 30 Estimated	Budgeted
Item				
Income:				
Dues	$200.00	$100.00	$ 300.00	$ 300.00
Donations	—	200.00	220.00	200.00
GSB allocation	480.00	240.00	720.00	720.00
Other	0	0	0	0
Total Income			$1,240.00	$1.240.00
Expenses:				
Phone — local	$ 51.00	51.00	$ 102.00	$ 102.00
Toll	20.00	40.00	60.00	70.00
Office Needs — postage	13.00	0	13.00	19.00
printing	40.00	25.00	65.00	65.00
supplies	0	10.00	10.00	15.00
Dues — regional	35.00	0	20.00	20.00
national	35.00	0	35.00	35.00
Publicity — advertising	25.00	30.00	55.00	65.00
posters	0	10.00	10.00	10.00
flyers	5.00	5.00	10.00	10.00
Travel	19.00	0	19.00	19.00
Competitions	120.00	400.00	520.00	600.00
Capital Expenses:				
Paddles	$100.00	$ 0	$ 100.00	$ 100.00
Nets	110.00	0	110.00	110.00
Total Expenses			$1,129.00	$1,240.00
Net Income (loss)			$ 110.00	0

The Sports Club
Current and Estimated Income and Expense Statement
Budget of 1977-1978

try would be made under liabilities. In this example, the "Sports Club" does not owe money to anyone.

6. *Projected Capital Expenditures*

The officers of a club should project the club's capital equipment needs for a period of three years. The club should specify all needs and if possible should give approximate prices.

7. *Club Officers*

The Student Finance Committee requires each club to list its current officers so that the SFC advisor will know whom to contact in case of budget complications such as apparent errors, revocation, or in the the case of an assessed penalty.

Figure 5

Item			
The Sports Club SCC and SFC Approved Budget 1977-1978			
Income			
Dues		$300	
Donations		220	
GSB Allocation		720	
Total Income			$1,240
Expenses			
Phone — local	$102		
toll	70	$172	
Office Needs — postage	19		
printing	65		
supplies	15	99	
Dues — regional	20		
national	35	55	
Publicity — advertising	65		
posters	10		
flyers	10	85	
Travel (See breakdown)	19	19	
Competition (See breakdown)	600	600	
Capital Expenses			
Paddles (4 @ $25.00)	100		
Nets (2 @ $55.00)	110	210	
Total Expenses			$1,240

8. *Sports Club Council Block Budget Request to GSB*

The Sports Club Council tabulates and collects the budget requests for all of the Iowa State University sports clubs and submits these requests collectively to the GSB.

BUDGET ADJUSTMENT

All sports clubs are required to follow the GSB approved budget once Student Activity Fee funds have been received for the club's operation, however, provision has been made for those clubs that find themselves with a necessary unbudgeted expenditure or have made accurate estimates regarding their expenses or income. This provision is called a budget adjustment and may be used only when no additional funds are needed.

Figure 6

Travel and Competition Breakdown
Budget of 1977-1978

Item			
Travel:			
Convention (Des Moines)			
September 3, 1977			
2 people, 1 day			
100 mi. x $.07 x 1	$ 7.00		
2 x $3.00 x 1	12.00	$ 19.00	
Total Travel			$ 19.00
Competition:			
Dubuque, November 10, 1977			
10 people, 2 days, 1 night			
440 mi. x $.07 x 2	$61.60		
10 x $3.00 x 2	60.00		
10 x $5.00 x 1	50.00	171.60	
Omaha, Neb., Jan. 31, 1978			
15 people, 2 days, 1 night			
320 mi. x $.07 x 3	$67.20		
15 x $3.00 x 2	90.00		
15 x $5.00 x 1	75.00	232.20	
Minneapolis, Minn., March 5, 1978			
10 people, 2 days, 1 night			
500 mi. x $.07 x 2	$70.00		
10 x $3.00 x 2	60.00		
10 x $5.00 x 1	50.00	180.00	
Des Moines, May 1, 1978			
4 people, 1 day			
60 mi. x $.07 x 1	$ 4.20		
4 x $3.00 x 1	12.00	16.20	
Total Competition			$600.00

Figure 7
The Sports Club Balance Sheet

		June 30 1977	June 30 1978
Assets			
Cash		$120.00	$231.00
Equipment:	paddles	0	100.00
	nets	0	110.00
	stopwatch	100.00	100.00
	RR Account xxxx	10.00	10.00
Total Assets		$200.00	$541.00
Liabilities:			
None			

Procedure

A club requesting a budget adjustment should submit eight (8) copies of the request to the Campus Recreation Office at least three weeks before the new expense is to be incurred and one week before the request is to be considered by the Sports Club Council. In addition, the club should bring thirty-two (32) copies of the request to the Sports Club Council meeting at which a decision is to be made. The Sports Club Council will vote on whether to accept or reject the proposed change. The Student Finance Committee advisor to SCC may approve the adjustment if the SCC choses to accept it. If the adjustment is for an amount in excess of $100, then the SFC Chairman may sign the change and if the adjustment is for an amount in excess of $300, then the GSB Senate may approve it. The club may appeal any decision by the Sports Club Council, the SFC advisor, and the SFC chairman to the GSB Senate.

Format

The budget adjustment request should consist of a copy of the current approved budget, a copy of the current and estimated income and expense statement, and a description of the proposed budget changes. The current budget and the income and expense statement should be the same as for the allocation request (figures 4 and 5). The proposed budget change statement is described below.

Example

The budget change statement consists of three major parts; the budget line items to be reduced (to act as a source of funds), the budget line items to be increased (to act as a use of funds and which should equal the sources), and an explanation for the change.

In the example shown in Figure 8, the club is reducing the budget line items "competition" and "telephone" by a total of $110 in order to attend a convention in Chicago using funds that would otherwise remain unused.

SPECIAL GOVERNMENT OF THE STUDENT BODY/SPORTS CLUB COUNCIL ALLOCATIONS

Any sports club may request a special allocation during fall, winter and spring quarters. This request is considered above and beyond their regular GSB yearly allocations or adjustments. For example, if a club has the opportunity to participate in a national tournament which is not in their current budget, they may submit a special budget request to cover expenses of the tournament trip. The same budget request procedures are followed as with the regular allocation process (refer to "how to budget request travels").

CRITERIA FOR EVALUATION OF SPORTS CLUBS AND OTHER CAMPUS ORGANIZATIONS FUNDED BY THE GOVERNMENT OF THE STUDENT BODY

Eligibility

1. The organization must be
   a. officially registered by the Office of Student Life and Campus Recreation Office.
   b. not affiliated with or dedicated to a particular political party or political movement, either domestic or foreign.

Figure 8

The Sports Club
Budget Adjustment Request

Line Items:	Current Budget	Change	Proposed Budget
From:			
Competition	$600.00	($100.00)	$500.00
Telephone	70.00	(10.00)	60.00
To:			
Convention, Feb. 1, 1977			
Chicago			
900 x $.07 x 1 = $49.00	0	$ 49.00	
3 x $3.00 x 7 = 18.00		18.00	
3 x $5.00 x 2 = 30.00		30.00	
Registration $6.50 x 2 = $13.00		13.00	$110.00

Explanation:

The regional association has called an emergency meeting to clear up some misunderstandings about club competition. Since not all of the competition money was spent due to a cancelled meet, we wish to utilize some of these funds to attend the conference.

Signed: _____

        Organization Treasurer   Date

_____

        For Sports Club Council   to   Vote

_____

           SFC Advisor

_____

           SFC Chairman

---

   c. neither affiliated with nor dedicated to a particular religion or religious movement, not advocating any particular religious point of view as its primary purpose as an organization.

   d. open, but not limited, to membership to all activity fee paying students and spouse card holders, regardless of sex, race, age, nationality, etc.

2. The organization must be providing a service for the students of which the Senate will "purchase."
3. The organization must attend an orientation meeting to be held at the beginning of each quarter by SFC and SCC.

Operating Expenses

1. Travel to Events
   a. Budget requests must be itemized according to events, dates and participants.
   b. Transportation
      (1) Mileage will be subsidized at 7¢/mile/car based on 5 people/car. Seven cents (7¢) for one car will be allowed if less than five are traveling.
      (2) Other modes of transportation will be subsidized at 50% of the cost of transportation.
      (3) SFC will not question the mode of transportation chosen by the organization.
   c. Travel will be decided upon an individual organization basis.
   d. Lodgings will be subsidized at $5/day/person.
   e. Meals will be subsidized at $3/day/person.
   f. Convention travel will be limited to two people per organization.
2. Office expenditures will be considered.
3. Advertising, publicity, newsletters and films will be considered if their necessity is justified in the request for funds.
4. Funds for speakers may be allocated to and will be under the jurisdiction of the Lectures Committee.
5. Three bids are required for items over $100.00 and may be requested for items less than $100.00, unless it is impossible to obtain this number.
6. Other items not covered in another section above will be considered.

Capital Expenditures

1. All Organizations
   a. Three bids are required for items over $100.00 and may be requested for items less than $100.00, unless it is impossible to obtain this number.

    b. Each organization must project capital expenditures for a three (3) year period.
2. Sports Club Capital Expenditures
    a. Class 1 equipment shall be defined to be "perishable equipment that must be replaced regularly as it is used up or wears out, i.e., tennis balls, golf balls, shuttlecocks, etc." Class 1 equipment will not be considered for funding by GSB.
    b. Class 2 equipment shall be defined to be "individual use equipment, normally individually owned." GSB will fund class 2 equipment under the following conditions:
      (1) only new members of a club may use the equipment.
      (2) new members are expected to provide their own equipment after a trial period of membership.
      (3) a user fee will be charged for use of the equipment.
      (4) thereafter Class 2 equipment shall be replaced with money collected from user fees where possible...this shall be the *only* use of such revenue.
      (5) funds for equipment and the equipment will be allocated to and under the jurisdiction of Campus Recreation.
    c. Class 3 equipment shall be defined to be "club equipment, used by all, either too expensive or impractical for individual purchase." Class 3 equipment will be considered for funding.
    d. SFC reserves the right to determine in which class a particular piece of equipment belongs.

Social functions, dances, banquets, retreats, and refreshments will not be funded.

All organizations must support *all* of their activities with membership dues which are reasonable with *respect to level of activity* of that organization. Organizations may not use these dues or other forms of income to 'cross-match' non-criteria items except in the case of income derived directly from a non-criteria expense.

Organizations may maintain a reserve fund no greater than 10% of their current yearly budget. Organizations which find it necessary to pay a staff may maintain a reserve fund of 50% of their yearly staff salary, plus 10% of the remaining budget. Additionally, if the organization has depreciable assets they may keep a reserve in the amount of accumulated depreciation plus 10% of remaining budget.

Organizations which find it necessary to collect user and/or rental fees, shall maintain the income of such fees in a separate "repairs and maintenance" account with the Campus Organizations Office. Funds arising from such fees may only be used with approval of Campus Organizations Auditor and the SFC Chairperson except when impractical.

Salaries for activities which provide academic credit will not be funded. Activities which provide research for nonstudent organizations will not be funded.

REFERENCES

[1]Palmateer, Donald, "Survey Showing Current Practices in Club Sports Funding," Colgate University, 1976.

[2]Phelps, Dale E., "Comparative Survey of Responses Between Selected Four-Year Midwest Colleges and Universities and Big 8 Conference Universities," unpublished Doctoral Dissertation, Indiana University, Bloomington.

[3]Sliger, Ira T., "Sports Club Survey," University of Tennessee, Knoxville, 1974.

[4]Sports Club Council Allocation Procedures and Information Guide. Prepared by Government of the Student Body, Student Finance Committee, and Sports Club Council, Iowa State University, 1977.

SPORT CLUBS PROGRAM
Definition, Purpose, Philosophy, Liability and Insurance

by Danny Mason, University of Tennessee Knoxville

A Sport Club may be defined as any group of individuals who are organized to further their interest and participation in a particular sport or activity. In most cases, the formation and guidance of a Sports Clubs program comes under a Sport Clubs Office which is an integral part of the campus recreation program. A Sport Clubs program should be a vital part of any college or university recreation program. The increase in the desire for sports participation has shown a tremendous growth and support for the Sport Clubs program in colleges and universities.

The purpose of a Sport Clubs program is to offer a sports activity for any interested student or staff who has a desire to participate, to develop skills in specific sports, and to provide an opportunity for extramural competition. In 1909, Woodrow Wilson stated, "It is felt that the mind cannot live by instruction alone. The real life of a student manifests itself not necessarily in the classroom, but in what they do and talk and set before themselves as their favorites objects between classes." This is still very true today as it relates to campus recreation.

The Sport Clubs program is student oriented with emphasis on student leadership. The program is "for the student and by the students." With an extensive Sport Clubs program there is a need for central planning, implementing, supervising, and evaluating. The most effective way this can be accomplished is through the supervision of a professional staff person, the Director of Sport Clubs. The Director's job is to insure that all phases of the Sport Clubs program are run smoothly and effectively.

Sport Clubs are organized when students express an interest in a certain sport or activity. Each club must have a faculty or staff advisor to provide expertise and mature judgment, and to help insure that the activities and undertakings of the club are sound and reflect favorably on the university. A constitution and by-laws are required of each club before it can be formally recognized by the University Student Activities Office. The most successful clubs are those with outstanding student leaders. Encouragement, guidance, and supervision is offered through the Sport Clubs Office, but without active student involvement and participation a club will not survive.

Because of high rising cost of insurance it is impossible for most schools to offer insurance coverage for its participants. All students should be encouraged to have adequate insurance to cover the expense of any injury. Student Health Insurance will often cover any student while participating in a club sport except those sports where there is intercollegiate competition. All club members should be required to sign a release and assumption of risk certificate before participating in any club activity. Advisors and club officers are responsible to insure that the release forms are signed by club members before participating in any club activity. All completed release and assumption of risk forms should be kept on file at the Sport Clubs Office.

Law suits are ever present in our day and Sport Clubs are not exempt. Student leaders (officers) of each Sport Clubs need to be aware of their responsibility when elected as an officer. Most colleges and universities do not provide liability insurance for student officers. It is recommended that student officers who are associated with high risk clubs, such as, canoe & hiking, flying, scuba, and parachuting obtain their own liabilty insurance coverage. Faculty & Staff advisors should be covered under the university blanket liability policy provided they are on the university payroll.

"SPORTS CLUBS AND FINANCING"

by Sheri L. Stewart, Purdue University

Even though the sports club concept is one of the oldest sporting concepts in the history of American forms of competion, it is a concept that has remained relatively unchanged. A continuum illustrating the financial support of sports clubs within institutions of higher education would begin with no support and end with virtual total support. Between the extremes are many variations of financial support. Variation occurs not only with the funding source but also with the administration of funds, the structure of the budget, and the allocation of budgets.

Typically, there are four sources for support. They include the general fund, student fees, membership dues, and state appropriations. Two other sources worthy of mention are gate receipts and gifts/contributions. Alternatives include combinations of these four basic sources. The most common singular source of support for sports clubs appears to be student fees. Usually a combination of student fees and membership dues supplemented with funds from state appropriations, or from the general fund provide support for the most lucrative programs.

The administration of funds varies with the hierarchy of delegation of responsibility. Funds may be distributed, issued, or spent through the school or department secretary, by any staff member, by a designated student. or by the administrator assigned the responsibility of the program. Spending may be accomplished by check, by cash issue, or by receipt reimbursement.

Actual structure of the budget will be built upon items that are considered legitimate requests. A list of items that are not acceptable is given to each club president with the budget request form. The list includes office supplies, telephone calls, personal game items such as mouthpieces and ball gloves, and awards.

Many sports clubs require little financial assistance once they are organized and in operation. The initial expense comes from developing the facilities and in purchasing the necessary equipment. When allocations of department budgets are given to sports clubs, answers must be given to the following six questions:

1. What type of financial support is to be given to each club?
2. Should an equal allocation of funds be made to each club?
3. Is the allocation to be made directly to the club or made within the bookkeeping system of the department?
4. Are the officers of each club to be given the opportunity to determine how their budget allocations are to be spent?
5. What controls are necessary over all monies spent by the club (i.e., requirements for check signing, approval of budget and auditing requirements)?
6. Is financial support to include reimbursement to extramural for their travel, lodging and meal expenses?

In answering these questions, many methods of allocating funds have been designed. A predetermined amount is often established per club regardless of differences or needs. An equal distribution of monies available is often the answer with budgets fluctuating according to the allocation. There is also the option of allocating a certain amount of money for every 10 students, 25 students, etc. The proportionate budgeting approach devised by Dr. George Haniford, Director, Division of Recreational Sports at Purdue

University, is an equitable manner in which to budget sports clubs. Upon the basis of budget requests submitted by each club the per cent basis of each club's request is determined by dividing the sum of all budget requests into each club's request. (i.e. Canoe Club request equals $500.00. Total sum of all requests equals $33,000.00 Divide $550 by $33,000 that equals .015.) Take the money available and multiply the money available times the per cent factor. If the total sum available was $32,000.00 then .015 × $32,000 equals $480.00 and that equals 96% of their request. It is not only a fair system but it is also one that is equitable according to club needs as determined by each club.

The actual budget appropriation process consists of the following steps:
1. Budget Request Forms are given to club presidents.
2. Individual appointments are scheduled with each club to discuss their request. In this discussion any item that will not be accepted is explained and justification is requested for any request that is not clear.
3. The analysis of the total request is reviewed by the Director.
4. A Budget Sheet is developed with all clubs and all appropriations represented based upon the total available monies.
5. Approved budgets are returned to each club on a form illustrating a breakdown according to what is requested, what is accepted, and what is budgeted.
6. The original request is held on file for a year.

SPORTS CLUBS:
A MULTI-FACETED EXAMINATION

by Sandy Stratton-Rusch, Glen Radde, Geneva Ormann, Jeanne Hilpisch, Sally Thornton and Margo Imdieke, University of Minnesota

Introduction

An important part in the life cycle of any program is to investigate and document its past and present in order to anticipate the future. The University of Minnesota's Recreational Sports Clubs Program was born in the Fall of 1974. (Clubs existed before that time but without the structure known as the Sports Clubs Council), and has founded its existence on a firm belief in student development and involvement in the programming and philosophy of Sports Clubs.

The following study is diverse in that it deals with four aspects of the University of Minnesota Sports Clubs: A Sports Clubs Officer Personal Development Inventory and results; an analysis of the cost breakdown and participation figures of Clubs as a means of determining the effectiveness of the Program; the Sports Clubs Fair, a special programming technique involving lots of student involvement; and "Habilis", a look at a Sports Club for physically limited students. Viewing the Development Inventory, and the Cost Analysis will provide an idea of Sports Clubs past, considering the Fair will display some present events undertaken and looking at "Habilis" will hopefully generate ideas for special populations to use a Sports Clubs program in the future.

SECTION I

SPORTS CLUBS OFFICER
PERSONAL DEVELOPMENT INVENTORY

by Glen Radde & Sandy Stratton-Rusch

There is more to student development in a college setting than merely acquiring information and technique understandings. Experiences in the classroom, as well as out of class experiences, are important in this development.

A specific out-of-class environment is a Sports Clubs Program. This feeling is finally becoming a reality as we have made one of the first attempts to ascertain and record a structure or ranking of a student development process occurring in a Sports Clubs setting. This task was accomplished through conducting a Personal Development Inventory of Sports Clubs' Officers at the University of Minnesota last Spring, 1977. (The Inventory can be found in the appendix of this Section of the study and will be referred to throughout this text). The following is a presentation and analysis of some of the data from the 21 female and 32 male Sports Clubs Officers who completed the survey.

ANALYSIS OF INVENTORY

The initial research hypothesis or assumption relates to the concept that differences exist between a student's experiences prior to and during a Sports Clubs experience. In some way, it was believed, the instrument or Inventory would quantify a great variety of previously expressed perceptions and attitudes regarding a student group and their opinions of a possible ongoing growth and developmental process affecting them in the Sports Clubs setting.

After the completed Inventories were filled out and returned from the Sports Clubs Officers, all the values were assigned particular number equivalents (e.g. Strongly Disagree-5 to Strongly Agree-1) to aid in statistical processing. In first handling the data, it was felt it would be interesting to discover whether or not there were differences within the students' pre and post Sports Clubs involvement. This was done in order to justify exploration with the data and whether or not it would be supportive of the initial hypothesis.

TABLE I

CALCULATED PERCENTAGES OF RESPONSES IN THE AFFIRMATIVE* OF BOTH SEXES TO THE TOTAL SAMPLE		
	QUESTION NO.	**% RESPONDED POSITIVE**
BACKGROUND INFORMATION	10 (large h.s.)	51%
	(highly involved-	
	11 involved)	75
	14 (excellently-very well)	34
SPORTSMANSHIP SKILLS	1	42
	2	36
	3	32
	5	28
	6	30
	7	38
	8	33
PEOPLE SKILLS	1	57
	2	49
	3	66
	4	68
	5	42
	6	32
MANAGEMENT SKILLS	1	66
	2	38
	3	55
	4	68
	5	62
	6	51
	7	77
	8	53
*Responses of Strongly Agree-1 and Agree-2		

In Table I, seventy-five percent of the respondents indicated they had been highly involved or involved in high school extra-curricular activities which might indicate a strongly motivated group of students. At least one third responded positively to all questions tabulated including "better identifying themselves as to who they are" (No. 6-"People Skills"). The highest positive response to a question was related to making decisions for the Club's future direction and goals (No. 7-"Management Skills"). Seventy-seven percent responded positively. This might indicate a deep concern for the continuation and well-being of the Club.

Fifty-seven percent of the Sports Clubs responded positively to No. 1-"People Skills", related to developing a greater feeling of confidence in themselves in a leadership role. The realization and belief in their ability to guide and lead is being reinforced in the Sports Clubs setting. Sixty-six percent and sixty-eight percent of the Officers responded positively to bettering their communication both verbally and through listening, respectively (No. 1 & 2)-"People Skills"). This could indicate that the respondent was placed in a position to clearly discuss issues and ideas and be able to get across what he/she was trying to say along with learning to become more sensitive and tolerant of others' ideas and opinions. Thirty-six percent felt an opportunity to improve their physical skills in their sport had occurred as seen in No. 2-"Sportsmanship Skills." This would show that people are working hard at their sport with a dedication and desire to better themselves.

In Table II, the Inventories were divided according to sex to discover whether or not there was a significant difference anywhere between male and female officers. One difference discovered was average age—males 22.4 years, women 21.9 years of age. Some of the following observations were made related to specific sexes: only nineteen percent of the male Club Officers viewed themselves as doing an excellent or very good job whereas females rated themselves high at fifty-seven percent, (No. 14-"Background Information"). Yet, forty-one percent males as compared to nineteen percent females felt they had identified themselves better as to who they are (No. 6-"People Skills"). This might indicate that organizationally, women perceive themselves as performing better and seem to have a higher esteem of their ability, but males seem to derive more identity in themselves from physical participation and place more emphasis on this than administrating the Club. This finding might be supportive of American Society where the male is often conditioned somewhat more than the female that physical activity is an integral part of identity. Males also have more confidence in their ability to instruct their sport as can be seen in No. 3-"Sportsmanship Skills," by forty-four percent to fourteen percent. This might indicate that women are at the point where they are becoming proficient in playing their sport, whereas men have gone beyond that to where they feel comfortable teaching it.

Women generally scored higher under "Management Skills" which indicates they might believe that they are organized. Both sexes scored par-

TABLE II

	QUESTION NO.	MALES	FEMALES
APPARENT SEX DIFFERENCES IN THE AFFIRMATIVE* RESPONSE IN THE ANSWERING OF SELECTED QUESTIONS			
BACKGROUND INFORMATION	10	56%	43%
	11	56	43
	14	19	57
SPORTSMANSHIP SKILLS	1	41	43
	2	34	38
	3	44	14
	5	28	29
	6	34	24
	7	37	38
	8	31	38
PEOPLE SKILLS	1	66	43
	2	53	43
	3	69	62
	4	69	67
	5	34	52
	6	41	19
MANAGEMENT SKILLS	1	44	52
	2	25	57
	3	43	71
	4	59	81
	5	56	71
	6	41	43
	7	84	67
	8	47	62

*Responses of Strongly Agree-1 and Agree-2

ticularly high under No. 4, related to promoting the Club through various contacts, with women agreeing by eighty-one percent to the men's fifty-nine percent. This might indicate that both are willing and aware of the need to obtain more members and draw attention to their Club.

METHODS

The *The Statistical Package for the Social Sciences* (SPSS) was used upon the recommendation of those in the field. The use of this book allowed us to analyze the data via the Factor Analysis and the Guttman Scaling techniques.

Factor Analysis

The exploratory factor analysis (with Varimax rotation and Kaiser normalization) was undertaken to reduce the questionnaire data set to see whether some underlying pattern of relationships that might exist could be organized, in some manner, to reveal a small set of *factors* (or dimensions).

The results of the Factor Analysis presented us with three major dimensions that would account for the variance that was present in the data in terms of a model of student development. These results are shown in Table III. The loadings on these factors and what we feel they indicate will be discussed later.

TABLE III

FACTORS	EIGEN VALUES	% VARIANCE
1	6.81	53.9
2	3.51	27.8
3	2.31	18.3

To answer questions of whether an ordering could be found within this student development structure, a Guttman Scaling technique was used. (Table IV). We believe we have found three developmental scales that cross the observed factoral dimensions.

After careful examination of the way the questionnaire responses are related to the factors derived from the analysis and to themselves, it was decided to name the factors in terms of selected dimensions of development. (The actual factor plots and numerical loadings are available, upon request, from the author.)

Since we sincerely believe that a three dimensional construct describes a development process ongoing in Sports Clubs, it was advantageous to define

TABLE IV

B = Background Section   S = Sportsmanship   P = People   M = Management

SELF-IDENTIFICATION SCALE

	Questions			
		P6	M4	S2	B10
	4	X	X	X	X
	3		X	X	X
Scale—Item	2			X	X
	1				X
0					

53 Cases

Coefficient of Reproductibility = 0.90
Minimum Marginal Reproductibility - 0.76
Percent Improvement - 0.13
Coefficient of Scalability = 0.56

'EXTROVERTIVE' SCALE

	Questions			
		M4	P1	S6
	3	X	X	X
	2		X	X
Scale—Items	1			X
	0			

53 Cases

Coefficient of Reproductibility = 0.91
Minimum Marginal Reproductibility = 0.80
Percent Improvement = 0.11
Coefficient of Scalability = 0.56

PLANNING SCALE

	Questions			
		P1	M7	S6
Scale—Items	3	X	X	X
	2		X	X
	1			X
	0			

53 Cases

Coefficient of Reproducibility = 0.95
Minimum Marginal Reproducibility = 0.86
Percent Improvement = 0.09
Coefficient of Scalability = 0.65

them as Factor 1—*Maturation*—the sum of the skills and actions that one acquires when dealing with other individuals in a Sports Clubs settings. Factor 2—*Somatic*—the acquisition of physically oriented skills of sports. Factor 3—*Origins*—the general experience acquired prior to college life. What is shown in the diagrams of the factoral plots is how the individual questions of the instrument (labeled in terms of their section) relate, in terms of direction and distance, to the probable three-dimensional factor model to describe a student's development via a Sports Clubs setting.

DISCUSSION

With these tools, we are looking for an underlying structure to help us document quantitatively student development within the Sports Clubs setting. The Factor Analysis allowed us to assume there existed an underlying structure within the data set (the factor plots located in the Appendix with the Table of Loadings illustrate the way the sections of the questionnaire relate to the three factors found) in terms of a simple model. We feel the factors are usable because they encompass not only Sports Clubs Officer's growth, but more likely, human growth in general. An awareness of these factors allows programming to take on a "feeling" sports experience approach long advocated by the University Recreational Sports Office. This means the program staff provides minimal administrative foundation and maximum assistance to the student in need of direction to foster the greatest growth for the participating individual.

For easy discussion, the Guttman Scales that were found exemplify certain specific characteristics and so they have been named appropriately the Self Identification Scale, the Extrovertive Scale and the Planning Scale, and these reflect most appropriately the original criteria.

The Self Identification Scale consists of four major components. The first is the participant's high school size, (Question 10-Background Information), the second, improvement of physical skills (Question 2-Sportsmanship Skills); the third, promotion of the Club in the University and business areas (Question 4-Management Skills); and the final component, better self identification (Question 6-People Skills). We offer this scale as a potential structure that may indicate the ordering of these responses in terms of a developmental process with self identification being the objective of the responses given.

The Extrovertive Scale consists of three components. The first, a greater appreciation of a physically fit body, (Question 6-Sportsmanship Skills); the second, making decisions about the Club's future (Question 37-Management Skills). This process is representative of 2 conditions needed for an individual to feel confident in a leadership role: the physical aspects of the sport and

312

setting goals. It must be emphasized here, that though the Scales presented are not absolutes, their main utility is that they present an ordering of responses, and therefore, yield a structure in terms of underlying development. Only the relative position of selected criteria can be determined (as distance cannot be inferred at this time).

With these three Scales and with supplementary information we offer, very tentatively, a Super Scale that has not been adequately tested. This Scale definitely yields a structure for development and might be used in a modeling process. We believe this Scale to be a five component scale. The first being the realization of the appreciation that everyone needs a physically fit body and becomes involved in Sports Clubs of their choice according to previous experience. The second component finds the individual expressing his/her interest in developing a physically fit body in terms of Sports Clubs membership and because of the emphasis placed on student management of the Sports Club, an individual then becomes involved in the determination of his/her Club's future. Because of the student's involvement in the planning aspect of a Club, as well as a committment in terms of time and expertise to that Club, we reach the third component of the Scale, achievement of confidence on the part of the participating individual. The individual's confidence now extends itself and not only administrative capabilities improve, but there is a greater emphasis at this time on the physical (technical) aspects of the Club and of the Sport, the fourth component. Confidence is further expressed in terms of competence and how articulate they are in their individual Club setting. Not only can they do the job but they are more effective and can demonstrate it to others.

IMPLICATIONS

Student Development is an important process that, in terms of Sports Clubs Officers, can be separated into 3 major dimensions with certain identifiable structures existing within those dimensions.

We also offer a very tentative developmental structure that might be evidence for a new model of development or evidence for proving previous models. (See T.H.E. Model A Student Development Model for Student Affairs for a previous model).

Not only have we been able to begin documenting some previous developmental processes in Officers, we also have looked at our past record and development related to fiscal management. Section II will see a brief breakdown and cost analysis of University of Minnesota Recreational Sports Clubs.

REFERENCES & ACKNOWLEDGEMENTS

[1]Nie, N.H., C.H. Hull, J.G. Jenkins, K. Steinbrenner, D.H. Bent, *Statistical Package for the Social Sciences.* McGraw Hill, Inc. N.Y. 1975.

[2]Anon., *T.H.E. Model,* from the S.A.C. Office, U. of MN. 1978.

[3]We greatly appreciate the advise and help provided by Professor Andrew Ahlgren (Associate Director of the Educational Development Center) and Professor Leo McAvoy, Jr. (Physical Education, Recreation and School of Health Education).

APPENDIX A

Dear Sports Club Officer:

The purpose of this Inventory is to find out whether or not you, as a Sports Clubs Officer, have experienced various physical, psychological, emotional, etc., stages because of and during your time in office.

Previously the idea that student development occurs in the Sports Clubs setting has only been an assumption. As an initial start, this survey hopes to actually document whether or not student development does indeed occur.

Your honesty and concern in filling out this survey will be greatly appreciated.

BACKGROUND INFORMATION

1. Age: _____   2. Sex: M _____ F _____
3. Year in College: Fresh. _____ Soph. _____ Jr. _____ Sr. _____ Grad. _____
4. I belong to the _____Club.
5. I have been a Sports Clubs Officer for_____quarters.
6. I have been a Sports Club member for_____quarters.
7. I helped form my Club? Yes _____ No _____
8. I spend an average of_____ administrative *hours* per *week* on my Club.
9. I spend an average of _____ participation *hours* per *week* on my Club.
10. The high school I graduated from was:
    small (50-300 people) _____ medium (300-500 people)_____
    _____ large (600 + people) _____
11. My involvement with high school extracurricular activities was:
    Highly involved_____   Involved _____
    Indifferent_____   Turned Off _____
    Other
    (please discuss other) _____
12. Regarding my role as a Sports Club Officer, I feel my dedication is:
    High _____   Medium _____   Low _____
13. I decided to run for Sports Clubs Officer because:
    It seemed challenging_____   No one else would do it _____
    I wanted to better by Club _____   It would improve my resume_____
    Other
    (please discuss other) _____

14. I believe I am performing my job as a Sports Clubs Officer in the following manner:
    excellently _____ very well _____ good _____
    satisfactorily_____ indifferently_____poorly_____
    other
    (please discuss other) _____

"SPORTSMANSHIP SKILLS"

Please indicate your degree of agreement with each of the following statements by *circling* the answer you feel is most related to your job as a Sports Clubs Officer.

Through being a member of a Sports Clubs and an Officer, I feel I have:

		Strongly Disagree	Disagree	Neutral	Agree	Strongly Agree
1.	developed a better knowledge of the rules and mechanics of my Sport.	SD	D	N	A	SA
2.	improved my physical skill level and ability to play my Sport.	SD	D	N	A	SA
3.	acquired the knowledge to instruct my Sport to others.	SD	D	N	A	SA
4.	acquired the knowledge to officiate or referee my Sport.	SD	D	N	A	SA
5.	learned the background and historical development of my Sport.	SD	D	N	A	SA
6.	appreciated more the need to develop a sound, physically fit body.	SD	D	N	A	SA
7.	learned my physical capabilities in my Sport.	SD	D	N	A	SA
8.	learned my limitations in my Sport.	SD	D	N	A	SA

"PEOPLE SKILLS"

Through being a Sports Club Officer I feel I have:

		Strongly Disagree	Disagree	Neutral	Agree	Strongly Agree
1.	developed a greater feeling of confidence in myself in a leadership role.	SD	D	N	A	SA
2.	learned to tolerate differences in other Club members.	SD	D	N	A	SA
3.	improved my ability to communicate my feelings and ideas to other Club members.	SD	D	N	A	SA

315

4.	learned to listen better to feelings and ideas of Club members.	SD	D	N	A	SA
5.	made companions, friends, socialized, had · fun with other Club members.	SD	D	N	A	SA
6.	identified myself better as to who I am.	SD	D	N	A	SA
7.	clarified goals for my college career.	SD	D	N	A	SA

"MANAGEMENT SKILLS"

Through being a Sports Clubs Officer I have learned to:

1.	conduct business meetings for Club.	SD	D	N	A	SA
2.	prepare agendas for Club business meetings.	SD	D	N	A	SA
3.	coordinate a practice schedule with the Recreational Sports Office.	SD	D	N	A	SA
4.	promote the Club through University, business, or community contacts.	SD	D	N	A	SA
5.	realize the necessity and reason for having a Club Constitution.	SD	D	N	A	SA
6.	write a Constitution.	SD	D	N	A	SA
7.	decisions connected with the Club's future direction and goals.	SD	D	N	A	SA
8.	conduct fundraising activities to raise money for the Club.	SD	D	N	A	SA

9. How do you apply some of your Sports Clubs experiences to other aspects of your life? (ie: classes, meeting people, family, etc.)

_____

_____

_____

10. What is your favorite gripe about Sports Clubs?

_____

_____

Thank you very much for your cooperation, effort, and time!

Please return this Inventory to:

Sandy Stratton—Student Sports Clubs Coordinator
Sports Clubs Office
101-A Bierman Building
373-1917

SECTION II

COST ANALYSIS OF SPORTS CLUBS 1974-77

Geneva Omann

As stated previously the Sports Clubs were organized under a Sports Clubs Council that took over the role of managing and developing the Sports Clubs Program on campus. In 1974, for the first time, Student Service Fees Monies were appropriated specifically for distribution to Sports Clubs.

The first year the appropriated money was distributed amongst the Clubs by the Sports Clubs Coordinator, and in the following years it was allocated to the Clubs by the Executive Board of the Sports Clubs Council.

The amount of money allocated to each Club is determined by the following method. Spring Quarter, each Club submits a proposed budget for the following year. The Executive Board reviews each budget and makes adjustments according to previously set criteria. The adjusted budget requests are then added to give a total budget request. Each Club's allocation is determined from the following formula:

$$\text{Club's adjusted budget request} \times \frac{\text{Student Service Fees Appropriation}}{\text{Total Budget Request}} = \text{Club's Allocation}$$

The amount of money typically given to each Club is approximately 45% of their adjusted budget request.

The purpose of this report is to analyze the effectiveness of the Sports Clubs program, as it now exists, in terms of number of students involved, amount of participation by students, and the cost per participation hour and per student.

Records of all money transactions involving allocated funds were maintained by the Rec Sports office. Data on the number of Club members and the number of participation hours was obtained by requiring each Club to submit this information for each quarter to the Rec Sports Office. One hour of participation to a Club activity per person is referred to as one participation hour. The number of Club members is the average number of members in the Club while the Club is active.

Figure 1 shows the number of participation hours per year from 1970-71 through 1976-77. There has been a 23-fold increase in the number of participation hours from 1970-71 to 1975-76. Participation during the first year of the Sports Clubs Council's operation approximately doubled compared to the previous year, and participation increased 1.8 times in the second year of the Council's operation. Participation hours decreased by 21% from 1975-76 to 1976-77, although the figures for 1976-77 were still considerably higher than for 1974-75.

Table I lists the cost figures from 1974-75 through 1976-77. The cost per member increased between 1974-75 and 1975-76 by 51%, however, the number of participation hours per member also increased by 41%. The cost per participation hour increased from 9 cents to 10 cents over the same period, which is consistent with an approximate 10% cost-of-living increase.

The cost per member and per participation hour increased significantly from 1975-76 to 1976-77. The increased allocation of $31,176 was given in anticipation of a participation increase similar to the previous years. However, in 1976-77, the number of members decreased somewhat and the number of participation hours per member decreased slightly, resulting in these increase cost figures.

The cost per participation figures for these 2 years indicate that the students of the Executive Board were as effective in allocating funds in 1975-76 as the Sports Clubs Coordinator in 1974-75. The positive trends observed over the time period from 1973-74 to 1975-76 correlate with the introduction of the Sports Clubs Council. Although it cannot be concluded that the Sports Clubs Council was responsible for these trends, it seems apparent that the Sports Clubs Council was effective in administering the program.

The decrease in participation hours for 1976-77 is probably indicative of a plateauing of participation rather than the beginning of a downward trend. Although the data for 1977-78 are incomplete, it appears that participation for this year is increasing compared to 1976-77. This plateauing may be the result of several factors. Enrollment rates are dropping at the University of Minnesota, although this is far from being significant in accounting for the participation plateau. The capacity limits of the Rec Sports facilities at the University of Minnesota may have been reached. Crowded Rec Sports facilities have been a matter of growing concern at this campus, although previously no one has been able to predict when the maximum limits would actually become evident. Alternatively, the Sports Clubs program may be approaching its maximum limit in terms of student involvement and interest. The data represent approximately 5% of the student population devoting four hours per week to his or her Club.

According to Section I, positive student development can be documented and discussed. Students who are responsible for formulating their Club's budget proposal develop fiscal management skills and accountability. The more highly motivated of these students generally seek out positions on the Executive Board of the Sports Clubs Council, where they become responsible for the budget evaluation and fund allocation of all Clubs. Data of participation hours and cost analysis is an important source of information for

TABLE 1:

COST ANALYSIS
FOR
RECREATIONAL SPORTS CLUBS
FROM
1974-1975 THROUGH 1976-1977

YEAR	NUMBER OF MEMBERS	NUMBER OF PARTICIPATION HOURS	PARTICIPATION HOURS PER MEMBERS	ALLOCATION	COST PER MEMBER	COST PER PARTICIPATION
74-75	1383	136,300	98.5	12,500	$ 9.04	0.09
75-76	1786	248,459	139.1	24,450	$13.69	$0.10
76-77	1571	196,735	125.2	31,176	$19.85	$0.16

319

FIGURE 1:

TOTAL NUMBER
OF
PARTICIPATION HOURS PER YEAR

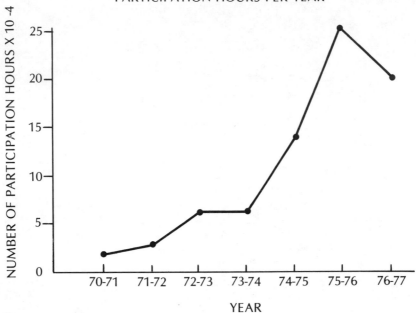

these students in evaluating the current status of the program and in determining the monetary needs of the future.

A concern of all programs is maintenance and a means of obtaining input and involvement.

Our first Sections speak to the reputability and soundness of our Program. Section III will deal with a very unique, successful way to program an event to involve as many students as possible and add to the well being of the Program — try a Sports Clubs Fair!

REFERENCES

[1]Omann, G., Froehlig, J., Kangas, M., Hilpisch, J., Bissonnette, R., Tonsager, G., Stratton-Rusch, S. *Finance Related Information for Sports Clubs,* University of Minnesota, 1977.

SECTION III

UNIQUE PROGRAMMING THROUGH A SPORTS CLUBS FAIR

Jeanne Hilpisch

During the building of our recreational Sports Clubs Program, the Executive Board of the Sports Clubs Council has tried to increase the involvement level which necessitated the establishment of unique programming to reach students. To achieve our goals, the Board experimented with a Sports Clubs Fair, which based upon its success, is now being integrated into our basic programming.

Preparation for the event began about one month in advance. A committee of fifteen people was formed to work with the Executive Board and Coordinator in planning. The total number of planning hours was approximately 50 hours. The initial contact with potential participants was a letter sent by the Chairperson requesting voluntary participation of Clubs in this event. About 50% of the Clubs responded to contacts.

The reasons that Clubs gave for non-participation were conflicts with class schedules or Club instruction times, difficulty adapting their sport to outdoors, lack of available members for an all day event, and basic skepticism as to whether it would work.

The second Club contact was personal verification. At this point the committee asked for the amount of necessary space and equipment. Clubs were responsible for independently preparing their activity; the activities were as broad as horse jumping to karate demonstrations to folkdancing to boxing. Extreme freedom was allowed in the demonstrations and creativity was strongly encouraged.

Overall co-ordination was provided by the committee. Concessions were divided up by the committee among Clubs to avoid duplication. The tent, which was for general purpose use and information distribution, was rented by the committee.

The total cost of the Fair was relatively insignificant. Approximately $500 was spent in direct Fair expenditures. Tent rental was $100 for a moderately sized tent. Concessions were $150—Clubs should be selective in type of concession. Uniqueness is the key to success. Refreshments can be obtained through any University vending machine, yet snow cones become a rare item when the Fair day is in the high 80's. The Ice Skating Club, selling snow cones, made over $100 at 15¢ a cone: that is equivalent to 660 cones. This type of planning points out the fundraising potential of such an event. Publicity for the Fair cost $75. This included one page ads in the student newspaper. In future planning we intend to double if not triple that figure.

Universities should also be aware that electricity and vehicles are billed to your department. These expenses can come to $250.00.

The execution of the Fair went smoothly because Clubs handled their project. Each Club did their own set. Overall setup took one hour. The total number of participating Club members was approximately 70.

The location of the Fair was our Northrop Mall which is a large, grassy mall that extends from our auditorium to our student union. It is approximately 600 feet long and 150 feet wide. It is a central location on campus because the science buildings, administrative offices, and our second largest campus library empty into this area.

The chosen date was a Friday in Spring. Friday was chosen because students have more available unscheduled time. The day was also Regents Day.. This meant our Regents were on campus and the news media would already be there; yet, press relations should not be neglected. This choice increased our publicity greatly because the Fair was made convenient. It is suggested that all important University administrators receive special invitations.

There were problems in the execution of the Fair, but solutions can be offered.

First, our campus has a unique problem of student involvement which is related to the size of our campus. Our health science students are located on the outside edge of campus, business students and social science students are located on the other bank of the river, and there is a separate campus in St. Paul for students in the agricultural fields. Making these students aware of the functions is extremely difficult. A possible solution would be to publish a specific schedule of events in the student newspaper and post schedules on campus. Continuous daylong programming of the Fair did not involve enough of these students.

A second problem area is equipment. Special equipment such as artificial ice and swimming pools were desired but they could not be obtained. Our Parachute Club wanted to skydive into the stadium. This needed three weeks for approval from a state agency. The best way to correct problems like these is to start planning for certain aspects of the Fair at least three months in advance. Long term planning would allow for special equipment allowances to be made.

A third problem is physical safety which involves several areas. Any university or campus considering this type of programming should investigate their college insurance policy. A minor incident occurred when our Board Chairperson broke his wrist while playing volleyball at the Fair. This evidences the importance of safeguarding the event. Since our program was an officially sanctioned University event, it was covered by University insurance. Another suggestion would be a first aid station should be set up so that if any problems did occur they could be dealt with immediately. Anyone running concessions should be aware that they must meet the State Board of Health Regulations. The Planning Committee should find out the state and local policies dealing with the selling of foods. At our Fair, our three concessions (beverages, candy floss and snow cones) were visited several times by a state inspector. A final aspect of the physical safety is that Clubs which are involved with animals (i.e. horses) would make provisions for the cleanup. Otherwise, the University Sanitary Department may charge for this function.

A fourth problem area is billing. Anyone contemplating a Fair should get advance written estimates of cost. Depending on the university, the activity could be charged for electricity, water, and all necessary equipment. University employees who are involved in the set may also charge for their time.

After these observations on the functions of the Fair, the issue needs to be addressed as to whether the Fair succeeded. As earlier indicated in the introduction our Executive Board concluded that the Fair did succeed. Therefore, what criteria was used for this evaluation?

The basic philosophy of a Sports Club should be noted. Sports Clubs try to offer the opportunity of participation to any person who desires to learn a sport regardless of his/her abilities. The purpose of the Fair was to advance this philosophy through trying to promote awareness within the University of our program.

Our goal was reached through the Sports Clubs Fair. The Board has no numerical figure to offer as to the number of students gained by the Clubs due to this activity. Yet, the Board can indicate that several Clubs expressed that they gained a significant number of members. Determining actual figures would be very difficult because people could join three or four months later and the membership cannot be casually linked to the existence of the Fair.

Second, the Fair improved Club cohesiveness among participants. Unified Clubs are very important to their long term existence. The Fair added stability to their membership.

Third, the Board achieved greater awareness because actual student participation is the best way to reinforce our existence. If a student is merely informed, by verbal or written means, he/she will most likely not remember. Active involvement is the best way to encourage membership.

Finally, our program achieved visibility on campus. Pictures appeared in the student newspaper and the local city paper, the *Minneapolis Tribune*. The day and location choice had special implications towards achieving visibility. The regents and media were on campus; and the students on Friday had more available time. The central mall location added convenience. Finally, the unique type of action drew attention which increased visibility.

Thousands of students saw the Fair that day.

For these reasons the Executive Board concluded that the programming was very successful with even more potential as the program evolved.

In conclusion, the Fair was a positive participation experience for all parties involved. The Clubs gained, the Recreational Sports Department of the University of Minnesota gained, and the general student body benefited. The Executive Board achieved the overall goal in promoting awareness of our program through visibility. Difficulties were minimized because the Clubs handled their own activities. A major suggestion is that the Fair should be long term planning. The planning does not have to be extensive, yet it should try to preclude major execution problems.

SECTION IV

"HABILIS", A NEW, INNOVATIVE DEVELOPMENT IN SPORTS CLUBS AT THE UNIVERSITY OF MINNESOTA

Part A— The Beginning of "Habilis"
Sally Thornton

"Happy are those who dream dreams and are ready to pay the price to make them come true."   L.J. Cardinal Suenens

I believe in dreams for without them, right now at the University of Minnesota a very unique and innovative Sports Club "Habilis" would not be in existence. The idea for the formation of "Habilis" Sports Clubs transpired Fall quarter 1977 because several "aware and disappointed" students (and staff) at the University of Minnesota felt that it was time the non-existent participation of "disabled" students in the Recreational Sports Club program was considered. (This will be the last reference I make to the word "disabled"—I prefer the words physically limited or mobility impaired because these words to me are not derogatory or restricting as I believe the words "handicapped" or "disabled" are).

The idea for a Sports Club for physically limited individuals, once introduced, caught on like a chain reaction. Sandy Stratton-Rusch, Coordinator for Sports Clubs, first mentioned the possibility at a Unicorn meeting (a student organization which unites people from the University community who have an interest in disability) where a member, Margo Imdieke decided to take on the project as a Unicorn representative, mainly because of her extensive background in wheelchair athletics. From there, Margo contacted me the third week of Fall quarter and we were off!

324

The start of Winter quarter marked an important event in the respect that on Wednesday, January 18th "Habilis" was accepted as an official University Sports Club. At this point we decided we needed to move out of the "planning" phase, and move into the "action" phase. For the remainder of the quarter this "action phase" consisted of 2-3 hours designated on Monday evenings for weight training, waterpolo & swimming.

The name "Habilis" was selected for many reasons, primarily because we felt the name itself would arouse curiousity. It is a Greek derivation meaning "able." This could be considered a "play with words" because unfortunately many people still have antiquated beliefs in the way they feel physically limited individuals are not able or capable of participating in recreational and/or competitive sports. The word "Habilis" and the Club "Habilis" will hopefully promote the breakdown of these negative attitudinal barriers at the University of Minnesota.

It's a "natural" that a Sports Clubs program would provide recreation activities for a special population. Not only can it act as a referral service for physically limited individuals by aiding them to seek out particular sports activities, it can also emphasize a sport activity itself. For example, the Habilis Sports Club will be concentrating mainly on inner tube waterpolo and weight training this Winter and this spring will switch to track. However, one who wants to learn archery or attempt badminton can be referred to those activities by the Habilis Club.

It is amazing how adaptive the lousiest weight room can become. All it takes is approaching someone with a physical limitation and saying, "Hey, let's work together on programming something for you." Try adapting Beep Baseball, tandem bike riding, table tennis, inner tube waterpolo or track and field. A Sports Clubs Progam can adapt to any of these readily and easily.

> There is a splendid urge all dreamers know,
> A splendid, driving urge to live—to grow!
> To fling the dream ahead and follow through—
> A splendid, thrilling urge to be—to do!
>
> And never did this world have greater need
> of people to dream great dreams, & hearts to heed
> That urge to scale the heights not scaled before,
> That splendid urge that bids the spirit soar.
>
> If you've a dream—hold fast, nor doubt its scope;
> One dream held high can rouse a whole world's hope
> One life, dream-powered, with a will to climb,
> Can lift the faith of people to heights sublime.
>
> A splendid urge—would that we all might know
> That urge to do—to be—to live—to grow!
>
> Helen Lowrie Marshall

Part B— Issues Concerning "Habilis"
Margo Imdieke

Habilis is a Greek word meaning "able". Greek is the language of Athens, the location where physical sports for leisure and competition first originated. The Habilis Sports Club was designed to accomodate the interests of individuals with physical limitations who until recently had not utilized the limited but somewhat accessible sports facilities at the University of Minnesota. The "A" Section of this report talked about some of the programming challenges being faced by Habilis. This section will concentrate more upon the issues of concern that a Club like Habilis wishes to address.

The first issue of concern I want to touch on is the main streaming versus special groups controversy for the disabled. Should physically limited individuals be treated like everyone else or treated special? Generally, my belief firmly supports mainstreaming, but in the case of physical participation in a recreational sporting experience, a unique situation is presented and one almost has to approach the situation from an alternative angle.

The situation is unique because traditional grade school and high schools, primary education centers, do not encourage physically limited children to participate in physical education activities. In fact most schools are inaccessible and most instructors are not well trained to deal with children of different abilities. On the other hand, people who are injured or physically limited from adolescence usually grow up having a stereotypic attitude concerning "the disabled". They believe "the handicapped" do not participate or can not compete in any kind of physical activity. In either case, by the time these individuals get to the college level, joining a Recreational Sports Club is beyond their consideration because they've been steered away from the experience. By organizing a Sports Club of this nature, each individual participating has the opportunity to reach his or her own comfort level. They hve an opportunity to realize their physical potential and awareness of their body increases, which are feelings they haven't necessarily experienced before.

The Club has two main functions; it provides an immediate recreational opportunity and it acts as a referral service. As an organized Club, its population is constantly being replenished by disabled freshmen and students who become injured while in college. The variety of activities offered also lends it uniqueness; the activities include, innertube waterpolo, weight training, wheelchair basketball and track and field. The referral services are incorporated when there is an existing Sports Club that serves a specific interest that can be easily modified to serve an individual with physical limitations.

In twenty years or so, when primary education centers incorporate accessible physical education programs into their schools, Sports Clubs such as "Habilis" might not be necessary. The greatest barriers in developing accessible programs have been both architectural and attitudinal.

In 1973 Congress passed Section 504 of the Rehabilitation Act which states that no federally funded institution can discriminate on the basis of "Handicap" in the areas of employment, programs offered or building accessibility. The Department of Health, Education and Welfare and other federal agencies are now coming out with strict guidelines for compliance. Hopefully, this legislation eliminates architectural barriers and this accomplished, outdated attitudes concerning sports and the disabled should change.

FINAL REMARKS

We are extremely excited about the information accumulated in this study regarding the University of Minnesota Sports Clubs. Hopefully, a look at our student personal inventory, cost and participation analysis, Sports Club Fair and disabled students Club will provide you with some new ideas and beliefs in Sports Clubs. It aids us greatly in capturing looks at our heritage and our direction. Sports Clubs really do make a difference.

CHAPTER IX

Women in Sport

"A WINNING COMBINATION"

by Linda Doering, The University of Texas

It's a goal!! The ball flew off her foot, sailed through the air—past the straining bodies of the defenders, over the goalie's out stretched arms and body—into the back of the net. A score for her team! And, best of all, now comes the congratulations from the teammates.

Soccer is a great game—very exciting and physically vigorous. Women are attracted to it in increasing numbers all of the time—with good reason. Not only is it great for getting in shape, it's also the basis of a social sub-culture all its own. Women are beginning to enjoy its many benefits as men have done for years.

Perhaps the most obvious benefit of playing soccer is the physical fitness aspect of the game. After playing two 45 minute halfs—with no time outs—a woman knows she has put out a lot of energy and burned up a lot of calories. She must be tired and she may be sore the next day, but she's made it through another uninterrupted hour and a half of running, kicking, passing and sheer excitement. And since most teams practice at least a couple of times a week, women can play soccer as a means of keeping in shape.

Through the medium of soccer with its physical activity, a women becomes more in touch with her body. What a thrill to know that she too can successfully play an active game that her men friends enjoy and that professionals play on TV. In addition, she is actively partaking in an area of sports previously forbidden to her and unattractive to her because of social taboos.

There is a sense of comraderie among soccer players, women and men alike. The social interaction of players is that of a large family. Women players are a respected part of that family. Team loyalties lose their importance at the social gatherings after the game.

Because 11 individuals make up a team, plenty of situations arise where the group must learn to work cooperatively. The satisfaction a "together" team derives is at least equal to that of winning a hard played game.

Besides the physical and social benefits of the game of soccer, it is an ideal game because of the low cost for a woman to come involved initially. All the equipment that is needed is a ball and some type of gym shoes. Of course, a team could get fancy and wear special shoes, uniforms, warm ups, etc.

In Austin, Texas, women's soccer has grown in 4 years from an initial group of 22 interested women to a present 16 team city league (Austin Women's Soccer League—AWSL) with over 300 players. The City Parks and Recreation Department provides 4 fields with goals. The rest is up to the women, who have organized into a league with a board of directors and a referee association. The league sponsors clinics for beginners, schedules weekly games throughout the year for teams and elects all star teams to play with visiting teams throughout the state. There is a place for women of every skill level and every interest level.

A recent development in the AWSL is the emergence of women coaches. When first organized, most teams in the league were coached by men. No women knew enough about soccer, were skilled enough, or brave enough to take on the task of coaching. But in the 4 years since the beginning of AWSL women have developed the knowledge, skill and assertiveness needed to coach their own teams. No longer will the male coaches claim the glory of victory.

Women have also become very involved in refereeing. Initially men refereed all games. But as with the coaching, women now have learned and practiced enough to be competent referces. They are compensated for their work with funds generated by team entry fees. In order to initiate new women into the rigors of refereeing, the association sponsors training sessions and internships.

Now only do women in Austin have the opportunity to play soccer and derive its direct benefits, they also have earned the right and chance to direct the destiny of their own league through coaching, refereeing and administering the league. Women and soccer, it's a winning combination!

WOMEN: CAMPUS RECREATIONAL SPORT (IM)

By Gail M. Yager, Michigan State University

Never before has the female been so free from cultural restraints and taboos as she is today. Women's new role in society is opening up uncountable opportunities for her to engage in play activities without the restrictions and discouragements she once had to face (Neal, p. 1)

The purpose and intent of this paper is to develop selected topics pertaining to women in sport, with specific emphasis on the female participant in the university Intramural program. In order to adequately discuss this, it is necessary to explore a brief history of women in sport, where we are now, and what the future holds for women in sport.

This writer feels that a well-rounded sports program, adequate facilities and equipment, and a professional staff are accepted prerequisites, and thus will devote a minimum of time to developing a foundation of an "adequate" intramural sports program. The main thrust will be to provide a philosophical basis for intramural programming, and will deal with cultural and sociological factors which have had an impact on the modern women's participation in sport and recreation activities.

A further assumption made by this writer is that the growth and development achieved by an individual, as provided by the basic objectives of education and the specific objectives of an intramural program, will enhance the person's contribution to society as a more capable, functioning human being. "When we speak of education . . . we mean teaching the whole man—the spiritual, physical, mental, social, emotional, recreational, and business ability to make a living and contribute something to his community." (Keen, p. 54)

To begin a discussion of the organization and administration of an intramural sports program, one must first examine an institutional philosophy of higher education. The President's Commission on Higher Education has established that such a philosophy focuses on the ". . . full, rounded, and continuing development of the student, and that it is committed to the furtherance of individual self-realization in its greatest glory." (Williamson, p. 11)

The American public has charged the schools "to foster the development of individual capacities which will enable each human being to become the best person he is capable of becoming." (Ed. Policies Commission, p. 1) In order to achieve this goal, each individual must attain optimal fitness: physically, mentally, socially, and emotionally. In an age of growing leisure time, individuals must be motivated and able to make positive and healthy use of free time. As a further extension of philosophy, it should be noted that "in 1918 the National Education Association Commission on the Reorganization of Secondary Education . . . listed health and worthy use of leisure time in the seven cardinal principles of education." (Kleindienst and Watson, p. 51)

Voluntary programs of physical education have traditionally been viewed as consisting of general recreational sports, intramural sports, and varsity athletics. The emphasis here will be with the intramural sports program, which provides organized competition and game play for the mass of students. The term "intramural" refers to Latin terminology "within the walls," and designates the services offered only those within a given institution. The goal in IM sports is for everyone to have an opportunity to play, with little importance played on winning and losing. Furthermore, it is a people-based program with a service philosophy, which encompasses current sports needs of the given population. (Beeman, Harding and Humphrey, p. 1)

The woman student is only now beginning to realize her true potential in regards to sport participation. History indicates that a negative attitude has pervaded through the years to curb women's interest in sports activities. From the beginning, women have faced barriers that discouraged their progress in the level of participation in sport. Attempts to differentiate between male and female roles in sport have abounded, with reference to the physical, psychological, and cultural nature. Women were conditioned to accept that "muscles, sweat, and competition of an athletic nature were to be admired in males but abhorred . . . among females. Historically, the choice was blatant—woman or athlete—it was not possible to be both." (Poindexter, p. 58-59)

Aristotle provided a theory which no doubt was a basis for society's thinking throughout the better part of history:

> The author of nature gave man strength of body and intrepidity of mind to enable him to face great hardships, and to woman was given a weak and and delicate constitution, accompanied by a natural softness and modest timidity, which fit her for sedentary life." (Boslooper, p. 115)

For a short period of time during the late 1920's, women enjoyed a bit of freedom and shed their chains of "feminine delicacy" to participate in such sports as tennis, swimming, horseback riding, and other "acceptable" activities. However, no significant progress was made because the thought of the day and culture was such that many still believed that intense physical training would result in strain and nervous tension. "Many women felt that the disadvantages so far outweighed any advantage that it was pointless to even consider a recreational program." (White, p. 75)

Dewey attempted to provide for an ideal of democracy in education when he defined education as: "1) the maximum development of all students; 2) equal opportunities for all, and 3) special privileges for none. While idealistically sound, cultural reality prevented women from realizing all their potential. Modesty, differentiation, and the mere "Female" or "feminine" concept kept them within the confines of a separate (sports and recreation) program with different needs, facilities, and finances." (White, p. 75-76)

Thus the myth of the "ideal woman" was taught and allowed to thrive at the expense of countless numbers of women who could not have known that to choose the role of woman (as prescribed above) was an "open denial of the pleasures of movement, competition, and comraderie accompanying sport and the development of the undefinable self-satisfaction that comes from skilled performance." (Poindexter, p. 59)

The evolution of the modern-thinking woman of today has come about within the last twenty-five years and is a direct result of women's liberation. Without dwelling upon the primary feeding ground for this movement, that being basic inequities between men's and women's opportunities, let it suffice to say that women are no longer willing to passively sit back and watch their world and the opportunities within it pass them by.

Several conditions have led to the growing acceptance of women's place in sport and recreational activities. Society has become very health conscious since recognition during and after World War II of the generally unfit male population, as well as increasing stress and strain of everyday living. Programs of health and physical fitness received support from the American Medical Association and during the Presidential terms of Eisenhower and Kennedy when recreational sports activities and fitness became the center of the national spotlight.

Becoming physically fit is no longer limited to men, however, and women are making attempts to overcome the double standard of previous years where they are expected to be "active, healthy and coordinated while still being dainty, fragile, and feminine . . . The cultural continuum with femininity on one end and athletics on the other has narrowed. The ideal female has become a physically fit one. Exercising is "in" and suddenly the sports woman is shown daily eating right, exercising and covering five miles a day needing only the right deodorant." (White, p. 77)

> Under these auspicious circumstances the gate has swung wide open for achieving new dimensions in intramural and recreational programs . . . in schools and colleges. Increasingly, they are viewed and accepted as an integral part of education. (Kleindienst, p. vii.)

Based on the rationale that Intramural programming is a viable means for achieving the philosophy and objectives of higher education, it is now necessary to establish criteria for specific goals and projectives of a stable Intramural program. The writer will then develop the values inherent in an intramural program (for the female participant), and the resulting personal growth and increased value of the participant as a contributing member of modern society.

In order to determine Intramural goals and objectives, this paper will incorporate the aims of education, which have been classified into four areas of objectives as defined by the Educational Policies Commission:

1. *Self-Realization:* . . . knowledge of health, disease, fitness, family and community health, skill as a participant and spectator in sports and resources for leisure time.
2. *Human Relations:* this is concerned with the importance of human relations, enjoyment of social relations, appreciation of cooperation, courtesy, fair play, family and home living.
3. *Economic Efficiency:* includes objectives relative to appreciation of good workmanship, vocational preparation and success, wise consumer and producer of goods.
4. *Civic Responsibility:* includes aims for improved humanitarianism, tolerance, conservation of natural resources, observation of law, civic responsibility and democratic living. (Kleindienst, p. 84)

The objectives of an Intramural program are conclusive not only of general educational philosophy, but also specifically with several advocated Student Personnel assumptions, most notably Chickering's seven vectors. (Chickering, 1972) Objectives and the resulting values of the Intramural program are developed under the following areas of consideration: (Kleindienst, Chapter 5)

Recreation: deals with the desire to satisfy competitive needs, as well as relaxation as a result of the physical activity and environment. This parallels Chickering's vector of competence concerning physical and manual skills, as well as developing autonomy. "Generally, if youth were left to their own inclination and fundamental urges, they would probably continue to be active throughout their lives. Unfortunately, however, the artificial social values of young adults and the competition for time and abilities change these natural desires . . . The young people of today need help in planning for present and future free time and in developing a discriminating sense of values with respect to recreation activities." (Goehrs, p. 51)

Physical Health: participation and physical activity should contribute to one's health and total fitness.

Mental and Emotional: sport provides opportunity for expression of and release from stresses, strain, and frustrations. This adequately supports Chickering's vector of managing emotions. "The Intramural program is a stabalizer of the mental and emotional life of the individual. It provides activities and situations that are very real to those who participate and may very well lay the cornerstone for that phase of the educational process concerned with developing mental and emotional stability . . . IM activities offer wholesome release of the emotions and an opportunity for personal expression, which may enhance the possibilities of avoiding many of the conflicts during the more serious environment of later life." (Wedemeyer, p. 47)

Social Development: this parallels Chickering's vector, freeing interpersonal relationships. Participation with others as opponents, partners, team members, or individuals with similar interests will aid the person in developing social skills. This is important when noting that . . . "education has been given the responsibility of providing experiences that will encourage participation by all, to the end that individuals may be fitted for wholesome living in an ever-changing society." (Wedemeyer, p. 48)

Ethics and Values: this parallels Chickering's vector, developing integrity. Participation in an Intramural program will hopefully strengthen the individual's personal code of ethics, ie. what is right, what is wrong conduct. " . . . values are a way of life and express an individual's beliefs and dictate his behavior, social and moral. These values are so closely related to social experiences and attitudes that when understood they lend stability and security to individual behavior." (Flory, p. 50)

Sports Interests and Appreciation: A variety of sport and activity offerings may result in increased interest in the wide range of the Intramural program. "The woman Intramural participant wants sport to remain relevant for her daily physical and emotional need for recreation, pleasure, and relaxation . . . Women of all ages and backgrounds are looking to Intramural sports centers and administrators to represent women's interest in traditional sports and to develop innovative sports experiences as well." (Harding, p. 93-95)

Recreation Skills: same connotation as Chickering's vector of competence. As the philosophy denotes, a sports for all attitude exists in Intramural programming and would provide activity for all levels of skill, as well as for the limited or handicapped student.

Appreciation of Physical Activity: The Intramural program should provide greater sensitivity for the value of physical activity as a lifelong endeavor.

The future of women in sport, specifically women's participation in the intramural sports and recreation program, is optimistic. Cultural and social restraints have been lifted and women are now free to engage in sports activities at their will. Society has accepted women as participants in sports activities to the extent that advertising medias are spotlighting attractive sports wear, and the physically fit and healthy woman is glamorized as "today's active woman" in order to sell the large array of consumer products. Women have more leisure time than ever before, and the time is right to develop sound values in the positive use of such free time.

No one facet of higher education is directed more diligently toward attaining the goals of education than the Intramural program. And inasmuch as the woman student of today is finding participation in sports and recreation as a rewarding, pleasurable experience, we as educators need to strive to make the educational process one which will lead to a more productive life in a better world.

> *Sport . . . for women is conditioned partly by the times, the mode of life, and the general conduct and moral quality of a people. Sport, however, need not be merely worked upon by society. Sport, with its leaders and its participants can, in part, mold the society. Sport can make a vital social, moral, ethical and physical contribution to the present condition of man and to his continuing and ultimate condition. Sport as planned action can and must be not only the result of society's change but must be an agent for planned change in individuals and society. (Holbrook, p. 43)*

Sports and recreation activities are a vital part of our American way of life. Sport will continue to be a vital part of women's lives, as a means of expression of self, socialization, recreation, and appreciation. Intramural programs in colleges and universities should continue to expand the emphasis and enlarge the opportunities for participation by the woman student.

The modern woman has voiced her needs and desires. We, as administrators, must develop the design for a program that will be unique to its own purposes and yet still contribute to educational and life purposes.

> *Be it remembered that until woman comes to her kingdom physically she will never come at all. Created to be well and strong and beautiful she long ago sacrificed her constitution. She has walked when she should have run, sat when she should have walked, reclined when she should have sat. She is a creature born to the beauty and freedom on Diana. (Poindexter, p. 63)*

ENDNOTES

[1]Neal, Patsy, *Coaching Methods for Women*, Reading, Mass., Addison-Wesley, 1969, p. 1.

[2]Keen, Paul V., *Contributions of Intramurals to the Education Program*, N.I.A. Proceedings, 1968, pp. 53-57.

[3]The President's Commission on Higher Education, *Higher Education for American Democracy*, Vol., *Establishing the Goals*. Washington: 1947, pg. 5, from *Student Personnel Services in Colleges and Universities*, E.G. Williamson, Editor, 1961, p. 11.

[4]Educational Policies Commission, *The Central Purpose of American Education*, (Washington, D.C.: The National Education Association, 1961), pg. 1.

[5]Kleindienst, Viola and Weston, Arthur, *Intramural and Recreation Programs for Schools and Colleges,* Appleton-Century-Crofts: New York, 1974, pg. 51.

[6]Beeman, Harris F., Harding, Carol A., and Humphrey, James H., *Intramural Sports,* William C. Brown Co. Publishers, 1974, pg. 1.

[7]Poindexter, Hally B.W., *Women's Athletics: Issues and Directions,* National College Physical Education Association for Men Conference Proceedings, 1973, p. 58.

[8]Boslooper, Thomas and Hayes, Marcia, *The Femininity Game,* Stein and Day Publishers, New York, 1973, p. 115.

[9]White, Janice L., *Women's Intramurals—Past, Present, and Future,* N.I.A. Proceedings, 1973, p. 75.

[10]*Ibid.,* p. 75.

[11]Poindexter, p. 59.

[12]White, p. 77.

[13]Kleindienst and Weston, p. vii.

[14]*Ibid.,* p. 84.

[15]Chickering, Arthur W., *Education and Identity,* Jossey-Bass, Inc., Publishers, 1969, Part One.

[16]Kleindienst and Weston, Chapter 5.

[17]Goehrs, Warren J., *Recreational Aspects of the Intramural Program,* N.I.A. Proceedings, 1968, p. 51.

[18]Wedemeyer, Ross, *Contribution of the Intramural Program to Education,* N.I.A. Proceedings, 1968, pp. 47-48.

[19]*Ibid.,* p. 48.

[20]Flory, C.M., *The Social Aspect,* N.I.A. Proceedings, 1968, p. 50.

[21]Harding, Carol A., "Women's Intramurals: Issues and Directions," *Intramural Administration: Theory and Practice,* edited by James A. Peterson, Prentice-Hall, Inc., Englewood Cliffs, New Jersey, p. 93-95.

[22]Holbrook, Leona, *Women's Participation in American Sport,* National College Physical Education Association for Men Conference Proceedings, 1973, p. 43.

[23]Poindexter, p. 63.

BIBLIOGRAPHY

[1]Beeman, Harris F., Harding, Carol A., and Humphrey, James H., *Intramural Sports,* William C. Brown Co. Publishers, 1974.

[2]Boslooper, Thomas and Hayes, Marcia, *The Femininity Game,* Stein and Day Publishers, New York, 1973.

[3]Chickering, Arthur W., *Education and Identity,* Jossey-Bass Inc., Publishers, 1969.

[4]Educational Policies Commission, *The Central Purpose of American Education,* (Washington, D.C.: The National Education Association, 1961).

[5]Fidler, Merrie A., *Women's Intramurals in Relation to Women's Extramurals: A Historic Viewpoint,* N.I.A. Proceedings, 1972, 180-184.

[6]Flory, C.M., *The Social Aspect,* N.I.A. Proceedings, 1968, 49-51.

[7]Goehrs, Warren J., *Recreational Aspects of the Intramural Program,* N.I.A. Proceedings, 1968, 51-52.

[8]Harding, Carol A., "Women's Intramurals: Issues and Directions," *Intramural Administrations: Theory and Practice,* edited by James A. Peterson, Prentice-Hall, Inc., Englewood Cliffs, New Jersey, 1976, pp. 92-98.

[9]Holbrook, Leona, *Women's Participation in American Sport,* National College Physical Education Association for Men Conference Proceedings, 1973, pp. 43-59.

[10]Keen, Paul V., *Contributions of Intramurals to the Education Program,* N.I.A. Proceedings, 1968, pp. 53-57.

[11]Kleindienst, Viola and Weston, Arthur, *Intramural and Recreational Programs for Schools and Colleges,* Appleton-Century-Crofts: New York, 1964.

[12]Neal, Patsy, *Coaching Methods for Women,* Reading, Mass., Addison-Wesley, 1969.

[13]Poindexter, Hally B.W., *Women's Athletics: Issues and Directions,* NCPEAM Proceedings, 1973, pp. 58-63.

[14]The President's Commission on Higher Education, *Higher Education for American Democracy,* Vol. 1, *Establishing the Goals.* Washington: 1947, from *Student Personnel Services in Colleges and Universities,* 1961, edited by E.G. Williamson.

[15]Vanderswagg, Harold, J., *Toward a Philosophy of Sport,* Addison-Wesley; Massachusetts, California, London, and Ontario, 1972.

[16]Wedemeyer, Ross, *Contribution of the Intramural Program to Education,* N.I.A. Proceedings, 1968, pp. 47-48.

[17]White, Janice L., *Women's Intramurals — Past, Present and Future,* N.I.A Proceedings, 1973, pp. 73-82.

WOMEN AND RUGBY

by Linda Bishop, Ohio State University

"Boys learn basic skills of teamwork and competition on the sports field, skills that later serve them well in business and political organizations. They are also introduced to buddyism in the locker room. In activities approved for girls, there has been little practice with competing and even less opportunity for comradeship. Girls rarely found themselves in situations comparable to a football game or military service, in which the adventure involved great enough risk to demand interdependence." (Passages, Gail Sheehy, 1976)

Women play the contact sport of rugby because they want to, they like the game and all that accompanies it. In response to the question, "Why do you play rugby?", The Ohio State University Women's team had varied responses.

For some women rugby is an aggression-reliever, physical conditioner, and a social event as expressed by one of the players.

"Rugby allows a woman to participate in a contact sport where she can release built-up tensions. It also enables her to develop better coordination, skill, good physical condition, and a close sense of team work and friendship. The parties are also an asset to the sport."

Some players enjoy striving for optimum physical fitness in order to meet the demand of the game.

"I like being part of a team. I like how good I feel after a hard practice. I like to get and be in shape, to push myself to improve. It is a challenge."

Although the physical aspect of rugby is readily apparent, it is the social aspects of the sport which attract many participants.

"The competition is intense on the field, but once completed the shaking of hands and sharing of beer are prevalent. These are aspects of rugby that are missed in other sports, aspects which bring to sport what it should be: friendly competition, hard work, comraderie, and pressures not too demanding on the individual."

Typically, players only know their opponents within the confines of the contest itself. Again, rugby is an exception to the rule.

"The aspect of both teams partying afterwards is definitely more friendly, as compared to other sports where you more or less hate your opponent and usually don't even get to know them. Basically, I enjoy being a member of a team."

Several of the women had played college varsity sports and have chosen rugby instead.

"The thought of being part of a club sport as opposed to an intercollegiate sport is appealing to me—due to the lack of restrictions and the emphasis of the activity being fun rather than a have to win thing."

The stress in varsity athletics seems to take away the enjoyment of the sport for many women. A former high school track star said:

"I attended both track and rugby practices for a week and finally made a decision. Rugby was to be my new adventure for several reasons. It was evident to me that the pressures in rugby were a lot less on the individual than in track. I handled the pressure all right in high school but I decided that rugby would be more enjoyable because the atmosphere is more relaxed."

The pressure to succeed in rugby comes solely from within due to the lack of pressure from coaches and departments to win games.

"I originally was a fielder for O.S.U. (2 years) and got tired of the pressure of varsity sports, such as throwing because we had to. Personally, I threw because I wanted to. Women's Varsity Sports are making the same mistakes as men: getting too competitive, losing the idea of why they're playing the sport. So I play rugby with a swell group of kids, who play for fun, and each other, for ourselves, and it's great to win—but the satisfaction is in playing together, as a team. As far as the roughness goes, women are just as rough and tough as men."

This sampling of reactions is representative of why thousands of women play rugby. Women ruggers are becoming a visible representation of that portion of the population, male and female, which insists that certain sports games, careers, and clothes aren't masculine or feminine. They are neither, and only tradition and cultural mores make us view them otherwise. Personality traits such as aggressiveness and competitiveness are not masculine—they are natural to both men and women and should be allowed to emerge. And above all, women refuse to be told what they can or cannot do, what they will be "allowed" to do by a benevolent hierarchy. Women will continue to play despite the frequent sexist remarks thrown at them because they *know* that they are women, and not any less feminine because of their activities in a previously male domain. Their feelings are reflected in the remarks of tennis star Helen Hull Jacobs when she said,

"I never thought being a woman athlete required an apology. I wouldn't know what to apologize for."

It is a fact of life today that women compete in contact sports such as rugby, football and ice hockey; the question yet remains for many people, "Why?" As discriminatory ideas about women's physical and athletic capabilities are proven incorrect, vast numbers of people remained uniformed and non-believers. To tell these non-believers that some women even participate in a contact sports adds insult to injury for these people are not prepared to see women in contact sport. Contact sports, after all, are aggressive and competitive—certainly not "feminine" or meant for women.

Yet, thousands of women throughout the United States and Canada play the contact sport of rugby. Rugby is an aggressive game, consisting of tackling, rucks, scrums, and a lot of running on a 100 x 75 yd. field. Women generally play rugby in halves varying from 20 to 35 minutes with a 5 minute half-time. Rugby is fast-moving competition with little break in the action. Play does not stop when a tackle is made; someone else picks up the ball and runs. Such continuation limits the amount of set "plays," and forces players to be aware of the action, think quickly and respond on the field.

A small percentage of people cannot see why *anyone* would want to participate in sport. Rugby is a challenging game—mentally and physically.

Women love to play it, even though some people find that difficult to believe. Societal prejudices and pressures remain strong. Actual reactions to women's rugby consist of the following: "Why does a nice-looking girl like you want to play rugby?" "What are you looking for, a bunch of bumps?" "Women in *Rugby*, isn't that like sweeping? Like house cleaning?" The idea of women in rugby amazes many people and even threatens them. Women ruggers learn to expect derogatory comments when they bring up their favorite sport.

Rugby has many components which make it attractive to women. In the past, in "activities approved for girls", there has been little practice of competing and even less opportunity for comradeship. Girls, unlike boys and womenlike men, rarely find themselves in situations where the high risks demand interdependency. Men and boys have had this domain culturally separating them from women. Rugby, though, offers them individual and team competition, extreme work, and comradeship. On the field, every player contributes equally to the success or failure of a game. There are fewer "stars" simply because anyone can run with or kick the ball. The same women play offense and defense, often quite quickly as play is continuous until there is a penalty. With such spontaneity, team work is a "must.' Rugby also offers comraderie to a degree that most women have never experienced. If an opposing team comes to town for a match, the home team provides them with their extra players. The main purpose of rugby is to play and enjoy. When the whistle blows ending a game of hard tackles and stopping actual fights for the ball and being stepped on or over in the "rucks" and "mauls", the winning team automatically breaks into a chant of "Three cheers for . . ." the opposing team. They also form two parallel lines of players at the side of the field through which the losing team passes. The women shake hands, laugh, hug, congratulate and party with the opposition to celebrate a game well-played.

The attractions of rugby are many and varied; just like the positions on the field there is something for everyone. Despite the fact that women and men play on separate teams, the commonality of rugby enjoyment exists between them. Several university and city clubs are joining forces, having the men's and women's teams playing and practicing games and parties together. So if the elements of rugby interest you, try it!

CHAPTER X

Program Evaluation

COST ANALYSIS IN RECREATIONAL SPORTS PROGRAMMING

by Jennifer Sue Larson, University of Minnesota

As Recreational Sports programs become more diverse; more staff, facilities, equipment, and therefore more monies, become necessary for their administration. In many cases, programs grow at a much more rapid pace than do budgets. Central administrations are demanding a greater accountability for funds allocated to student activities and cost-benefits are closely examined. Because of an ever increasing need for Recreational Sports departments to carefully budget their money, administrators are searching for methods of evaluating their programs in order to better plan and budget.

Cost analysis is a management tool which may benefit programs in several ways. The same principles of economy which industry prizes so highly may also be useful in recreational sports programming. A cost analysis allows administrators to objectively look at the cost of the various segments of their total program. Benefits of each segment may then be matched with the cost, and evaluated. From the cost figures obtained, it is possible to determine the economic impact of each segment on the total program. Information gained from a cost analysis can also be used as a valuable tool in formulating policies for support of the program. Are you doing what you say you are doing? How much can be done for what amount of money? What are the costs for services provided for participants? How will projected budget changes affect programming? The answers to these questions shape your strategy when dealing with budget requests. The type of support a program receives often depends on the appreciation of that program by those who provide the money for it. The use of a cost analysis is one method of assessing offerings and potentially increasing quality, thereby providing participant satisfaction and support. Cost analyses are also valuable tools for long range planning in Recreational Sports. Future costs may be calculated from current ones, and the cost of new offerings may be predicted from the costs of similar ones in process.

In order to obtain cost analysis information which is both accurate and useful, four steps are necessary. First, the specifications of the analysis must be determined. Programs and functions to be covered must be stated, a time limit for the study set, the extent of direct and indirect expenses defined, and to decide if the analysis is to stand as a single piece of information or to be comparative in nature. (Hungate, p. 107)

Secondly, cost data must be obtained. Direct costs must be identified, and indirect costs that are part of programs being studies must be included in the data. (Hungate, p. 108) Items such as salaries, maintenance, equipment and hourly wages are examples of direct costs. Such costs are those incurred exclusively for the benefit of the program under analysis and during the time specified. Indirect costs may be more difficult to determine. The basic means of determining such costs is benefit to the program which is non-exclusive. (Hungate, p. 96) This may include such items as secretarial or staff assistance not directly attached to the program, staff benefits, and cost for the use of capital assets (interest, depreciation). It is most important that the allocation of indirect costs be carefully thought out. Staff members own job time analysis records can be most helpful, as are other departmental financial records.

Also, suitable procedures must be used. The results of the analysis should remain the same if the study was duplicated. Procedures must be carefully identified and defined. Consistency is a must. If the results of the analysis are to be useful, the study must be valid.

Lastly, appropriate allocation of indirect expenses must be made. This requires careful study of all components of the programs analyzed. Step-by-step walk-throughs of the program may be helpful in determining such costs.

In all cases, simplicity of the cost data is desirable (Hungate, p. 116). The analysis is only useful if it is understandable and applicable to the department's needs. The analysis itself is not the complete solution to any budget problem, but may be used as a method for objective evaluation of programs and their alternatives. Costs may be met in one of two ways, either by increasing revenues or by introducing economies (Millett, p. 154). The cost analysis is a tool to be used in both cases. As an aid in future planning, budgets can be prepared in a knowledgeable manner. In situations where economy is a necessity, areas of concern can be found and evaluated.

Cost analyses are time consuming to prepare and, therefore, costly. There are no standardized forms for Recreational Sports programs to use at the present time. It is only through the administrator's interest in serving the participant through effective and efficient quality programming that such tools will be developed and used for the benefit of all concerned.

REFERENCES

[1]Hungate, Thad L., *Finance in Educational Management of Colleges and Universities*, New York, Columbia University Bureau of Publications, 1954.

[2]Lynden, Fremont J., and Ernest G. Miller (ed.), *Planning, Programming, Budgeting: A Systems Approach to Management*, Chicago, Illinois, Markham Publishing Company, 1971.

[3]Meeth, L. Richard, *Quality Education for Less Money*, San Francisco, California, Jassey-Bass Publishers, 1974.

[4]Millett, John D., *Financing Higher Education in the United States*, New York, New York, Columbia University Press, 1952.

THE BEST INTRAMURAL PROGRAM

by B. C. Vendl, California State University, Long Beach

Once upon a time, while Director of Intramurals at the University of Chicago, I was in attendance at a dinner gathering of distinguished alumni, Nobel prize winning faculty, and illustrious university trustees. A vice-president was at the podium reaching high gear on the current accomplishments of the university in hopes of getting additional donations for the current fund drive. As I took the last swallow of coffee from my cup it suddenly stuck in mid-throat as I heard the university's intramural program was now ranked as the best in the country. Wasn't that great? How come *I* hadn't been told? And, by the way, who did the ranking? As my life flashed through my mind, and I was now choking on that last swallow of coffee, I fantasied, why not? Who can dispute it?

The next morning with a clearer and more realistic outlook, I met with the vice-president and discussed his statement. He sincerely believed what he said and based it on recently published statistics which I had presented to him. He had surmised that since they were of such proportions, OBVIOUSLY they must be the best in the country.

That entire episode stuck with me, and as I dwelled upon it I realized that all the statistics I had could tell me nothing by way of comparison with other colleges or universities. There is no standardization of measurements between institutions. "Numbers of participants" might, or might not, give equal status to a one race 50 yard freestyle swimmer, and a complete season for a basketball player. "Participants" might, or might not, distinguish equality among actual different names or by numbers on a team. "Number of activities" raises the question of time equity between frisbee and football. And once you get into the realm of finances, all sorts of manifestations are conjured up. The word "budget" may or may not, include salaries and shared facilities. What items are included when you calculate the "cost of an activity?" If this weren't enough, try management-by-objectives methods and any semblance of standardization goes right out the window. Where do I go for help? Why am I so concerned?

Is there anywhere a single Director of Intramurals who has not been approached by one of his administration people searching for intramural statistics to justify something or other? And the inevitable question—how do we compare to Brand X University? To answer this, I obtained funding for our department to hire one person to do nothing but statistics for one year. In June of 1975, I had the end result of that survey—a pile of great statistics, like "91% of all undergraduate male participated in at least one I-M activity." It told me a great deal about the students on our campus, but nothing about comparisons to other intramural programs. As suddenly as this quest had begun, the terrible truth was beginning to be realized. It DIDN'T matter how we compared. I had fallen into the bureaucratic nightmare of statistical comparisons between institutions. To satisfy an administrator's needs, we had lost sight of the trees for the forest.

My search for excellence now led to the philosphical principles which were peculiar to our institution, our department, our program. With professional staff and student imput, these were stated in a position paper, and, after review, approved by the university.

We reviewed the local history of our intramural program for two reasons. First, we wondered if a pattern of progress could be distinguished by the written evidence in the department files. Secondly, we wondered if student needs had been considered and met. Both staff and students from the Intramural Council explored this and found favorable evidence for both.

Through the Intramural Council student representatives, we then conducted an extensive survey of students needs. This included ranking types of activities distinguishable by sex, tournament types, degrees of physicalness, and time. Because of the uniqueness of the institution we were able to design a measuring instrument that avoided the pitfalls we felt inherent to this type of survey. The student representatives were able to actually poll students—not a mere sample—but the entire population. Although warned of the danger that this survey might "prove to be nothing more than a popularity poll," we were delighted since that was exactly what we were after. The survey results were reviewed by the professional staff. Based upon information and expertise received from intramural workshops, conferences, and conventions, we sifted through current trends in programming, activities, procedures, etc., and rendered subjective judgment as to which were suited to our situation. The diverse background of our staff allowed for healthy controversy and argument. No one felt restrained in expressing their views. Our decisions were self-evaluated based upon comparison with our statements of philosophical principles. We reviewed programming from various points of view—institutional policies, state and federal laws, finances, equipment needs, facilities available, number of officials available—each area adding its own limitations. Alterations and adjustments were made. The "bottom line" always reflecting the students' needs and desires.

After weeks of review and preparation, the survey results and proposals were presented and endorsed by the Intramural Student Council. The entire package was taken to the administration for budgeting changes. Even in days of budget squeezes, administrators not only listen, but approve budget increases when the voice of the student population is documented and verified. Facility priority usage can be rearranged when you are forced to play the numbers game. But probably the best outcome of this whole project was the increased sensitivity to the students' communications.

For years, intramurals had maintained an "open door" policy to communicate with students—not talk, but listen—not just intramural participants, but non-participants. Now, others were starting to humanize their relations, doors started to open, and ears started to listen. No large turnover, but a crack started to appear in the ivory tower structure.

After the dust of preparation settled, the hub-bub of activity came and went, we evaluated the circumstances and statistics. We could honestly say that for our institution—for that period of time—we presented the BEST IN-TRAMURAL PROGRAM possible.

As students and time turn over, factors change—an annual review is necessary. The activities are altered, personnel is changed, finances adjusted—but the intramural population is served to the limit of the resources. The BEST INTRAMURAL PROGRAM is not in competition with any other institution or program, but in competition with the challenge within its own walls—which after all is what "intramurals" is all about.

And the participants of the BEST INTRAMURAL PROGRAM lived happily ever after.

SIX APPROACHES TO EVALUATING YOUR CAMPUS
RECREATION PROGRAMS

by Christine Z. Howe, University of Illinois

Introduction

For each different purpose of evaluation, there is a different definition of evaluation. There are also a variety and diversity of evaluation designs. The evaluation of campus recreation programs has been limited to but a few of the evaluation approaches that exist. The evaluation approaches most frequently employed by campus recreators appear to be: (1) surveys of needs, interests, and satisfaction, (2) checklists of compliance with standards, (3) professional or expert judgment of merit, and (4) participation ratings (Bannon, 1976, pp. 268-273). However, there are several other approaches to the evaluation of recreational programs that are also useful.

Clearly, campus recreation programs and activities must exist before they can be evaluated. But, evaluation should not necessarily *always* be the last act. Early or formative evaluation may be used for program improvement while the program is still occuring. Summative evaluation may occur (usually near the end of a program) to judge its merit or worth (Scriven, 1975). Before the evaluator goes to work, he or she must know what questions are going to be asked—what information is desired. Then the evaluator can choose the best means to answering these questions (Caulley & Dawson, 1978).

Why Evaluate

Campus recreation programs usually take place under the auspices of post-secondary educational institutions. The call for accountability has been heard by people in higher education. Not so long ago, decisions affecting college and university operations were roughly made on the basis of the un-challenged assumptions and feelings held by experienced administrators. Today, those same people are being required to provide a variety of evaluative information to support their decisions. (Gardner, 1977, pp. 571-572)

In addition to meeting the demand for accountability, evaluation is useful for: (1) determining the effectiveness of a program. (2) improving a program, (3) planning programs, (4) explaining the successes and failures within a program, (5) describing a program, (6) obtaining and communicating information to guide-decision-making, and (7) ascertaining the worth of a program. The aforementioned represents only the more common purposes of evaluation.

Figure 1: A Taxonomy of Models for Educational Program Evaluation[1]

APPROACH	MODELS	PURPOSE	PROPONENTS	METHODOLOGY	RESULTS	PROBLEMS
Evaluation as Professional Judgment	ART CRITICISM MODEL	Approval of a program	Eisner, 1975	Critical review by individual	Subjective appraisal of product	Diversity of reviews
	ACCREDITATION-BLUE RIBBON PANEL MODELS	Those with experience and/or training judge programs	NCA Henry, 1975	Critical review by visiting panel, interviews, self study and observation	Professional/peer acceptance	Disagreement on who is "expert" and criteria
Evaluation as Measurement	SYSTEMS-MANAGEMENT ANALYSIS MODELS	Rational decision making, quantitative outcome measures	Rivlin, 1971 Burnham, 1973	PPBS, MBO, Cost benefit analysis, statistical treatments, head counts	Efficiency, feedback for decision making	Non-humanistic, overlooks values, emphasis on quantification
Evaluation As Congruence Between Performance and Objectives	BEHAVIORAL OBJECTIVES EVALUATION MODELS	Behavior specified into measurable performance	Tyler, 1950 Popham, 1969 Provus, 1973	Statements of behavioral objectives and criterion referenced tests	Productivity, accountability	Disagreement on criteria and measures of achievement
Decision-oriented Evaluation	DECISION MAKING MODELS	Decisions to be made from basis of policy to be developed	Alkin, 1967 Stufflebeam, 1970	Surveys, questionnaires, inverviews and document analysis	Effectiveness, quality control, social choices	Neglects minority interests
Goal Free Evaluation	GOAL FREE EVALUATION MODEL	Reduction of effects of bias in program evaluation	Scriven, 1973	Logical analysis and observation	Client choice, minimal co-optation	Psychological discomfort of those involved
Transaction-Observation Evaluation	TRANSACTION-OBSERVATION EVALUATION MODELS	Portrayal of what has occurred	Stake, 1975 MacDonald, 1977 Pearlett & Hamilton, 1972	Observation in case-study interviews and participation-observation	Understanding of picture, diverse views	Unfamiliarity with qualitative methods.

Evaluation Defined

In as much as there are many purposes of evaluation, there are according-ly, many definitions of evaluation. The six definitions of evaluation that establish the general famework for most evaluations in *education* today are: (1) evaluation as professional judgment, (2) evaluation as measurement, (3) evaluation as the determination of congruence between performance and objectives (or standards of performance), (4) decision-oriented evalua-tion, (5) goal free evaluation and (6) transaction-observation evaluation (Ban-non, 1976; Gardner, 1977; House, 1977; Stake, 1974; Worthen & Sanders, 1973). These six titles compose the basic categories of evaluation, with one to three evaluation models falling under each of them. The definitions that form the basis for each of the six approaches are borrowed from the evalua-tion of educational programs and adapted for use in evaluating campus recreation programs. Figure 1 shows each of the six approaches based on taxonomies developed by Stake (1974), House (1977), and Gardner (1977).

The Six Approaches Explained

The six evaluation approaches are explained in terms of comparing and contrasting the models within each category. The taxonomy itself represents an outline of the characteristics of the models. The models in reality are not discrete. Instead, they have some overlap, especially in the areas of methodology and purpose (Hoemeke, 1977, pp. 68-72). Each model's pro-ponents recognize that different evaluators have different styles and resources. Thus, evaluation is one tool to aid in understanding for a specific function—according to what questions are being asked.

The models under the first category, Evaluation as Professional Judgment, include the Art Criticism model and the Accreditation-Blue Ribbon Panel models. The Art Criticism model is similar to a critic evaluating a play. A limitation centers around "knowing" the critic and his or her evaluative criteria, so that the criticism can be examined and weighed (Gardner, 1977). Evaluation as criticism is the process of critically describing and judging a program through critical guideposts that are intrinsic to the critic or con-noisseur. The connoisseur is the evaluation instrument who judges effec-tiveness.

Accreditation and Blue Ribbon Panel models are among the broadest of approaches. The accreditation model is used by regional educational associations, such as the North Central Association, to certify that their member schools meet certain minimum educational standards (Taylor, 1976, p. 1) based on the judgments of a panel of prestigious and/or expert outsiders who visit and observe a program to approve or disapprove it. Another aspect of these models is self-study. An example of this would be a campus recreation staff effort to internally review programs and to increase effectiveness while meeting the demand for public accountability. The blue ribbon panel is a group of experts who are brought in to resolve crises, preserve programs, or make other decisions about programs.

Ratings to be used for comparative and decision making purposes often-times results from the Accreditation and Blue Ribbon Panel models. However, disagreement exists over standards, criteria, and definitions of "expert." The standards are not empirically validated, the criterion tends to be intuition or professional judgment alone, and there is no assurance that the experts possess any special insight. An accreditation panel could be considered to be a group of connoisseurs, thereby facing problems similar to those of the art criticism model. Without a doubt, program evaluation under this approach is based on the subjective judgment of individuals either internal or external to the campus recreation program.

In the Evaluation as Measurement category, the Systems-Management Analysis models appear. Taylor (1976, p. 2) states that the models do not assess merit directly but focus on gathering information for the use of decision-makers. The purpose of systems-management analysis as an evaluation model is to enhance rational decision making. In these models, the programmer determines information needs, collects and analyzes quantifiable data, and organizes and reports data to his or her director. This is most often accomplished through the use of quantitative measures, such as participation rates and cost-effectiveness studies. Quantifiable data are emphasized due to the appearance that they can be easily defended. Judgment boils down to a number. However, the models are limited by their potential to over-value numbers at the expense of qualitative information. Using this approach the evaluator has minimal, if any, involvement with value judgments, has primarily numerical concerns, and uses systems analysis to gather information for day-to-day operational decisions (Hoemeke, 1977, p. 80).

The category of Evaluation as Congruence Between Performance and Objectives includes several models. The cornerstone of these models is that the important purposes of a program can be expressed as behavioral objectives. Thus, evaluation may consist of comparing actual participant performance to the levels specified in the objectives. This approach could be used by campus recreators to help establish program goals and objectives, to find situations in which the achievement of the objectives are shown, and to develop measurement techniques to compare the stated objectives with the measured degree of achievement. A limiting factor is the adequacy and appropriateness of the goals and objectives and the way in which they are compared with reality (Worthen & Sanders, 1973).

The fourth category, Decision-oriented Evaluation, contains the Decision Making models. They are evaluation models based on the decisions to be made via rational thinking. This approach contains elements of others in terms of its goal orientation and specification of criteria for decision making. However, here, the major emphasis is on informed judgment in decision situations (Dressel, 1976). The role of the evaluator is to supply information to persons in leadership positions to help guide programmatic or organizational action. Stufflebeam (1970) advocates these approaches and summarizes them as follows, "Evaluation is the process of delineating, obtaining, and providing useful information for judging decision alternatives." (p. 129)

The guiding paradigms for the decision making approaches are the models of decision making and the scientific method. These approaches focus on the rational model of decision making and ignore the human relations orientation, the pluralistic and idealogical bargaining models, and the organizational models of decision making (P. L. Peterson, 1976). Thus, they are limited by their assumptions or rationality and the need to identify decision makers.

In Scriven's (1973) Goal Free Evaluation model, the fifth approach, the evaluator who is usually an outsider, enters a program with absolutely no information about its goals to render a judgment upon the program. The model assumes that some consensus of opinion exists about the evaluative criteria and consequences. The lack of goal knowledge on the part of the evaluator is thought to help insure freedom from bias or co-operation. This is also thought to enhance the likelihood of his or her perceiving unanticipated effects. The methodology is based on logical deduction and observation. Concern over the evaluator's freedom from bias and unintended effects led to the development of this model.

This model has been infrequently employed due to evaluators' feelings of discomfort in judging a program without knowing its goals. The program developers also feel discomfort when evaluators interpret their programs without knowledge of their goals. There is thus a need for basic information from which judgments can be made (Gardner, 1977).

The last category, the Transaction-Observation Evaluation models, concentrate on program processes. Stake (1975, p. III-9) writes that the activities of programs are studied with special attention to settings and milieu. In the transaction-observation approach, attention is given to the pluralistic nature of values. Hamilton (1977) writes:

> Compared with the classical models they [transaction-observation models] tend to be more extensive (not necessarily centered on numerical data), more naturalistic (based on programme activity rather than programme intent); and more adaptable (not constrained by experimental or pre-ordinate designs). In turn they are likely to be sensitive to the different values of pro-

350

*gramme participants; endorse empirical methods which incor-
porate ethnographic fieldwork; develop feed-back materials
which are couched in the natural language of the recipients; and
shift the locus of formal judgement from the evaluator to the participants. (p. 30)*

The transaction-observation evaluation models have drawn increasingly
on the case study as their major methodology. The case study method is
used for the purpose of providing a variety of points of view to portray what
has occurred in a program. The main components of the models are description, interpretation, and judgment.

The limitation of these models is that the evaluator has to be able to work
with the program developer or director in order to be used effectively
throughout the evaluation process. Also, the methodology used is subject to
question by those who advocate the quantitative, numerically oriented approaches. The judgments appear to be subjective, because they are based
on the accounts of others, as opposed to an index number.

The models and approaches represent the more theoretical aspects of
evaluation. They are directly linked to some operational concerns.[1]

Conducting An Evaluation

While specific evaluation purposes may vary, the general goal of evaluation is to ascertain the worth of something. The procedures used in conducting an evaluation must take into account the uniqueness of the particular
program being evaluated. The procedures used depend upon the question
addressed, the desired techniques for data collection, and the audience to
whom the data will be reported. The role of evaluation is to obtain and communication information that will guide judgment and assist in the consideration of issues relevant to various people: programmers, participants, and administrators.

In general, evaluation is conducted in response to a need expressed by
either the people within a program, or by administrators, individuals, or
groups interested in a program but external from it. Evaluation may focus on
what has been done, what is being done, and/or what might have been done.

Oftentimes people involved with or anticipating the implementation of
some form of evaluation run into unexpected opposition from those who
misunderstand the purpose of the evaluation project. They tend to fear the
evaluation and perceive it as something threatening because it has the
potential to harm them. The evaluation should be undertaken for program
improvement, not to do personal damage, assign blame, or find fault. Care
must be exercised to alleviate the fears of those involved, to steer far from
the environment of suspicion that seems to accompany most evaluation attempts, and to concentrate on the facts which best portray what happened,

why, how, and to what ends. One of the best ways to alleviate the fears of those engaged in the program which is to be evaluated is to involve them in the early planning stages of the evaluation and to enlist their aid in the determination of the issues which are to be examined. Individuals should not be threatened by evaluation, but should see it as a tool for improvement, planning, and accountability.

Through discussion with people involved in the program, an appropriate range of issues can be identified. From these, a priority list should be made to determine which things are of greatest importance to the purpose of the evaluation. The focus and scope of the evaluation provides guidelines as to the types of data to be gathered and the best means for gathering it. The methodology is inherent in the model or approach chosen.

Information Gathering Tools

As each evaluation approach is examined, the diversity of evaluation methods becomes apparent. The methods range from a strong emphasis on quantitative information, to a strong emphasis on qualitative information. Likewise, a variety of data gathering techniques are available to obtain the information.

It is critical that the evaluator's first consideration is what is most significant and revealing about the program. Collection of masses of data without any focus or purpose is an inefficient use of time, energy, and resources. Care should be given to the collection of data and evidence which can benefit future programs and serve to improve present efforts.

Evidence may take a variety of forms: descriptions of personnel, events, program goals, reactions from participants or target populations, descriptions of the social milieu, etc. Once a decision is made as to the type or types of data to be gathered, the corollary decisions of how much data and from what sources also need to be made. Data sources are the people, documents, and records that provide evidence about the program. Each of these sources can yield some information about a program. The evaluator should tap only the most beneficial sources while at the same time being careful not to examine just one side of an issue.

Some methods of data-gathering may be more useful than others for evaluating a given program. Every approach has a methodology, each with its relative merits and demerits. The evaluator should think through what method best answers his or her questions and then choose a model accordingly whether he or she is on the campus recreation staff or an external person.

Data Analysis

Good data analysis will describe the program being evaluated highlighting aspects of the description that are important for addressing issues or audiences. There are many ways to analyze evaluation data. The choice of an analysis technique depends on the nature of information to be analyzed, the purpose of the analysis, and the resources available for the analysis. In some instances, statistical techniques may be appropriate, while in many other instances, qualitative techniques are more appropriate. The success of a program need not be measured by attendance figures or profits alone, for individual gains may become obscured if the evaluator concentrates solely upon the quantifiable. In general, the type of data analysis conducted should be directly linked to the concerns of the audience or groups involved, the type of evidence, and the desired utility of the final report (Issac & Michael, 1971).

People have different abilities and different experience which influence the way they receive and use evaluations. It is important to understand what criteria various people use to judge programs, what standards are relevant and meaningful, what indicators people accept as legitimate, and in what form and in what language all of these things are meaningfully discussed.

Practical Aspects

Conducting an evaluation will cost in terms of money, time, and personnel resources. However, some form of evaluation can fit into any budget. The time has come when judgments about program excellence must be based on evidence. Therefore, people must be encouraged to use evaluation. The process of evaluation, as well as the use of evaluation results, requires a clear understanding of the social, personal, and political dynamics surrounding any activity. If satisfactory use is to be made of evaluative information, an evaluation plan should show how the results can be used. People will be more likely to use evaluation information if they perceive the process and/or resulting information as relevant to their needs, if they see the potential benefits to be derived from the evaluation, and if they find the evaluation results to be available when needed. Don't make the evaluation a cloak and dagger operation. Explain it and fully involve the staff. The time for evaluation in campus recreation has arrived.

REFERENCES

Bannon, J. J. Leisure resources: Its comprehensive planning. Englewood Cliffs, N. J.: Prentice Hall, 1976.

Caulley, D. N. & Dawson, J. A. Quantitative versus qualitative program evaluation. In L. Rubin (Ed.), Critical issues in education policies: An administrator's overview. Boston: Allyn & Bacon, 1978.

Dressel, P. L. Handbook of academic evaluation: Assessing institutional effectiveness, student progress and professional performance for decision making in higher education. San Francisco: Jossey-Bass, 1976.

Gardner, D. E. Five evaluation frameworks. Journal of Higher Education, 1977, 48, 571-593.

Hamilton, D. Making sense of curriculum evaluation: Continuity and discontinuities in an educational idea. In L.S. Schulman (Ed.), *Review of research in education.* (Vol. 5). Itasca, Ill.: Peacock, 1977.

Hoemeke, T. H. *Evaluation of cross-cultural programs of technical assistance to education.* Unpublished doctoral dissertation, University of Illinois, 1977.

House, E. R. (Ed.). *School evaluation: The process and the politics.* Berkeley: McCutchan, 1973.

House, E. R. *Assumptions underlying evaluation models.* Paper presented at the annual meeting of the American Educational Research Association, New York, April 1977.

Isaac, S. & Michael, W. *Handbook in research and evaluation.* San Diego: Robert K. Knapp, 1971.

Peterson, P. L. *School politics-Chicago style.* Chicago: University of Chicago Press, 1976.

Scriven, M. Goal-free evaluation. In E. R. House (ed.), *School evaluation: The politics and the process.* Berkeley: McCutchan, 1973.

Scriven, M. *Evaluation bias and its control.* Evaluation Center Occasional Paper #4, College of Education, Western Michigan University, 1975.

Stake, R. E. *Nine approaches to educational evaluation.* Unpublished manuscript, University of Illinois, 1974.

Stake, R. E. *The responsibility to evaluate educational programs.* Unpublished manuscript, prepared for the Organization for Economic Cooperation and Development, University of Illinois, 1975.

Stufflebeam, D. L. Frameworks for planning evaluation studies. In B. R. Worthen & J. R. Sanders (Eds.), *Educational evaluation: Theory and practice.* Worthington, Ohio: Charles A. Jones, 1973.

Taylor, D. B. Eeny, meeny miney, meaux: Alternative evaluation models.*North Central Association Quarterly.* 1976, *50*, 353-358. (Reprint)

Worthen, B. R. & Sanders, J. R. *Educational evaluation: Theory and practice.* Worthington, Ohio: Charles A. Jones, 1973.

[1]The contents of the following sections were greatly aided by the writings of the Office of Continuing Education and Public Service of the University of Illinois at Urbana-Champaign.

DEVELOPING A COST ANALYSIS PROCEDURE FOR RECREATIONAL SPORTS PROGRAM

By Kathy Pedro Beardsley, University of Maryland

Introduction

At the present, a precise measure for determining a cost analysis for Recreational Sports programs does not exist.

Satryb proposes a cost analysis model which serves two important functions: "1) it gives a quantitative measure for internal evaluation of current programs, and 2) it gives an understandable justification vehicle for resource allocation"[2] Satryb's basic premise is to assign a dollar figure to each service and function the department offers which can be very difficult to determine. He suggests that the staff determine a dollar figure for each activity based on direct and indirect costs. Once this is done, the number of participants for each activity must be determined.[3]

A variation of Satryb's model will be used to determine cost procedure for various recreational sports programs such as self-service swim programs and intramural sports activities. These two programs will serve as examples to illustrate application of Satryb's model to cost analysis.

Cost Analysis of a Self-Service Swim Program

Following Satryb's model, the number of participants in the swim program must be estimated. This can be determined by lifeguards compiling an hourly log of the participants in the pool. To determine an average number of participants per hour, the total number of participants using the pool is divided by the number of hours the pool is utilized. Since records are not always accurately compiled during each hour or sometimes even recorded, the average participant is determined by what was actually logged.

Figure 1

Pool	Number of participants logged	Hours logged	Average participant Per Hour
A	10,038	713	14
B	7,723	664	12

The approximate cost per hour for the swim program is determined by listing the costs involved in implementing a swim program and determining a dollar figure.

Figure 2

Item	Cost
Lifeguards	$2.50/hr.
Maintenance and Supply	$2.00/hr. a
Staff time in scheduling and maintenance	$2.00/hr. b
Equipment	$0.40/hr. c
Office expenses	$0.40/hr. d
Total cost to implement self service swim program	$7.30/hr.

$$\frac{\$1,500}{750 \text{ hrs}} = 2.00$$

a) based on $1,500 per year for 750 hours to be schedule;

b) based on $7.50/hr. for 5 hrs. per week or $37.50/week: 40 weeks are scheduled

$37.50 X 40 = $1,500 per year;

$$\frac{1,500}{750 \text{ hrs.}} = 2.00$$

c) based on $300 per year; $\frac{\$300}{750 \text{ hrs}} = \frac{1}{2} 4]$

d) based on $300 per year, $\frac{\$300}{750 \text{ hrs.}} = .40$

355

The cost per participant is determined by dividing the approximate hourly cost for the self-service swim program and dividing that cost by average number of persons who participate per hour. (figure 3.)

Figure 3

Pool	Approx. Cost per Hour	Average Number of Persons per hr.	Cost per participant
A	$7.30	14	$0.52
B	7.30	12	$0.61

To determine the approximate number of participants per quarter, the number of hours per week the pool is scheduled is multiplied by the average number of participants per hour and the number of weeks in the school year the pool is utilized.

Figure 4

Pool	Number of Hours Per Week	Average Number of Participants per Hour	Number of Weeks in School year	Approx. # of participants
A	65	14	36	32,760
B	54	12	36	23,328

The approximate cost per year for the self service swim program is determined by taking the cost assigned per participant and multiplying this figure by the average time allotted per person and the total approximate number of participants. The average time allotted per person may vary from institution to institution.

Figure 5

Pool	Cost Assigned Per Hour per Participant	Average Time Allotted Per Person	Participants Served	Total Cost for services
A	$0.52	1	32,760	$17,035.20
B	0.61	1	23,328	$14,230.08

Cost Analysis of Intramural Program

The cost analysis of an intramural program is determined by the cost of each intramural activity in relationship to the number of participants, number of teams, number of participants and number of games.

Activity Cost

Approximate activity costs are done by listing each activity and assigning a specific cost for each given category which, can include a) office personnel costs, b) equipment costs, c) official and activity supervisor costs, d) maintenance costs, e) office costs, f) publicity, g) awards, and h) miscellaneous costs.

Staff Costs

The approximate staff time spent in programming a specific intra-mural activity is determined by having each staff member tabulate on a weekly basis the number of hours spent programming intramurals. A staff planning form can be developed to help the staff compile their hourly programming responsibilities. (figure 6)

Figure 6

Activity Description	Responsibilities	Weekly Workload
Co-rec basketball	Programming	4
Co-rec volleyball	Supervising	2

Each activity is listed in a similar manner as above. The categories which can be used for the different time allotment desginations include: 1) programming—the actual scheduling and planning of a specific activity; 2) supervision—the time spent in supervising others at an activity including being at the event; 3) office work—the office time taken to do draw sheets, scorecards, flyers, etc., for each activity; 4) phone calling—the time it takes for personnel to call the participants for each activity; 5) assigning officials—the time it takes to schedule the officials for each activity; 6) answering questions—questions which occur during the week from participants regarding a specific activity; 7) miscellaneous—time spent on a specific activity that cann ot be identified.

The office personnel costs are determined by multiplying the number of hours per week by the approximate cost per hour (see Figure 7) The per hour cost is determined by taking the number of hours per week and dividing this into the total cost per week.

Figure 7
Activity: Co-Rec Basketball

Personnel	Number of Hours Per Week	Staff Hourly Cost	Total
Staff Programmer A	5	$8.50	$ 42.50
Staff Programmer B	7	$6.50	$ 45.50
Secretary A	8	$5.00	$ 40.00
Student Office Worker A	5	$2.50	$ 12.50
Student Office Worker B	7	$2.50	$ 17.50
Total	32	$4.94	$158.00/week

Equipment Costs

Equipment costs are determined by listing equipment purchases and determining the equipment's life. Once the yearly cost is determined, the weekly cost is determined by dividing the number of weeks the activity is scheduled. The hourly cost is then determined by dividing the weekly cost by 40 hours. This hourly figure can also be determined by dividing this into the total yearly cost.

Item	Cost	Life of Equipment	Yearly Cost
basketballs	$200.00	1 year	$200.00
whistles	$ 10.00	1 year	$ 10.00
official uniforms	$150.00	2 years	$ 75.00
Total yearly cost			$285.00
Total weekly cost (36 weeks)		7.92	
Total hourly cost (40 hours per weeks)			$ 0.20

Officials and Supervisor Costs

These costs are determined by using time cards that can include the activity that is being officiated and supervised as well as the number of hours a person works. Most time cards only include the person's name and hours worked. By revising the time card to include activity description a more accurate cost of what it costs for this service can be determined. (figure 9).

Figure 9

Personnel	Weekly hours	Salary/hour	Total
Official A	5	2.50	$12.50
Official B	10	2.50	25.00
Official C	7	2.50	17.50
Supervisor	10	3.00	30.00
Total cost per week			$85.00/week
Total cost per hour (40 hours per week)			$ 2.12/hour

Maintenance Costs

Maintenance costs are harder to define if there is one single sum which is paid to maintain the entire intramural program. Depending upon its situation, each institution needs to derive some type of dollar figure. For example, let's say that the total cost per year for maintenance for the entire Rec Sports Progam is $5,000, and there are 20 activities that operate at so many hours an activity, then each total hourly figure per activity can be divided into the maintenance cost. For example, basketball may operate 500 hours of the total 2,000 hours intramural activities operate. Since basketball accounts for one-fourth of the time for all activities, it is responsible for one-fourth the maintenance cost of ¼ × $5,000 = $1,250. The problem with this method is that it does not take into consideration the varied amount of time it takes to maintain specific activities.

Office Costs

Office costs are the costs of paper, pencils, stencils, phone calls, etc. These costs can be very difficult to determine but an estimation can be determined by recording items that are used at the time they are used. (see figure 10)

Figure 10

Date	Item	Intramural Activity	Number	Costs	Total
1/4	Mimeograph paper	basketball	4 rooms	$1.69	6.76
1/7	Stencils	basketball	3	.20	.60
1/8	Xerox copies	basketball	25	.05	1.25
1/10	Mailings	basketball	50	.13	6.50
1/12	Envelopes	basketball	50	.01	.50

Awards

The cost of awards is figured out by multiplying the cost of each award given in a sport by the total number of awards which are awarded. For example: 100 basketball awards X $2.50 © $250.00

Publicity

Handbooks, student newspaper advertisements, flyers, etc. are all publicity materials that must be considered in the costs of a specific intramural program, if the cost is incurred by the department. (see figure 11)

Figure 11

Item	Number	Cost	Total
3 X 80 basketball Ads	2	$95.00	$190.00
Flyers for basketball	300	$55.00	$ 55.00
Total			$245.00

Intramural Cost Summary Sheet

Once all the costs for an activity are identified the cost analysis of the intramural program can be prepared. The weekly cost is multiplied by the number of weeks in the school year. Each cost area is then added together to get the total amount spent for an intramural activity. A summary cost sheet can then be developed (Table 1).

INTRAMURAL COST SUMMARY SHEET

Table 1

Activity	Office Personnel	Equip.	Super./Official	Office Supplies	Maint.	Awards	Publicity	Miscellaneous	Total Costs
Basketball	2000.00	300.00	1500.00	100.00	100.00	20.00	10.00	50.00	$ 4080.00
Ice Hockey	500.00	200.00	150.00	25.00	200.00	50.00	15.00	5.00	$ 1145.00
Softball	6000.00	3000.00	12000.00	500.00	700.00	1500.00	300.00	50.00	$24050.00

Table 2

Activity	Approximate Total Cost For Activity	# of Partic.	Cost Per Partic.	# of Teams	Cost Per Team	Number of Participations	Cost Per Participations	# of Games	Cost Per Game
Basketball	4080.00	2000	2.04	70	58.29	14,000	.29	490	8.33
Ice Hockey	1145.00	400	2.86	20	57.25	2,400	.48	140	8.18
Softball	24050.00	8000	3.01	700	34.36	42,000	.57	2200	10.93

Cost per Participants, Teams, and Participations

The number of participants, teams, and particiations needs to be determined in order to estimate how much money is being spent for these three areas. The number of participants, teams and participations is divided into the total cost per participant, cost per team, and cost per game (Table 2).

Conclusion

The main disadvantage of this cost analysis model is that it is a qualification of services, rather than the benefits of the services. In addition, this model is only as accurate as the information gathered by the person doing the research. However, this method is simple to use and interpret. It provides a definitive output for evaluation of goals and objectives, and it can be easily understood by non-student personnel and professional staff members.

In implementing a cost analysis procedure, it is important to remember that it takes approximately three to four years of cost analysis research to get an accurate picture of costs of programs. By using a three to four year cost analysis pocedure the Recreational Sports administrator has enough information to 1) facilitate long-term planning, 2) increase the organization's efficiency, 3) redirect its priorities, and 4) evaluate if the activities offered are cost-efficient, etc.[4]

The goal of cost analysis is to demonstrate the costs of a given service.[5] Using such a system, the expense of student activities, such as intramural basketbasll and volleyball can be determined. Features of a good cost analysis system include: 1) staff input in designing the system, 2) a system that is flexible, 3) data being generated is specific, 4) it requires as little time as possible to maintain and 5) the data produced is easy to compile and report.[6]

Since Recreational Sports Departments are support services of an University, they need to justify their existence in terms of cost and benefits of their programs. Hopefully, this cost analysis procedure will provide Recreational Sports administrators with a system to collect data needed for the cost portion of this task.

NOTES

[1]Satryb, Ronald P.; "A Budget Model for Student Personnel;" NASPA Journal; v. 12; p. 1; pp. 51-56; Sum. 74.

[2]Ibid, pg. 53.

[3]Ibid, pg. 54.

[4]Hoenack, Stephen A. "A Evaluation of Management Techniques," NASPA, v. 12; n. 3; pp. 195-201.

[5]Bishop, John B.; "Some Guidelines for the Development of Accountability Systems," NASPA, v. 12, n. 3, pp. 190-194; Winter, 1975.

[6]Ibid, pp 194.

BIBLIOGRAPHY

Bishop, John B. "Some Guidelines for the Development of Accountability Systems," *NASPA Journal,* v. 12, n. 3, pp 190-194, Winter, 1975.

Hoenack, Stephen A. "An Evaluation of Management Techniques," *NASPA Journal,* v. 12, n. 3, pp 195-201.

Satryb, Ronald P. "A Budget Model for Student Personnel," *NASPA Journal,* v. 12, n. 1, pp 51-56, Sum. 74.

COMPUTERIZED EVALUATION OF INTRAMURAL BASKETBALL OFFICIALS

By Mark Sobotka, Gerry Maas and M. Steven Reed, Iowa State University

In an effort to provide an additional avenue of student input into the intramural program, it was decided to have each team rate the officials in the sports in which officials were used. A common complaint in many intramural sports is the quality of the officiating. This was to be an effort which would allow teams to evaluate officiating as perceived by participants.

The first year all data was collected on the back of scorecards (Figure 1). Each official was rated on six different categories by each team. The intramural staff was then presented with the problem of putting the data into a form that would be useful with a minimum expenditure of time and money.

A computer assisted method of handling the officials' evaluations was needed. A computer science undergraduate/intramural official suggested a system which would not have to be keypunched.

THE SYSTEM

Input

A machine readable format was needed. Regular punched cards still required large amounts of manual labor. A 'marked sense' card was decided upon. "Marked sense' cards are the same size as a standard 80 column computer card. Each card provides for 40 columns of data. Data is entered on the card by a standard No. 2 pencil. This system also allowed for additional comments by allowing the teams to make comments on the back of the card.

The information to be put on the card was:

Columns:
1 - 4	Team ID
5 - 19	Officials Name
20 - 25	Officials Rating (one category per column)
26	Win - Lose indicator

27 - 29	Team score
30 - 32	Opponent's score
33 - 36	Opponent's identification number
37 - 40	Sportsmanship rating by officials (four categories)

Additional data was included in the input in the event that additions would be made to the system for sportsmanship rating of teams and a computerized score reporting system.

Some points worth noting:

1. Detailed, easy to understand instructions on proper data input should be provided to the teams and officials.
2. The system must be 'sold' to the participants and officials or they will not take the time to insure that the data is property entered. Results are only as good as the input.

Hardware Notes: Marked sense cards require a special card reader or an additional feature on the card reader. The problem as it is written will accept key punched data in the above format if a marked sense card reader is unavailable.

Software

The program was written in cobol and assembled with an IBM OS American National Standard Cobol Assembler. The code should be compatible with most cobol assemblers available at the college or university computing center. Cobol was chosen because it is widely used and most colleges and universities have someone on its staff who can program and debug programs in cobol.

The program uses the data cards as its only input. The program reads the data cards and then sorts them by official's name. Each data record is then read and edited to make sure a valid rating is in each field. If not, the data card is rejected and a message is output telling what the error is and an image of the card is output. If the ratings are valid (0-9) and the win/lose indicator is W or L or determined from the score then the data record is ready for processing. Team ID's and official's names cannot be edited because we wanted to allow the officials the choice of using any combination of characters and number they wanted and team ID's were a combination of letters and numbers. Teams and officials should be warned to always double check their ID or name to insure than it is properly coded, otherwise the rating may be split among two or more output ratings. After editing, the ratings are added to various internal work areas, depending on win/lose status, that are used to compute the officials' averages and overall averages. This procedure is followed for each data record until a new official's name is encountered. Then the averages for the previous official are computed and

Figure 1

| PLEASE COMPLETE THE FOLLOWING RATINGS FOR YOUR GAMES OFFICIALS. THANK-YOU |

REFEREE 1   R. Bass   REFEREE 2   D. Bubke

TEAM (top)	TEAM (bottom)		TEAM (top)	TEAM (bottom)
1.5	2.0	1. HUSTLE, AGILITY	2.5	2.0
2.0	2.5	2. AUTHORITY (sureness of calls)	3.0	2.5
3.0	3.5	3. CONSISTENCY OF DECISIONS	3.5	3.5
2.5	3.0	4. DIPLOMACY (tactfulness, manner in handling players, fans, etc.)	2.5	3.0
2.0	2.5	5. SELF-CONTROL and POISE	3.0	2.5
2.0	2.5	6. OVERALL PERFORMANCE	3.0	3.0

RATING SCALE: 1 - Superior
                 2 - Good
                 3 - Average
                 4 - Weak, unsatisfactory
                 5 - Inferior

COMMENTS:

GAME PROBLEMS/OFFICIALS NOTES (protests, ejected players, etc.):

output. The internal work areas for the individual official are zeroed out. When the end of the data is encountered the averages for the last official are output and averages for all of the officials combined are computed and output. (Figures 2, 3, 4, and 5 show system data flow.)

Output

Output for each official is four lines
1. Official's name
2. Average ratings by winning teams
3. Average ratings by losing teams
4. Average ratings by all teams

TABLE 1

OFFICIALS RATING BY TEAMS AVERAGE OFFICIALS RATINGS

Name	Number Ratings	Hustle	Authority	Decision Consistency	Tactfulness	Self-control Poise	General Overall	Average
Black, A.								
Winning	3	1.33	2.00	3.00	2.33	2.00	2.00	2.11
Losing	3	2.00	2.67	3.33	3.00	2.67	3.00	2.78
TOTALS:	6	1.67	2.33	3.17	2.67	2.33	2.50	2.44
Blue, A.								
Winning	3	2.67	3.00	3.33	2.33	3.00	3.00	2.89
Losing	3	2.33	2.33	3.33	3.00	2.67	3.00	2.78
TOTALS:	6	2.50	2.67	3.33	2.67	2.83	3.00	2.83
Brown, A.								
Winning	3	2.67	3.33	3.33	2.67	3.00	3.33	3.06
Losing	3	2.33	2.33	3.33	3.00	2.67	3.00	2.78
TOTALS:	6	2.50	2.83	3.33	2.83	2.83	3.17	2.92
Green, A.								
Winning	1	2.00	3.00	3.00	2.00	3.00	3.00	2.67
Losing	2	2.00	2.00	1.50	2.00	2.00	1.50	1.83
TOTLAS:	3	2.00	2.33	2.00	2.00	2.33	2.00	2.11
Orange, A.								
Winning	3	2.67	2.67	3.00	3.33	2.67	3.00	2.89
Losing	2	2.50	3.50	1.50	3.50	2.50	3.00	2.75
TOTALS:	5	2.60	3.00	2.40	3.40	2.60	3.00	2.83
Red, A.								
Winning	2	3.00	3.00	3.50	3.00	3.00	3.50	3.17
Losing	1	3.00	3.00	5.00	4.00	4.00	5.00	4.00
TOTALS:	3	3.00	3.00	4.00	3.33	3.33	4.00	3.44
GRAND TOTALS:								
Winning	15	2.40	2.81	3.20	2.67	2.73	2.93	2.79
Losing	14	2.28	2.57	2.92	3.00	2.65	2.93	2.73
TOTALS:	29	2.34	2.69	3.06	2.83	2.69	2.93	2.76

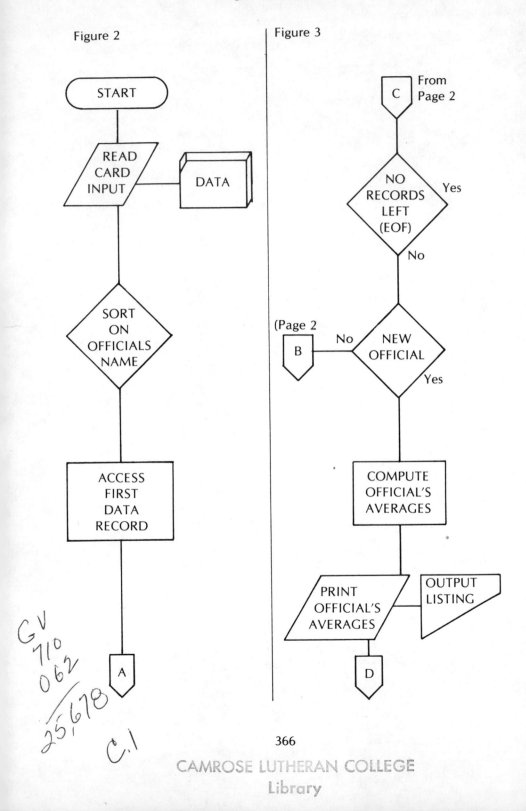

Figure 2

Figure 3

START

READ CARD INPUT

DATA

SORT ON OFFICIALS NAME

ACCESS FIRST DATA RECORD

A

C — From Page 2

NO RECORDS LEFT (EOF) — Yes

No

(Page 2) B — No — NEW OFFICIAL

Yes

COMPUTE OFFICIAL'S AVERAGES

PRINT OFFICIAL'S AVERAGES

OUTPUT LISTING

D

366

Figure 4 | Figure 5

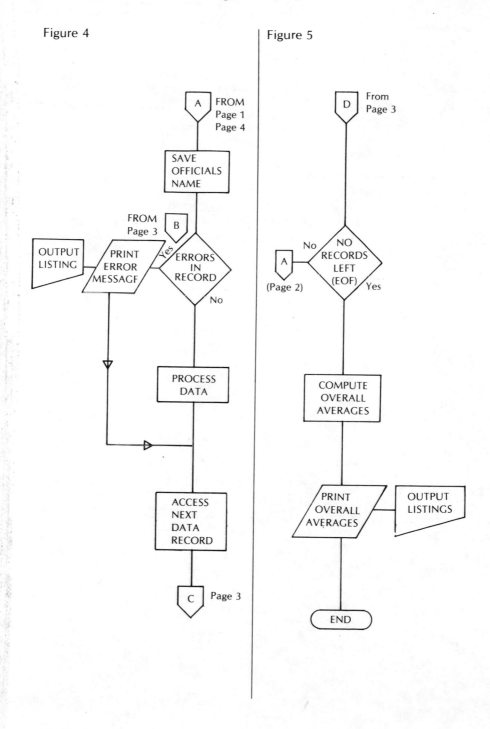

Figure 4

A — FROM Page 1 Page 4

SAVE OFFICIALS NAME

FROM Page 3 — B

OUTPUT LISTING

PRINT ERROR MESSAGE

Yes — ERRORS IN RECORD

No

PROCESS DATA

ACCESS NEXT DATA RECORD

C — Page 3

Figure 5

D — From Page 3

A (Page 2) — No — NO RECORDS LEFT (EOF) — Yes

COMPUTE OVERALL AVERAGES

PRINT OVERALL AVERAGES

OUTPUT LISTINGS

END

Each rating line has the following information
1   Number of ratings
2 - 7 Average ratings in each of the six categories
8   Average overall rating (computed from six categories)
9 - 12 Average sportsmanship ratings given by the official
13 Average overall sportsmanship given by the official (computed from 4
      sportsmanship ratings)

Sample Data

Data from officials ratings are illustrated in Table 1. Data for each official is listed with grant means at the end of each run to compare student officials' ratings. Student supervisors ratings of officials could also be handled on this format. The computer prints an alphabetized listing of student officials   results to the intramur